Hands
Netscape

David Sachs ■ Henry Stair

PRENTICE HALL PTR
UPPER SADDLE RIVER, NJ 07458

For book and bookstore information

http://www.prenhall.com

Production team: *Camille Trentacoste, Joanne Anzalone, Patti Guerrieri*
Cover design director: *Jerry Votta*
Cover design: *CopperLeaf Design Studio*
Back cover and flap design: *Anthony Gemmellaro*
Manufacturing manager: *Alexis R. Heyd*t
Acquisitions editor: *Mary Franz*
Editorial assistant: *Noreen Regina*

 © 1996 by Prentice Hall PTR
Prentice-Hall, Inc.
A Simon & Schuster Company
Upper Saddle River, New Jersey 07458

The publisher offers discounts on this book when ordered in bulk
quantities. For more information, contact Corporate Sales Department,
Prentice Hall PTR, One Lake Street, Upper Saddle River, NJ 07458.
Phone: 800-382-3419; FAX: 201- 236-7141.
E-mail: corpsales@prenhall.com

The Netscape Navigator and logo, Netscape Corp.'s home page, and all other Netscape-related images
and URLs are reproduced on the cover and throughout this book by courtesy of Netscape
Communications Corporation. All other product names mentioned herein are the trademarks or
registered trademarks of their respective owners.

Printed in the United States of America
10 9 8 7 6 5 4 3 2 1

ISBN 0-13-240284-X

Prentice-Hall International (UK) Limited, *London*
Prentice-Hall of Australia Pty. Limited, *Sydney*
Prentice-Hall Canada Inc., *Toronto*
Prentice-Hall Hispanoamericana, S.A., *Mexico*
Prentice-Hall of India Private Limited, *New Delhi*
Prentice-Hall of Japan, Inc., *Tokyo*
Simon & Schuster Asia Pte. Ltd., *Singapore*
Editora Prentice-Hall do Brasil, Ltda., *Rio de Janeiro*

About the Authors

David Sachs is Professor of Office Information Systems and Assistant Dean in Pace University's School of Computer Science and Information Systems in New York. He has been actively involved in developing and teaching computer science courses since 1984. He has co-authored *Discovering Microsoft Works, Hands-On Internet, Hands-On Mosaic*, and *Instant Internet with WebSurfer*. He frequently presents workshops and courses about the Internet and the World Wide Web to corporate clients around the world, and participates actively in the Internet World conferences sponsored by Mecklermedia. Dr. Sachs is particularly interested in the field of telecommunications and its impact upon our world. His interests include racquetball and downhill skiing. He can be reached at dsachs@ibm.net

Henry (Pete) Stair is a senior consultant with Mycroft Information in New Canaan, Connecticut, where he specializes in high-performance global telecommunications and internetworking. He co-authored the post-graduate textbook *Megabit Data Communications* as well as *Hands-On Internet, Hands-On Mosaic*, and *Instant Internet with WebSurfer*. He is a registered professional engineer (CA) and a member of the IEEE and the Internet Society. He frequently presents workshops and courses about the Internet and the World Wide Web to corporate clients around the world, and participates actively in the Internet World conferences

sponsored by Mecklermedia. His interests include demystifying technology, cross-country skiing, consciousness research, wine, and classical music. He can be reached at `stair@mycroft.com`

Dedication

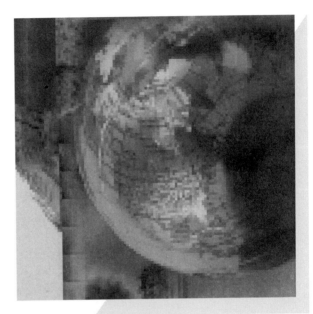

Hands-On Netscape is dedicated to my wife, Linda, whose commitment to the Appalachian Service Project for the past two years has been a wonder to behold. Her energy and enthusiasm have been boundless as she has worked hard to help the many participants in this program to create a world that is warmer, safer, and drier for those less fortunate than they.

—David Sachs

Hands-On Netscape is dedicated with love, to my wife Lorrine.
Et, sans savoir pourqoi, disent toujours: Allons!

—Henry H. Stair

Acknowledgments

Hands-On Netscape is the product of many hands. Our gratitude goes out to all who have been so supportive and encouraging. There have been several individuals who deserve special thanks.

At Prentice Hall PTR, our acquisitions editor, Mary Franz, continues to be an inspiration. Mary knows her subject, understands the software, and has willingly committed herself to lots of support that goes above and beyond the call of duty. Camille Trentacoste, production editor, is funny and bright and does a magical job of taking our prose and pictures and transforming them into the book you now hold in your hands. Gail Cocker-Bogusz has once again created a set of graphics that wonderfully enhances our prose.

Martha Williams, our copyeditor, has added many important and useful suggestions to our writing. Martha's attention to detail is impressive, and although we have never met face-to-face, she is an important member of our virtual team.

Thomas Powell has provided the technical reviews for *Hands-On Netscape* in a thorough, timely, and caring fashion. Thomas clearly knows both the content and the potential readers, and has shared his perceptions with us throughout the creation of this text. Many of his helpful suggestions to us have been incorporated into *Hands-On Netscape*.

As always, we are grateful for the help and support that we have received during the past few months from the personnel at Prentice Hall PTR and others. Even with all of this help, we and we alone, are responsible for any remaining goofs, glitches, and gaps. Please be sure to let us hear from you if there are any suggestions to make the next edition of this book even better.

David Sachs	dsachs@ibm.net
Henry Stair	stair@mycroft.com

Contents

About the Authors, iii

Dedication, v

Acknowledgments, vii

Installing the Hands-On Netscape CD-ROM, xvii

Installation, xvii

Netscape Video Tutorials, xviii

Introduction, xix

Movie: *Authors*

Movie: *Netscape Navigator*

What Is Netscape Navigator and What Can It Do?, xix

Why Have We Written This Book for the Microsoft Windows User?, xx

Introduction, xx

For Whom Is This Book Intended?, xxi

How Is This Book Organized?, xxii

Conventions Used throughout the Book, xxiii

How to Use This Book, xxiv

Part One: Netscape Ready

Session 1

What You Need to Start, 3

Movie: *Internet Growth*

Movie: *WWW Growth*

The Internet: A Quick Review, 3

Activity: *Getting Started—A Road Map, 11*

Activity: *Checking Your Hardware and Software, 12*

Activity: *Finding and Installing TCP/IP Software, 14*

Activity: *Selecting Your Internet Service Provider, 15*

Session Summary, 19

Session 2

Getting Netscape Installed, 21

Movie: *Extracting Netscape*

Movie: *Installing Netscape*

Getting Netscape Navigator—Choices, 21

Activity: *Downloading Netscape Navigator Using ftp, 22*

Activity: *Installing Netscape, 25*

Activity: *Purchasing and Installing Netscape, 30*

Session Summary, 35

Session 3

A Glimpse of the Web, 37

Movie: *HyperLinks*

Movie: *What's New*

What Is the World Wide Web?, 37

Activity: *Starting Netscape Navigator, 40*

Activity: *Touring Netscape's Home Page, 43*

Activity: *Netscape's What's New! Button, 44*
Activity: *Visiting Web Sites, 47*
   Session Summary, 55

Part Two: Netscape Set

Session 4

Touring Netscape, 59
   Movie: *Netscape Control Bars*
   Movie: *Alt and Ctrl Keys*
   Movie: *Right Mouse Button*
   Movie: *Security*
   Activity: *A Grand Tour of Netscape, 59*
   Activity: *Controlling Netscape, 67*
   Activity: *Keystrokes and Mouse Clicks, 81*
   Activity: *The Right Mouse Button, 82*
   Activity: *Netscape Security, 84*
      Session Conclusion, 85
      Session Summary, 85

Session 5

What's Out There?, 87
   Movie: *Uniform Resource Locators*
   Movie: *History List*
   Movie: *Bookmark List*
   Activity: *What's Out There on the World Wide Web?, 87*
   Activity: *Uniform Resource Locators—URLs, 90*
   Activity: *Using URLs to Probe the Web, 93*
   Activity: *History and Bookmarks: An Introduction, 102*

Activity: *Setting Netscape's Options, 109*
  Session Summary, 115

Session 6

A Tour of the World Wide Web, 117

Movie: *Web Tour List*
Movie: *Editing the Bookmark List*
Activity: *Touring the Web, 117*
Activity: *How to Build Your Bookmark List, 145*
Activity: *Organizing Bookmarks, 151*
Activity: *Editing Your Bookmark List, 162*
  Session Summary, 163

Part Three: Netscape Go!

Session 7

Searching with Netscape, 167

Movie: *Yahoo*
Movie: *Searching*
Activity: *Internet Browsing and Searching, 168*
Activity: *Directory Searches—Yahoo, 175*
  Searching for Particular Topics Using Netscape, 179
Activity: *Searching with WebCrawler, 181*
Activity: *Searching with Lycos, 184*
Activity: *Searching With InfoSeek, 189*
Activity: *Finding People with Netscape, 195*
Activity: *Searching Tips and Tricks, 210*
  Session Summary, 211

Session 8

Using Netscape for telnet, ftp, gopher, E-mail, and Usenet, 213

Movie: *File Transfer Protocol*

Movie: *Gopher*

Activity: *Using Netscape for telnet Sessions, 214*

Activity: *Using Netscape for ftp Sessions: Getting an ASCII File, 224*
Compressed Files, 232

Activity: *Using Netscape and ftp to Get a Copy of pkz204g.exe, 235*

Activity: *Getting pkz204g.exe Ready to Use, 239*

Activity: *Using Netscape and ftp to Get Virus Protection Software, 239*

Activity: *Using PKUNZIP to Get scn-212e.zip Ready to Use, 243*
Summary of ftp Activities, 244

Activity: *Using Netscape for gopher Sessions, 244*

Activity: *Using Netscape for E-mail, 247*

Activity: *Using Netscape for Usenet, 252*
Session Summary, 257

Session 9

Using Multimedia with Netscape, 259

Movie: *Visiting the White House*

Movie: *Adobe Acrobat Examples*

Activity: *Accessing the IBM Welcome Page, 262*

Activity: *Getting the PC Speaker Driver and WPLANY, 264*

Activity: *Viewing Images on the World Wide Web, 276*

Activity: *Viewing Documents Using Adobe Acrobat Reader, 279*

Activity: *Getting and Installing Movie Players, 288*
Session Summary, 305

Session 10

Getting Started With Hypertext Markup Language (HTML), 307

Movie: *HTML Document*
Hypertext Markup Language Introduction, 307
Activity: *Setting Up an HTML Document, 311*
Activity: *Creating a List, 317*
Activity: *Adding Hyperlinks, 320*
Activity: *Checking Hyperlinks, 327*
Session Summary, 328
Activity: *Additional HTML Resources, 328*

Session 11

Netscape, Your Way, 331

Movie: *Preferences*
Activity: *Customizing Netscape - Preferences, 331*
Activity: *Staying Up-to-Date, 348*
Session Summary, 349

Appendices

Appendix A

Internet Service Providers, 353

Internet Service Providers (Courtesy of the Internet Society), 353

Appendix B

TCP/IP Background, 453

The TCP/IP Program, 453
What TCP Does, 454

What IP Does, 454
Internet Addresses, 455
Internet Names, 456
Domain Nameservers, 457
An Internet Gateway or Provider Connection, 458
SLIP and PPP, 458

Appendix C
Downloading and Installing win32s Software, 461

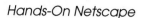

Installing the Hands-On Netscape CD-ROM

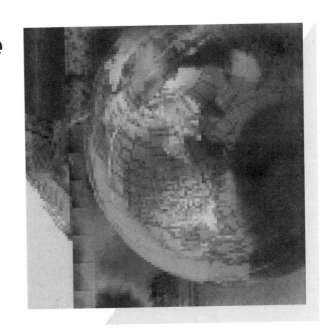

Overview

The CD-ROM that is included with *Hands-On Netscape* contains many important files that you will use as you work through the activities included in *Hands-On Netscape*. In order to access them quickly and easily, you will have to install the CD-ROM Menu onto your hard disk. Once you have done that, you will be able to access the Netscape Video Tutorials and the Netscape Helper Applications at your convenience. Be aware that when it is uncompressed, the menu will occupy approximately 1 MB on your hard disk.

Installation

To install the software, you must have Windows 3.1 or later. Here is how to install the Hands-On Netscape CD-ROM Menu:

1. Insert the CD-ROM in your CD drive.

2. From the Windows Program Manager, click on **File** and then on **Run...**

3. In the Command Line box, type `d:setup` (if 'd' is the letter of your CD drive; otherwise use the proper drive letter.)

Once the installation process begins, the main installer screen will appear. You will be asked where you want the menu to be installed. You can accept the suggested location, which will place the program on your c: drive in a directory called 'ho_netsc,' or you may designate another location of your choosing.

4.   Click the **OK button**, and installation will proceed. (You will be notified if you have insufficient hard disk space in which to install the software.) You can exit the installation process at any time by clicking the button in the lower-right-hand corner of the main installer screen.

When installation finishes, the "Hands-On Netscape" program group opens.

5.   Double-click the **Hands-On Netscape icon** to run the program.

6.   Double-click on **Hands-On Netscape** and you will be greeted by the Hands-On Netscape CD front page.

7.   Click on the **Next button** in the lower left-hand corner and you will see the Contents screen. We will return to this screen frequently throughout the book.

Netscape Video Tutorials

The CD-ROM included with *Hands-On Netscape* contains 25 video tutorials designed to help you better understand the concepts being taught in each session. An icon at the beginning of each session indicates which video tutorials (movies) are associated with that session.

On the Contents screen of the CD-ROM, you will find a list of all the movies. Just point and click on the one that is of interest to you and it will immediately play. Take a few moments to experiment with the movies and to adjust the volume to your liking. Enjoy!

Introduction

Movie 1:	Authors
Movie 2:	Netscape Navigator

What Is Netscape Navigator and What Can It Do?

The Netscape Navigator is an Internet information browser with a very user-friendly, windows-like appearance. It was developed by many of the same people who first developed the now famous Mosaic browser at the National Center for Supercomputing Applications (NCSA) at the University of Illinois at Urbana-Champaign.

An information browser like Netscape allows you to roam the Internet's immense world of multimedia information. And, you are able to do all of this without having to learn or remember the many commands that have always made the Internet a little complex and uncomfortable for beginners.

Using this extremely friendly and powerful tool, you will have access to all the information and resources provided by traditional Internet tools, such as gopher, ftp, and telnet. In many cases, you won't even have to know the details of how these older tools work; you will be able to just point and click at the resources you desire.

In addition, the multimedia aspect of Netscape Navigator means that you will be able to find and use art work, maps, photos, sounds, music, and even movies!

Why Have We Written This Book for the Microsoft Windows User?

Microsoft Windows PC users are accustomed to having a friendly, powerful interface for their software. Many commands can often be invoked by pointing and clicking at them. Until now, this has not been true for most Windows PC users who have been Internet users as well. If you have been using what is known as terminal access, then the interface you have had to use is one filled with many UNIX commands, a command-line interface, and no ability to have color, sound, or graphics. Using Netscape Navigator as your multimedia navigator for the Internet will change all that.

Netscape Navigator is available for free evaluation from many locations on the Internet and for a small fee at software stores. However, even if you have heard about Netscape Navigator, you may not have known where to get it. And, even if you have downloaded a copy, you may have been somewhat perplexed as to what to do next. Suddenly, you encountered discussions about SLIP and PPP connections (we will explain them shortly) as well as something known as TCP/IP software. All of this can be very confusing, at least at first.

We believe that the Netscape Navigator for the Microsoft Windows family is an extremely powerful multimedia tool with which Windows users can navigate the Internet. We have written this book to show you how you can have access to this multimedia software and the global Internet on your Windows PC. We will show you how to "surf the Web" with the Internet's most popular software tool.

Introduction

Welcome to *Hands-On Netscape*. This book contains everything you need to explore the world's greatest network of networks—the Internet—using Netscape Navigator. In a series of online sessions, you learn to

1. Establish (or verify) the special type of Internet connection that is needed to use Netscape Navigator

2. Obtain and install your own copy of Netscape Navigator

3. Use Netscape Navigator to navigate the multimedia Internet.

For Whom Is This Book Intended?

Novice Internet Users

This book has been written with both current Internet users and Internet beginners in mind. The wonder of Netscape Navigator is that it allows both beginners and experienced users to "surf the Net" with almost equal ease. Gone is the need to use obscure UNIX commands. This is truly point-and-click Internet navigation.

Internet Users from Information Services

If you have been accessing the Internet from services such as America Online or Prodigy, you have seen a bit of what the World Wide Web is about. If you have been wishing for full access to the entire Internet, this book is intended for you. *Hands-On Netscape* will teach you about the type of Internet service provider connection and software you need to use Netscape Navigator.

We then will help you find and install the TCP/IP type of software required by Netscape Navigator. Finally, we teach you all about the many powerful opportunities Netscape Navigator can provide. All of these will enable you to learn how to access the entire Internet. In addition, you will have the ability to quickly and efficiently download and use multimedia files of all shapes and sizes.

Experienced Internet Users

If you are an experienced Internet user who would like to significantly upgrade your Internet capabilities, *Hands-On Netscape* should provide you with much valuable information. As soon as you change your terminal account to a SLIP or PPP account and install TCP/IP software and Internet tools like Netscape Navigator, you will be able to use gopher, ftp, and telnet far more easily. In addition, you will then find that you have access to a wide array of multimedia resources that were previously unavailable.

If you are already using another Web browser, you will discover the many advantages of the Netscape Navigator. You will learn why it has become the Web's most popular browser.

How Is This Book Organized?

In the text and graphics that follow, we will guide you hands-on through three parts: "Netscape Ready," "Netscape Set," and "Netscape Go!"

Part One: Netscape Ready

To use Netscape Navigator, you will need two things. First of all, your computer must have a SLIP or PPP connection that provides you with a connection to the Internet. This can be a dial-up connection with a modem or a direct connection from your school or business.

Second, you must have installed TCP/IP software. We show you how to do both of these in "Netscape Ready." First, we provide instructions so that you can find and install the TCP/IP stack of software. Next, we help you to locate an Internet service provider who can provide you with SLIP or PPP access.

Then we will show you how to install Netscape Navigator for Windows 3.1.

For a quick and fun start, we visit a few World Wide Web sites on the Internet. In Part Two, we will provide more detail, but here we take a quick spin using our newly installed browser. By the end of Part One, you will truly be Netscape Navigator ready!

Part Two: Netscape Set

In "Netscape Set," we take you on a guided tour of the Netscape Navigator software. You will learn all the features and hidden tricks of this wonderful Web browser. We detail the menu bar, the toolbar, and the directory buttons. We show how you can control Netscape as well as some hidden features.

We explain how things on the Internet and particularly the Web are addressed. You will discover all about Uniform Resource Locators (URLs). Very importantly, we will discuss network and information security.

Then we go together out on the World Wide Web for a guided tour of the Web. We have prepared a special file to guide you, so you won't have to key in long and sometimes complex addresses. Our Web Tour file will take us to a dozen places, but you can use the file to go to well over 100 interesting, fun, and educational sites all around the world.

And we will show you how to keep track of where you have been and how to build your own bookmarks list. In anticipation of the day when your bookmarks list becomes too large (as it surely will), we will show you how to edit it for easy use.

Part Three: Netscape Go!

In "Netscape Go!" we lead you through many hands-on sessions, including ones that show you how to use the classic Internet tools. You will see how Netscape can be used for telnet, ftp, gopher, and Usenet news.

We will use file transfer protocol (ftp) to get some files you will use repeatedly, such as a virus scanner and a program to "unzip" compressed files. We also explain the E-mail capabilities of the Navigator.

Beyond E-mail, you will be able to find the classic text files as well as an enormous array of multimedia files, including art work, maps, satellite photos, voices, and music! And we will lead you through finding and installing a variety of multimedia programs to play the sounds, see the pictures, and play the movies!

Finally, we show you how to customize the Netscape Navigator to your own tastes. There are many different ways to fine-tune Netscape and we will show you how to do them all. We conclude by showing you how to keep Netscape Navigator up to date. We'll show you where to look and how to download the latest versions of this ever-changing and growing program.

Conventions Used throughout the Book

Sessions—There are 11 sessions in this book, each of which is intended to be done online and hands-on so you can work along with us as you first put your Windows PC directly onto the Internet and then install your own copy of Netscape Navigator.

Session Hotlists—As you will see, once you have Netscape Navigator up and running, session hotlists will provide you with an overview of the options awaiting you each step of the way.

Hands-On Activities—In each session, you will find many hands-on activities in which we lead you carefully through the steps that are necessary to complete each activity successfully.

Hints—From time to time, there are suggestions about ways to make particular activities flow more smoothly.

Heads Up!—There are times when what you are about to do will be somewhat complicated, or more technical, than you may have experienced previously. We would like you to be fresh, alert, and paying close attention when we get to these activities.

Tips—Sometimes we provide some commentary about what may have just happened.

Movies—Each session has two movies that are intended to provide you with an overview of the materials that you will encounter while working through that session. The movies are on the accompanying CD-ROM. If your PC has a CD-ROM and audio capabilities, you can play these movies before beginning each session.

CD-ROM—Software programs have been included on the accompanying CD-ROM. We provide directions on how to obtain this software in the event that your computer does not have a CD-ROM, or in case you would like to make sure that your version is the latest one available. We will use this symbol to let you know when to check the CD-ROM for the particular software.

How to Use This Book

If you presently have no connection to the Internet, *or* if you presently have a connection to an information service, *or* if you presently have a connection to an E-mail service, *or* if you are a modem user you will need to purchase a SLIP or PPP connection from an Internet service provider. Then you will need to install TCP/IP software. You will learn how to do both of these activities in "Netscape Ready." If you are already an Internet user, you may also need to install TCP/IP software and arrange to have an Internet connection.

Then you should proceed through this book in the order in which it is written. We will take you through all of the needed steps.

If you presently have a SLIP/PPP connection and installed TCP/IP software, then you should move directly to Session Two, "Getting Netscape Installed."

If you presently have a SLIP/PPP connection and installed TCP/IP *and* have already installed Netscape Navigator, you should start at Session Three, "A Glimpse of the Web," or at Session Four, "Touring Netscape."

Now let's get started!

Hands-On Netscape

In this first part of Hands-On Netscape, *we will:*

1. *Briefly review what the Internet is, Internet access methods, and what it means to be "on the Internet."*

2. *Walk through a road map to help find the right place to get you started.*

3. *Ensure that you have all the computer hardware, memory, hard disk storage, and software you will need to actually be up and running on the Internet.*

4. *Help you, if necessary, find and install a TCP/IP program that will be your "window" on the Internet.*

5. *Help you find an Internet service provider if you don't already have one.*

6. *Show you several ways to get the Netscape Navigator and then install it on your Windows-based computer.*

7. *Show you a first glimpse of the World Wide Web and investigate "hypertext" and "hyperlinks."*

- ❍ What You Need to Start
- ❍ Getting Netscape Installed
- ❍ A Glimpse of the Web

PART ONE

Session

1

Activity 1:	Getting Started—A Road Map
Activity 2:	Checking Your Hardware and Software
Activity 3:	Finding and Installing TCP/IP Software
Activity 4:	Selecting Your Internet Service Provider

Movie 1:	Internet Growth
Movie 2:	WWW Growth

What You
Need
to Start

Session Overview

In this first session, we will review the Internet and how it is accessed. Next we will provide you with a road map to guide you in your choices about how to begin. Then we will check the computer hardware, software, and storage you need to use Netscape Navigator.

If you need to obtain TCP/IP software, we will present you with several options of where to find it and indicate how you should install it. Finally, we will give you some ideas about selecting and connecting to an Internet service provider.

If you are already familiar with the Internet, jump ahead to Activity 1.

The Internet: A Quick Review

To many newcomers, the Internet is confusing because it is unlike anything else in the world. We all like the idea of some kind of order and structure. Order and structure are present in the Internet, but they are harder to find.

The Internet's structure is distributed. The design and operation are distributed so widely that no one is quite sure how many people are actually involved or how many people actually use the Internet at any given time. This idea takes a little getting used to.

The Internet is actually an interconnection of a very large (and still rapidly growing) number of computer data networks. Some networks may have only one or a few computers and some networks may have hundreds of thousands. Each of these networks is owned and operated by someone, but no one "owns" or "runs" the entire Internet.

There are a number of people who set the standards for what we call the Internet and many of them belong to an organization called the Internet Society. But the society doesn't run the Internet and is not really "in charge." The Internet Society is largely made up of volunteers from around the globe. Their interest is keeping the Internet working and improving both what it does and how it does it.

What we do know about the Internet is its growth. The statistics that follow (from the Internet Society) give some idea about the Internet's stupendous growth.

Figure 1-1 shows the actual and projected number of computer networks that make up the Internet. Notice that the word NOW refers to January 1995 and that, based on what has happened during the past five years, the graph projects values until the year 2000. The Internet Society believes that a rather amazing number of networks will exist by the year 2000!

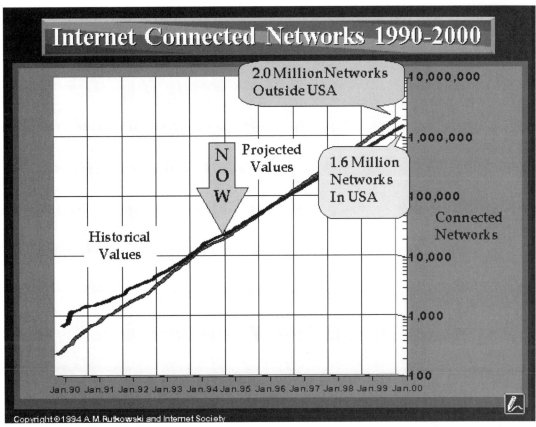

Courtesy of the Internet Society

Figure 1-1
Internet Connected
Networks 1990-2000

If we look at the number of computers on each network and add them, we find the growth to be even more amazing. Figure 1-2 projects that the number of computers (called *hosts*) that will be on the Internet in the next few years will exceed 100 million! Notice that the projected growth in Figure 1-2 is based on what has been happening since 1990.

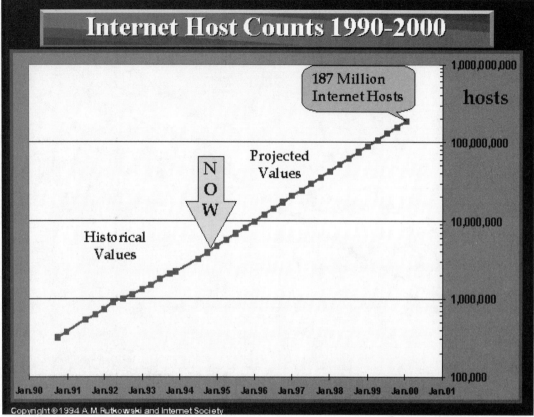

Figure 1-2
Internet Host Counts
1990-2000

Courtesy of the Internet Society

The most amazing growth, however, is that of the *World Wide Web. The Web*, as it is often called, really began growing in early 1993. Its growth has been far beyond anyone's wildest guesses.

What caused this astounding growth? Most people attribute it to the release of a Web browser called *NCSA Mosaic* in late 1993. Mosaic made the Internet easier to use in much the same way that Microsoft's Windows and Apple's Macintosh interfaces have made personal computers easier to use. Figure 1-3 illustrates the phenomenal growth of traffic on the World Wide Web since late 1993. Notice the start date of the graph is January 1993. The measurement is the amount of traffic *per month*, measured in bytes, transferred over the World Wide Web. Where we are now, in mid-1995, represents only a small percentage of the traffic that is expected to exist on the World Wide Web by the end of this century.

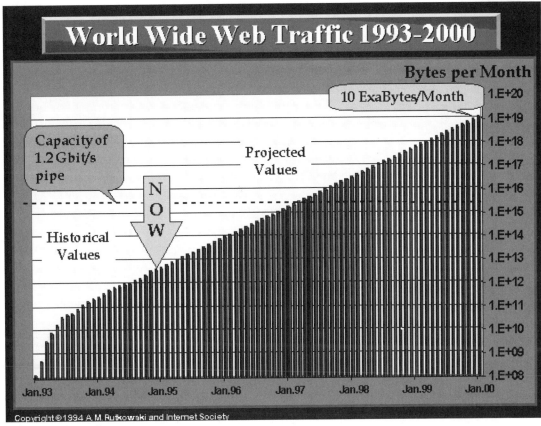

Courtesy of the Internet Society

Figure 1-3
World Wide Web
Traffic 1993-2000

The World Wide Web concept was really invented (by Tim Berners-Lee) from 1989 to 1991 as a new way to use information and the Internet. The Web and Web browsers allow us to visit both the older places on the Internet as well as all the new Web sites. Web sites are designed to offer their information to browsers. The offered information may include not only text, but also sounds and music, pictures and photos, and even videos. It's these extra bits for images and sounds that add much of the traffic to the Web. The Web is also responsible for making a (mostly) serious information medium more fun to use!

You may ask: Won't we run out of capacity to carry that traffic? We may encounter some delays, like a highway at rush hour. But there are no fundamental physical limitations to prevent the anticipated growth.

It looks as if we had better begin to understand and use the Web!

Netscape's Navigator is a tool that allows us to *browse* this World Wide Web. It is actually a second-generation graphic browser as many of the developers of the original NCSA (National Center for Supercomputer Applications) Mosaic are also the developers of Netscape's Navigator.

Netscape's Navigator is the real name of this browser. But that's a bit clumsy to say and to read. Like the rest of the industry, we will now begin to call it just Netscape.

To use Netscape, you will need to be "on the Internet." This means that you will need to access the Internet directly with *your* computer being a full part of the Internet.

Internet Access Methods

According to a recent article in *Internet Society NEWS*, there are four types of Internet access. We will focus on three of them.

Method One: Gateway (Information Service) Access

If you have America Online, CompuServe, Genie, or Prodigy, you already have an Internet connection available to you. You may have an easy-to-use Windows-type interface to your service provider. However, even with one of these connections, you will be limited in getting information directly to your computer. This is really *indirect* access to the Internet.

You will have an E-mail address and will be able to communicate with those on the Internet through what is known as a gateway. But, you are really going through the information service's special software to get to the Internet. This is diagrammed in Figure 1-4.

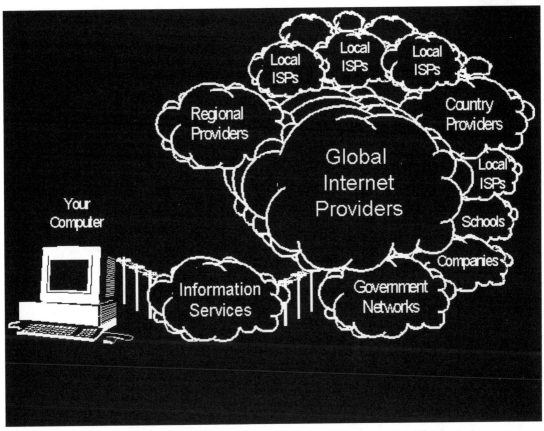

Figure 1-4
Information Services Access

As we write this, the information services are scrambling to offer and improve their access to the Internet and the World Wide Web. By the time you read this, some may have adopted Netscape as their browser. If you have an account with an information service that offers you Netscape as a browser, you may now jump ahead to Session Three.

Method Two: Terminal Emulator (or Shell Account) Access

You may be connected to an Internet service provider by using a dial-up modem line. You may be using simple asynchronous communications software such as ProComm, SmartComm, or Telix that lets you connect to a host computer on the Internet by having your personal computer emulate a "dumb terminal," such as a VT-100. You may have been struggling with strange typed commands to use the Internet.

Binary files can be moved to your computer only through additional
file transfer steps or encoding schemes. You can use ftp, telnet, gopher,
and E-mail, but while you are on the Internet, you cannot use full
graphic Web browsers such as Netscape.

A few Internet service providers are offering very specialized access using names such as SLIRP or TIA. If your provider uses something like these, you will still need TCP/IP software in your computer.
You will not have to change providers, however. If you think your
provider may offer one or more of these, contact the provider and
ask. Be sure to ask whether you can use Netscape's Navigator with
these.

Method Three: Internet Host Access via SLIP or PPP Accounts

Internet Host access assumes that you have a computer and TCP/IP
software. (If you really want to know a lot more about TCP/IP software and SLIP/PPP, we explain them in Appendix B.) TCP/IP software provides the full range and power of Internet services, limited
only by the capability of your computer. This is what the Internet Society calls *host access*. By the way, all computers connected this way,
regardless of size or power, are called *hosts*. Host access is the focus of
this book. Once you have TCP/IP software, you will be capable of
being fully on the Internet.

Internet Connections

To have Host access, and to *really* be on the Internet, you must have
three things:

1. An Internet service provider (ISP)

2. TCP/IP software for your PC

3. A telephone (dial-up or leased line) connection to your Internet
service provider

If you have these three things, you are really on the Internet and can be
part of all of the information, excitement, resources, and tools now
available from the Web to browsers such as Netscape.

We will now look at a road map to help you find your way to the
Internet.

Activity One

Getting Started—A Road Map

The road map starts at several different places. You should pick your starting place from the following list:

a. If you presently have Netscape, TCP/IP software, and a SLIP/PPP connection to an Internet service provider, go to 1 below.

b. If you presently have TCP/IP software and a SLIP/PPP connection to an Internet service provider, but do not have Netscape, go to 2 below.

c. If you have a Local Area Network (LAN) connection with Internet access through your school, business, or agency, go to 3 below.

d. If you presently have an Information services connection with AOL, CompuServe, Prodigy, or others offering Internet access, go to 4 below.

e. If you presently have a terminal or Internet shell connection with an Internet service provider, go to 5 below.

f. If you presently have no online connections, go to 6 below.

The Starting Places

1. If you presently have Netscape, TCP/IP software, and a SLIP/PPP connection to an Internet service provider, jump now to Session Three to begin learning more about Netscape.

2. If you presently have TCP/IP software and a SLIP/PPP connection to an Internet service provider but do not have Netscape, jump now to Session Two to obtain Netscape.

3. If you have a Local Area Network (LAN) connection with Internet access through your school, business, or agency, verify that obtaining and using Netscape is permitted by your enterprise, and jump to Session Two and obtain Netscape.

4. If you presently have an information services connection with AOL, CompuServe, Prodigy, or others with Internet connectivity, you have several choices. You may, of course, purchase the Netscape Navigator Personal Edition as described in Activity 6.

If your service allows file transfer protocol, you may also get a TCP/IP program as described in Activity 3. You will then need to select an Internet service provider as detailed in Activity 4. You can then move on to Session Two to obtain Netscape.

You should still check your hardware and software setup in Activity 2 in this session. You should then go directly to Session Two.

5. If you presently have a terminal or Internet shell connection with an Internet service provider, you may choose to use your shell account to obtain a TCP/IP program as detailed in Activity 3.

You should still check your hardware and software setup in Activity 2 in this session. You should then go directly to Session Two.

You can then proceed to get Netscape by file transfer protocol (ftp) as explained in Session Two.

6. If you presently have no online connections, the easiest choice for you is to purchase the Netscape Navigator Personal Edition either from a software store or by calling Netscape sales at 1-415-528-2555. The cost at this writing is U.S. $44.95. Street prices may be lower.

This will give you a complete TCP/IP program, an E-mail program, the Netscape Navigator, and a Registration Wizard allowing you to register automatically with any of a number of national Internet service providers.

You will still need to check your hardware and software setup in Activity 2 in this session. You should then go directly to Session Two.

Checking Your Hardware and Software

Hardware

To install and run Netscape you will need an IBM compatible PC with the following hardware:

Hardware	Minimum	Recommended
Processor Type	386 or later	486 or later
RAM Memory	4 megabytes	8 megabytes or more
Hard Disk Space	12 megabytes free	18 megabytes free

Note: These requirements are for Netscape Navigator; additional hard drive space will be needed for the TCP/IP program and for multimedia programs discussed in Session Nine.

Communications

To communicate with your Internet service provider (ISP), you need a telephone line connection. This will usually be one of the following:

a. An ordinary dial telephone line and a modem attached to your PC. We strongly recommend a 28,800 bits-per-second modem due to the amount of multimedia information you will be receiving once you are using Netscape. (The faster your modem, the quicker the information will be transferred to your computer.) Try not to get a modem with speeds below 14,400 bits per second.

b. An Integrated Services Digital Network (ISDN) adapter connected to your PC and an ISDN connection from your telephone company. Your ISP must also support ISDN. ISDN is now becoming available from many telephone companies and offers higher speeds than a modem connection.

c. A local area network (LAN) adapter in your PC connected to an Internet router or gateway. These connections are most often found in schools, businesses, or government agencies. Although, this is the highest speed connection, some organizations place administrative or technical limitations. You should contact your systems or network administrator to see if it is possible to use Netscape on your network.

After you have verified that you have the right equipment, you will need to check your software.

Although our focus here is on IBM compatible PCs, Netscape Navigator is also available for Macintosh and UNIX-based X-Windows systems. If you have one of these systems, many of the instructions that we provide beginning in Session Three and continuing throughout the rest of the book will apply to your system.

Software

There are several different versions of Windows operating systems that will permit you to run Netscape on your PC. As of this writing, they include:

Operating System:

Microsoft Windows 3.1 or 3.11 or

Microsoft Windows for Workgroups 3.1 or 3.11 or

Microsoft Windows 95

The examples in this book use the Windows 3.1 version of Netscape. You will also need TCP/IP software compatible with your operating system.

Finding and Installing TCP/IP Software

If you are using Windows 95, we believe that it includes TCP/IP. (It has not had its final release as this is being written.) After verifying that TCP/IP is included in Windows 95, you should jump ahead to Activity 4.

TCP/IP Shareware

There are many TCP/IP software programs or "stacks" available for purchase or as shareware. *Shareware* is offered at no charge over the Internet, but if you continue to use it, a (usually) small license fee is requested. It is considered "good form" to send in this license fee and it often grants you rights to upgraded programs and support.

The most popular shareware TCP/IP program is called *Trumpet Winsock*. Trumpet is the name that Peter Tattam (Trumpet's creator) of the University of Tasmania has given his program.

The program has the filename winsock.zip

It should be available by file transfer protocol (ftp) from many anonymous ftp servers, among which are the following:

Host	Path
ftp.utas.edu.au	/pc/trumpet/winsock
ftp.ucdavis.edu	/win-public/Winsock

Host	Path
ftp.tas.gov.au	/pc/winsock
ftp.sunet.se	/pub/vendor/microsoft/developr/MSDN/NewUp
ftp.std.com	/customers2/src/pc/winsock
ftp.waiariki.ac.nz	/pub/msdos/windows/winsock
ftp.cic.net	/pub/Software/pc/winsock
ftp.deakin.edu.au	/pub/pc-net/windows/winsock
ftp.mr.net	/pub/dialip/win/winsock
ftp.bhp.com.au	/pc/msoft/bussys/lanman/public/winsock

If downloading programs using ftp is still a bit daunting for you, you may wish to contact Netscape (see number 6 in Activity 1) and save yourself the bother.

Peter Tattam has also prepared additional applications such as telnet and these are available from many of the same sites. The filename of these additional applications is usually winapps.zip.

Internet Service Providers

Internet service providers may also offer TCP/IP programs as part of their services. You may wish to contact prospective providers in your area and ask them about TCP/IP packages. Be sure to tell them that you plan to use Netscape's Navigator.

Selecting Your Internet Service Provider

Activity Four

As illustrated in Figure 1-5, Internet service providers come in many flavors and sizes. The largest are global providers such as the IBM Global Network or CompuServe's Internet connection. Many providers are local or regional or national. The interconnection of all these providers forms what we call the Internet. Figure 1-5 shows you this array of providers.

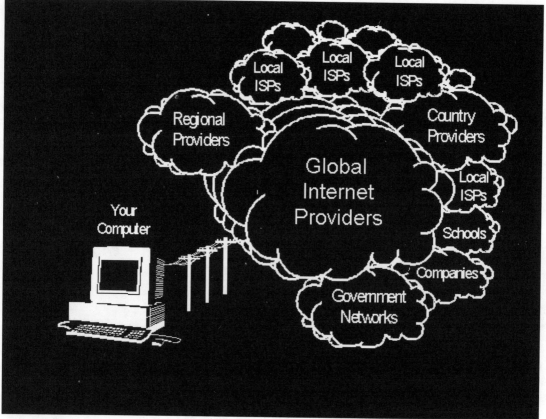

Figure 1-5
Internet Provider
Access

What the figure tries to show is that your connection is direct to an Internet service provider, not through any specialized gateway. The connection may be to a global, national, regional, or local provider. We will discuss how to find a provider at the end of this session.

There are, however, many special cases. You may fall into one of these and still wish to use Netscape.

1. Your school, agency, or business may offer a full Internet connection through a "firewall" or security protection computer.

2. Your school, agency, or business may use Netscape only for an internal closed Web for local purposes only.

3. You may need to be on a special local area network (LAN) to gain access to the open Internet.

If you suspect that you are in one of these situations, you will need to contact a system or network administrator at your school, agency, or business to determine how to proceed.

Most of us will probably access the Internet through a dial-up telephone line and a modem (or an ISDN adapter). For that reason, we will focus on dial-up access providers. Almost all these providers will also offer leased line Internet services to businesses, schools, and agencies.

Appendix A lists many Internet service providers (ISPs). The lists have been taken from public sources. You may want to look at these sources for their most current lists.

Selecting Your Internet Service Provider (ISP)

You will be looking for an Internet service provider to connect you to the global Internet. Since you will be using TCP/IP in your PC, your ISP must support compatible connections. There are different kinds of connections and many ISPs will offer several. Some providers, however, offer just the most basic.

The three types of connections are

> **SLIP**—*Serial Line Internet Protocol.* Almost all PC-based TCP/IP programs and almost all providers support SLIP.

> **CSLIP**—*Compressed SLIP.* Again most packages support this.

> **PPP**—*Point-to-Point Protocol.* This is a newer way to connect to the Internet. PPP handles telephone line errors better than does SLIP or CSLIP. Not all providers support this method.

This need not be a complex choice, but you must be sure that your ISP supports the protocol you are intending to use. More often than not, you will select the protocol based on what your ISP will offer.

The deciding factor may be the cost of the service to you.

Suggestions for Selecting Providers

For SLIP, CSLIP, and PPP services, most providers offer about the same service. There are not large differences in the service itself. Almost all providers offer connections for the highest speed modems available. The biggest difference may be in the total cost to you.

For most of us, cost is a key issue when selecting a service, Internet or otherwise. There are three cost elements to consider when accessing Internet service providers by using dial-up telephone services:

1. Monthly service charges for the service;
2. Additional per-hour service charges, if any;
3. Telephone call costs to reach your provider.

Some providers charge an initial sign-up fee, but this is usually small compared to a year's worth of service and telephone costs.

Depending on where you live, the actual telephone costs may be the most important cost element. If you live near the provider's access telephone number, the per-minute cost of the call may be zero. That is, you will be making a local call. Many of us, however, must make toll or long-distance calls.

Our first suggestion is to find a provider with telephone access numbers that are local calls for you. However, if you travel the United States and want to use Netscape on your laptop, you may want to consider an ISP with countrywide local numbers.

Our second suggestion is to find a local provider with a "flat rate" charging structure. This means that there is no per-hour charge and that you will be permitted to have unlimited usage for the monthly fee.

If you travel internationally, there are fewer choices. As we write this, the IBM Global Network and CompuServe offer a wide range of local access telephone numbers around the world.

Some service providers offer 800-number service, but that adds to their cost and they pass those costs along to you, the customer. You may want to calculate how many minutes a month you plan to use the Internet and then see if an 800 number is cheaper for you than a long-distance call might be.

Other service providers offer lower rates on weekends and at night. If most of your use will be at times other than during the business day, this could save you money.

Some long-distance telephone companies offer discounts to frequently called numbers. You might investigate making the service provider one of your frequently called numbers.

Finding and Contacting Internet Service Providers

Service providers usually have voice telephone numbers for new account sales. Some, however, prefer E-mail. If you do not yet have any E-mail or Internet accounts, you will have to contact them by telephone. Almost all will take Mastercard or Visa charge cards to set up and bill your account.

Check Appendix A for the list of Internet service providers.

Session Summary

This introductory session has been intended to provide you with the background information required for you to get started on the Internet. We have provided a brief overview of the Internet and a road map to get you started. We have listed the minimum and desirable needs for your PC software and hardware. We have shown several places to get TCP/IP if you need it and how to select an Internet service provider.

Session

2

Activity 1: Downloading Netscape Navigator Using ftp

Activity 2: Installing Netscape

Activity 3: Purchasing and Installing Netscape

Movie 1: Extracting Netscape

Movie 2: Installing Netscape

Getting Netscape Installed

Session Overview

In this session, we will show you how to obtain and install Netscape's Navigator (also commonly referred to as Netscape). We list the several ways you can find Netscape and give you the details you will need to get your own copy of this World Wide Web browser. If you choose to purchase Netscape, we will give the facts and contacts. If you decide to download Netscape from the Internet, we will show you how and where to acquire it. Finally, we tell you how to install the browser and register your copy with Netscape Communications Corporation.

Getting Netscape Navigator—Choices

There are several ways of getting the Netscape Navigator.

The fastest method is to use file transfer protocol (ftp) and to download it directly from Netscape Communications Corporation.

The easiest method is to purchase Netscape either from a software or computer store or directly from Netscape.

The choice is yours and may be made based on your experience with using the Internet and ftp in particular. It is not difficult to download Netscape using ftp, and we will show you how if you choose that route.

We will begin with the process of how to download Netscape using ftp. If you have decided that you would rather purchase Netscape, then skip ahead to Activity 3, Purchasing and Installing Netscape.

Downloading Netscape Navigator Using ftp

In their online documentation, Netscape states that "Netscape Navigator 1.1 is subject to the terms detailed in the license agreement accompanying it."

If you choose to download Netscape, you must do so under the terms of the license. The license can (and should) be downloaded and read. If you fit one of the categories in the license, then you are permitted to use Netscape without a license fee.

The online Netscape license begins:

> GRANT. Netscape Communications Corporation ("Netscape") hereby grants you a non-exclusive license to use its accompanying software product ("Software") free of charge if (a) you are a student, faculty member or staff member of an educational institution (K-12, junior college or college) or an employee of a charitable non-profit organization; or (b) your use of the Software is for the purpose of evaluating whether to purchase an ongoing license to the Software. The evaluation period for use by or on behalf of a commercial entity is limited to 90 days; evaluation use by others is not subject to this restriction.

Please read the complete license.

If you have decided to download Netscape, you must be careful to select the correct version. At this time, there are several different versions of Netscape for different versions of Windows. You will probably want to choose the simplest version at first until you gain familiarity with Netscape's operation. You may then wish to return to an ftp site and download a later version.

The way to determine which version you should download depends on which Microsoft Windows version you are running. Briefly, this means

If you have	Then download
Windows 3.1	n16e11n.exe (or later equivalent)
Windows for Workgroups 3.11	n16e11n.exe (or later equivalent)
Windows NT	n32e11n.exe (or later equivalent)
Windows 95	the 32-bit version that supports Windows 95. As we write, this version is in final beta test.

You may want to download the 16-bit version and visit Netscape's Home Page to get information about the latest release of this version.

If you have upgraded Windows or Windows for Workgroups with a program called WIN32S, you must be using either WIN32S version 1.20 (or later) or you must remove WIN32S. In either case, you need to download the 32-bit Netscape version. The README.TXT file we will download gives full details about how to do this.

Downloading Netscape Using ftp

To download Netscape, you must have a program that will allow you to use *file transfer protocol* or *ftp*. Simply, *ftp* is a program that will allow you to move a file (such as Netscape) from one computer to another over the Internet. In other words, you can use ftp to transfer a copy of Netscape to your computer's hard drive. If you have any of the following, you can use ftp to get Netscape.

1. An account with America Online, Compuserve, Prodigy, or a similar information service that allows ftp

2. A shell (command line) account with an Internet service provider

3. A SLIP/PPP account with an Internet service provider and ftp client software on your computer

Since we cannot know what type of account you have, we will tell you where to look for the files and then ask you to get them using your own particular account type.

All Information services and Internet service providers offer much in the way of help. If you are having difficulty using ftp, contact them or use their help facilities.

Here are the files you should download. You should download all three. Then read the README.TXT and LICENSE files first for current information and licensing details.

The text files and Netscape's Navigator can, of course, be found at one of the following ftp sites:

ftp.netscape.com *or* ftp2.netscape.com

You will be looking for the directory   /netscape/windows

You will be looking for the files

LICENSE

README.TXT

N16E11N.EXE   (or N32E11N.EXE, see above)

Note that the first two should be downloaded using the ASCII setting with ftp, and the Netscape program should be downloaded using the BINARY or IMAGE setting.

We suggest that you put these files in a separate directory on your PC, such as C:\INCOMING.

If you are using Windows 95, look for directories indicating that there is a Windows 95 version. At the time of writing, this had not yet been established.

Once you have successfully downloaded and read the README.TXT, and LICENSE files and downloaded the Netscape program, you are ready to install Netscape under Windows.

Installing Netscape

The steps in this activity will illustrate how to install Netscape. There may be slight variations as later versions of Netscape are released. However, the process should remain the same. We will assume that you now have the N16E11N.EXE file in your C:\INCOMING directory. Make whatever adjustments you need to make if you have the file elsewhere.

Here's the installation procedure.

1. Start Windows

2. Click on **File** and **Run**

3. Type C:\INCOMING\N16E11N

A number of files will be extracted and expanded. You will then return to your Windows screen.

4. Click on **File** and **Run**

5. Type C:\INCOMING\SETUP

You should then see the following sequence of screens. You may accept the suggested directories and group names or you may change them if you wish. Figure 2-1 shows the Windows File, Run screen.

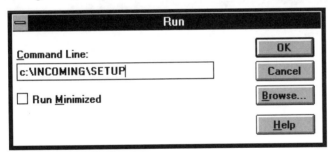

Figure 2-1
Windows\File\Run
Screen

Figure 2-2 shows the Netscape Setup as it begins.

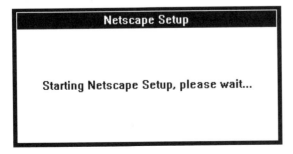

Figure 2-2
Starting Netscape
Setup

Figure 2-3 shows the Netscape Setup: Welcome screen. As indicated, just click on **Continue** and the installation will begin.

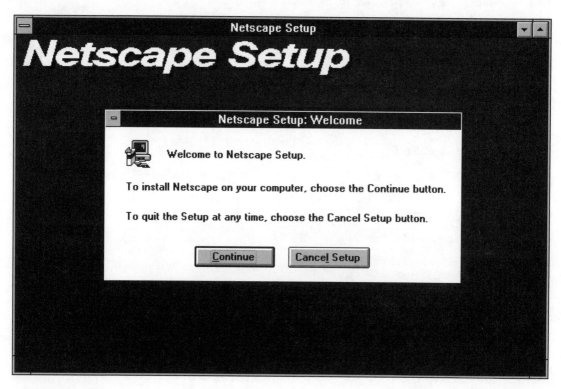

Figure 2-3
Netscape Setup:
Welcome Screen

Figure 2-4 shows the Netscape Setup: Installation Location screen in which you can determine where to have Netscape installed. The default is to put it into a directory called Netscape.

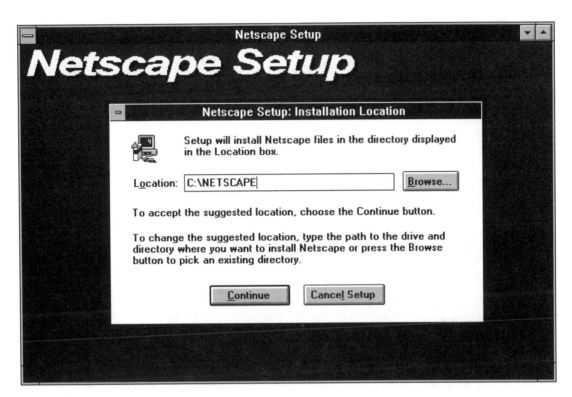

Figure 2-4
Netscape Setup:
Installation Location
Screen

Figure 2-5 shows the Netscape Setup: Program Group Screen in which you are told which Program Group will be constructed for Netscape. If you would rather have the Netscape Icon elsewhere, here is where you would make that choice.

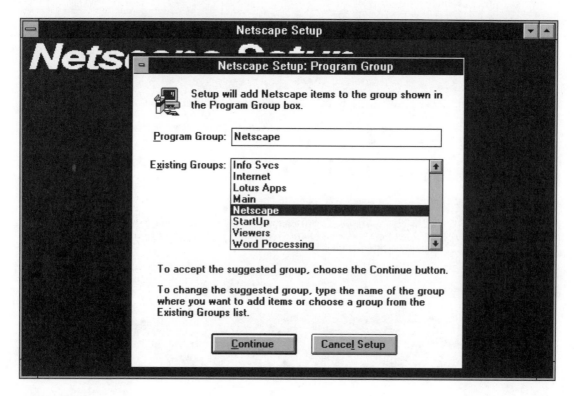

Figure 2-5
Netscape Setup:
Program Group
Screen

Figure 2-6 shows the Netscape Setup screen that indicates the progress of the installation as the files are being installed.

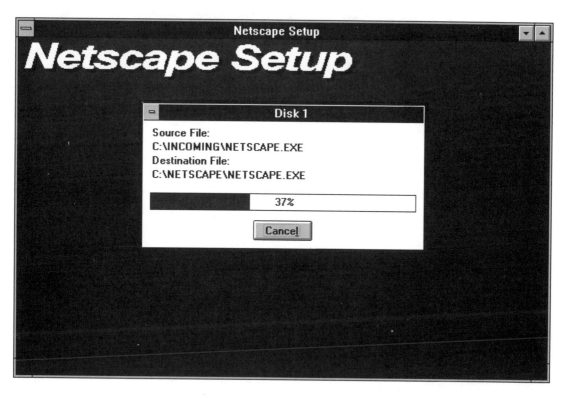

Figure 2-6
Netscape Setup
Progress Screen

Figure 2-7 shows the Netscape Setup at the conclusion of the installation. You can choose to read the README file at this time.

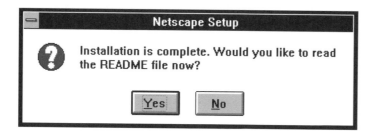

Figure 2-7
Netscape Setup
Screen at Completion
of Installation

Figure 2-8 shows the Netscape Icon group that has been created for you.

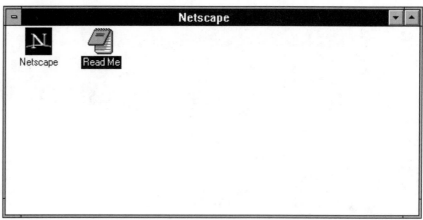

Figure 2-8
Netscape Icon Group

Netscape has now been installed and you are ready to skip ahead to Session Three and your first glimpse of the Web using Netscape.

Purchasing and Installing Netscape

As we write, there are two versions of the Netscape Navigator for Windows users available for purchase. We expect that by the time you read this, the Windows 95 version will be available as well.

The two current versions are *Netscape Navigator* and *Netscape Navigator Personal Edition*.

The two versions both include the Netscape Navigator, but the Personal Edition also provides you with additional programs. Included in the Personal Edition is a sign-up program for an Internet connection called the *Registration Wizard*, TCP/IP software, an E-mail program called Eudora Light and, of course, the Netscape Navigator.

Here's how to decide which version is for you.

1. If you already have an Internet SLIP or PPP account, this implies that you already have an Internet connection, you already have TCP/IP software, you (most likely) have an E-mail program, and you are only lacking Netscape Navigator. Assuming that all of this is true, you should just purchase Netscape Navigator.

2. If you have only a Windows PC and a modem (you may also have America Online, Compuserve, or Prodigy), you should purchase the Netscape Navigator Personal Edition. You will need to have the Registration Wizard to sign you up for your Internet connection. You will need to have the TCP/IP software so that you can have either a SLIP or PPP connection. And, you would certainly wish to have Eudora Light, a fully-functional E-mail program. Most importantly, you will want to have Netscape Navigator. All of these programs are included in the Netscape Navigator Personal Edition.

Either one can be purchased by telephone from Netscape. In addition, the Netscape Navigator Personal Edition is available from major software and computer stores. At press time, it had a list price of $44.95 but could be found for less at "street" prices.

If you choose to purchase either one of these software packages directly from Netscape, you can call them in Mountain View, California at 1-415-528-2555.

The installation process for Netscape Navigator is very similar to the one that was detailed in Activity 2. In any case, you will be following the printed instructions that come with the package.

For Netscape Navigator Personal Edition, we have shown the series of screens you will see while installing the program in Figures 2-9 through 2-15.

Netscape Navigator Personal Edition Installation

The Netscape Navigator Personal Edition comes with two disks and a small manual. The package is shown in Figure 2-9.

Figure 2-9
Netscape Navigator
Personal Edition
Package

After unpacking the diskettes, read the installation instructions, and following them, install the disks. The installation process follows a normal Windows installation sequence using File and Run.

After you have completed the instructions, you will see a new program group in Windows that looks like Figure 2-10.

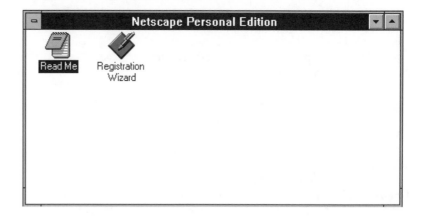

Figure 2-10
Netscape Personal
Edition Icon Group

If you do not have an existing SLIP or PPP account, you should now click on **Registration Wizard**. You will see a screen like Figure 2-11.

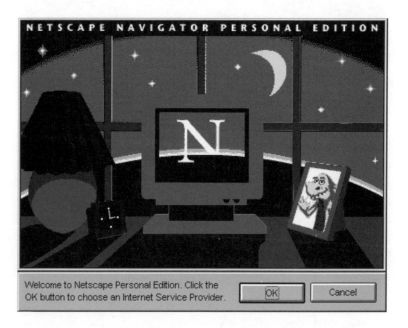

Figure 2-11
Netscape Personal
Edition Welcome
Screen

If you click on **OK**, you will be taken to the Overview of the Registration Wizard as shown in Figure 2-12.

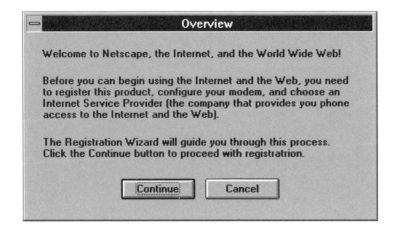

Figure 2-12
Overview of the
Registration Wizard
Screen

A series of screen prompts will guide you in selecting an Internet service provider. Fill each box in completely. (Remember to use your name, not mine.) You will be asked for a major credit card number and its expiration date. Figures 2-13 through 2-15 show much of the rest of the process. After you look at the information about each provider, you may select a provider and then you can register.

As shown in Figure 2-13, you will have to provide your name, and information about the type of modem you will be using to access the Internet service provider. Clicking on the **Service Provider... button** will permit you to choose the service provider of your choice and to set up your Internet account.

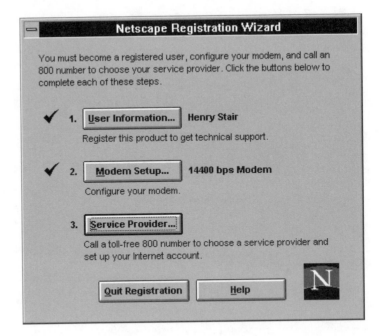

Figure 2-13
Netscape Registration
Wizard Screen

Figure 2-14 shows the Dialing Settings screen in which you will have to provide some information about the actual way that your computer will be dialing the Internet service provider. Follow the instructions in the "Getting Started" manual and the prompts on the screen.

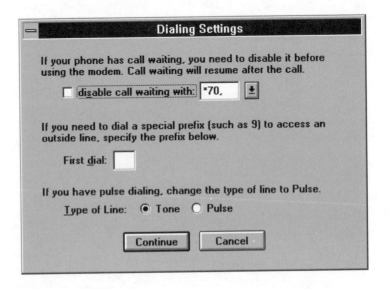

Figure 2-14
Dialing Settings Screen

As indicated in the What's Next? screen shown in Figure 2-15, your modem will dial an 800 number to register the product and to help you to choose an Internet service provider. You will need to have your credit card ready for this step!

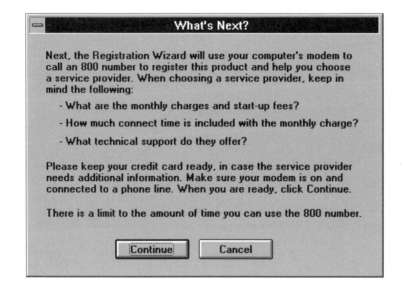

Figure 2-15
What's Next? Screen

The major Internet service providers usually charge both a sign-up fee as well as a monthly fee. The monthly fee usually covers a fixed number of hours online. After you have used that fixed number of hours, they will charge a per-hour fee. You are not, however, getting married to any provider. After a period of time, you may choose to change to another provider, should you wish to do so.

You should now have Netscape installed and you should be registered with an Internet service provider! You are ready for your first glimpse of the World Wide Web.

Session Summary

In this session, you completed the installation of Netscape, which was acquired either by using ftp or by purchasing it. You are now through with the installation process and are ready to actually use Netscape. We will begin to do that in the next session.

Session

3

Activity 1: Starting Netscape Navigator

Activity 2: Touring Netscape's Home Page

Activity 3: Netscape's What's New! Button

Activity 4: Visiting Web Sites

Movie 1: HyperLinks

Movie 2: What's New

A Glimpse of the Web

Session Overview

Before we begin to use Netscape, we will pause for a moment to learn about the World Wide Web, Web servers, and Web browsers. Then we will take our first excursion out onto the Web with Netscape Navigator. Without worrying about the actual details of how Netscape does all that it does (that comes in the next session), we will just point and click with our mouse to get our first taste of this amazing new resource. We conclude this session with an exploration of a simple Web directory.

What Is the World Wide Web?

The Global Internet

There are many books and articles that explain the history, nature, and culture of the Internet. We will not try to repeat that here. Let's just say that the Internet consists of millions and millions of computers of all kinds and sizes all connected by a common language. (The language, or protocol suite to be precise, is TCP/IP and is described briefly in Appendix B.)

Your computer is now one of these computers and it (and you) can reach all the other computers on the Internet. This Internet has been around under various names since the 1970s. The Internet provides the underlying transport mechanism for the World Wide Web. You now have your Internet service provider, TCP/IP software, and Netscape and your computer is now connected to (or can dial) the Internet.

Your computer is now capable of many of the traditional Internet activities, such as telnet, ftp, gopher, and E-mail. We are going to focus on the newest of these: the World Wide Web. Later in the book, in Session Eight, we will show you how to use Netscape to do these more basic Internet activities.

The World Wide Web

While the Internet has been around for over 25 years, the World Wide Web was invented fairly recently, in March 1989. Its inventor is Tim Berners-Lee and he did the initial work at CERN, the European Particle Physics Laboratory. He is still very much involved with the Web, as it is commonly called, through the World Wide Web Consortium.

According to the World Wide Web Consortium, the Web contains "the universe of network-accessible information, an embodiment of human knowledge."

Yes, but what is the Web?

The Web is made up of all the computers around the world (Web servers) containing hypertext and hypermedia (HTML) information connected to the Internet. The information is accessed over the Internet using a transport scheme called *Hypertext Transport Protocol* (HTTP) by computers with Web clients or browsers known as Mosaic or Netscape or WebSurfer.

Simply put, the Web is a way for you to get information (text, data, pictures, sounds, movies, programs, and so forth) from all over the world. It is a way for you to do this right from your computer without your having to know "computerese." The Web allows you to navigate this exploding new world of information with only a mouse.

How did this happen?

The inventors of the World Wide Web wanted to find a way to share information using what is known as hypertext. *Hypertext* allows us to create documents with built-in references to other information. These references, or *hyperlinks* as they are called, allow us to jump directly to a reference word, phrase, or picture by just selecting it.

However, unlike Windows Help screens (also hypertext), clicking on the hyperlink can take you instantly to information that is located anywhere on the global Internet. At first this was done using text screens and cursor keys. These were called text-only browsers. A *browser* is a program that talks to Web servers in HTTP (Hypertext Transport Protocol) and receives and presents the responses on your screen. The responses are sent from the server in a form called Hypertext Markup Language (HTML).

We will describe HTML in greater detail and show you how to create some of your own HTML pages in Session Ten.

While this was successful in a limited way, by early 1993, there were still only about 50 Web servers in the world with HTML information.

Graphic Browsers

In 1993, a team at the National Center for Supercomputer Applications at the University of Illinois created something new for the Web. It was called Mosaic and was a *graphic browser*. Late in 1993, they made it freely available over the Internet. The team also made it available for the three most popular computer types: PCs with Microsoft Windows, Apple Macintosh, and UNIX X-Windows systems.

Mosaic captured the imagination of the Internet world and the Web was "discovered." Soon, graphic Web browsers caught the attention of the whole world.

In less than two years, the number of Web sites (Web servers with information in HTML) exceeded 5,000. It is still growing at an incredible rate. As you read this, it will have passed 50,000 and perhaps far more.

Netscape

In 1994, many of the NCSA Mosaic team moved to the Silicon Valley in California and formed Mosaic Communications Corporation, now known as Netscape Communications Corporation. It is their graphic browser that we present.

Starting Netscape Navigator

By now, you have installed Netscape Navigator and are ready to start. First, you must establish your connection with the Internet. If you are using a dial-up connection, you should get this going first. If you are using Netscape Navigator Personal Edition, starting Netscape will automatically start your dialer connection. If you are using another dial-up method, such as NetManage's Web Sampler, double-click on the **Custom Icon** and click on **Connect**.

Once connected, you can then start Netscape like any other Windows application program, by double-clicking on the **Netscape Icon.** If all is working well, you should see Netscape Communications Corporation's Home Page.

A *home page* is what we call a starting place. The initial screen that you view from a Web server is called a home page. You can think of it as the front door or lobby. Once we actually journey beyond the initial home page, we may find a wealth of information (or just a little).

Some home pages may only have one page to look at. The home pages for some large companies are more like the front lobbies of huge office buildings that provide an entry to enormous information resources.

When using Netscape, by default we start out at the home page of the Netscape Communications Corporation. From this initial starting point we can explore the resources of the Netscape program and the Netscape corporation or even travel out to other pages on the Internet.

Later, we will show you how to change Netscape so that when it begins, it will go to another place (or no place at all) when you start. For now, we will leave the default as Netscape's Home Page.

The Netscape Home Page will look similar to Figure 3-1 but will have been updated from what is shown in the figure.

Figure 3-1
Netscape Home Page

Name Resolution

The Internet works by allowing us to use human readable names such as

```
home.netscape.com
```

But, the computers actually use Internet Protocol (IP) addresses which are numbers, such as

```
192.27.245.16
```

At your Internet service provider and at many other places on the Internet are special computers called *domain name servers* (*DNS*). These computers convert the human readable names to computer numbers. At times, these computers are heavily loaded and may be slow to respond to requests from your computer.

Sometimes the Internet (or your Internet service provider) gets a bit overloaded. When this occurs, the DNS computers that are supposed to look up host names may appear to fail. If this happens, you may get an error message that looks like Figure 3-2.

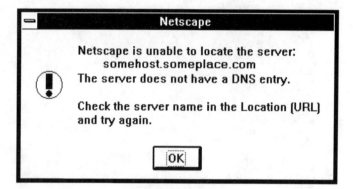

Figure 3-2
Name Lookup Failure

One of four things may be happening.

1. Your connection with your ISP is not really working properly. If you click on the **Home button** many times and get an error message like the one shown in Figure 3-2, your connection may need to be verified or restarted. You may need to contact your ISP if this always happens when you are starting.

2. The name resolution process is a little slow. After you are sure that your ISP connection is functioning correctly, just try accessing a given location a second time. Usually this will work if you try once (or twice) again.

3. The connection to that host is temporarily broken or that host is temporarily unavailable (maintenance, power failure, and so forth).

4. There really is an error in the name.

If you have been unsuccessful in connecting to your ISP several times, the failure will, more often than not, be the second reason. Trying once or twice again will usually get you through. You do this (for now) by clicking on the **Reload button** that is the circular-arrow button near the top left of your screen (see Figure 3-1). You may also click on the **Home button** (the button with the little house).

If this is your first time connecting to the Internet and the World Wide Web and you receive the error message shown in Figure 3-2, you probably have an ISP connection problem. Contact your ISP and ask them to help you get your connection working well.

Now that the Netscape Home Page is visible, let's take a quick tour of it so that you might better understand what you are seeing.

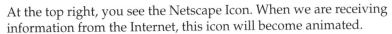

Touring Netscape's Home Page

We will take a much more complete tour of Netscape in Session Four. Let's just hit the highlights here. Look either at your screen or back at Figure 3-1. At the top of your screen, you see several rows of text and buttons. These rows of text and buttons are used to control Netscape.

At the top right, you see the Netscape Icon. When we are receiving information from the Internet, this icon will become animated.

The large central area of the screen is the document area where we can actually look at text and pictures coming in from a Web site.

At the right side is a normal Windows-type scroll bar. This allows us to move up and down a page that is too long to fit on our screen.

At the bottom is a status line. This will tell us what, if anything, is happening at the moment. Right now it may be saying "Document: Done." (This will not be there if you have moved your mouse or pressed the cursor keys.)

Netscape's What's New! Button

Let's start our quick tour by using our mouse to click on the **What's New! button** at the top left of our screen. A new document or page will appear on your screen in the document area. While it may not look exactly like the one shown in Figure 3-3, it will be similar.

What's New? is a selection of Web servers that are new (or new to the people who prepare this page at Netscape). The list is updated regularly.

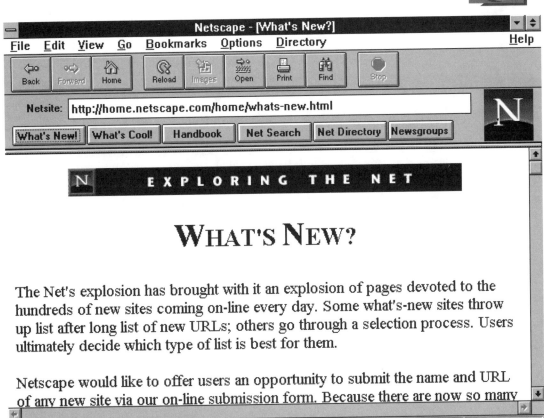

Figure 3-3
What's New?

Now we will use our first hyperlink. Remember that a hyperlink is really a pointer to another place on the Internet. By clicking on it, we tell Netscape to contact that Web server.

Understanding Hyperlinks

Look at the What's New? page on your screen and find a hyperlink. The hyperlink should be in color (usually blue) and will be underlined. Looking back to Figure 3-3, there are two hyperlinks:

submission form in the second paragraph

What's New on Yahoo near the bottom of the document area

Now move your mouse pointer to the lower one (or a similar one on your screen). Notice that the shape of your mouse pointer changes when it goes over this colored, underlined phrase or word. Your mouse pointer is now on a hyperlink. We have shown this in Figure 3-4.

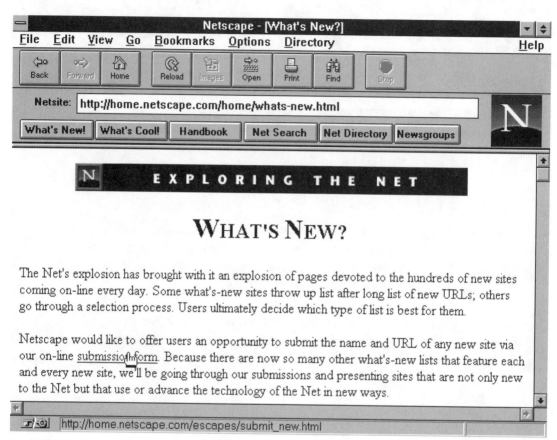

Figure 3-4
Pointing to a Hyperlink

Notice also that the status line at the bottom of your screen now shows a complex line of text. This is the actual host address of the Web server you are trying to contact. This address will be sent out over the Internet in search of your information. It may also include additional information about specific files or pages to retrieve. For now, you can ignore it; we will explain these addresses in greater detail later.

If you just single-click the **mouse button**, Netscape will come to life and go off in pursuit of the Web site for the information. The new information will arrive and will itself contain many hyperlinks to other interesting places.

You have just started surfing the Web. We should caution you that this can become habit forming and that some hours may pass before you come back to us here. Please do come back, there's lots more to do.

You can use the Back button at the top left of your screen to "navigate" back to where you have been. If you get totally lost, you can always return to the Netscape Home Page by clicking on the **Home button.**

Welcome back! Even if you have already gone off to many Web sites, we want to finish our glimpse of the Web using a somewhat more structured approach. We will take you to a popular Web directory and illustrate quickly one way to find interesting Web sites. Later in the book, we will show you many ways to do this.

Visiting Web Sites

You can always return to Netscape's Home Page (unless you have changed the default) by clicking on the button on the top row marked "Home" which has an illustration of a little house on it. If you do that now, we will take you on a quick tour of the other directory buttons on Netscape's screen.

What's Cool?

Like What's New!, What's Cool! is a selection of cool (or hip or attractive or interesting) pages prepared by the folks at Netscape.

If you click on the **What's Cool! button**, you will be taken to the most current version of Netscape's What's Cool? page. When we did this, the page looked like the one shown in Figure 3-5.

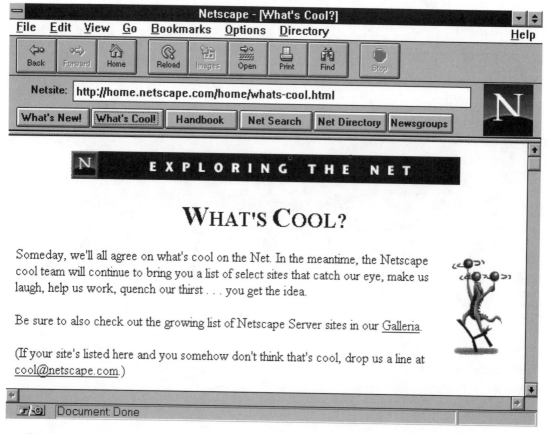

Figure 3-5
What's Cool? Page

This page will contain many hyperlinks, but please don't dash off.

The Handbook—Online Help

You can return to the What's Cool? page in a moment; it will be right
there. Right now, however, let's next click on the **Handbook button**.
The Netscape Online Handbook provides you with a set of reference
materials from Netscape. It should look similar to Figure 3-6.

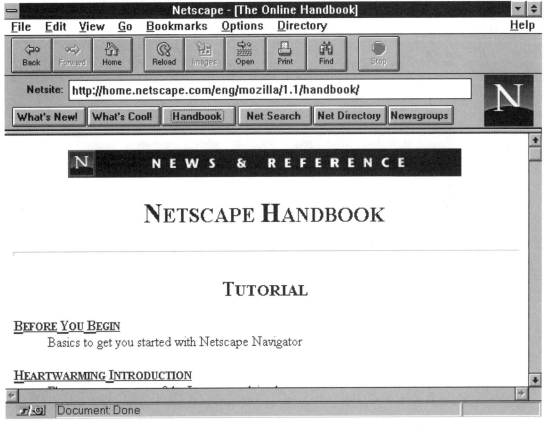

Figure 3-6
The Online Handbook

Notice that the Online Handbook and its references are not located
on your computer. Unlike most program help facilities, Netscape
keeps its help programs at the factory. Thus, they can fix mistakes
and add new information at any time. This is one of the real
strengths of the Web. The information will always be as fresh as the
provider wishes to make it. You might want to take a few moments
to explore the wonderful resources that are provided by the Online
Handbook. Once you have had a chance to do so, join us as we
explore the Net Search page.

Net Search

If you now click on the **Net Search button**, you will be taken to a selection of World Wide Web search tools. The page may look something like the one depicted in Figure 3-7.

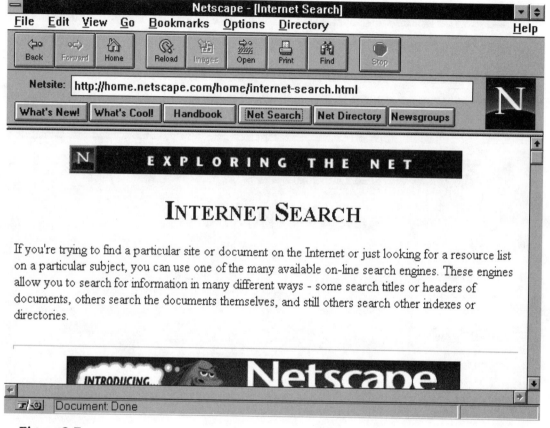

Figure 3-7
Internet Search

We will return to this page during Session Seven when we explore Web searches and search tools in greater detail. For our last stop on this quick overview tour, we will visit a site that is known as Yahoo.

Net Directory

Click on the **Net Directory button** and you will be taken to Netscape's Internet Directory page. At the time of writing, the Internet Directory page was provided by Yahoo.

It seems likely that Yahoo will continue to provide the Internet Directory page. However, if that is not the case at the time when you are reading this, try typing the following URL. Type

`http://www.yahoo.com`

This should take you to the same set of information that is shown in Figures 3-8 and 3-9.

The Internet Directory page provided by Yahoo looks like the one that is displayed in Figure 3-8.

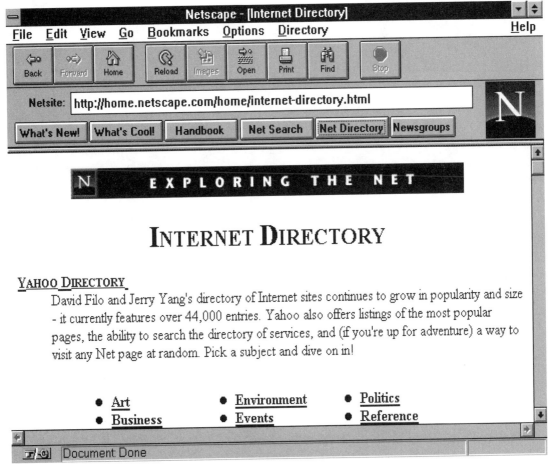

Figure 3-8
Internet Directory

As a brief demonstration of the Yahoo Internet Directory, we will move through a series of hyperlinks and illustrate each one with a figure. To keep this simple, we will pick from the top of each list. We will begin by clicking on the hyperlink **Art** in the directory. This will take us to a page similar to the one shown in Figure 3-9.

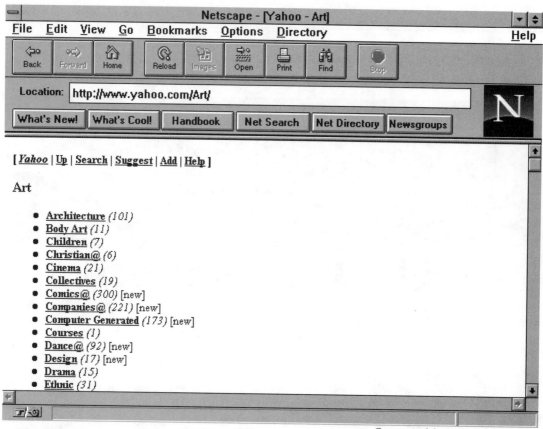

Figure 3-9
Yahoo—Art Page

Courtesy of the Yahoo Corporation

As you can see, we have moved down a level in the directory or index of sites. We have now arrived at a page devoted to Art-related Web sites. Next we click on **Architecture** and move down another level. We are now at a directory page listing sites related to Architectural Art. This is shown in Figure 3-10.

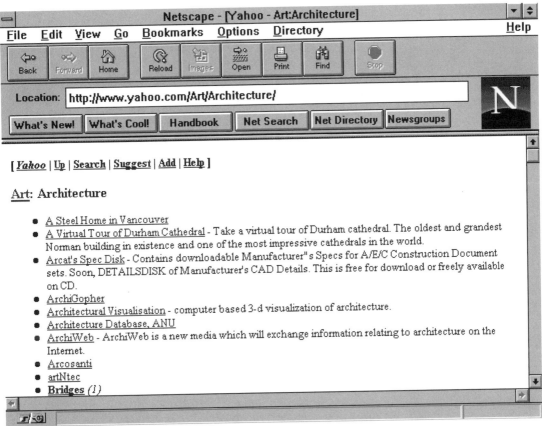

Courtesy of the Yahoo Corporation

Figure 3-10
Yahoo—
Art:Architecture Page

For our next jump, we move down this page to Bridges. After we click on the **Bridges hyperlink**, we are sent a directory page with just one listing (at least that was true at the time when we did this). It looks like Figure 3-11.

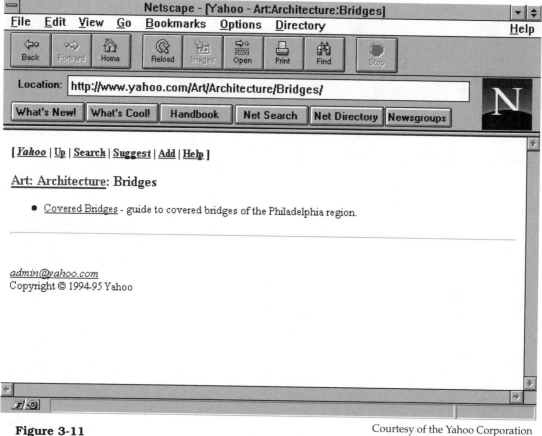

Figure 3-11
Yahoo—
Art:Architecture:
Bridges Page

Courtesy of the Yahoo Corporation

We click on the **Covered Bridges hyperlink** and arrive at the page illustrated in Figure 3-12.

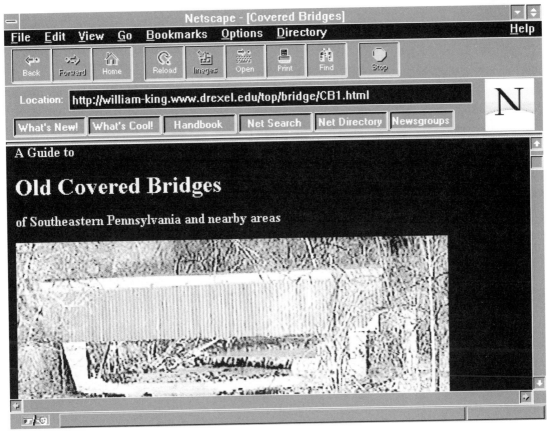

Figure 3-12
Covered Bridges Page

Our example and quick tour are now complete. In our next session, we will take you on a more detailed tour of Netscape's Navigator and teach you how to control various aspects of the program.

Session Summary

This session introduced you to the World Wide Web and has allowed you to take a quick and easy tour of a few Web sites. We hope you have discovered that Netscape is really a very intuitive tool. It is very easy to learn and to use, as is the Web itself.

In this second part of Hands-On Netscape, we will:

1. *Take a tour of the Netscape screen so that you can better control your copy of Netscape.*

2. *Teach you about URLs.*

3. *Introduce you to History and Bookmarks.*

4. *Take you on a tour of the World Wide Web.*

5. *Teach you how to add to, organize, and edit your Bookmarks List.*

○ Touring Netscape

○ What's Out There?

○ A Tour of the World Wide Web

PART TWO

Session

4

Activity 1:   A Grand Tour of Netscape

Activity 2:   Controlling Netscape

Activity 3:   Keystrokes and Mouse Clicks

Activity 4:   The Right Mouse Button

Activity 5:   Netscape Security

Movie 1:   Netscape Control Bars

Movie 2:   Alt and Ctrl Keys

Movie 3:   Right Mouse Button

Movie 4:   Security

Touring
Netscape

Session Overview

In this session, as we start detailing Netscape Navigator and its many features and tools, you will begin to see how Netscape allows us to access the Internet in a very friendly way. All the classical (read-difficult and complex) tools of the Internet can be used much more easily with Netscape. In Session Eight, we will show you how to use many of these classical tools while using Netscape. First, however, we will want to tour Netscape itself and learn how to control it. By the way, although the formal name of this wonderful Web browser is the Netscape Navigator, we will usually refer to it as Netscape.

A Grand Tour of Netscape

In the last session we began to have a taste of the World Wide Web by using some simple buttons on Netscape's screen. Now that you have seen a few example screens from Netscape, we will pause for a moment to take a tour of the screen. This tour will explain all the parts of the screen and what you can do with each feature. Let's start with an overview of the screen that's shown in Figure 4-1.

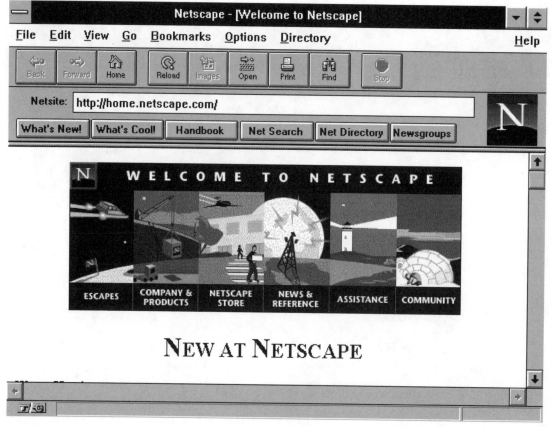

Figure 4-1
Welcome to Netscape

The Netscape Navigator was developed by the Netscape Communications Corporation. We have chosen to use their home page to explain their Netscape screen. It may appear automatically when you start Netscape (if you are connected to the Internet) or you may choose to go to this location.

Take a look now at Figure 4-1 or else launch the Netscape program and then click on **File** and **Open Location**. Once the Open Location box is open, type
```
http://home.netscape.com
```
You can follow along either using the figures in the text or your own screen.

The Title Bar

We will start at the top of the screen. Notice that Netscape has many of the features we are used to from Microsoft Windows. The title bar in Figure 4-2 tells us the program we are using and the location we are viewing. In this case we are using Netscape Navigator for MS Windows and we are viewing a document whose title is "Welcome to Netscape."

Netscape - [Welcome to Netscape]

Figure 4-2
Netscape Title Bar

At the left end of the title bar is the usual Control Menu box, often called the File Drawer. A single click on this box will produce the Windows-type drop-down menu. A double-click on this box will close the window. At the right end of the title bar are the minimize and maximize buttons.

The minimize button will shrink Netscape to a small icon at the bottom of your screen. It does not stop the program; it merely minimizes it. Double-clicking on the minimized icon will bring back Netscape as an open window. The maximize button will allow Netscape to occupy your entire screen. Once Netscape occupies the entire screen, the maximize button will then change to a double-arrow button to allow you to return the program to a smaller window.

The Menu Bar

Going down the screen, we see the familiar Windows-type menu bar. This is illustrated in Figure 4-3.

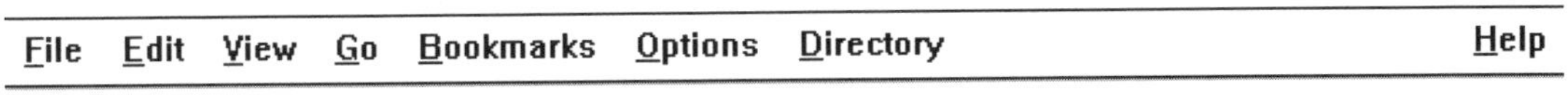

File   Edit   View   Go   Bookmarks   Options   Directory   Help

Figure 4-3
Netscape Menu Bar

Here we see individual words, each with a single letter underlined. We can either single-click on a word or hit the ALT key and the underlined letter to activate a drop-down menu. You may be aware that these underlined letters are sometimes referred to as accelerators.

We will look at each of these drop-down menu boxes in greater detail in Activity 2 in this session.

Netscape Toolbar

Continuing down the screen, we come to the toolbar that is shown in Figure 4-4.

Figure 4-4
Netscape Toolbar

The toolbar contains buttons that provide a fast path to many Netscape commands. Not all are active, but let's look at a few that are.

Back, Forward, and Home

Netscape not only shows us pages from the World Wide Web, but it also keeps track of the pages we have already viewed. This "history" allows us to go *back* that is, to a previous page. We can also go forward to later pages. *Forward* will be active only if we have gone back to see a previous page. This movement is done with the Back and Forward buttons.

Clicking on the far-left Back button takes us directly back to a preceding page (if there is one to go back to). Clicking on the Forward button takes us directly forward to the following page (if there is one to go forward to). And clicking on the Home button takes us (for the moment) to the Netscape Home Page (where we are right now). Later we will show you how to set this Home button to the location of your choice.

Reload

The Reload button permits you to reload the page that is presently active. This is particularly helpful if you are looking at a page where information may have changed since the last time you looked at it (more about that later). It is also very handy if you get a page with images missing. If you see a broken image icon, you can try to "reload" the page and see if the image will come in the second time.

Images

The Images button permits you to view images that are affiliated with the current page. If you are concerned about the time it takes to download images to your computer, then you might initially choose to turn off the Images button. Should you decide to view them at a later time, you would click on the Images button to do so.

Open

The Open button will open the Open Location dialog box that you may have used earlier in this session.

Print

Clicking on the Print button will cause the current document to be printed.

Note: The entire document will be printed, not just the portion that is visible on your computer's monitor.

Find

Clicking on the Find button will open a Find dialog box where you will be prompted to enter one or several words in the Find What box. Netscape will then search through the current document for the word or words that are indicated. This is particularly helpful if you have downloaded a lengthy document containing a lot of text.

The Find function will only work with the page that is currently being displayed. It will not try to search other pages or hyperlinks.

Stop

Clicking on the Stop button will cause the document being downloaded to your computer to stop. This is very useful if you see that little or no activity is taking place, or if you change your mind about where you wish to go with Netscape, or if there are too many graphics and the download is taking too long.

Continuing down the screen, we come to the Location Box which is depicted in Figure 4-5.

| Location: | http://www.whitehouse.gov/ |

Figure 4-5
Netscape Location Box

The Location box provides us with important information. This is the actual address of the page we have downloaded. Also known as the *URL* (the *Uniform Resource Locator*), this address provides us with the following information:

The protocol being used. In this case, it is *http*, which is an abbreviation for *HyperText Transport Protocol*. (We will discuss the other protocols that can be used in Session Eight.)

The name of the host computer on which this file can be found. In this case, it is home.netscape.com.

The directory information where the file can be found. In this case, there is none.

The Location box has several other functions as well. If you place your cursor in the text area of the box and type in a new location, the words to the left of the box change to "Go To:" followed by what you have typed. This is another way to go to a new location. We can also use the Open button or the File, Open Location choice from the menu bar. The change in the Netscape Location box words is shown in Figure 4-6.

Go to: http://www.whitehouse.gov

Figure 4-6
Netscape Location
Box—Go To:

Yet another function of the Location box is to show if Netscape has detected a *Netsite server* at the distant World Wide Web (WWW) site. Netsite was the original name for the family of server products also made by Netscape Communications Corporation. They now simply call them *Netscape communications servers*.

Notice the word Netsite in Figure 4-7.

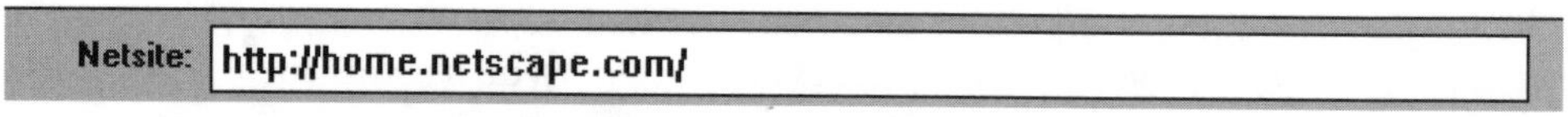

Netsite: http://home.netscape.com/

Figure 4-7
Netscape Location
Box—Netsite:

Continuing down the screen, we come to the directory buttons that are shown in Figure 4-8.

What's New! **What's Cool!** **Handbook** **Net Search** **Net Directory** **Newsgroups**

Figure 4-8
Directory Buttons

Directory Buttons

The directory buttons are, for the most part, a repeat of what can be found in the menu bar under either Directory or Help. As we have already seen in the previous session, they are provided for the convenience of new users. You will learn shortly, if you would like to see more of the document which is displayed, how you can hide them if you wish.

The last button, Newsgroups, needs additional information before you can see Newsgroups. We will show you how to add that information in Session Eight.

The Directory Buttons are:

What's New!	Same as Directory/What's New
What's Cool!	Same as Directory/What's Cool
Handbook	This will take you to a reasonably good set of information about Netscape
Net Search	Same as menu bar Directory/Internet Search
Net Directory	Same as menu bar Directory/Internet Directory
Newsgroups	Same as menu bar Directory/Go to Newsgroups

To the right of the Directory buttons is the Netscape icon, shown in Figure 4-9.

Figure 4-9
Netscape Icon

The Netscape icon serves two purposes. First, it is the Netscape logo. Second, the Netscape icon also tells you when Netscape is communicating with the Internet. You may have already noticed the stars flying through the air while Netscape is downloading a file to your computer. Look closely at the icon in Figure 4-10 and you will see the shooting stars.

Figure 4-10
Netscape Icon with Stars

Moving down the screen, we arrive at the document area. The entire center of your screen is the working document area (Figure 4-11) that displays documents and images from Internet sources. Here you will find the blue underlines and blue boxes that indicate hyperlinks to other information.

Figure 4-11
The Working
Document Area

At the right side of the screen, you sometimes find a Windows-type scroll bar (Figure 4-11). This will tell you that there is more information above or below the screen you are viewing. You can click on the up or down arrows to move slowly up or down, or you can put your cursor on the button and hold down the left mouse button to drag the button. You can also click on the scroll bar above or below the button to move in bigger jumps. If a wide screen of data arrives, you may also get a scroll bar at the bottom of your screen. It works the same way but moves to the right or to the left.

Finally, we come to the bottom of Netscape's screen. Here we find the multipurpose status bar that is shown in Figure 4-12.

Figure 4-12
The Status Bar

The status bar is worth noting whenever you are requesting a new hyperlink, waiting for something to come in, or just looking to see what is happening. At the right end of the status bar a red thermometer line appears. This *thermometer* provides you with a visual representation of how much of your data has been downloaded.

The thermometer can, however, be a bit misleading. Netscape has the ability to bring in many different streams of data and the bar will alternately show them all. Sometimes, just when you think everything is in, the bar drops back to show that more is coming.

The status bar will show "Document Done" when all of the data has been completely downloaded to your computer. The numbers in the center of the status bar are also used to indicate the progress of the streams of data as they arrive.

The status bar has another function in Netscape: to indicate security. Notice the small broken key at the left end of the status bar. The broken key is a reminder that Netscape believes that transactions between your computer and the remote site are not secure.

Netscape Communications Corporation, as mentioned earlier, also offers their Netscape server products with the capability of conducting secure transactions with your Netscape software. When your Netscape software detects a secure Netscape server, the small key in the status bar changes to a solid gold key on a blue background. This is shown in Figure 4-13.

Document: Received 512 of 1708 bytes 523×20

Figure 4-13
The Secure Status Bar

We will cover security in more detail at the end of this session.

This completes our grand tour of Netscape. We will now take a more detailed look at the menu bar and each of its menus.

Controlling Netscape

Each of the menu bar items contains a drop-down menu box which you can use to control the actions of Netscape. In this section, we will do a quick review of each menu bar item. (Discussion of some of the more detailed actions in Options will be saved for the Appendix.)

You will notice that some items in each of the drop-down menus are dimmed or are not as dark as others. This means the dim or grey item is not available at the present time as there is nothing to apply it to.

Like Windows, each of the menu choices and drop-down boxes have several ways to control Netscape.

Mouse Control

You can use the mouse to point to the menu bar and click to open the drop-down box. You can then use the mouse to select the action.

ALT Key Control

You can, however, also select the drop-down box with the ALT key and the underlined letter on the menu bar. When the box drops, you can select the action by pressing the key matching the underlined letter in the box.

CTRL Key Control

A third method is also useful. As you look at each of the drop-down boxes, notice that many actions can also be performed by pressing the CTRL key and another key. Using just two keys, CTRL and an accelerator, you can cause the desired action immediately.

The File Menu

Let's start with the File Menu as shown in Figure 4-14.

Figure 4-14
The File Menu

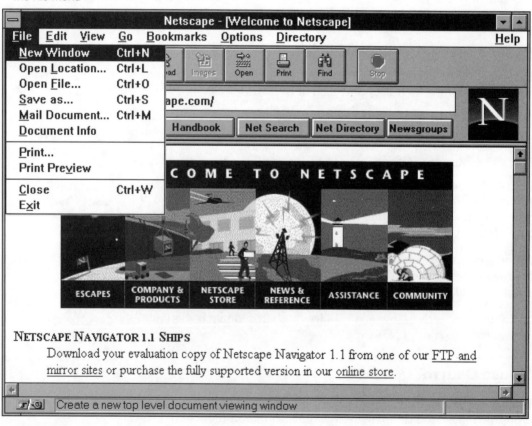

File allows control of Netscape's windows, connections, file saving, and printing. As you can see from the figure, the first choice is **New Window.** Netscape allows several simultaneous windows to be open, although this capability will be limited by the memory, storage, and speed of your computer.

You may wish to experiment with several windows to see what your particular limits are. You may also want to use Windows tools, such as the Help function which is included with Program Manager. If you have too many Netscape windows open, click on **Help** on the menu bar in Program Manager and then click on **About Program Manager**. Look at the bottom line, System Resources, and be sure that the number has not dropped below 20 percent. If it has, you may wish to close several Netscape (or other) windows.

Open Location and **Open File** will each open Netscape dialog boxes to allow you to select Internet sites or local files.

Open Location pops up a dialog box asking what location to open. In this box, you can type the address (URL) of the Web site you wish to visit. We will explain more about URLs later, but for now you just need to understand that URLs are location addresses out on the World Wide Web.

Open File pops up a familiar Windows dialog box asking what local file we wish to open. Selecting a file here will cause it to be opened by Netscape.

Netscape is expecting to find a file written in HyperText Markup Language or html. If you attempt to open another kind of file, you will get very weird results. html files will use the file extension of. HTM Files with the.TXT extension may also be read with Netscape.

Save As permits you to save the document currently being viewed. Note, however, that only the text of the document will be saved. Later in this session, we will point out the functions of the right mouse button which may permit you to save images.

Mail Document allows users to send documents or brief E-mail messages. You must specify your return E-mail address in Netscape's Options and Preferences as described in Session Eight.

Document Info gives both document source and date information and will tell you about any security information used to receive the current document.

Print and **Print Preview** do just as they say. Printing in Netscape works exactly as it does in other Windows applications; the entire contents of the current document will be printed (limited only by the capabilities of your printer).

Close will close only the current Netscape window and Exit will terminate Netscape.

The Edit Menu

Next we will look at the Edit menu as shown in Figure 4-15.

Figure 4-15
The Edit Menu

Edit follows the usual Windows customs of Cut, Copy, and Paste and adds two additional Netscape functions: Undo and Find. Of the three—Cut, Copy, and Paste—Copy will be active most often. With

Copy, you can copy selected items of text from the current page to Windows Clipboard. Undo will attempt to undo anything you have just completed, if this is possible.

Find will offer a Find What dialog box permitting you to search long documents for specific words, numbers, or phrases. In very long documents, this can be a real time saver.

The View Menu

The View menu offers ways for you to bring a document in again or for you to load images if you have deferred them until later. View offers several choices: Reload, Load Images, Refresh, and Source.

Reload returns to the current Web site and downloads the page again over the Internet. **Load Images** will be active only if you have turned off (no check mark) Auto Load Images in Options. You can then use View, Load Images to get the images when you wish.

Refresh brings the current page back in from your computer's memory; that is, it does not go back to the disk or to the original Web site.

A powerful feature of View is the ability to look at the real html source information. The View menu is illustrated in Figure 4-16.

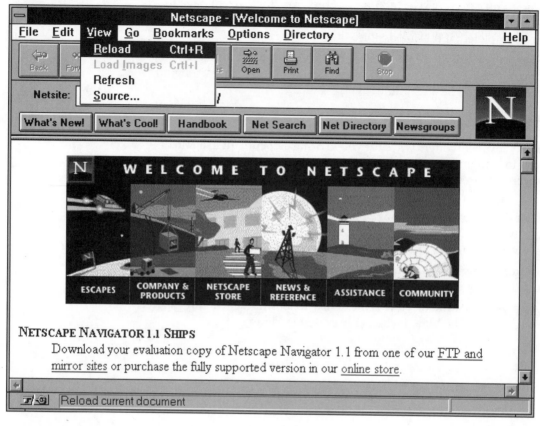

Figure 4-16
The View Menu

If you click on View Source you will be able to see the HyperText Markup Language (html) that has been used to create the document you are currently viewing.

The Go Menu

The Go menu is your navigational aid in Netscape. Its choices are shown in Figure 4-17.

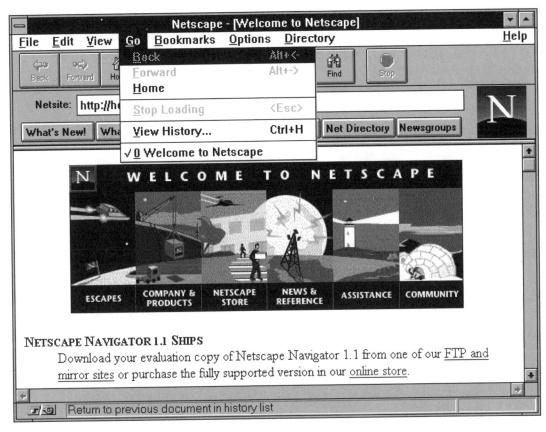

Figure 4-17
The Go Menu

Back, **Forward**, and **Home** move you about the pages currently open in Netscape. Stop Loading performs the same function as the Stop button does. View History will tell you exactly where you have been during a particular session.

The Go Menu in Figure 4-17 shows only one entry below View History, but as you accumulate more "history," each document you have visited will be listed here. A fast way to return to a site is to use the ALT key and then press the number of the item below View History. Figure 4-17 shows only "0 Welcome to Netscape."

History will be kept only while you have Netscape active. If you exit Netscape, the current history list will be gone. If you want to keep an address of a site for future reference, you will need to use the Bookmarks feature of Netscape.

The Bookmarks Menu

The Bookmarks menu and the *Bookmarks* which are entered into it are one of Netscape's most powerful features. Simply put, Bookmarks compile a record of the places to which you would like to return. Figure 4-18 shows what your Bookmarks menu will look like before you add any of your Bookmarks.

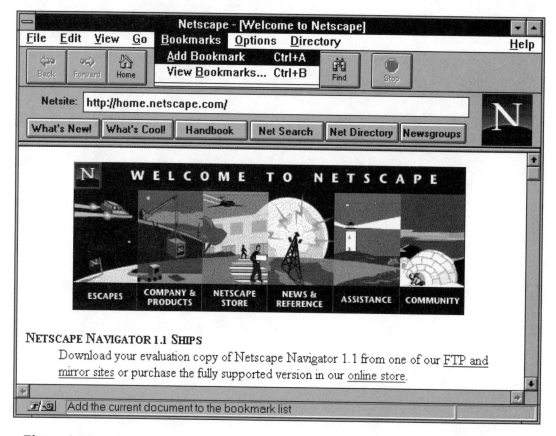

Figure 4-18
The (Empty)
Bookmarks Menu

As shown in Figure 4-18, there are no bookmarks shown in the menu. To begin to add bookmarks, you can select Bookmarks, Add Bookmark, or you can use CTRL + A to add the current document's location to your Bookmarks list.

When you have collected many bookmarks, your menu may look like the one which is shown in Figure 4-19. In Session Six, we will show you many of the sites in this list and will also show you how to manage your Bookmarks list.

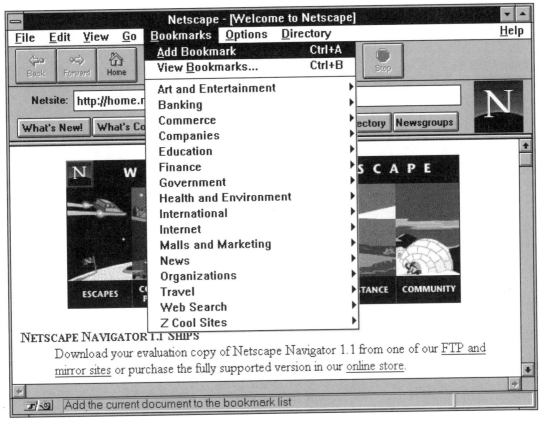

Figure 4-19
The Bookmarks Menu

The Options Menu

The Options menu gives you many ways to customize Netscape to your needs. The Options menu is shown in Figure 4-20.

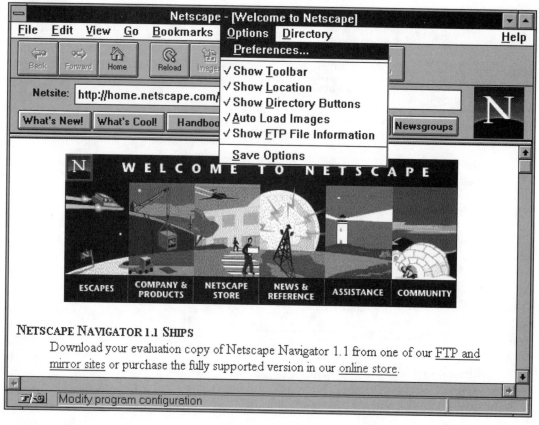

Figure 4-20
The Options Menu

The first item in the list, Preferences, offers a very large set of items that can be changed. In fact, there are so many possible options that we will defer discussing many of the possible Preferences choices until the Appendix.

Without going into great detail about Preferences here, it is important for you to realize that you can use the Options menu to turn several of the top bars in Netscape on or off. Notice that you are given the choice of showing (or hiding) the Toolbar, the Location bar, and the Directory Buttons. Hiding one or more of these will give you more screen area in which to view documents.

If you make changes to the Options, remember to click on Save Options or your changes will not be kept for your next Netscape session.

The Directory Menu

The Directory menu largely parallels the actions offered by the Directory buttons, but it is preferred by some who are more comfortable with Windows File menus. The Directory menu is shown in Figure 4-21.

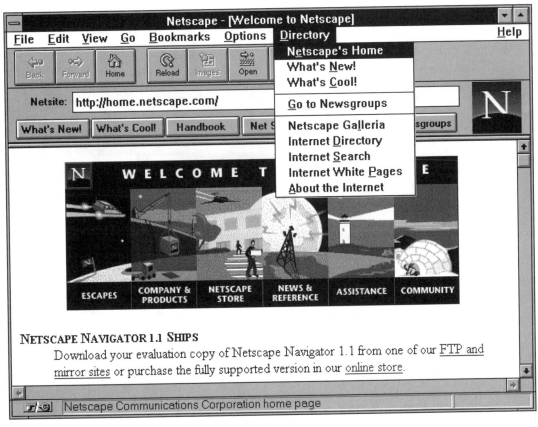

Figure 4-21
The Directory Menu

As you can see, the items in this menu closely resemble the ones offered by the Directory button choices. Also, there are several additional items. These are the Netscape Galleria, the Internet White Pages, and About the Internet. We will look at each of these in turn.

Netscape Galleria is a listing of companies that have built their sites using Netscape products. It's an impressive list and you should take some time to study it.

The *Internet White Pages* form a collection of search tools for people on the Internet. Take a look here to see if you can locate yourself or some of your friends.

About the Internet is a set of links to places where you can learn more about the Internet. Like the other listings, they change constantly, so you may wish to check back here from time to time to see what's new.

The Help Menu

Figure 4-22
The Help Menu

Finally we reach the Help menu as shown in Figure 4-22.

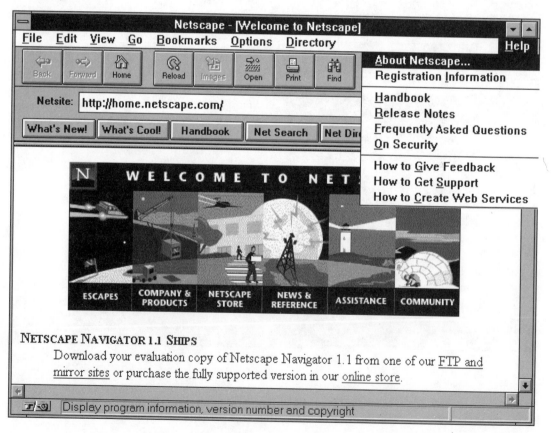

The Help Menu offers a number of ways to learn more about Netscape, Registration Information, and other topics.

If you have downloaded an evaluation copy of Netscape, you may wish to register it, so that you will receive information about new releases of the software, as well as some additional documentation. The cost, as of this writing, is $39 for individuals, and the entire registration process may be done securely over the Internet using the form which has been provided by Netscape.

You may want to look at About Netscape to learn what version you have. Also hidden on that screen behind the Netscape logo is a list of some of the people at Netscape who have contributed to this marvelous product. We have included the list in Figures 4-23 and 4-24. See if you can find this list in Netscape.

The Mozilla Team
1995

Front End Client Development
Macintosh
- **Tim McClarren**
- **Aleks Totic**

MS Windows
- **Garrett Blythe**
- **Troy Chevalier**
- **Chris Houck**
- **Ken Thomaston**

X Windows
- **Jamie Zawinski**

Cross Platform Client Development
- **Eric Bina** - Parser/Layout engine
- **John Giannandrea** - Imagery
- **Hagan Heller** - Gooey Stuff
- **Kipp Hickman** - Network Security
- **Lou Montulli** - Networking, Bookmarks and News
- **Michael Toy** - Whatever
- **Jeff Weinstein** - Crypto-Grunt

Figure 4-23
The Mozilla Team
(Part 1)

Iñtërnâtiônàlizætiøn

- **Bŏb Jüng**
- **Tønÿ Xûe**

Support

- **Rod Beckwith** - The Forgotten Network Deity
- **Sharon Iimura** - Testing (chimp wrangler)
- **Scott Kronick** - Documentation
- **Darin May** - Scapegoat
- **Jon Mittelhauser** - Marketing Droid
- **Dan Mosedale** - Systems Exorcist

Management

- **Marc Andreessen** - the Hayseed with the Know-How
- **Jim Barksdale** - The New Guy
- **Jim Clark** - Uncle Jim's Money Store
- **Joy Lenz** - Quality Assurance
- **Tom "Pacman" Paquin** - Client Development Manager
- **Rick Schell** - Vice President of Stuff

All human actions are equivalent ... and ... all are on principle doomed to failure.
Jean-Paul Sartre (*Being and Nothingness*, Conclusion, sct. 2)

Figure 4-24
The Mozilla Team
(Part 2)

Keystrokes and Mouse Clicks

As a summary and as a reference, we have included many of the controls for Netscape in Table 4-1. Each activity is listed by the various methods already outlined in this session.

Table 4-1

Activity	With a Mouse	ALT Key Commands	CTRL Key Commands
Go to or Open a new site	Click on the **Open button**	Alt F, L	CTRL L
Open a local file	Click on **File**, then **Open File**	Alt F, F	CTRL O
Save a document	Click on **File**, then on **Save as**	ALT F, S	CTRL S
Open a new Netscape window	Click on **File**, then on **New**	ALT F, N	CTRL N
Close the current window	Click on **File**, then on **Close**	ALT F, C	CTRL W
Exit Netscape	Click on **File**, then on **X**, or double-click on the **Control icon**	ALT F, X	
Find something in a document	Click on **Edit**, then on **F**	ALT E, F	CTRL F
Go Forward one document	Click on **Go**, then on **F**	ALT >	
Go Backward one document	Click on **Go**, then on **B**	ALT <	
View History	Click on **Go**, then on **View**	ALT G, V	CTRL H
Add the current location as a bookmark	Click on **Bookmark**, then on **Add**	ALT B, A	CTRL A

As you become more familiar with Netscape, you will discover your own ways of working with this wonderful product. One not so obvious way is to use the right mouse button.

The Right Mouse Button

One feature of Netscape that easily escapes attention is the use of the right mouse button. This button can be very helpful in several ways.

Clicking on a Hyperlink

Figure 4-25
The Right Mouse Text Menu

If you position your mouse on a text hyperlink (usually blue and underlined) and click the right mouse button, you will see a menu. An example of this menu is shown in Figure 4-25.

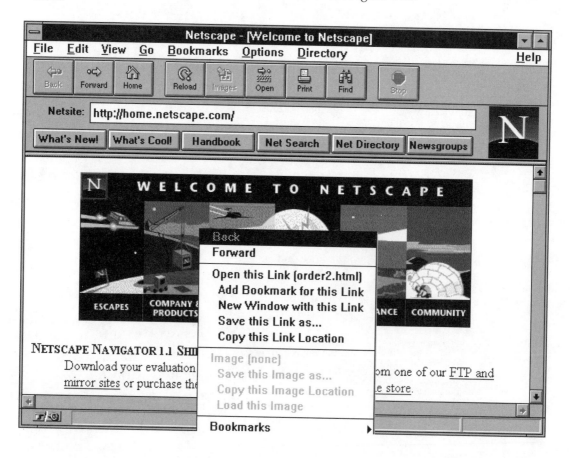

As you can see, this text menu provides you with navigational choices or many other options.

1.   You can go forward or back or you may choose to open the hyperlink.

2.   You can open a new window for just this link.

3.   You can save this complete link address to a file.

4.   You can copy this complete link address to the clipboard.

5.   You can open your Bookmarks list.

This right mouse button menu allows you yet another way to control the actions of Netscape. If you position the mouse over a graphic hyperlink (rather than a text hyperlink), different options of the right mouse menu are offered. In Figure 4-26 we show what appears when the mouse is over the "Welcome to Netscape" graphic.

Figure 4-26
The Right Mouse
Graphic Menu

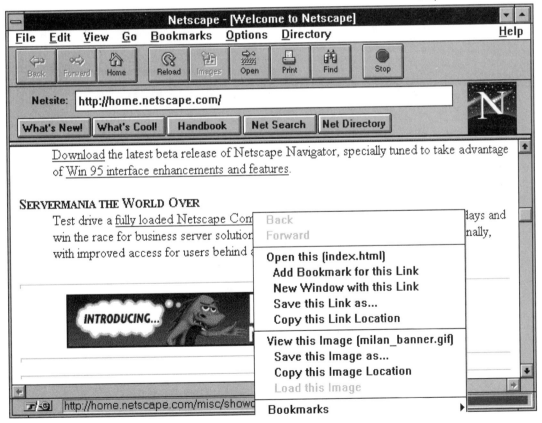

This right mouse graphic menu offers us additional choices if we click on a graphic image. The additional choices include

1. View this image by itself without any text
2. Save this image to a file of your choice
3. Copy the location (address) of this image to the clipboard

In the next session, we will discuss location addresses also known as Uniform Resource Locators or URLs more thoroughly.

Netscape Security

One of the useful features that is provided by Netscape is that it is capable of providing transaction security. We have all heard that the Internet is not a secure place in which to send credit card numbers or financial transactions. Netscape offers a secure, encrypted way to travel on the Internet.

When the Netscape software on your computer detects a Netscape server, it can set up an encrypted data flow between your computer and the server. This encrypted flow is sort of like using an armored car to transport money on public streets.

Netscape uses a series of warning pop-up windows to alert you to the security status of what you are about to do. For example, we will later discover that some World Wide Web pages allow you to fill in blank forms and send information across the Internet. Netscape will warn you that you are about to send information that is either secure or not secure.

Netscape also alerts you when you begin a secure transaction. An example of this is shown in Figure 4-27.

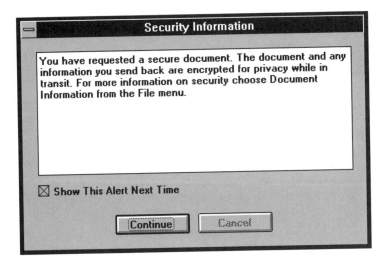

Figure 4-27
The Secure Warning
Window

Additional reminders are given when you are in a secure transaction. As noted earlier in this session, the broken key icon at the left end of the bottom status bar becomes solid. In addition, a thin bar just above the document area turns blue to remind you of the secure status.

Session Conclusion

As the development of Netscape continues, there will be changes to the screen. We hope this first tour has given you a start on using the screen and its tools.

In our next session, we will explain URLs and http and will define the other new terms you will encounter in greater detail. We'll also show you how to begin to customize Netscape.

Session Summary

Congratulations! You have begun to experience some of the power that Netscape and the World Wide Web can provide. You have learned about the various components and controls of the Netscape screen. Netscape is an extremely powerful software program; in the next few sessions, we are going to help you explore all the treasures that Netscape has to offer you.

Session

5

Activity 1: What's Out There on the World Wide Web?

Activity 2: Uniform Resource Locators—URLs

Activity 3: Using URLs to Probe the Web

Activity 4: History and Bookmarks: An Introduction

Activity 5: Setting Netscape's Options

Movie 1: Uniform Resource Locators

Movie 2: History List

Movie 3: Bookmark List

What's Out There?

Session Overview

In this session you will have an opportunity to broaden your understanding of the World Wide Web and Netscape. We will first examine the addressing scheme of Uniform Resource Locators— URLs. Then we will look at some of the many resources that are available and we will bring in a wide array of home pages. Next we will go over Netscape's History function and see how you can use it. Later we'll see how to create and use bookmarks. Finally in this session you will learn how to begin to fine-tune your copy of Netscape. Let's get started!

What's Out There on the World Wide Web?

The short answer is everything! There are many tens of thousands of places to go on the Web with an unbelievable richness of topics.

The longer, and probably more useful, answer would give you some sense of the wide array of resources that can be found on the World Wide Web.

While we can give you only some small hints about what's out there, here are just a few samples:

General Information about the World Wide Web

Information about the Global Internet
Information about the World Wide Web
Lists of World Wide Web Clients (or browsers)
Lists of World Wide Web Servers (or Web sites)

Mailing Lists

Hypertext Discussion Lists
Hypertext Archives

Courseware

World Wide Web Courseware
World Wide Web Literature

Lists of Tools and Programs

Commercial Sites

Wired Magazine
CommerceNet
Global Network Navigator
Silicon Graphics

Country Sites

Guide to Australia
Spain Web Sites
Austria
Chile
Costa Rica
Czechoslovakia
Germany

Educational Sites

Honolulu Community College
The University of Notre Dame
The Chinese University of Hong Kong

Interactive Sites

Michigan State University Weather Movies
Interactive World Map Interface

Legal Information and Government Sites

> Legal Information at Cornell
> U.S. Bureau of the Census
> U.S. Department of Commerce
> NASA and Its Many Labs
> The City of Palo Alto, California

Literature

> English Server at Carnegie-Mellon University
> Internet Book Information Center

Museums and Art

> San Francisco's Exploratorium
> University of California Museum of Paleontology

Music and Audio

> Internet Music Resources
> Internet Talk Radio

Organizations

> Electronic Frontier Foundation
> Association for Computing Machinery
> World Health Organization

This short list is intended to make you aware of some of the many resources that can be found on the World Wide Web. As we will show you shortly, you can use Netscape to help you find all of these resources from among the many that exist.

How Do We Address These Places?

The Internet uses two kinds of addresses: computer names and computer numbers. We do not need to concern ourselves here about the numbers (actually Internet Protocol addresses,) but we do need to know about the names. The Internet calls computers *hosts* and gives them unique names so that we may find them.

The names take the form of *subdomains*, *domains*, and *top-level domains*. An example is:

```
home.netscape.com
```

home is the computer at Netscape and *netscape* is in the *.com* top-level domain.

Let's look at some top-level domains to help you become familiar with them.

`.edu`	educational	`.au`	Australia
`.com`	commercial	`.ca`	Canada
`.gov`	governmental (U.S.)	`.de`	Germany (Deutschland)
`.mil`	military (U.S.)	`.fr`	France
`.net`	networks	`.jp`	Japan
`.org`	organizations		and so on...

You can recognize many host names when you see that they use *www* as the first part to identify their World Wide Web site. Here are a few examples for you to figure out:

www.harvard.edu   www.ibm.com   www.whitehouse.gov

Not too hard, eh? Some, of course, are not as obvious, but this will give you some idea about the host computer part of the uniform naming scheme.

Uniform Resource Locators—URLs

This uniform naming scheme goes by the acronym *URL* which means *Uniform Resource Locator.* According to Kevin Hughes,

> The World Wide Web uses what are called Uniform Resource Locators (URLs) to represent hypermedia links and links to network services within HTML documents. [More about HTML in a moment.] It is possible to represent nearly any file or service on the Internet with a URL.

A simple URL might look like `http://www.harvard.edu`

URLs are made up of three components.

1. The first part of the URL (before the two slashes) specifies the Internet tool or method of access, such as http: or gopher: or telnet: or ftp: (these tools are explained in more detail in Session Eight). The two slashes divide the tool from the next part, the Internet host computer.

2. The second part is the host name of the distant computer on which the data or service is located, such as `www.harvard.edu` Sometimes a computer port is shown in the second part. An example is `http://www.caltech.edu:80`

3. The third part (not always used) shows directories and specific files at the distant host computer or web server. A complete example is

`http://home.netscape.com/netstore/index.html`

If we tease this apart, it becomes:

`http:`	HyperText Transport Protocol— the tool or protocol
`home.netscape.com`	the host computer name
`netstore`	a computer directory
`index.html`	an HTML file in that directory at that host

A URL is always a single, unbroken line with no spaces.

Here are some more examples of URLs:

• `http://www.hcc.hawaii.edu`

Connects to Honolulu Community College World Wide Web Service

• `http://www.eff.org`

Connects to the Electronic Frontier Foundation

• `http://www.xerox.com`

Opens a connection to Xerox, the document company

• `gopher://gopher.uiuc.edu:70/1`

Connects to the gopher server at the University of Illinois at Urbana-Champaign

As you can see, all of these URLs have the same general format, and, in fact, look remarkably similar to Internet host addresses you may have seen before.

Hypertext Transfer Protocol: http

You will notice that several of these URLs begin with the initials

`http`

You will frequently see this term used at the beginning of URLs. *http* is an abbreviation for *Hypertext Transfer Protocol*, which refers to the language that is used on the World Wide Web.

Two kinds of computer programs use http—World Wide Web clients or browsers (such as Netscape) and WWW servers or Web sites. All Web clients and servers must be able to use http if they are going to "speak" to each other.

Thus, the most common form of a URL is

`http://www.hostaddress.domain/directory/file.html`

where *hostaddress* is often an abbreviation for a company, agency, or educational institution as we showed above. Or the computer might be located in another country, in which case the host address will end with the country domain.

The final part of the URL is often one or more directories and a file with the extension or ending of *html* for Hypertext Markup Language.

Hypertext Markup Language: html

One of the examples in the previous section contains the file extension html. You will see this extension used frequently and you will learn a lot more about *html* in Session Ten. *html* is the abbreviation for what is known as *Hypertext Markup Language*.

This is the text markup language that is used by the World Wide Web for creating and recognizing hypermedia documents. html permits those who are interested in doing so to take standard ASCII files and mark them up with all the formatting codes that are necessary to describe their layout and any hyperlinks they might have.

Now, let's look at several URL addresses again.

1. Main CERN World Wide Web Home Page

`http://info.cern.ch/Hypertext/WWW/TheProject.html`

`http://` tells us that this document adheres to the Hypertext Transfer Protocol. The colon and the two forward slashes are separators.

`info.cern.ch` is the host address that will take us to Switzerland.

`Hypertext/WWW/TheProject.html` provides us with the names of the directories and the name of this file and indicates that it was created using html, the Hypertext Markup Language.

2. CommerceNet

`http://www.commerce.net`

`http://` tells us that this document adheres to the Hypertext Transfer Protocol.

`www.commerce.net` tells us that this is a World Wide Web server, provided by commerce.net

3. U.S. Bureau of the Census

`http://www.census.gov`

`http://` tells us that this document adheres to the Hypertext Transfer Protocol.

`www.census.gov` tells us that this is a World Wide Web server provided by the governmental organization known as the Bureau of the Census.

Using URLs to Probe the Web

This activity will actually comprise many short exercises. We will take a few minutes to sample some of the many World Wide Web servers that exist. As we have noted, all of them communicate with each other using the Hypertext Transfer Protocol (http)—which is why you will notice that the places we will visit during this session begin with http.

Before beginning our first exercise, let's take a minute to dissect the address we are given. This is for the Netscape What's Cool? page.

The address is

`http://home.netscape.com/escapes/whats_cool.html`

Reading from left to right:

`http://` refers to the Hypertext Transfer Protocol used to address this server.

`home.netscape.com` is the host name for this World Wide Web server.

`/escapes` is the name of the directory containing the file whats_cool.html.

`/whats_cool.html` is the name of the file we will retrieve; the extension html indicates that the file is in Hypertext Markup Language.

Now, let's go look at this page.

Exercise A: Netscape's What's Cool? Page

URL:

`http://home.netscape.com/escapes/whats_cool.html`

1.   If your computer is already connected on the Internet, skip to step 2; otherwise connect to the Internet.

We will assume that you have some form of local network or dialup connectivity to the Internet. Our purpose here is to demonstrate Netscape and the World Wide Web. Please see Session One if you do not have an Internet Connection.

2.   Double-click on the **Netscape Icon**

3.   Once the Netscape for MS Windows main window is open, be sure to maximize it by clicking on the **up arrow** in the upper-right-hand corner

4.   Click once on **Open** on the toolbar

5.   In the Open Location: box, type

`http://home.netscape.com/escapes/whats_cool.html`

You actually do not need to type `http://` in Netscape, but we will continue to show it in our examples. Netscape will usually assume an http type of connection. You may also type the URL directly into the Location/Netsite box above the Directory buttons.

6.   Then click on **Open**

You should see a screen that resembles Figure 5-1, although you will see a more current version of this page.

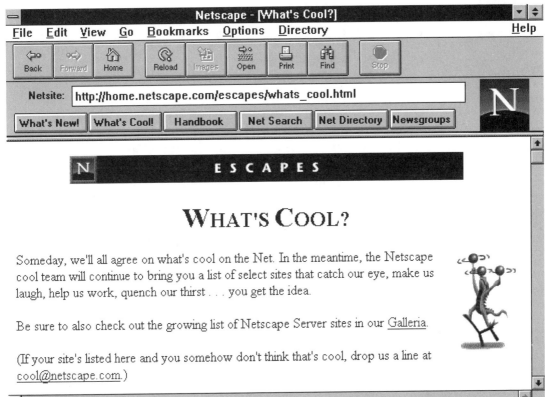

Figure 5-1
Netscape's What's
Cool? Page

For the rest of the examples, we will *not* repeat steps 1 through 4; we will just assume that the Open Location window is open or that you are typing into the Location/Netsite bar.

Take some time to wander through this first example. Click on the **down arrow** in the scroll bar on the right-hand side of your screen to scroll down through the Netscape What's Cool? document. As you might imagine, clicking on the **up arrow** in the scroll bar will take you back to the beginning.

NAVIGATION HINTS

a. As we noted in the last session, when you move your cursor across one of the items that is in blue, your cursor becomes a hand with a pointing forefinger. Clicking once will take you to the item printed in blue.

b. If you have chosen one of the words or boxes or names printed in blue and then decide you would like to return to the home page where you began, just click on the **back arrow** on Netscape's toolbar at the top.

c. If you decide you would like to save this URL in what is known as your Bookmarks list, just click once on **Bookmarks** and then once on **Add Bookmark**. We will go into more detail about Bookmarks in Session Six.

Exercise B: PCWEEK

URL:
`http://www.zdnet.com/~pcweek`

1. Click once on **Open**

2. In the Open Location box, type

`http://www.zdnet.com/~pcweek`

You may have to look hard to find the ~ (tilde) key. It's one of those keys that is in different places on various computer keyboards.

3. Click on **Open**

Your screen should be the latest edition of *PC Week* online and should resemble Figure 5-2.

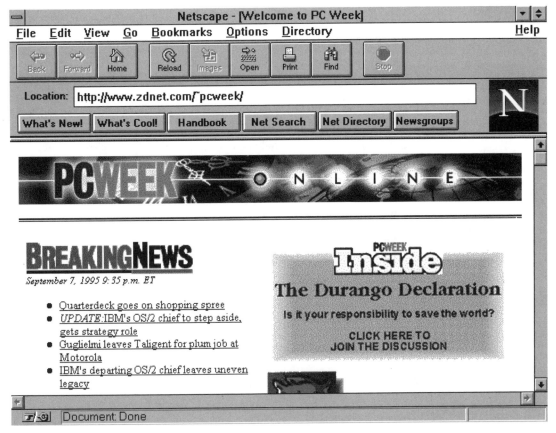

Figure 5-2
PCWEEK Online

NAVIGATION HINTS

a. Use your up- and down-arrow keys (on the right-hand scroll bar) to navigate through the articles provided by this magazine.

b. Use your Back button (located at the top on the toolbar) to jump back to the last document(s). Once you have done that, use your Forward button to jump forward to this one.

Exercise C: Guide to Australia

URL:
http://life.anu.edu.au/education/australia.html

1. Click once on **Open**

2. In the Open Location box, type

http://life.anu.edu.au/education/australia.html

3. Click on **Open**

NAVIGATION HINTS

a. Use your up- and down-arrow keys (on the right-hand scroll bar) to navigate through the Guide to Australia.

b. Use your Back button (at the top) to jump back through the last few documents. Use your Forward button to jump forward to this one.

You should see the Guide to Australia Home Page as shown in Figure 5-3.

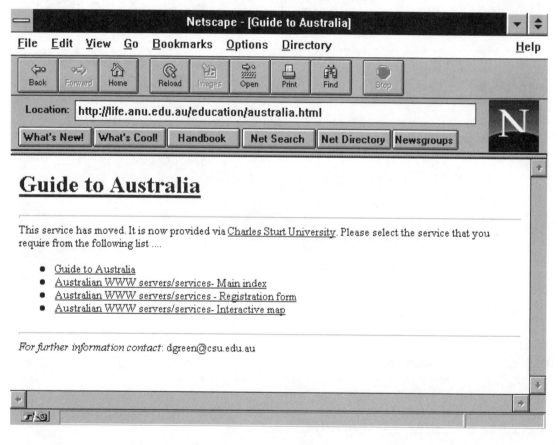

Figure 5-3
Guide to Australia

Exercise D: The City of Palo Alto, California

URL:
`http://www.city.palo-alto.ca.us/home.html`

1. Click once on **Open**

2. In the Open Location box, type

`http://www.city.palo-alto.ca.us/home.html`

3. Click on **Open**

4. Use your up- and down-arrow keys (on the right-hand scroll bar) to learn an enormous amount of information about the City of Palo Alto, California.

Figure 5-4 shows the home page that Palo Alto presents to the world.

Figure 5-4
City of Palo Alto Home Page

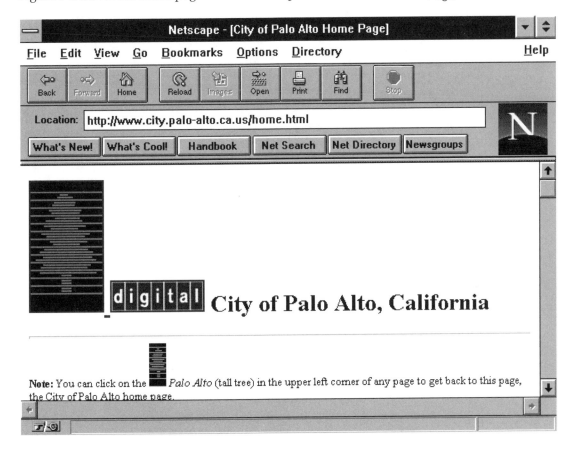

Exercise E: The Internet Book Information Center

URL:

http://sunsite.unc.edu/ibic/IBIC-homepage.html

Many World Wide Web sites use computers that are *case sensitive*, that is, they treat upper- and lower-case letters differently. Make sure when you are typing these exercises that you notice and type them exactly as shown.

1.   Click once on **Open**

2.   In the Open Location box, type

http://sunsite.unc.edu/ibic/IBIC-homepage.html

3.   Click on **Open**

Click on the up- and down-arrow keys (on the right-hand scroll bar) to learn an enormous amount about the amazing array of Internet resources that are related to books.

You should see a home page resembling Figure 5-5.

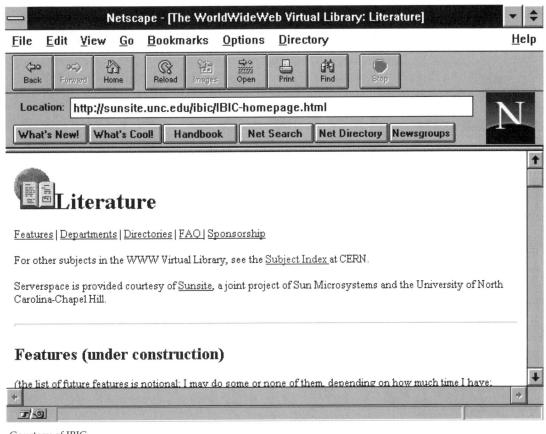

Courtesy of IBIC

Figure 5-5
The World Wide Web
Virtual Library:
Literature

Exercise F: Comprehensive List of Sites

URL:
`http://www.netgen.com/cgi/comprehensive`

NOTE: This exercise is included as a way of introducing you to the awesome number of http sites that exist on the World Wide Web. Note the number of hosts listed here!

Feel free to browse through this comprehensive http site list following the directions on the page. Here is how to do so.

1. Click once on **Open**

2. In the Open Location box, type

```
http://www.www.netgen.com/cgi/comprehensive
```

3. Click on **Open**

Use your up- and down-arrow keys (on the right-hand scroll bar) to learn about all of the many http sites that are available to you. Your screen should resemble the one shown in Figure 5-6.

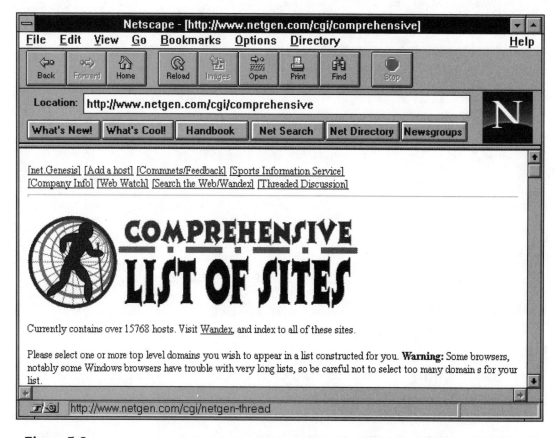

Figure 5-6
The Comprehensive
List of Sites

Hands-On
Activity
Four

History and Bookmarks: An Introduction

It quickly becomes apparent that URLs are often composed of extremely long lines of information. Certainly, it is possible to type the complete URL each time you need it. However, for many of us, this becomes a real chore, especially if there are URLs you find yourself using repeatedly. Netscape provides you with some tools—History and Bookmarks—for short- and long-term easy access to URLs.

History

History is created for you automatically each time you have a Netscape session. Netscape keeps track of the locations you have visited and puts them in a history list that is easily accessed. The history list is a summary of the last ten pages you have visited. If you have been following along during this session, your history list should resemble Figure 5-7. Just click once on **Go** on the menu bar to see this screen. (You will see in this figure that the sixth item in the history list is denoted as 404 Not Found. 404 Not Found usually results from errors in typing a file or directory name.)

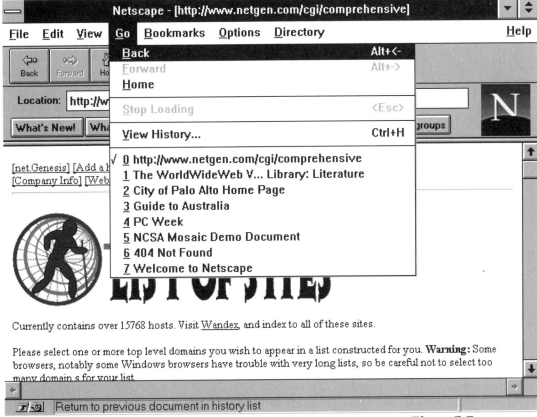

Figure 5-7
History List

Should you desire to go to any one of the listed sites, just click on it and you will be taken there (almost instantly)! The files have been cached or stored on your hard disk, and the response time should be quicker the second time around.

The history list is temporary storage and lasts only during the time that Netscape is running. It will be lost when you close Netscape.

Should you desire to keep any of these locations for viewing during a later Netscape session, you will have to store the locations in what is known as the Bookmarks List. You will learn more about bookmarks in Session Six.

Figure 5-8
View History

If you would like to see a more detailed listing of the sites you have visited, including their URLs, just click on **View History...** You should see a screen resembling Figure 5-8.

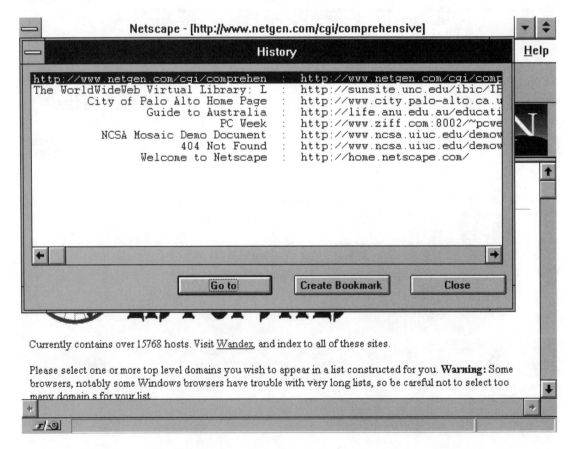

'Each one of these URLs can be accessed quickly by just clicking on the particular title and then clicking on the Go to button.

Bookmarks

As we mentioned earlier, information in a history list is present only during a particular Netscape session. Should you wish to save any or all of the sites you have visited, you will have to put them into what is known as your Bookmarks List.

1. Click once on **Home** to return to the Welcome to Netscape screen.

2. Click once on **Bookmarks** on the menu bar.

3. When the Bookmarks window appears, it should resemble the one in Figure 5-9.

Figure 5-9
Bookmarks Window

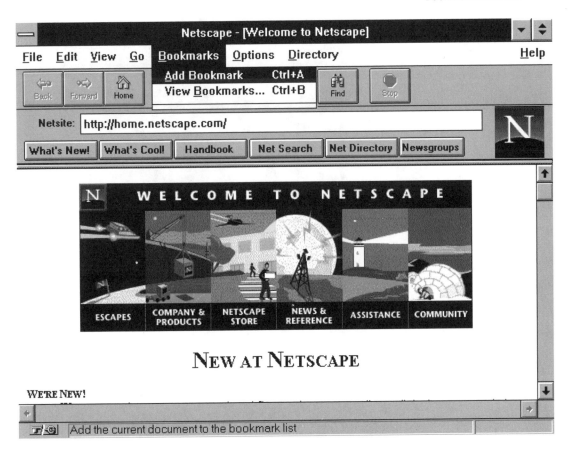

As you can see, clicking on Bookmarks enables you to either add a bookmark or to view your bookmark list.

Add Bookmark permits you to add the current document to the bookmark list. The title of the document (if there is one) will be listed in your bookmark list and the URL will be recorded as well. Best of all, you will not have to type any of this information!

View Bookmarks... permits you to view all the bookmarks that have been entered into your bookmark list.

Click once on **View Bookmarks....** Since we have not yet added any bookmarks, you should see a window resembling Figure 5-10.

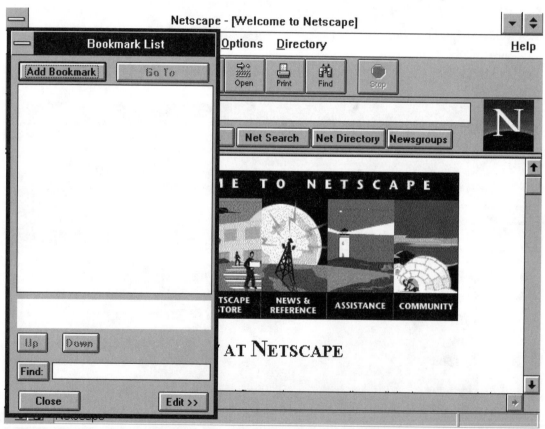

Figure 5-10
Bookmark List

Adding URLs to the Bookmark List

As you know, the Bookmark List is empty at the moment, since we have not yet chosen to add any URLs to it. However, adding URLs to the Bookmark List is remarkably easy to do. One way to add URLs to the Bookmark List is to click on **Bookmarks** and then on **Add Book-mark** when you are at a particular location which is of interest to you.

A second way to add URLs to the Bookmark List is to click on **Go** and then on **View History**. When the History window is open, you can highlight any of the URLs that are shown and then click once on the **Create Bookmark button** to have them added to your Bookmark List. Let's try this now!

1. Click on **Go** and then on **View History**

2. Click on each of the URLs visible in the History window

3. As each one is highlighted, click on **Create Bookmark**

4. When you have finished, click on **Close**

5. Click on **Bookmarks** and then on **View Bookmarks...**

Your Bookmark List should now resemble Figure 5-11. (Don't worry about the question marks for now. We will explain more about them when we organize your bookmarks in the next session.)

Figure 5-11
Bookmark List with URLs

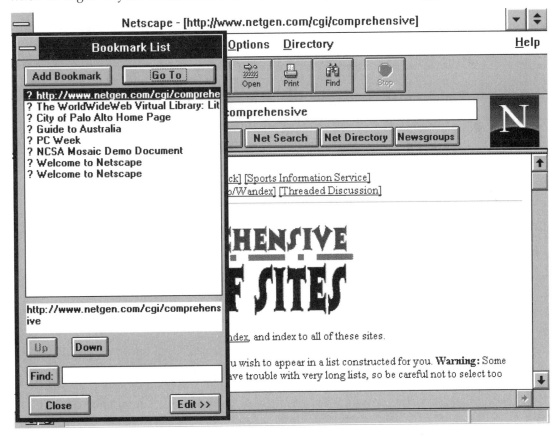

NOTE: The Bookmark List is automatically stored by Netscape on your hard drive in the Netscape directory as a text file called book-mark.htm. (*htm* is the DOS/Windows version of html.) The file takes up very little storage space and can be edited using the editing features that are built into Bookmark List. As you will see in the next session, a well-organized Bookmark List is a very valuable resource for your World Wide Web browsing!

Yet another way to add bookmarks to your list is to use the right mouse button when your mouse is resting on a hyperlink. The right-mouse-button menu allows you to add a bookmark directly.

You can also use the CTRL and A keys to add the current document to your Bookmark List.

Using the Bookmark List

To go to any of the URLs that are listed,

1. Click once on **Bookmarks**

2. Click once on any bookmark in the list

Try doing this several times now to see how this works.

Adding Additional URLs to the Bookmark List

You can add additional URLs to the Bookmark List at any time.

1. When you are on a page you wish to save, just click once on **Bookmarks** and then click on **Add Bookmark**

2. You can also use the CTRL and A keys or the right mouse button to add the current Web server to your Bookmark List.

This is really a very simple way to create a list of your favorite Web sites. After a while, however, your Bookmark List may get very large and will even slide partly off the screen. In the next session, we will show you how to organize a large Bookmark List and also how to manage your Bookmark List as it grows.

Activity
Five

Setting Netscape's Options

As you continue to use Netscape, you may wish to view more of the
information being presented to you in the main document viewing
area. In addition, you might wish to see the documents that are being
sent to you more quickly. In this activity, you will learn how to do both.

1.   Return to the Netscape Home Page

2.   Click once on **Options** on the menu bar. As it states in the status
     bar, this permits you to modify program configuration. You
     should see a screen which resembles Figure 5-12.

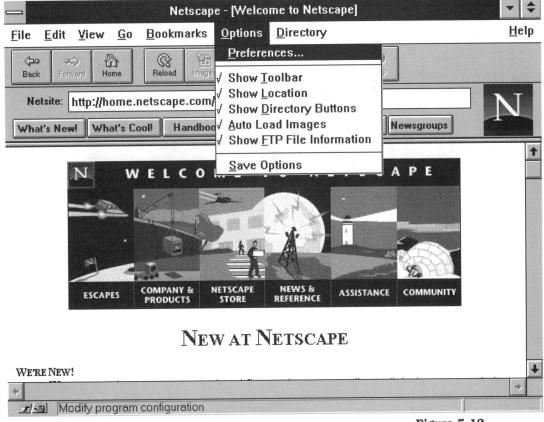

Figure 5-12
Options Window

We will focus on all the options that presently have check marks next
to them (which means they are on). Should you wish to turn any of
them off, you will have to click on them once. And, you can always
reverse this process by clicking on them again!

1. Show Toolbar

If you click on **Show Toolbar**, the toolbar will disappear from view. This will permit you to see significantly more of the screen, but you will then have to make your selections from the pull-down menu bar or by using some of the hot keys (usually a two-key combination) that are affiliated with various commands. Figure 5-13 illustrates what the screen looks like when you choose to hide the toolbar.

Figure 5-13
Toolbar Turned Off

2. Show Location

If you click on **Show Location** to turn it off, you will no longer be able to view the Location or Netsite information (the URL) that is provided on your screen. Some users choose to leave this option off unless they are particularly interested in knowing more about a given URL. Figure 5-14 shows what your screen will look like with this option turned off.

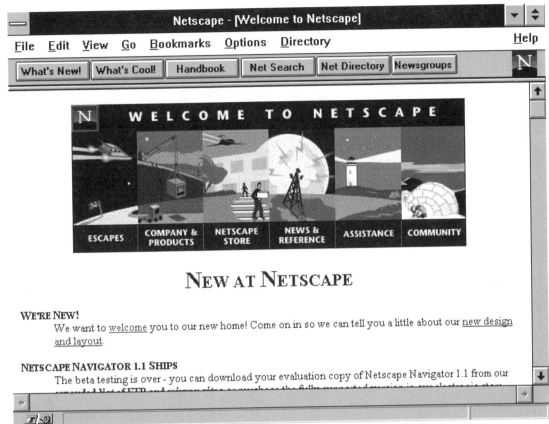

3. Show Directory Buttons

Once you are familiar with Netscape, you will probably find little or no need to keep this row of buttons visible. The commands may be accessed from the Directory command on the menu bar, and you gain even more of the screen by keeping it off. As you can see in Figure 5-15, we can see lots more of the screen with all of these options turned off!

Figure 5-14
Show Location
Turned Off

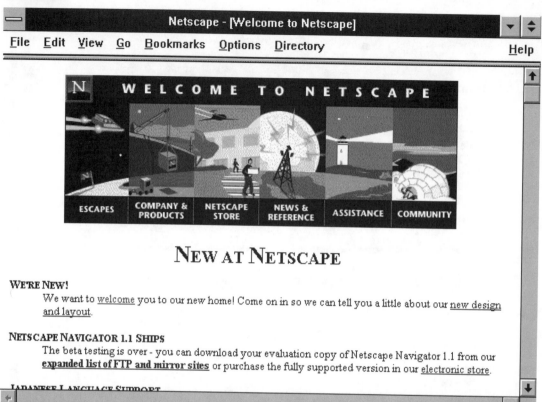

http://home.netscape.com/misc/home.map

Figure 5-15
Show Directory
Buttons Turned Off

4. Auto Load Images

The Auto Load Images option provides the capability of downloading files without seeing the full graphics that are affiliated with them. If your modem speed is slow, or if you are in a hurry, or if the graphics being downloaded add little or no value to the information you are seeking, it is advisable to turn this option off. You will be provided with icons that will indicate that graphics are present, but you will not have to look at them unless you choose to do so. A perfect example is provided by The Amazing Fish Cam site (URL: `http://www2.netscape.com/fishcam/fishcam.html`).

When we download this document with the Auto Load Images turned off, we see the image shown in Figure 5-16.

If we click on the **Images button** on the toolbar (or use View, Load Images), we see quite a bit more. The document shown in Figure 5-17 is certainly quite a bit prettier than the one shown in Figure 5-16, but it takes quite a bit longer to download. The good news is that you can make this decision "on the fly"; that is, you can leave Auto Load Images turned off and should you decide to see the images after all, you can just click on **View** and then **Load Images** as we have done here, and the images will appear on your screen.

Figure 5-16
The Amazing Fish Cam with Images Off

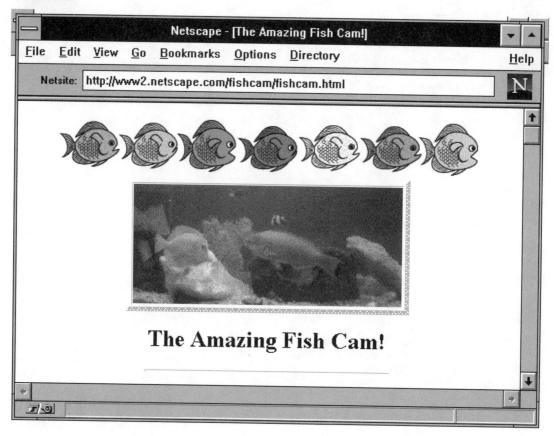

Figure 5-17
The Amazing Fish Cam
with Images Loaded

5. Show FTP File Information

When you access a file transfer protocol site, you will see full details of the files at that site; that is, you see dates, times and file sizes and descriptions. If you want to see more files (but less information about each file), you can turn off Show FTP File Information.

6. Save Options

Should you choose to save your window position and other options, just click on **Save Options**. This will save the options you have selected for the next time you start Netscape. You may always return and change the options again.

Options Summary

You have an enormous amount of control over the size and appearance of the document viewing area by selecting various options. You will have to determine the particular selections that make the most sense for you. The good news is that it is remarkably easy to turn these options on and off, none of the choices are permanent, and no harm can be caused by experimenting. Enjoy!

Session Summary

As we have seen in Sessions Four and Five, you can do an amazing number of things with Netscape and you have complete access to all the Hypertext Transfer Protocol hosts out there on the Web. In the next session, we will take a tour of the Web to get you comfortable with "surfing." Surfing, as you will discover, is roving the World Wide Web by jumping from link to link. One caution: It can be addictive! But it can also be fun and very instructional.

Session

6

Activity 1:   Touring the Web

Activity 2:   How to Build Your Bookmark List

Activity 3:   Organizing Bookmarks

Activity 4:   Editing Your Bookmark List

Movie 1:   Web Tour List

Movie 2:   Editing the Bookmark List

A Tour of the World Wide Web

Session Overview

In this session we will tour sites from all over the World Wide Web. We have already built a list of sites known as a Bookmark List so you can follow along. As you do so, you will create a history list. We will explain how you can construct your own Bookmark List from this history. We will then show you how to add places to your Bookmark List and ways to organize your list (or lists). We will also demonstrate how to use Netscape's bookmark editing features to edit your Bookmark lists.

If your company, school, country or site isn't shown in the following examples, please note that our choices illustrate only some uses of the Internet. We are not making judgments here about sites or about any one site over another. In Session Seven, we will show you how to search the World Wide Web. Then you can look up your favorite sites, add them to your Bookmark List and we'll all be happy.

Touring the Web

When you first install Netscape, your Bookmark List window will be empty. If you click on **Bookmarks** on the menu bar, you will see only the Add Bookmark and the View Bookmarks... choices. Later in this session we will review the ways you can add bookmarks to your own list.

This tour allows you to use a list of Web sites by just pointing and clicking along with us as we visit a number of places. To get our tour underway, we will use our already prepared file that is on the CD-ROM at the back of the book. The file is called WEBTOUR.HTM.

The same file is also located out on the World Wide Web if you do not use the CD-ROM. We will show you two ways to get the file: from the CD-ROM and from the World Wide Web. First, let's look at the CD-ROM method.

Exercise A: WEBTOUR.HTM

CD-ROM Method

1. If your computer is already connected to the Internet, skip to step 2, otherwise connect to the Internet.

2. Double-click on the **Netscape Icon** and maximize Netscape

3. Click once on **File** on the toolbar and again on **Open File**

4. Locate the Drives: in the area to the lower right of the Open box.

5. Insert the CD-ROM in your computer's CD-ROM drive and select that drive on the Open File dialog box.

6. Find the file called WEBTOUR.HTM and double-click on it.

The Web Tour List should appear in the Netscape document area as shown in Figure 6-1.

Internet Method

1. If your computer is already connected to the Internet, skip to step 2, otherwise connect to the Internet.

2. Double-click on the **Netscape Icon** and maximize Netscape.

3. Click once on **Open** on the toolbar (or **Open Location** in File)

4. Type the following in the Open Location box:

    ```
    http://world.std.com/~stair
    ```

5. When this Web page comes in, you should find a hyperlink called The Web Tour List.

6. Click on the Web Tour hyperlink and you will see our Web Tour List.

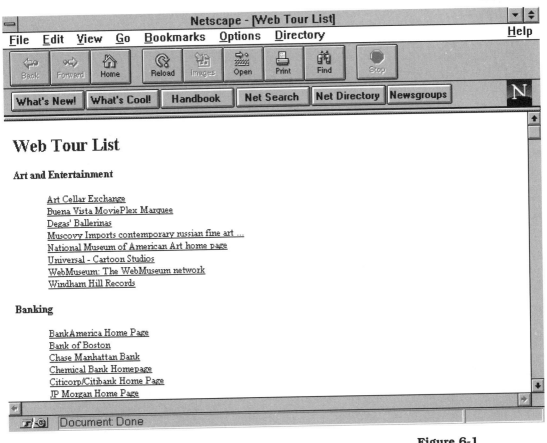

Figure 6-1
The Web Tour List

With either method, you can click on **File** and **Save as...** to put a copy of the Web Tour List on you own computer's hard disk. If you choose to do this, be sure to use the name WEBTOUR.HTM as we will create a bookmark file later.

The Web Tour List

This is a Web site list we have created to demonstrate Netscape and the World Wide Web. It has well over 100 sites in it although we will show only one from each category. Sites and addresses are continually changing on the Web. Some of these sites may have moved or changed addresses since we listed them here. In Session Seven we will show you how to search the Internet and the Web to find sites, both old and new.

Our Web Tour List was created with headings we chose to demonstrate the variety of the Web. Now let's visit a few sites from our Web Tour List.

Art and Entertainment

If we look at the Art and Entertainment heading, we will see a number of hyperlinks. Our Art and Entertainment list is shown in Figure 6-2.

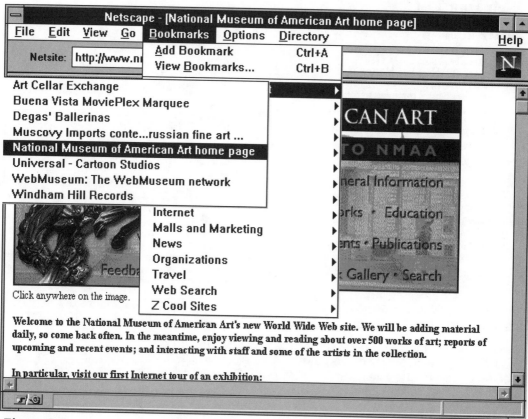

Figure 6-2
The Art and
Entertainment List

We have elected to visit the National Museum of American Art. Clicking on this item tells Netscape to go to this site. Notice that we don't have to type anything; we just point and click.

Figure 6-3 shows the document that is received from the National Museum of American Art.

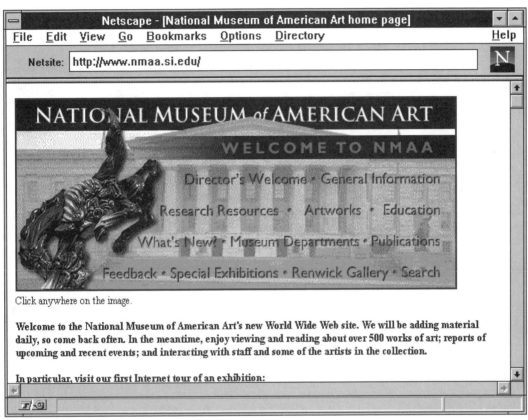

Figure 6-3
The National Museum of American Art

Banking

The next category in our tour list is Banking. We will visit the Bank of America's Home Page by clicking on the entry which is called Bank-America in our list. The Banking category is shown in Figure 6-4.

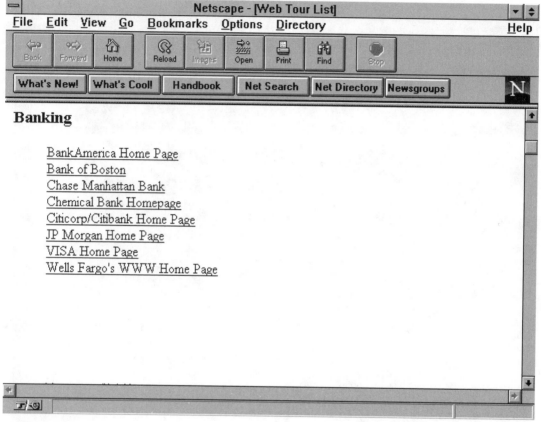

Figure 6-4
The Banking List

We have already noted that pages may move and addresses may change. Here we should also remind you that the contents of pages change regularly to reflect the newest information. When you visit the Bank of America's Home Page, it will have changed from what is shown in Figure 6-5.

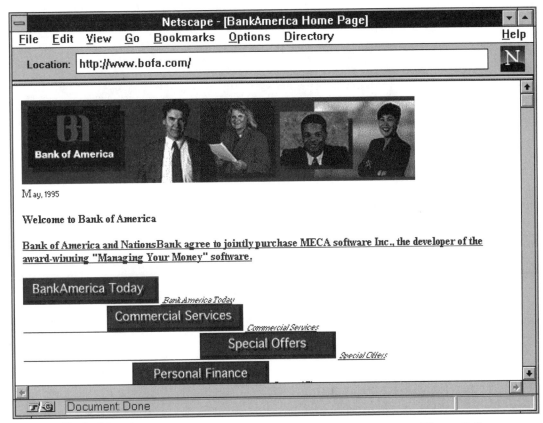

Courtesy of Bank of America

Figure 6-5
BankAmerica Home Page

Commerce

Our next heading, Commerce, is where we have chosen to list a number of advertising, marketing and publishing pages. The Commerce list is shown in Figure 6-6.

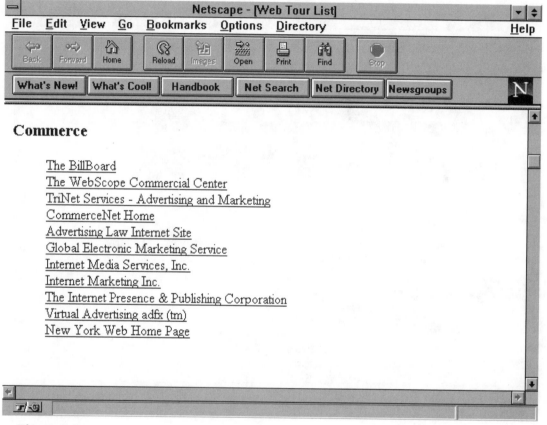

Figure 6-6
The Commerce List

A group that has been very active in promoting business and commerce on the Internet and the Web is CommerceNet. The CommerceNet Home Page is depicted in Figure 6-7.

Figure 6-7
The CommerceNet Home Page

Companies

The list of companies on the World Wide Web is huge and growing at a stupendous pace. We have chosen a very small set just to illustrate the group. If you choose to have a companies list, you will need to subdivide it into many different headings. In Session Seven, we will illustrate a Web directory site known as Yahoo that uses many categories in each heading.

Our short list of companies is shown in Figure 6-8.

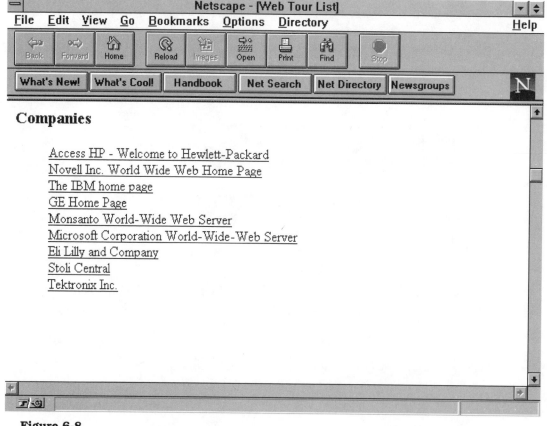

Figure 6-8
The Companies List

We picked the Stolichnaya Vodka Home Page as an illustration of creative page design. When you visit this page and can view it in full color, you will see how they have created a very attractive page setup. The Stolichnaya page is shown in Figure 6-9.

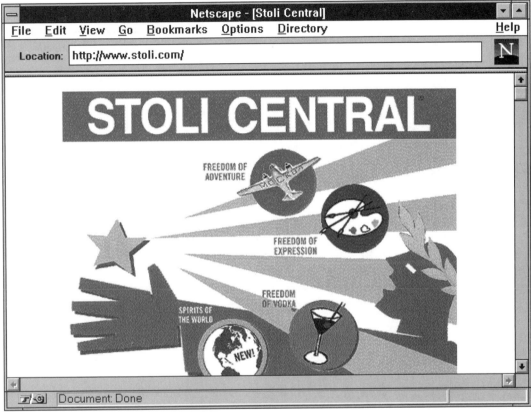

Courtesy of Carillon Importers Ltd.

Figure 6-9
The Stoli Central Home Page

Education

As you may imagine, educational institutions represent a large percentage of Web sites. The Internet really grew up in colleges and these schools still have a tremendous presence on both the Internet and the Web. Colleges and universities have been a major source of Internet development and interest.

We have chosen a few of these to illustrate this category in our Web Tour List. Figure 6-10 shows our limited selection for education.

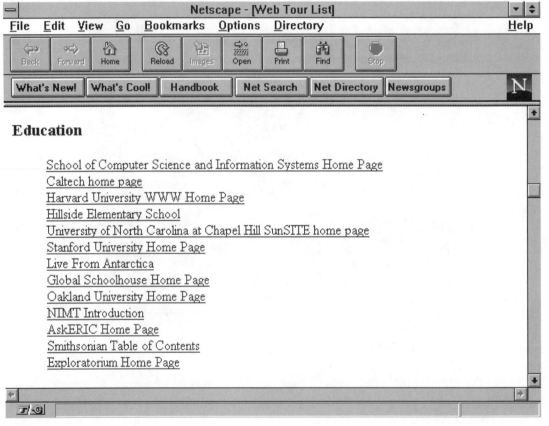

Figure 6-10
The Education
Heading

The Smithsonian Institution is surely one of the world's treasures and it is well represented on the Web. Here you can learn almost as much about the Smithsonian as you would if you were to go there for an actual visit. We would still, of course, recommend a visit, but you can prepare for that visit with their home page; it's shown in Figure 6-11.

Figure 6-11
The Smithsonian
Institution Home Page

Finance

The finance industry may be a more recent arrival on the Internet, but it is quickly becoming well represented. Here are a few of our choices including some companies specializing in electronic money handling over the Internet. Figure 6-12 shows our selections.

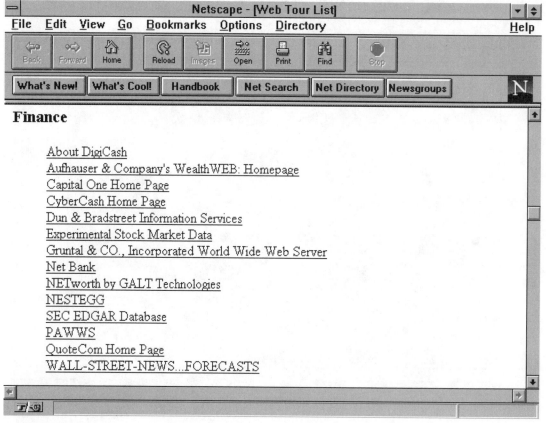

Figure 6-12
The Financial
Category

As we can show only a limited number of pages, we picked an experimental page that allows access to company reports. The EDGAR project permits you (and anyone else on the Web) access to recent filings with the United States Securities and Exchange Commission. Here you can look up information about companies that used to require a trip to Washington, D.C. to view. Look up your favorite company and see what they have been telling the SEC. The SEC EDGAR page is shown in Figure 6-13.

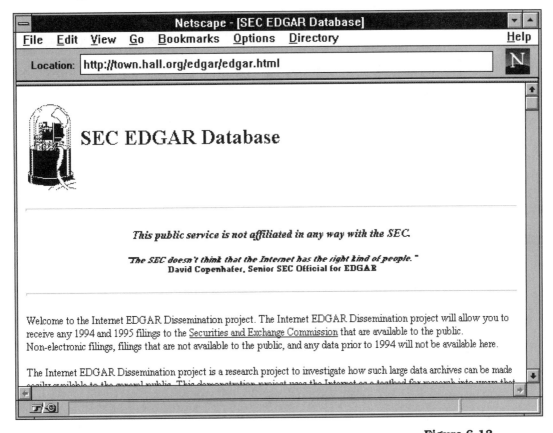

Figure 6-13
The SEC EDGAR
Database

Government

It's well known now that the United States federal government and the state governments have become very active on the Web. There are several very good reasons for this.

1. Immediacy of information: Up-to-date information is available as things change.

2. Reduction of expenses: fewer paper brochures to print and distribute and fewer calls, letters and FAXs to answer.

We can expect all levels of government to become even more active as they understand the benefits of distributing key information on Web pages.

Figure 6-14 shows our short list of government sites.

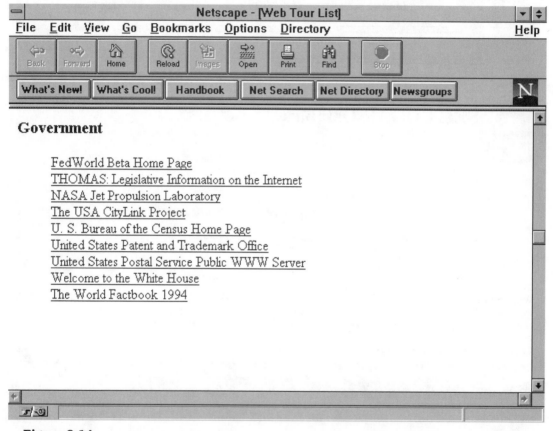

Figure 6-14
Government
Information

Many sites, such as the White House Home Page and the newer Thomas service from the Library of Congress have received much publicity. We have chosen a relatively unknown site with great value. The Central Intelligence Agency has provided public information about its unclassified geo-political data for some years. Many school librarians have known this for some time.

For most of us, however, it comes as a bit of shock to contact the CIA and find this treasure trove of information. We have selected the CIA's World Fact Book as our government illustration in Figure 6-15.

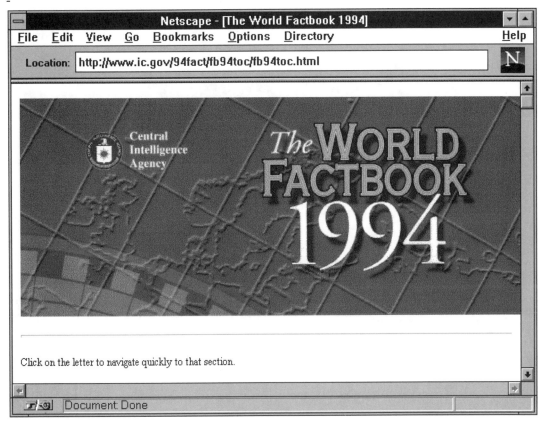

Figure 6-15
The CIA World Fact
Book

If you need detailed information about any country or region in the world, you will want to check out the CIA's World Fact Book.

International

It's easy for us to think of the Internet and the Web as United States centric. While this may have been true many years ago, the Internet and the World Wide Web are truly world wide. Our International list could easily be the largest in the book. We have selected just one page to cover this vast territory. Our International grouping is shown in Figure 6-16.

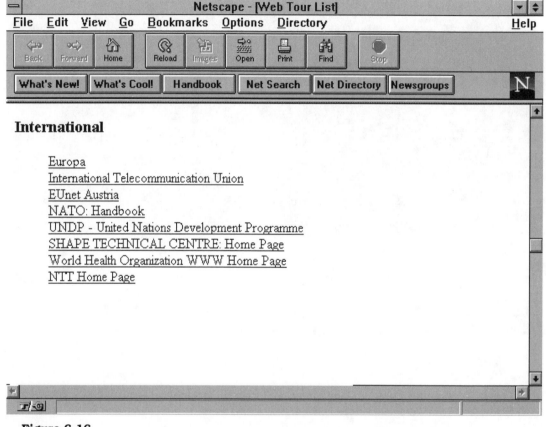

Figure 6-16
The International
Group

The European Commission, or Europe, represents what we are learning to call "Europe." One of the largest trading blocks in the world, Europe is key to the world's economy. Here is a rapid way to see what data they are making available to us all. It's also a very colorful page with hyperlinks all over Europe. Figure 6-17 shows Europa.

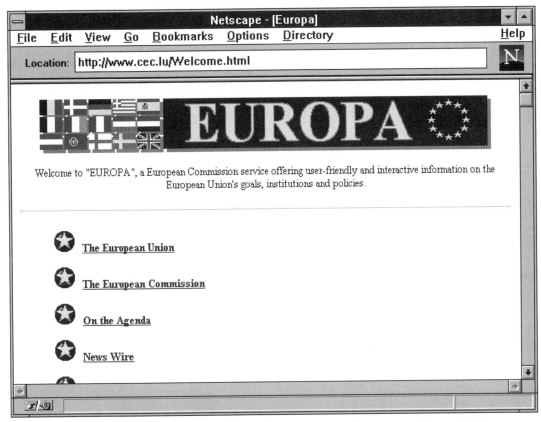

Figure 6-17
Europa

Internet

When we think of the Internet, we think of a global anarchy. It seems as much a "happening" as an exploding new technology. We are told that no one is in charge and that it all just comes together. We have listed just a very few sites in our Internet heading in the Web Tour List which is shown in Figure 6-18.

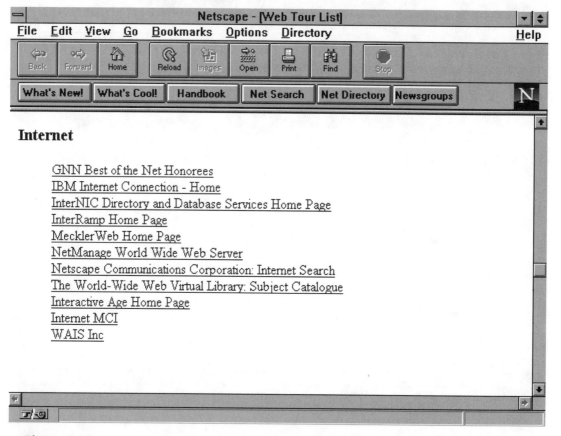

Figure 6-18
The Internet List

While some "anarchic" behavior does indeed exist, there are several small groups that work very hard to make sure that the Internet can actually function. The two that come to mind most quickly are the Internet Society and the Internet Network Information Center or Inter-NIC.

The Internet Society (URL: http://www.isoc.org) is largely a volunteer organization. It is dedicated to improving the Internet and ensuring that standards exist to keep newer and better things coming our way. We recommend that serious "Internauts" consider joining the society as either individual or organizational members. Certainly a visit to their site is very worthwhile.

The other group is much smaller and is known as the InterNIC. It operates under broad guidance from the Internet Society's various volunteer bodies. Among its most important tasks is the assignment of globally unique Internet names and addresses.

While the Internet may be anarchic, it can function only if names and addresses are really unique. The InterNIC performs this task and is the one force that really keeps things orderly. Actually, the InterNIC assigns blocks of names (domains) and addresses (Internet Protocol or IP addresses) to other organizations that make the detailed assignments. The InterNIC's page is shown in Figure 6-19.

Figure 6-19
The InterNIC Directory and Database Services Home Page

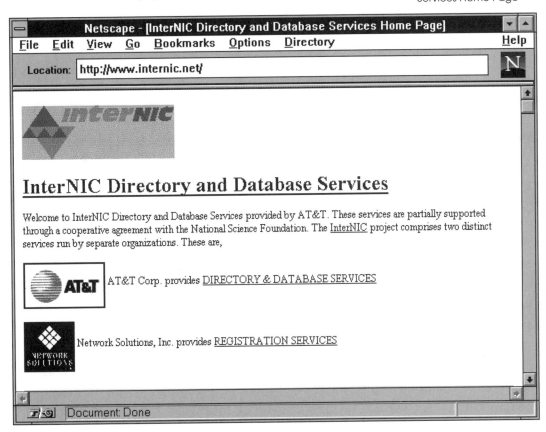

As you can begin to see from the InterNIC's Home Page, there is a wealth of information here about the Internet. The Directory and Database Services will enable you to find data for both the novice and the seasoned Internaut. The Registration Service will permit you to find domain names, such as ibm.com or caltech.edu as well as key contact names and E-mail addresses. It can also tell you who has already been assigned what addresses.

Malls and Marketing

The "new" Internet is increasingly commercial. How about some of the shopping we have all heard about? Our next category is Malls and Marketing, perhaps the fastest growing area of the World Wide Web. While we can show but a few, we have picked some of our favorites to list as shown in Figure 6-20.

Figure 6-20
Malls and Marketing

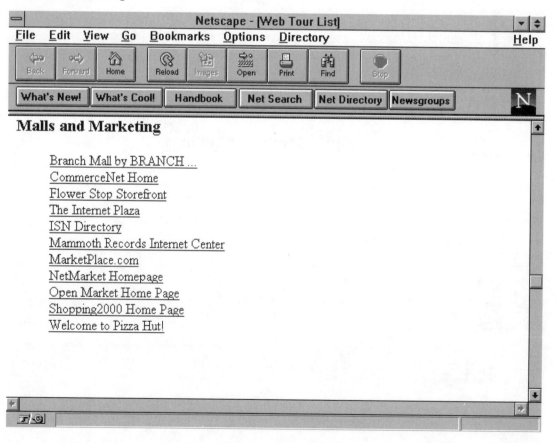

It's very hard to pick only one here, but we have chosen Shopping 2000 as our example. ContentWare, the producer of this page, has collected an amazing array of both little-known and well-known retailers. Here you can browse online catalogs with stunning graphics and sound bites. If you are prone to browsing catalogs, you will find a home here. One caution: You may end up buying something (don't say we didn't warn you).

The Shopping2000 Home page is illustrated in Figure 6-21. As with all our sample pages, you are seeing only the top of the page. When you visit there with Netscape (or if you are doing so now), you can scroll down the page to see all the parts we can't fit onto our book's page.

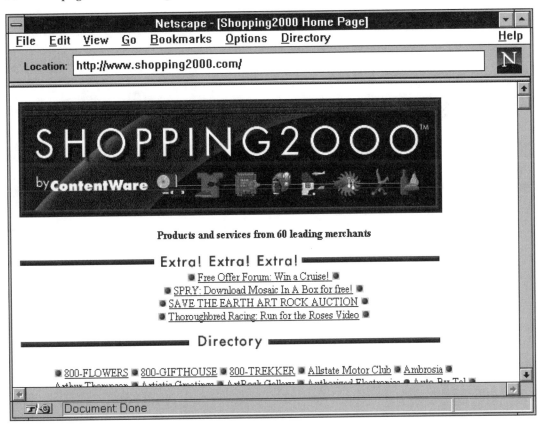

Figure 6-21
The Shopping2000
Home Page

The News

Newspapers, television, and radio today bring us the news and many different features. We can select to follow whatever we like on any given day. Now the Internet and the Web are beginning to deliver the news. As you can see from our sample list, many things you would normally expect to find are there. In addition, there are a few other new items worth mentioning.

While we will show a weather map as our example, you could expect to see that on TV or in your newspaper. Things you might not expect to see are near-real-time freeway conditions or quick FAX editions of major papers such as the *New York Times*. Our list of the News category is provided in Figure 6-22.

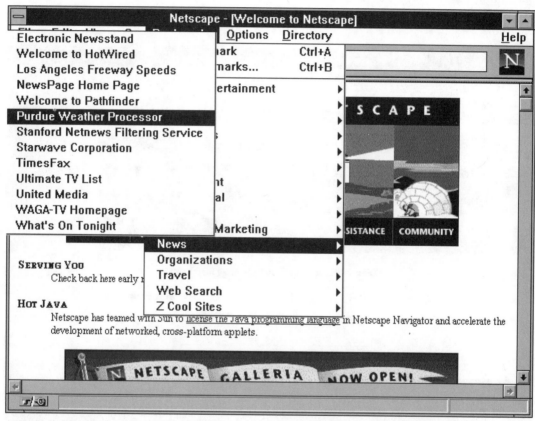

Figure 6-22
The News Sample
Group

You can, of course, see the weather map on the morning or evening news (or all day on the cable weather channel). But you won't get the detail or range of weather forecasts or images that you can find at several weather Web sites. If you are following along online, scroll down and note the images below our main map in the figure. Then note that you find not only your weather forecast, but also forecasts from all over. And they will be as current as if you were there. If you are traveling or just browsing places to go, this is a real source of wonderful information. Figure 6-23 shows a weather map from the Purdue Weather Processor.

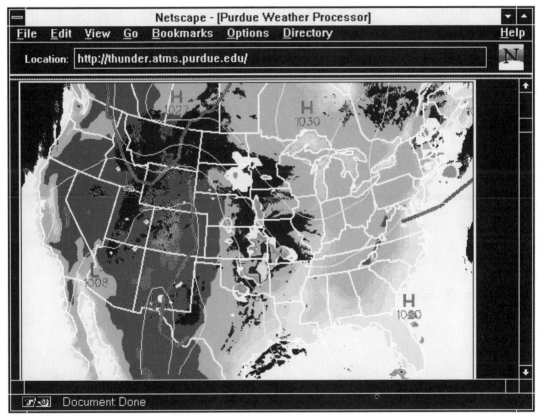

Figure 6-23
The Purdue Weather Processor

Organizations

Continuing our very high-level browse of the Web Tour List, we come to Organizations. Here we find many different groups with a very wide range of interests. Some of the names do not immediately bring the organization to mind; for example, Electronic Pathways calls itself "The Native American On-Ramp to the Information Highway." Women from the Comanche and Chippewa Nations have helped bring this Web site to life. Our Organizations category of the Web Tour List is shown in Figure 6-24.

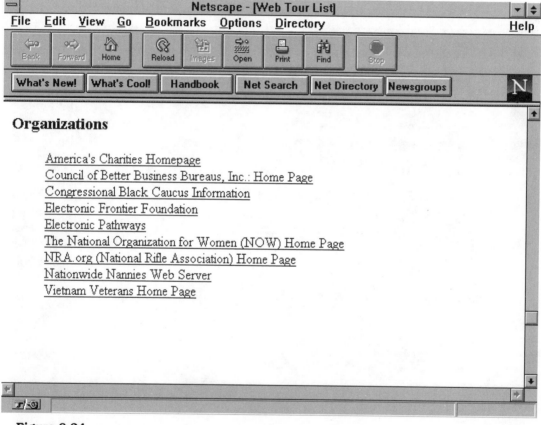

Figure 6-24
The Organizations List

For our Organizations example, we have selected the National Organization for Women. As you can see in Figure 6-25, they focus on providing information about their organization to the public.

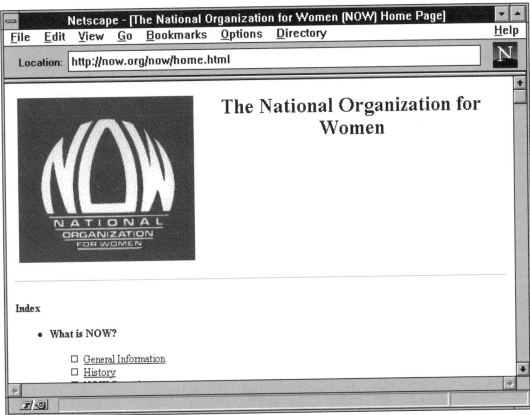

Figure 6-25
The National Organization for Women (NOW) Home Page

Travel

Our last Web tour example is Travel. Travel agencies and tourist boards around the world have discovered this new tool to reach potential travelers. Our example list literally goes around the world and covers nearly every continent. Travel sites on the Web are another fast growing segment as it is relatively easy to convert colorful travel brochures to Web pages. In addition, the information is (we hope) really up to date and immediately available. The travel list is shown in Figure 6-26.

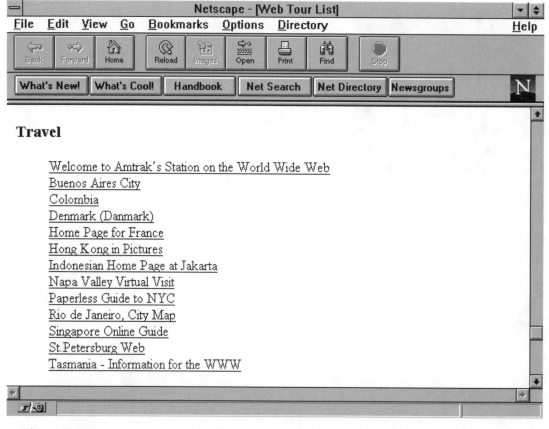

Figure 6-26
The Travel List

Each of these travel sites will attempt to persuade you to travel. And each will give not only enticement, but also many excellent suggestions about where to stay, where to eat, what to see and so on.

Snap Quiz: Do you know where Tasmania is? (Just kidding.)

As an illustration of one travel entity that has chosen to put itself on the World Wide Web, we have chosen Amtrak. Amtrak is the United States passenger railroad service and, like many other travel-related services, it wants to reach those who are savvy about the Internet. Here in Figure 6-27 is the Amtrak Home Page.

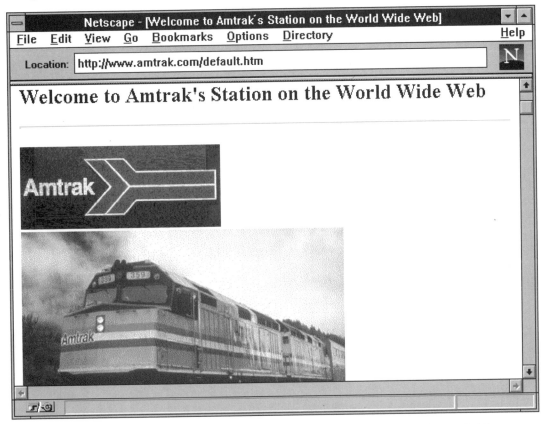

Figure 6-27
Amtrak's Station on the World Wide Web

We have now concluded our Web tour and will next show you how to build your own Bookmark List.

How to Build Your Bookmark List

In Netscape, there are many ways to add bookmarks. We will take a moment to review them. First, you must remember that Netscape keeps a file called BOOKMARK.HTM in its directory. If Netscape resides in a directory called C:\NETSCAPE on your computer, then the BOOKMARK.HTM file will be in that directory.

Netscape itself manages this file under your directions. As you add additional sites (or pages or URLs) to your list, the list grows. In Activity 3, we will show you how to organize and edit your bookmarks. First we have to see how to add bookmarks to your list.

Adding Bookmarks

When you are displaying a page, you can add it to your Bookmark List in one of several ways. You can use whichever method is the most natural and comfortable for you.

To add bookmarks to your list while you are displaying a page, use one of the following four methods:

1. Click on **Bookmarks** on the Menu bar and then click on **Add Bookmark**

2. Hold down the Control (**CTRL**) key and press the **A key**

3. Click on **Bookmarks** on the menu bar, click on **View Bookmarks...**, and then click on **Add Bookmark** (More about this method later.)

4. Click on **Go** on the menu bar, click on **View History...**, and then select the current (or a previous) item in the list. Then click on the **Create Bookmark button**

You may want to try each of these just to get a feel for them. It is also possible to add a bookmark to your list while you are pointing at a hyperlink. If you position your cursor on a hyperlink and click on the **right mouse button**, you will be offered a pop-up menu. One of the choices is "Add Bookmark for this Link."

Adding Bookmarks -- Method #1

We will illustrate the easiest of these methods in Figures 6-28 and 6-29.

1. First click on the **Home button** to display the Netscape Home Page

2. Then click on **Bookmarks** and again on **Add Bookmark**

In Figure 6-28, you see the Netscape Home Page and the mouse pointing at Add Bookmark in the Bookmarks drop-down menu bar.

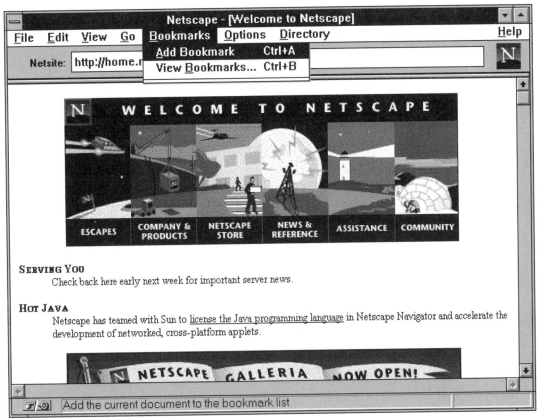

Figure 6-28
Add Bookmark

3.   Click on any other item to close the Bookmarks drop-down
menu.

When we click on Bookmarks again, we will see that "Welcome to Netscape" has been added just below View Bookmarks.... This is shown in Figure 6-29.

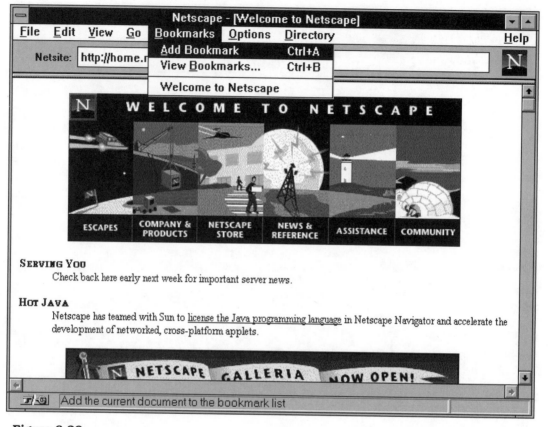

Figure 6-29
Bookmark Added

You can add bookmarks as you travel about the World Wide Web, or you can try another method. Rather than add a bookmark at each site and end up with an overly large list in a hurry, you can use Go, History. Here is how to do so.

Adding Bookmarks -- Method #2

When you finish a session on Netscape, you will have created a history list for that session. One good way to add bookmarks is to review that list and select your desired sites to add to your Bookmark List. Let's take a look now at the history list that has been created during this session.

1. Click once on **Go**

2. Click on **View History...**

Figure 6-30 shows the History list that has been created during this session.

History	
Welcome to Amtrak's Station on the	:	http://www.amtrak.com/default.
The National Organization for Women	:	http://now.org/now/home.html
Purdue Weather Processor	:	http://thunder.atms.purdue.edu
Shopping2000 Home Page	:	http://www.shopping2000.com/
InterNIC Directory and Database Ser	:	http://www.internic.net/
Europa	:	http://www.cec.lu/Welcome.html
The World Factbook 1994	:	http://www.ic.gov/94fact/fb94t
SEC EDGAR Database	:	http://town.hall.org/edgar/edg
The Smithsonian Institution Home Pa	:	http://www.si.edu/
Stoli Central	:	http://www.stoli.com/
CommerceNet Home	:	http://www.commerce.net/
BankAmerica Home Page	:	http://www.bofa.com/
National Museum of American Art hom	:	http://www.nmaa.si.edu/
Welcome to Netscape	:	http://home.netscape.com/

| Go to | Create Bookmark | Close |

Figure 6-30
The History List

As you can see, this list shows where we have been during Session Six. We can now select the pages that we want to save. Here is how to do so.

1. Select each page to be saved by clicking once on its line with the mouse. You will notice that on the left-hand side you are provided with the title of the page and on the right-hand side is the actual URL.

2. Then click on **Create Bookmark** to add the selected page and its associated URL to the Bookmark List.

We have done this for all the items that have been created in this session's history list and have created a new Bookmark List as shown in Figure 6-31.

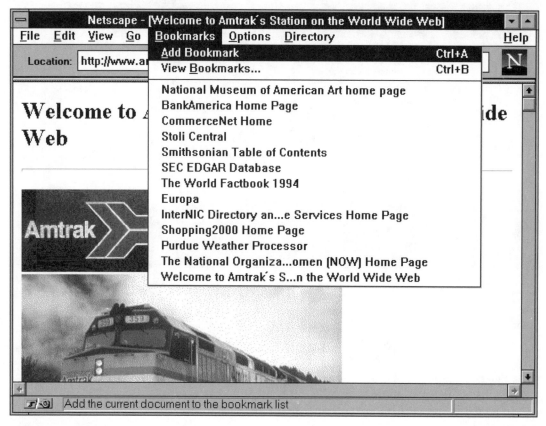

Figure 6-31
The New Bookmark List

That's really all there is to adding bookmarks. You can visit sites all over the World Wide Web and record your favorites in your own personal Bookmark List. There is, however, one problem.

As you visit more and more sites and add more and more items to your Bookmark List, it grows. And grows. And grows! Soon you have a Bookmark List that won't fit on your screen. Current versions of Netscape just add the word "More..." to the bottom of your list when you have too many bookmarks to be shown on one screen. Older versions of Netscape used to bump the list to an unreadable position off to the left of your screen.

Neither of these situations is easy to work with. What you will eventually (or quickly) need is a way to organize your bookmarks into categories. But how do you go about doing this? We will show you.

Organizing Bookmarks

As you continue to add bookmarks, they will be added to the bottom of your list. This means they are organized by the order in which you visited the sites. After a while, this won't make a lot of sense. You will probably want them organized by some groupings or categories.

We have taken our newly created list and entered the View Bookmarks choice from the Bookmark menu bar. As you can see, the menu shows the various locations in the order in which we visited them earlier in this session. Figure 6-32 shows this Bookmark List box.

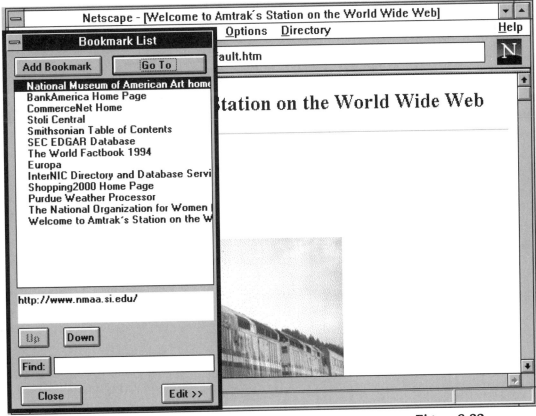

Figure 6-32
Bookmark List

You will find that you will use this box as a fast way to move items around in your list. First, however, we must enter the full Edit box and create some categories. We reach the full Edit box by clicking on the **Edit>> button.** The full Edit box contains a great deal of information about each of our bookmarks. When we first arrive at this box, it looks like Figure 6-33.

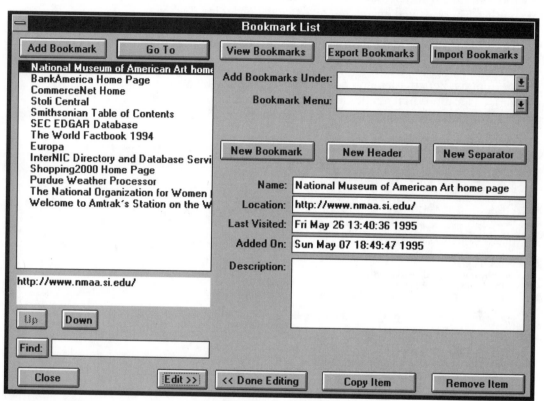

Figure 6-33
Bookmark List Edit

This is the box where you will do most of your work on organizing your list. Let's pause for a moment and examine this powerful Netscape tool. Across the top are five buttons. Here is what they enable you to do.

1. *Add Bookmark* is fairly obvious. Clicking on this button will add the currently viewed page to the bottom of your Bookmark List.

2. The action of *Go To* is not obvious, although it means go to the URL of the selected item in your list. The reason it's not obvious is that the Edit window covers Netscape and you can't see what

is happening. You will have to close the Edit window to see the results. You can also use <<Done Editing to see a part of the new screen in Netscape's document area.

3.   *View Bookmarks* puts your bookmarks on Netscape's main screen. You will have to press **Close** (or **<<End Editing**) to see them.

4.   *Export Bookmarks* and *Import Bookmarks* allow you to do just what they say. They will enable you to save your bookmark file in another file or bring another file to your Bookmark List.

   a.   Exporting is simple enough; it allows you to store your file under another name.

   b.   Importing brings in another file (it should be in .htm format) and places it at the bottom of your existing bookmark list. If you do this, you may note that the new entries have question marks to their left. The question marks only mean that some information is missing from the set of fields on the right of your screen: Name, Location, Last Visited, or Added On. Once the data is added (or the bookmark moved with the Up or Down button), the question marks will disappear.

The window on the left under the Add Bookmark button is your bookmark name list. The actual URL of the selected location is shown just below the bookmark name list.

Below the URL window are the Up, Down, Find:, and Close buttons. *Find:* locates words or phrases in the Bookmark List and *Close* returns you to Netscape's main screen. We will describe the Up and Down buttons when we discuss headers.

At the top right, just below Export Bookmarks and Import Bookmarks, are two selection blocks: Add Bookmarks Under:, and Bookmark Menu:. We will return to these at the end of this session.

The right side of the Edit window has three buttons: New Bookmarks, New Header, and New Separator. We will describe their use shortly.

The Name:, Location:, Last Visited:, Added On:, and Description: boxes come next on the right side.

Below them are the <<Done Editing, Copy Item, and Remove Item buttons. *<<Done Editing* returns you to the smaller Edit list window (Figure 6-32). *Copy Item* and *Remove Item* do just that to the selected item in your Bookmark List.

Now that we have toured the full Bookmark List Edit window, let's get started organizing your bookmarks.

If we click on **New Header** (with the top item selected), we will get a screen looking like Figure 6-34.

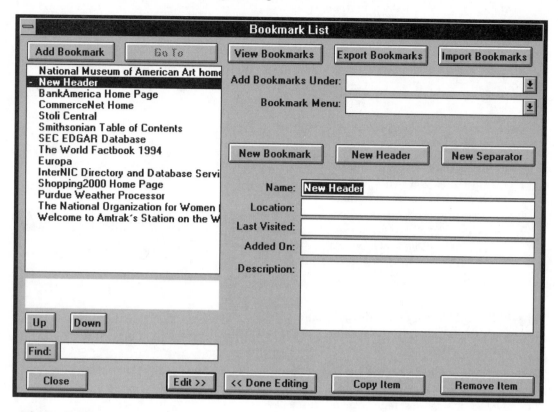

Figure 6-34
Add New Header

Notice the words New Header in the list near the top. Also notice that the Name:, Location:, Last Visited:, Added On:, and Description: blocks are largely blank. Although you should change the name of New Header to a more meaningful name, we have left it as New Header for our example. We will now add items under this New Header. This is where we use the Up and Down buttons.

If you select New Header and click on **Up**, the New Header will move up as you might have expected. The Up button is then dimmed as it is no longer active.

Please pay attention, it gets a little tricky here.

1. Select the item just *under* New Header; in this case, it is National Museum....

2. Click once on the **Up button**, and National Museum will be indented from the left.

Note: If we were to click again, National Museum would move above New Header. What we really want is for it to be indented from the left.

---

3. Move down through each of the next three items and press the **Up button** once to indent each from the left. The result looks like Figure 6-35.

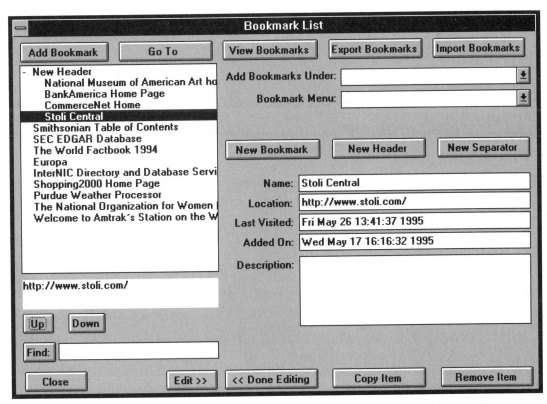

Figure 6-35
Indents under New Header

4. Continue this process with two additional New Headers.

5. Use the Name block to rename them to

1st Header
2nd Header
3rd Header

6. Using the same process with the Up and Down buttons, we place the bookmark items under, that is indented under, the Headers. If we have done this correctly, it will look like Figure 6-36.

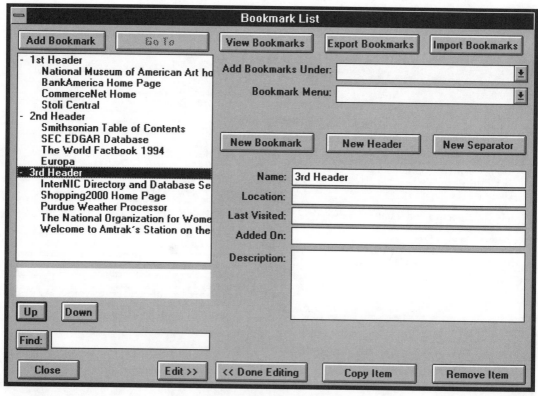

Figure 6-36
Indents under Three
Headers

All our bookmark items are now organized into three categories: 1st Header, 2nd Header, and 3rd Header. Let's see what this has done to the appearance of our Bookmark List on Netscape's main screen.

1. Press **Close** to return to the Netscape main screen and then click on **Bookmark**

You should see that we have compacted our 13 bookmarks into three categories or headings. The result should look like Figure 6-37.

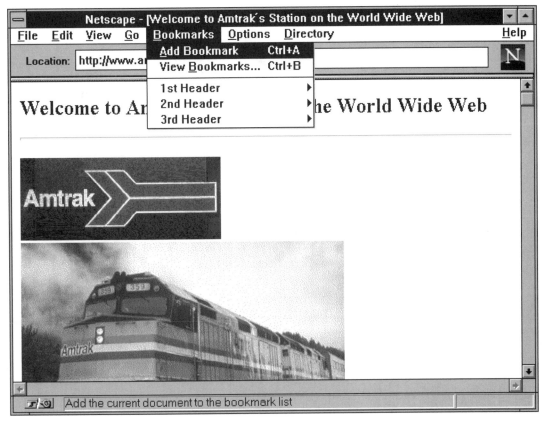

Figure 6-37
New Bookmark
Display

All you see now are the headers, but notice the little arrows at the right side of each line of the new bookmark display. These small arrows indicate that there is more to be seen if you were to click on the line. Let's do that now and see what happens.

1. Click on the line called **2nd Header**, and you will be able to see the four actual bookmarks in that category. We are now able to move the mouse to any of these bookmarks. By clicking on any of these four, we will be taken to that location. This new submenu is shown in Figure 6-38.

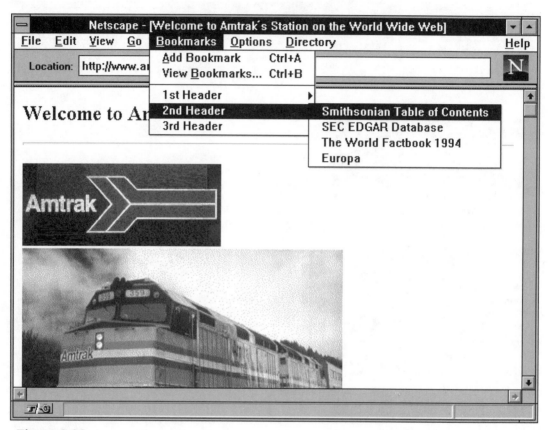

Figure 6-38
New Bookmark
Display

This process of adding (and naming) new headers can become as deep as we wish. The major limitation will be our patience in going down through a large hierarchy. After four or five levels, we lose patience and need to thin out our list. For those places we rarely visit, it is perhaps better to omit them from our list and to use a search tool. We will describe searching in Session Seven.

There is one more thing we can do to organize our list. We can add separators between categories. (You can add separators between items, but they do not add much.) To add a separator, select the item *above* a header and click on **New Separator**. You get a dashed line just *below* your selection. The New Separator is shown in Figure 6-39.

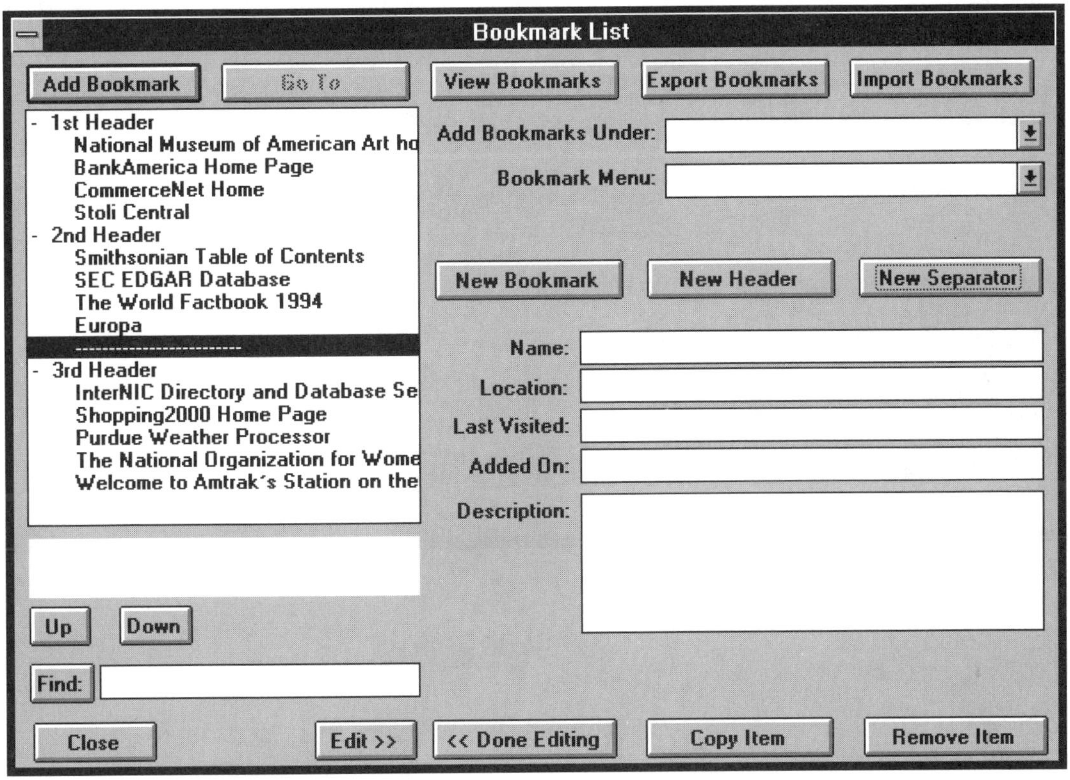

Bookmark List

| Add Bookmark | Go To | View Bookmarks | Export Bookmarks | Import Bookmarks |

- 1st Header
  - National Museum of American Art ho
  - BankAmerica Home Page
  - CommerceNet Home
  - Stoli Central
- 2nd Header
  - Smithsonian Table of Contents
  - SEC EDGAR Database
  - The World Factbook 1994
  - Europa

- 3rd Header
  - InterNIC Directory and Database Se
  - Shopping2000 Home Page
  - Purdue Weather Processor
  - The National Organization for Wome
  - Welcome to Amtrak's Station on the

Add Bookmarks Under:

Bookmark Menu:

| New Bookmark | New Header | New Separator |

Name:

Location:

Last Visited:

Added On:

Description:

| Up | Down |

Find:

| Close | Edit >> | << Done Editing | Copy Item | Remove Item |

Figure 6-39
New Separator

This may not look too interesting on the full edit screen, but let's close the edit screen and return to Netscape's main screen. Here we see that a solid line has been placed between our 2nd Header and 3rd Header. If you like to have separator lines, this is how it is done. Figure 6-40 shows how the separator line looks.

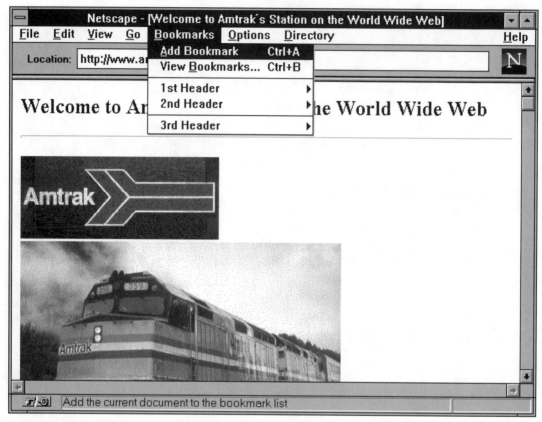

Figure 6-40
The Separator Line

We will conclude our discussion of the full Edit screen with the two boxes just below Export and Import. These are Add Bookmarks Under: and Bookmark Menu:.

Add Bookmarks Under:

Add Bookmarks Under: is a handy way to keep new bookmarks organized as you add them. When you click on **Bookmarks, Add Bookmark** on the main menu bar, the new bookmark is placed at the very end of your entire Bookmark List.

You may, instead, click on **Bookmarks, View Bookmarks** and go to the full Edit screen. Then click on the small **down arrow** of Add Bookmarks Under: and click on the category for this new bookmark. Then click on **Add Bookmark**. The Add Bookmarks Under: list is shown in Figure 6-41.

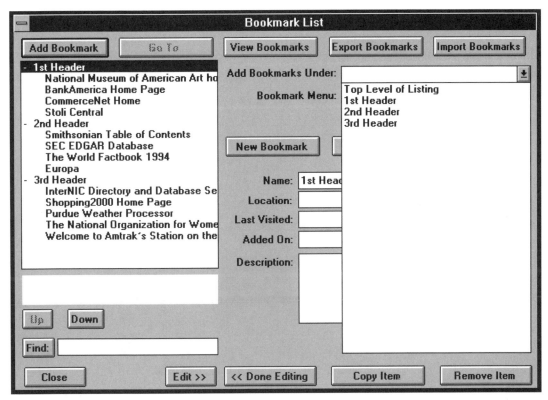

Figure 6-41
Add Bookmarks Under:

The new bookmark will be added to the end of that category. One minor bug: If you have used separators, the bookmark will be added after the separator. You will then have to move the separator.

If you select a category in Add Bookmarks Under:, it remains in force until you change it. That is, all new bookmarks will be added there until you make another change in Add Bookmarks Under:.

You can, of course, just add new bookmarks to the end of your list and then use the Up button to place them in the correct category.

Bookmark Menu:

The *Bookmark Menu: selection list* tells Netscape which list to display on the main Netscape screen. If you select 2nd Header under Bookmark Menu:, then that will be the only part of the Bookmark List which will be shown by Netscape.

This feature is invaluable when more than one person is using the same copy of Netscape. Each person can then choose to have their own portion of the Bookmark List and show only their own bookmarks. Another use would be for an individual who wants to have, perhaps, a personal Bookmark List and a business Bookmark List.

Editing Your Bookmark List

You can edit your Netscape Bookmarks in three ways, but we recommend only the first two. The three methods are:

1. Click on **Bookmarks, View Bookmarks...** and use the smaller Edit box to select and move bookmarks up or down. That is, you can choose to move them to other categories. You can also use this method to add and move new bookmarks.

2. Click on **Bookmarks, View Bookmarks..., Edit>>** and use the full Edit screen to move, copy, remove (delete), or export your bookmarks.

3. Use an ASCII editor (not a word processor) to edit Netscape's BOOKMARK.HTM file following HTML rules.

Method 2 is the most powerful and easiest way to edit your Bookmark List. We recommend that you practice with this method until you are comfortable with it.

Neither we nor Netscape recommend that you use method 3. If, however, you are really familiar with preparing and editing Hypertext Markup Language (HTML) files, you may wish to try this method.

Always back-up your original BOOKMARK.HTM file before editing it with method 3.

To give you a feeling for the complexity of method 3, we have shown the Bookmark file. Figure 6-42 shows part of what the actual BOOKMARK.HTM file looks like when viewed in Windows Notepad.

```
─                    Notepad - BOOKMARK.HTM                    ▼ ▲
File  Edit  Search  Help
<!DOCTYPE NETSCAPE-Bookmark-file-1>                              ↑
<!-- This is an automatically generated file.
    It will be read and overwritten.
    Do Not Edit! -->
<TITLE>Personal Bookmarks</TITLE>
<H1>Personal Bookmarks</H1>
<DL><p>
    <DT><H3 ADD_DATE="801511617">1st Header</H3>
    <DL><p>
        <DT><A HREF="http://www.nmaa.si.edu/" ADD_DATE="799886987" LAST_VISI
        <DT><A HREF="http://www.bofa.com/" ADD_DATE="796171094" LAST_VISIT="
        <DT><A HREF="http://www.commerce.net/" ADD_DATE="799464386" LAST_VIS
        <DT><A HREF="http://www.stoli.com/" ADD_DATE="800741792" LAST_VISIT=
    </DL><p>
    <DT><H3 ADD_DATE="801511838">2nd Header</H3>
    <DL><p>
        <DT><A HREF="http://www.si.edu/" ADD_DATE="796920476" LAST_VISIT="80
        <DT><A HREF="http://town.hall.org/edgar/edgar.html" ADD_DATE="800741
        <DT><A HREF="http://www.ic.gov/94fact/fb94toc/fb94toc.html" ADD_DATE
        <DT><A HREF="http://www.cec.lu/Welcome.html" ADD_DATE="796443947" LA
    </DL><p>
    <HR>
    <DT><H3 ADD_DATE="801511856">3rd Header</H3>
    <DL><p>
        <DT><A HREF="http://www.internic.net/" ADD_DATE="796443816" LAST_VIS
        <DT><A HREF="http://www.shopping2000.com/" ADD_DATE="796343836" LAST
        <DT><A HREF="http://thunder.atms.purdue.edu/" ADD_DATE="796171608" L
        <DT><A HREF="http://now.org/now/home.html" ADD_DATE="796264729" LAST ↓
←                                                                            →
```

Figure 6-42
The BOOKMARK.HTM File

Session Summary

In this session we covered bookmarks in great detail. This is a truly powerful Netscape tool which, when used properly, will permit you to keep, organize, and go to your favorite places on the World Wide Web quickly and efficiently. We traveled to some of our favorite places to illustrate how we keep our bookmarks organized. Then we described how you can add, organize, and edit your own Bookmark List.

Happy surfing!

In this third part of Hands-On Netscape, we will:

1. *Teach you how to search the World Wide Web using search engines such as WebCrawler, Lycos, and InfoSeek.*

2. *Show you how to use Netscape for all of the traditional Internet activities such as telnet, ftp, gopher, E-mail, and Usenet groups.*

3. *Provide you with detailed instructions that will enable you to hear sounds, view images, and watch movies using Netscape.*

4. *Provide you with an introduction to HTML, the HyperText Markup Language.*

5. *Teach you how to use HTML to create a useful searching document.*

6. *Teach you how to customize Netscape for your individual preferences.*

7. *Teach you how to stay current with Netscape as it continues to evolve.*

○ Searching with Netscape

○ Using Netscape for telnet, ftp, gopher, E-mail and Usenet

○ Using Multimedia with Netscape

○ Getting Started With Hypertext Markup Language (HTML)

○ Netscape, Your Way

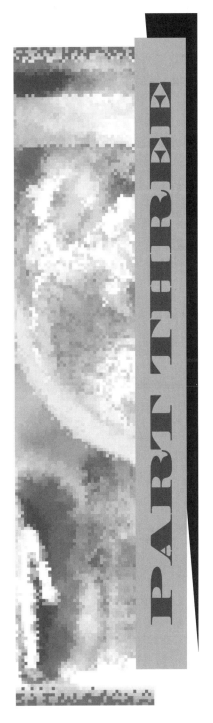

PART THREE

Session

7

Activity 1:   Internet Browsing and Searching

Activity 2:   Directory Searches–Yahoo

Activity 3:   Searching with WebCrawler

Activity 4:   Searching with Lycos

Activity 5:   Searching with InfoSeek

Activity 6:   Finding People with Netscape

Activity 7:   Searching Tips and Tricks

Movie 1:   Yahoo

Movie 2:   Searching

Searching
with
Netscape

Session Overview

In this session, you will learn how to find things on the World Wide Web. In fact, you will learn how to browse and search the entire Internet using Netscape.

We will delve into browsing and searching for topics and will look at Web sites and for information of all kinds. We will introduce many different kinds of directories and search tools that exist out on the Web. Some are free (or limited searches are free) and some cost a few cents per search. We will show you both types.

You will also discover how to find people and their addresses. You will learn that finding people is harder than finding topics, places and other information. But, we'll talk about several different ways to find people.

Finally, we will provide you with some of the tricks of the trade. These will speed and simplify your searches and will take you where you want to be quickly!

Internet Browsing and Searching

As we have already noted, the Internet is forever in a state of rapid change. Perhaps it will help if we think of the Internet as an electronic world road system. As we know, people and places on the world's real road system are constantly moving. So it is also with people and places on the electronic road known as the Internet.

Finding people and places on the real road system is a little easier with the telephone and postal systems. But as with real roads, we can lose them if they move. Sometimes they leave forwarding addresses. You see that also on the World Wide Web when the person managing a site that has moved remembers to leave the listing of their new URL, but sometimes they neglect to do that.

Places also go out of business or change their names through mergers or business acquisitions. More importantly, new people and places are joining the Internet and the Web in huge numbers every day. A key reason to browse and search the Web and the Internet is to find these new people and places. The Web can be searched to find things ranging from a site dedicated to your favorite TV show to the E-mail address of your Aunt Bessie.

Let's pause for a moment and relate all of this to Internet and World Wide Web information mining.

Looking for Information

There are three basic ways to look for information on the Web:

1. *Casual browsing* or *Web surfing* lets us travel as the mood strikes us to see where we can go and what we can discover that we didn't know was there before.

2. *Topic browsing* with a directory permits us to find a particular kind of information that we want.

3. *Subject* or *keyword searching* enables us to use a "search engine" to find information on a specific topic.

If you don't know how to browse or search quickly and effectively, you will soon become bored and frustrated. Our purpose here is to show you how to find the topics and people you wish to locate quickly with a minimum of time and effort.

Once you have found the Web sites you are seeking, you can put them in your bookmark files (see Session Six). After you actually find people, you can put their E-mail addresses in your mail lists (see Session Eight).

As an introduction to searching, we can begin with almost no effort by using Netscape's built-in Directory bar and the Net Search button. Figure 7-1 reminds us of the Directory bar and the Net Search button.

Figure 7-1
The Net Search Button

If we click on the **Net Search button**, we will see a screen similar to the one shown in Figure 7-2.

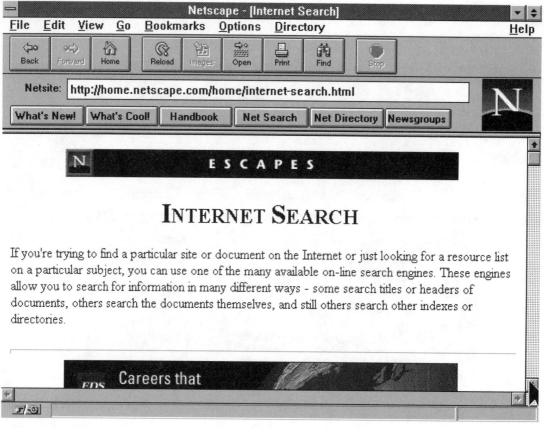

Figure 7-2
The Netscape Search
Screen

Search Engines

As we scroll down this Netscape screen, we arrive at an area called
Search Engines. *Search Engines* is just another name for a computer program that helps you to search the Web. Search engines usually have
names like worms, crawlers and wanderers.

How They Work

Search engines are really large databases containing addresses of Web
and Internet sites. They usually are organized by *keywords*. The databases are built by allowing simple programs to "crawl" or "worm"
through the Web looking for Web addresses and keywords. These programs periodically go out onto the Web to refresh and extend their

databases. When you use a crawler, worm or spider, you really are looking up items in their database.

Because each search engine operates differently and "crawls" at different times and rates, each one will produce different results. No one search engine is better or worse than any other; they differ from each other as printed reference works do. Figure 7-3 shows one engine that is known as InfoSeek.

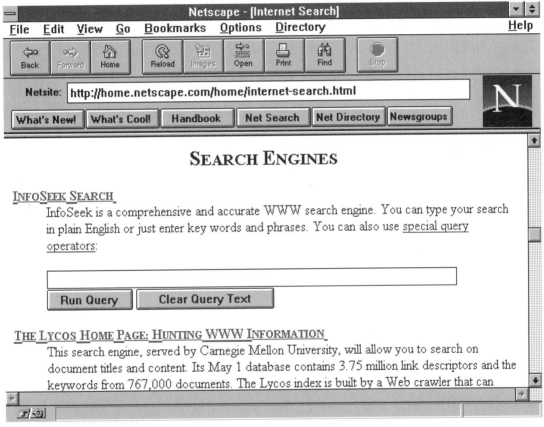

Figure 7-3
The InfoSeek Search Engine

Let's pause for a moment before using these tools to note a few things. In order to conduct a search, search engines use a World Wide Web technique called *forms*. That is, they request you to type some words into a blank space and then click on a button that sends your words. At the search engine Web site, your words are then used by the directory or search program. When results (or no results) are found, they are returned to you on your Netscape screen.

When you first begin searching, you may find you are receiving either far too many or far too few results. This means you will have to change your keywords or phrases to close in on your desired results. At the end of this session, we will give you some hints, tips, and tricks to "narrow" (fewer results) or "expand" (more results) your search.

Search Engine Searching

Before we leave this introduction to searching, you should notice that additional search engines can be found with a Search Engine Search. Figure 7-4 shows a lower section of the page that was illustrated in Figure 7-3.

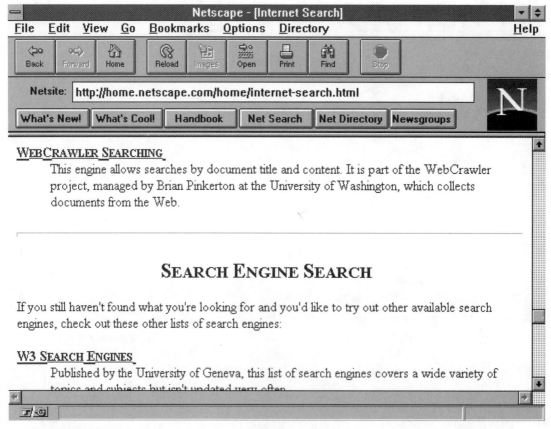

Figure 7-4
Search Engine Search

Using a Search Engine Search is simply a way to find more search engines. Note that in all cases, every search engine is presented to us as a hyperlink. If we click on that hyperlink, we are taken to that Web site. If we do that now with W3 Search Engines, we will go to the University of Geneva in Switzerland which keeps pointers to many search engines. This site is shown in Figure 7-5.

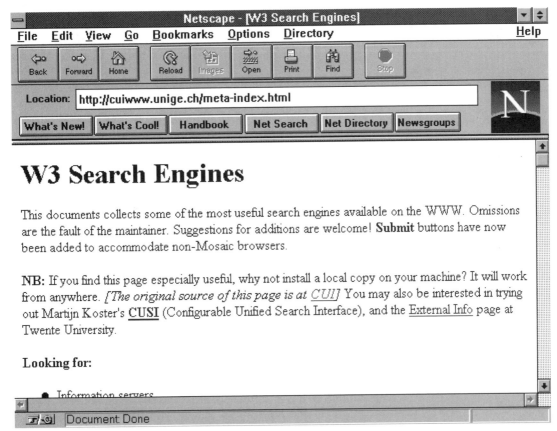

Figure 7-5
W3 Search Engines

While the page you see may differ from the one shown in our figure, the concept remains the same. The W3 Search Engines page is organized to help you to find different things on the Internet and the Web. Figure 7-6 shows the W3 Search Engines page when we visited and displays a list of suggestions of what you may be looking for: Information servers, software, people, and so forth.

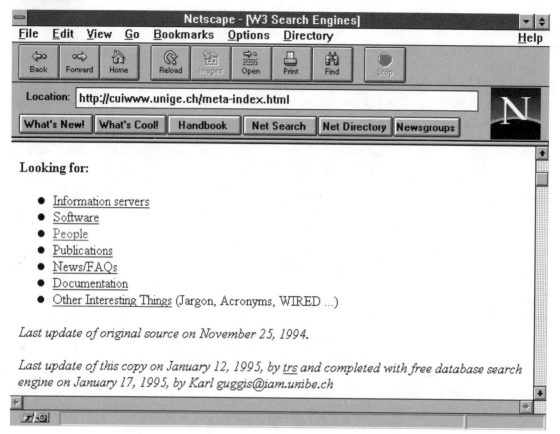

Figure 7-6
Looking for:

The process we have been following is similar to using a library. We began in the reference section (search engines). When we asked for reference books, we were asked a typical question: What are you looking for? We will find that many Internet and Web searches will work this way at first. As you become more familiar with search engines, you will discover the ones that work best for you.

In the following activities, we will point to many of the tools that have worked very well for us. As you become more experienced, you will find other tools and will increase your search speed and capabilities. We begin with a simple and popular directory called Yahoo.

Directory Searches—Yahoo

When you use directory searches, you will be following a hierarchical search tree. You will start with a top category and then follow the category down many levels until you arrive at your desired topic. There are many directories now on the Web, but as we write this, the best one is *Yahoo*. We will use Yahoo to illustrate a hierarchical directory search.

If you click on Netscape's **Net Directory button** you will be taken to an introductory Yahoo page. You are still really at Netscape, but the Netscape developers have given you an idea of what the Yahoo page offers. The top-level Yahoo categories (as shown by Netscape) are illustrated in Figure 7-7.

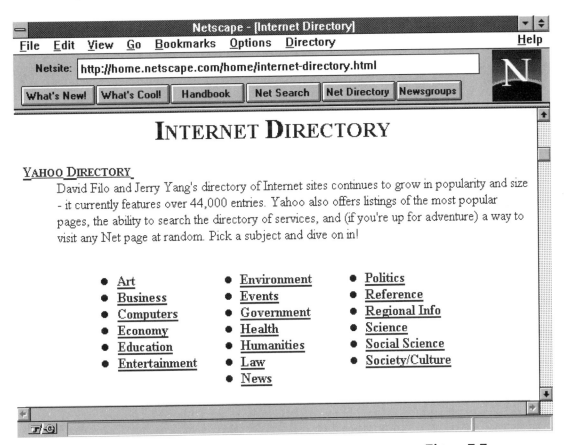

Figure 7-7
Netscape's Internet Directory

If we click on **Yahoo Directory** near the top of our screen at the left, we will go to Yahoo's Home Page. Here we will begin a simple hierarchical search as an illustration. When we have completed this search, you might wish to go back to the top level of Yahoo and try several other searches. Our simple example search will go down only about three levels, but many of the categories go down much further. The Yahoo Home Page is shown in Figure 7-8.

We have used Netscape's menu bar Options to turn off many of the top Netscape bars. This gives us greater visibility for our search screens. When we need to put them back to show something, we will do so.

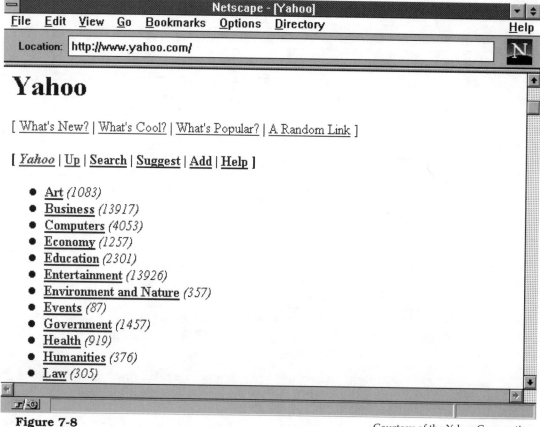

Figure 7-8
The Yahoo Home
Page

Courtesy of the Yahoo Corporation

Yahoo

Yahoo was developed by two Stanford students, David Filo and Jerry Yang. Yahoo's tremendous initial success caused its developers to become a commercial enterprise. When you read this, it may become a service for which there is a charge, but at the moment, it is a free service.

Before we begin our directory search, let's explain what you are looking at on the Yahoo main page. There are two rows of hyperlinks above the main categories. The first row is self-explanatory as to New, Cool (their judgment), Popular (most accesses) and Random. The Random link will take you to a Web site chosen by a random number generator. You never know where you will be going and you won't return twice to the same place. Try it; you will go to some pretty interesting places!

The next row remains constant during your travels throughout the Yahoo directory. *Yahoo* always takes you back to the top of the directory. *Up* takes you back one level, which is handy for backing out of false starts.

Search is a search engine built into Yahoo that enables you to search the Yahoo directory. Yahoo is a directory and as such is not similar to the search engines we will see later. In Yahoo's case people add their own listings. It's more like a telephone company's Yellow Pages directory with search capabilities.

Suggest is an E-mail interface permitting users to suggest ideas to improve Yahoo. And they do listen!

Add allows you to put your own page in their directory. They do have a checking process to ensure that your home page will be entered into the Yahoo directory.

Help produces a well-structured set of help information about Yahoo. It also gives some background about Yahoo.

The top level of categories, starting with Art, continues down the page. Beside each category is a number representing the number of entries in that category. In Figure 7-9, you will see several lower level categories with the word [new] after them. This signifies that the category has new items in it. When you reach the lowest level, you can then see which item has been marked as new.

Follow along with us as we descend through the Yahoo hierarchy. We have picked an easy example. As we follow down the tree, we will see

Art *(1083)*

Children *(4)* [new]

Art: Children

Adriana's Artwork
Kids' Space
Michelle and Zachary's ArtWorks
The Refrigerator [new]

This progression is shown in Figures 7-9 and 7-10.

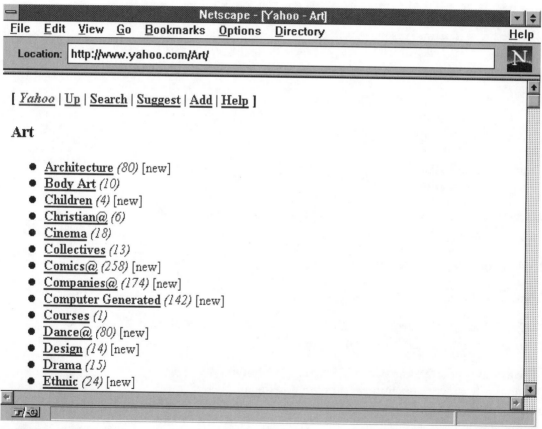

Figure 7-9
The Art Category

Courtesy of the Yahoo Corporation

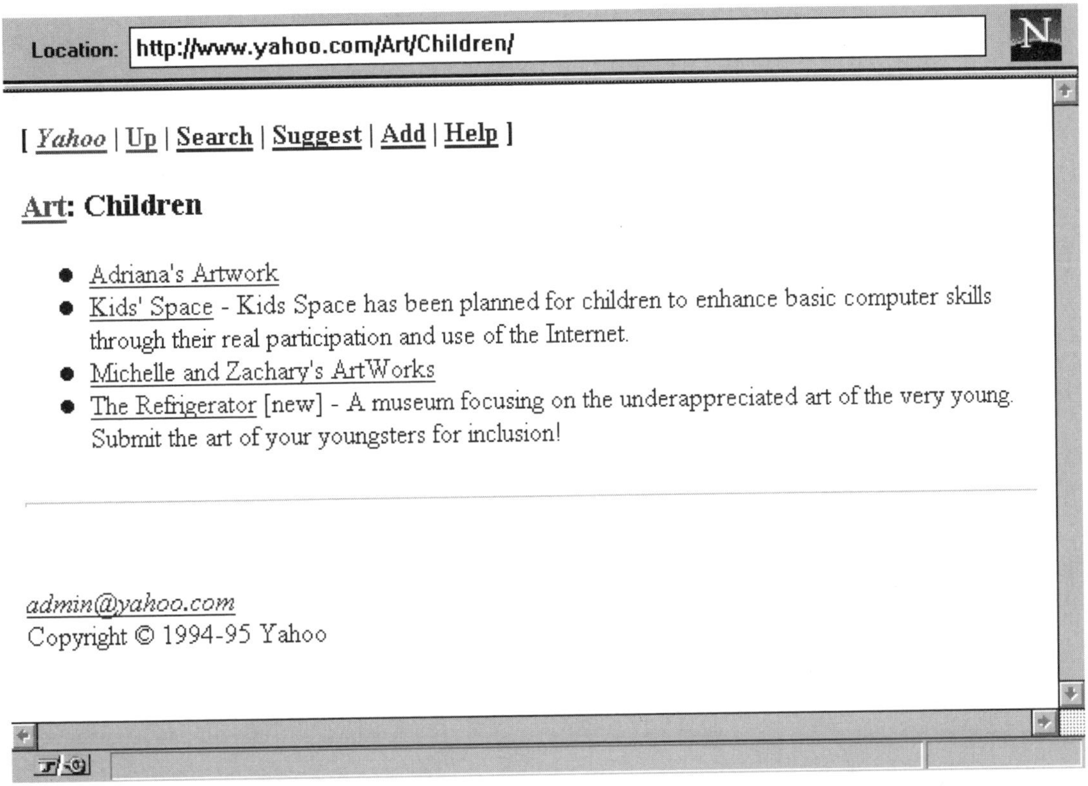

Location: http://www.yahoo.com/Art/Children/   N

[*Yahoo* | Up | Search | Suggest | Add | Help]

Art: Children

- Adriana's Artwork
- Kids' Space - Kids Space has been planned for children to enhance basic computer skills through their real participation and use of the Internet.
- Michelle and Zachary's ArtWorks
- The Refrigerator [new] - A museum focusing on the underappreciated art of the very young. Submit the art of your youngsters for inclusion!

admin@yahoo.com
Copyright © 1994-95 Yahoo

Courtesy of the Yahoo Corporation

Figure 7-10
The Art: Children Page

You should now use the Yahoo hyperlink at the top of the page and pick several categories of your own to explore. Have fun!

Searching for Particular Topics Using Netscape

Every week a new set of topic search tools for the Internet and particularly the World Wide Web seems to appear. In the following sections, we will illustrate some excellent search engines. You may find after you practice with these tools that newer ones are available. Here we hope to make you familiar with the concepts of Web searching. Then you will be able to use the concepts with the tools that we have shown you, as well as with the ever-evolving sets of new tools.

Let's begin by returning to the Netscape Internet Search that was shown previously in Figure 7-2. We will use each of the tools shown under Search Engines, but we will go in reverse order. Look now at Figure 7-11. We will begin with the WebCrawler; then we will use the Lycos Home Page and finally we will try out InfoSeek.

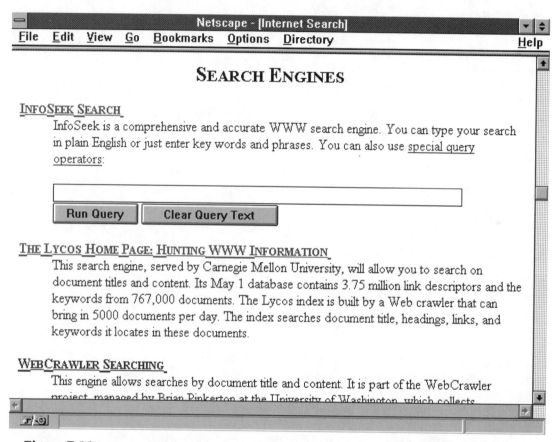

Figure 7-11
The Search Engines

Searching with WebCrawler

Hands-On
Activity
Three

We begin by clicking on the hyperlink **WebCrawler Searching** which takes us to the WebCrawler Home Page. The use of the word "Web" in World Wide Web has spawned a number of tools with arachnid or spiderlike allusions. The WebCrawler and its spider logos are examples of this. The WebCrawler page is illustrated in Figure 7-12. Their URL is `http://Webcrawler.com`

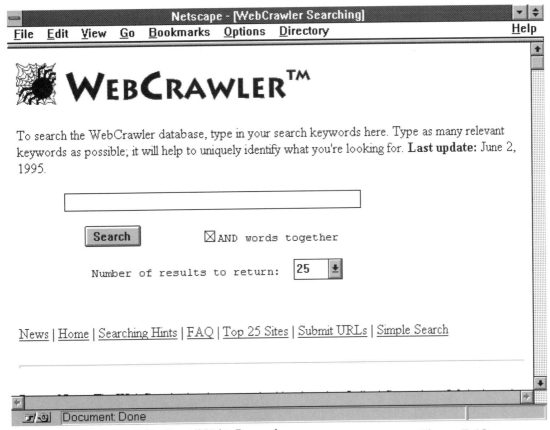

Figure 7-12
The WebCrawler

The WebCrawler is a wonderful place to start as it presents an easy-to-understand screen. Their instructions are clear and simple. They tell you that whatever keywords you use will be ANDed together (if you leave the default AND box checked). They also tell you that the default is for them to report the first 25 results to you. Before you change any of the defaults, let's try a search.

For our search keyword we will use the term `Maine lobster`

Most search tools start out being case insensitive. That is, you don't have to worry about upper- and lowercase in your search keywords. Some tools will tell you this and some will give you the option of changing this setting. Figure 7-13 shows the search term already entered and the cursor ready to click on **Search**.

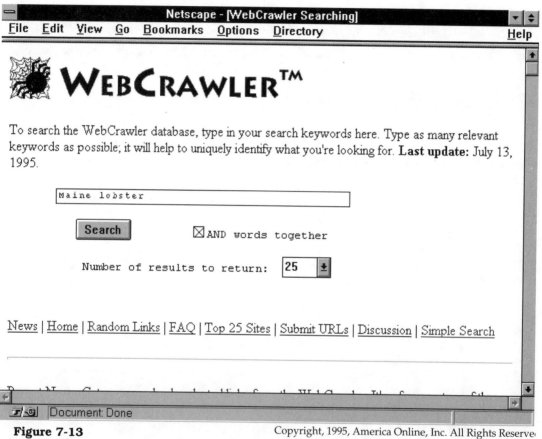

Figure 7-13
WebCrawler
Searching `Maine`
`lobster`

In almost no time (WebCrawler is very fast), a number of results are returned. Notice that they are all in the form of hyperlinks! This means that you do not have to scribble the addresses on bits of paper. As you can see from the results that are displayed in Figure 7-14, we are ready for our next jump.

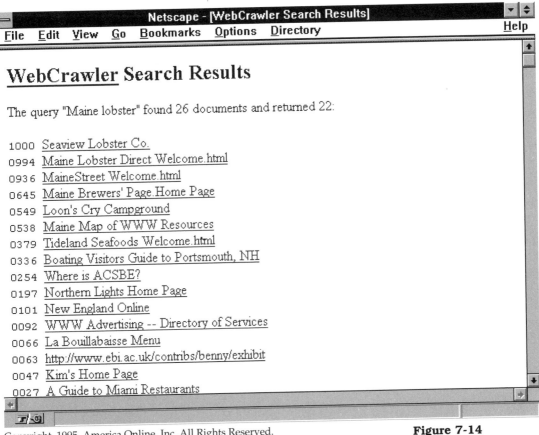

Figure 7-14
Search Results for "Maine lobster"

If you move about the WebCrawler pages, you will note that Web-Crawler has been acquired by America Online. We hope they continue to maintain and improve this lovely tool. You may wish to experiment now with some of your own search keywords. Just remember to come back to us here. We have warned you before that jumping from link to link (surfing the Net) can be habit forming!

Next we move on to the Lycos search engine. Their URL is
`http://lycos.cs.cmu.edu/`

Activity
Four

Searching with Lycos

If we return to the Netscape Search Engines page, we can select the Lycos Home Page. When we click on that hyperlink, we are taken to the main Lycos page that is located at Carnegie Mellon University. This page is illustrated in Figure 7-15.

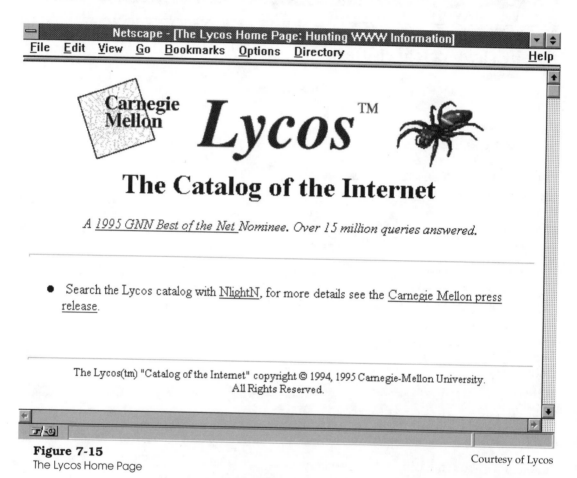

Figure 7-15
The Lycos Home Page

Courtesy of Lycos

You will have to read carefully to find the "Lycos search form" hyperlink. There is a lot of information on this particular home page. We recommend that you read through all of it to get a feel for what they have to offer. One item to which we will return shortly is known as *NlightN* (pronounced "enlighten".) While Lycos is a free service, NlightN is a "fee" service. We will discuss more about fee services later in this session.

Let's move on now to Lycos searching. Find the hyperlink Lycos search form and click on it. It should take you to a page similar to Figure 7-16.

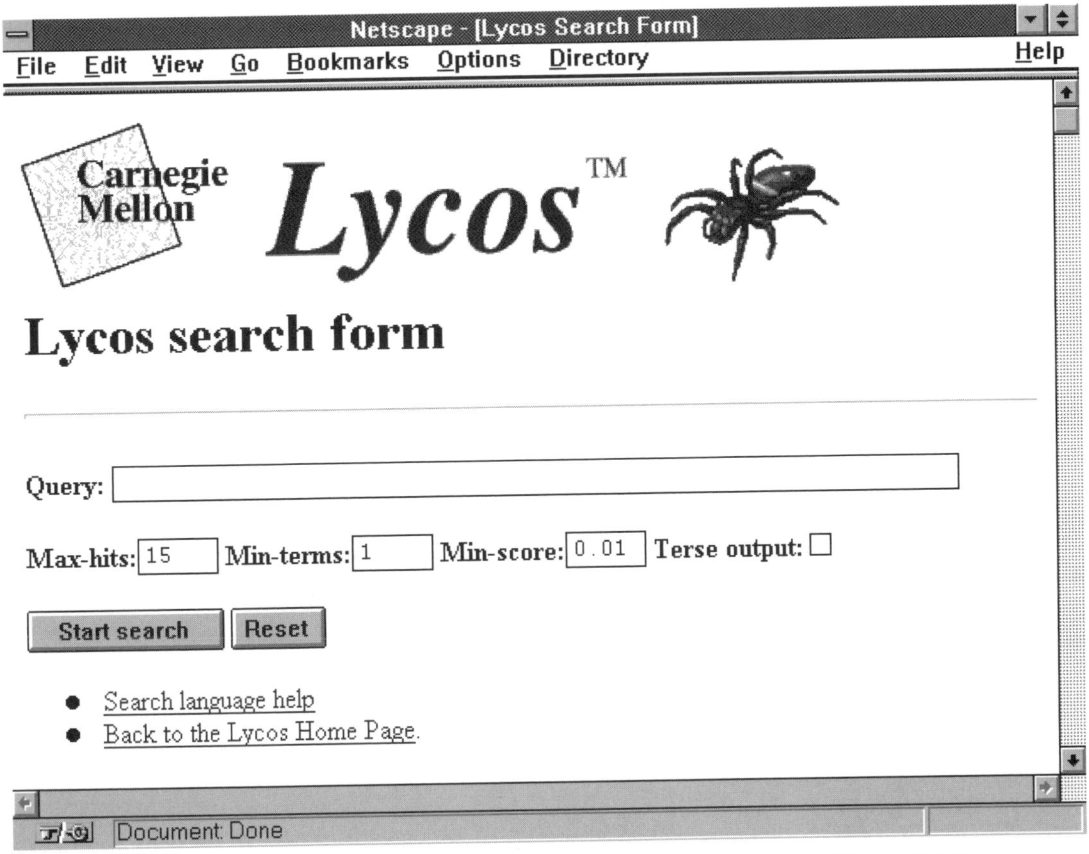

Netscape - [Lycos Search Form]

File   Edit   View   Go   Bookmarks   Options   Directory   Help

Carnegie Mellon *Lycos*™ 🕷

Lycos search form

Query: [   ]

Max-hits: [15]   Min-terms: [1]   Min-score: [0.01]   Terse output: ☐

[Start search]   [Reset]

- Search language help
- Back to the Lycos Home Page.

Document: Done

Courtesy of Lycos

Figure 7-16
The Lycos Search Form

Lycos is a somewhat more complex tool to use than WebCrawler, but it's easy to learn the basics. Like WebCrawler, Query: is where you will type your keywords. Unlike WebCrawler, unless you change the number displayed in the Min-terms: box, Lycos will return results for *anything* that it finds that matches *any* of the search keywords or terms. That is, the keywords will not be ANDed.

To fix this, you need to change the number of Min-terms, or the minimum number of search terms to be included in each result. For instance, if you want to AND oranges and apples you would type those words as the search terms. Then you would set Min-terms: to the number 2. This would tell Lycos to return hits that include *both* oranges and apples.

The next box, Min-score:, requires a little more explanation. When Lycos compares your terms to its data, it scores 1.00 for an *exact* match and a fractional number for less than an exact match. You can see that the default score of 0.01 is quite low. You may want to enter a different number in this box in order to change Lycos's search behavior.

If you are quite sure of your terms and want fewer hits, choose Min-score: to be at or close to 1.00. If you are not so sure, pick a lower fraction. We'll experiment with two examples.

For our first try, we will search for the words "Webcrawler" and "experiences." We will type in these two words as our query terms and set Min-terms: to 2 which will ensure that we have ANDed the two. Then we will set Min-score: to 1.00 so that we will receive only *exact* matches. Our query screen is shown in Figure 7-17.

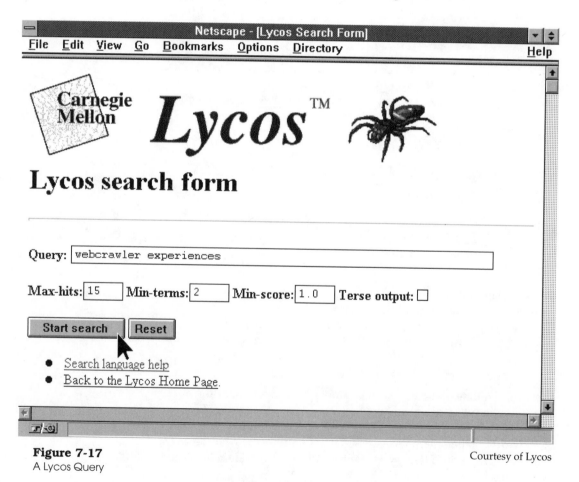

Figure 7-17
A Lycos Query

Courtesy of Lycos

Now we click on **Start search** and see what we get. Lycos returns our results shortly and we see that we have one, and only one, hit. Lycos shows us that 6,304 documents have partial results, but only the one shown below the statistics actually matched our criteria. This first Lycos result is displayed in Figure 7-18.

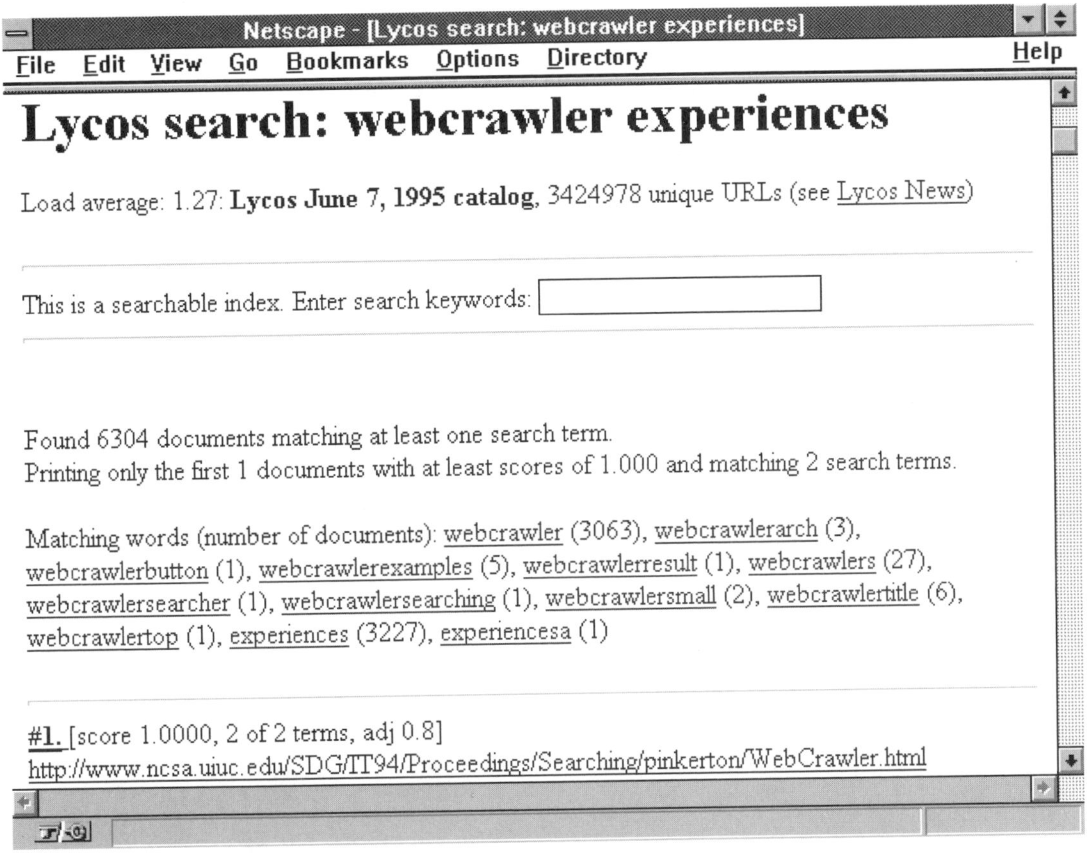

Netscape - [Lycos search: webcrawler experiences]

File   Edit   View   Go   Bookmarks   Options   Directory   Help

Lycos search: webcrawler experiences

Load average: 1.27: **Lycos June 7, 1995 catalog**, 3424978 unique URLs (see Lycos News)

This is a searchable index. Enter search keywords:

Found 6304 documents matching at least one search term.
Printing only the first 1 documents with at least scores of 1.000 and matching 2 search terms.

Matching words (number of documents): webcrawler (3063), webcrawlerarch (3), webcrawlerbutton (1), webcrawlerexamples (5), webcrawlerresult (1), webcrawlers (27), webcrawlersearcher (1), webcrawlersearching (1), webcrawlersmall (2), webcrawlertitle (6), webcrawlertop (1), experiences (3227), experiencesa (1)

#1. [score 1.0000, 2 of 2 terms, adj 0.8]
http://www.ncsa.uiuc.edu/SDG/IT94/Proceedings/Searching/pinkerton/WebCrawler.html

Courtesy of Lycos

Figure 7-18
The First Lycos Results

You will have to read this figure (or your screen) carefully to find these details.

Now we will make a slight change to our query. The only item we will change is the Min-score:. During our last query, we used 1.00 to assure an *exact* match. In this next query, we will change Min-score to 0.50 and see how it alters our results.

We have not repeated the query screen, but it is the same as the one shown in Figure 7-17. In that figure, we showed 1.00 as the value for Min-score:. We will now repeat the query, but will change the Min-score: to 0.500. The results of this new query are shown in Figure 7-19.

Netscape - [Lycos search: webcrawler experiences]

File   Edit   View   Go   Bookmarks   Options   Directory   **Help**

Lycos search: webcrawler experiences

Load average: 1.28: **Lycos June 7, 1995 catalog**, 3424978 unique URLs (see Lycos News)

This is a searchable index. Enter search keywords:

Found 6304 documents matching at least one search term.
Printing only the first 7 documents with at least scores of 0.500 and matching 2 search terms.

Matching words (number of documents): webcrawler (3063), webcrawlerarch (3), webcrawlerbutton (1), webcrawlerexamples (5), webcrawlerresult (1), webcrawlers (27), webcrawlersearcher (1), webcrawlersearching (1), webcrawlersmall (2), webcrawlertitle (6), webcrawlertop (1), experiences (3227), experiencesa (1)

#1. [score 1.0000, 2 of 2 terms, adj 0.8]
http://www.ncsa.uiuc.edu/SDG/IT94/Proceedings/Searching/pinkerton/WebCrawler.html

Figure 7-19
The Second Lycos
Results

Courtesy of Lycos

Again, Lycos found 6304 documents, but this time we were provided with seven documents that had scores of at least 0.500 and matched 2 search terms. The greater number of matches (or what is sometimes known as "hits") was due only to our reducing the exactness of the Min-score: from 1.000 to 0.500.

You can see that you can fine-tune Lycos to a much greater degree and thus broaden your search. The main advantage here is that you can look more broadly at your topic or conduct searches in instances in which you are less sure of the exactness.

It is important to realize that the word "exactness" refers to both the precision of your terms and the exactness of the documents that are being searched. All of us have misplaced papers occasionally by putting them in the wrong place. Electronic information is no different. People make keystroke errors and a tool like Lycos (and the flexibility of the exactness measurement) helps us surmount these problems.

Searching With InfoSeek

A more recent entry on the Internet search scene is *InfoSeek*. This tool offers both a free and a commercial (for fee) service. You can use (at this time) the free service for limited searches or the commercial service. The commercial service offers a wider range of sources and more hits for a small charge.

Although we show both free and fee services, the authors wish it known that we have no financial or any other interest in any of the tools described in this session. In a few years, we may wish that we did!

InfoSeek Search is available from the Netscape search page as is shown in Figure 7-20.

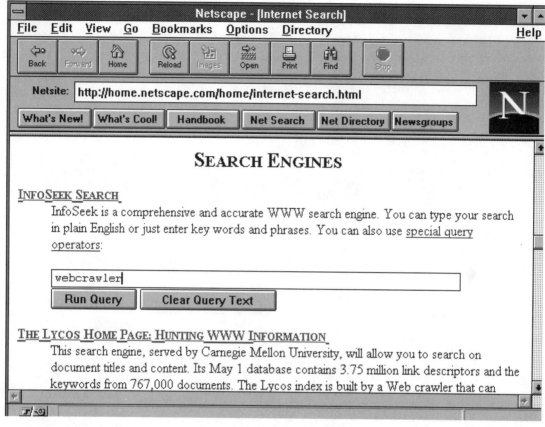

Figure 7-20
InfoSeek Search

This is the free or limited InfoSeek search engine. As we did in the preceding activity, we will use the word `webcrawler` as our search term.
We do this to show you how different search engines present information resulting from similar searches.

As you can see in Figure 7-20, all we have to do is to place our cursor in
the blank form and type the word `webcrawler`. Then we click on **Run
Query** and await our results. They are returned in just a moment and
are shown in Figure 7-21.

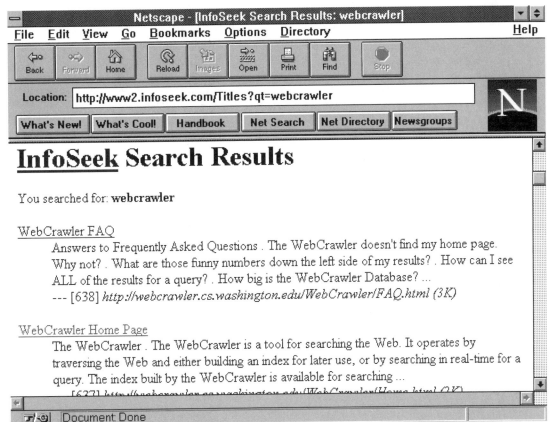

Figure 7-21
InfoSeek Search
Results: webcrawler

InfoSeek presents the results in an easy-to-read format. The hyperlink of each document is shown first, followed by an easy- to-read description of the resulting page's contents. In addition to all this information, the results also tell us how large a file will be downloaded if we click on the title hyperlink. The actual hyperlink is also shown.

As with many of the other search tools, we can jump directly to any one of our search results. Just click on the title of a particular result and you will be taken immediately to that page.

Now we will click on the large **InfoSeek hyperlink** on the upper left of
our screen to learn more about InfoSeek. This will take us to InfoSeek's
Home Page. It is shown in Figure 7-22. The InfoSeek URL is
`http://www.infoseek.com/Home`

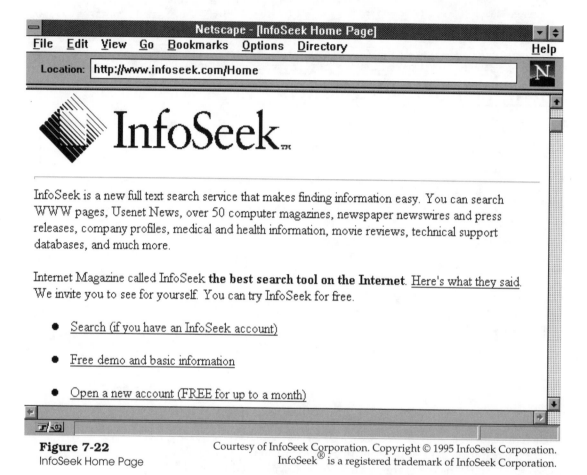

Figure 7-22
InfoSeek Home Page

Courtesy of InfoSeek Corporation. Copyright © 1995 InfoSeek Corporation.
InfoSeek® is a registered trademark of InfoSeek Corporation.

Here is the heart of InfoSeek. The three choices visible in our figure
show that we can search if we have an InfoSeek account, try out their
free demo and learn more about their services, or open a new account.

In order to use the search facility that is provided on the InfoSeek Home Page, you must have previously signed up for an account with InfoSeek. The cost at the time of this writing ranges from $2 a month for 10 searches to $10 a month for 100 searches.

Your authors have already signed up for an account. If we click on the **Search hyperlink**, we are presented with an account screen as shown in Figure 7-23.

Figure 7-23
The InfoSeek
Username Box

Courtesy of InfoSeek Corporation. Copyright © 1995 InfoSeek Corporation. InfoSeek® is a registered trademark of InfoSeek Corporation.

After our name and password have been entered (you didn't think we would show that here, did you?) we arrive at the main InfoSeek commercial search page. We have scrolled down this page a little bit below the query form so we can show you the choices that are offered. If you choose to sign up for an account, you can search any one of a number of different information sources including World Wide Web pages and help screens. In addition, InfoSeek offers a number of standard and premium collections. These are shown in Figure 7-24.

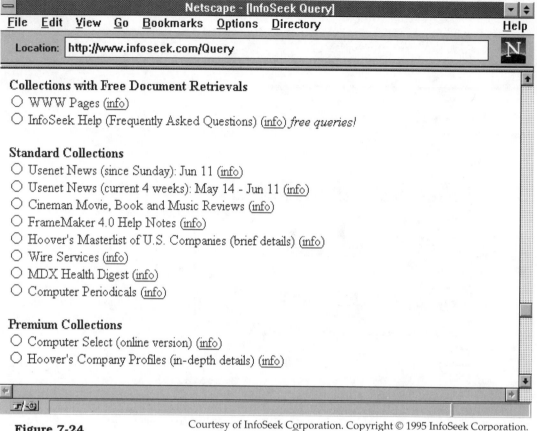

Figure 7-24
InfoSeek's
Commercial Choices

Courtesy of InfoSeek Corporation. Copyright © 1995 InfoSeek Corporation.
InfoSeek® is a registered trademark of InfoSeek Corporation.

You can select one of these for each search and InfoSeek will return the first 20 results to you. You are then asked if you would like to see the next 20 results that were found.

Notice the small *(info)* hyperlink to the right of each collection choice. You can click on that hyperlink (after you have arranged for an account) and get a full description of each of the choices. Observe that you have access to both the Internet's Usenet newsgroups and also to commercial wire (or news) services. These include the Associated Press, Reuters, and several other commercial news services. Note that the Premium Collections require additional subscription charges.

Beyond World Wide Web searching, two very valuable collections in InfoSeek are Usenet News and Wire Services. In an age when TV and newspapers limit themselves to high profile news, InfoSeek can often bring you the fine details.

As mentioned above, InfoSeek charges a very small amount for each search it conducts for you. The InfoSeek Home Page also offers a free one month trial period. The trial account is very low risk as InfoSeek doesn't (currently) even ask for a charge card number until the end of your trial period.

Finding People with Netscape

In addition to finding topics and specific information using directories and search engines, it is also possible to use Netscape and the World Wide Web to locate people. This activity shows you how to do this.

The Quick Method

Before we detail methods of finding people on the Internet, we should point out that there is a very simple way to find the E- mail address or URL for most people.

Simply call them up and ask them for their E-mail address or URL. If you can reach people by telephone, this is by far the fastest and most effective method to locate people on the Internet!

In addition, once you obtain their E-mail address, there are two other very important questions you should ask them. Do they actually read their E-mail? And, if so, how often? E-mail is a very fast and effective tool, but only if people look at it.

People Searching

We'll start our people search using the help provided to us by Netscape. Here is how to follow along.

1. Click once on the **Net Search directory button** or click on **Directory** and then on **Internet Search**.

2. When you arrive at the Internet Search page, move down that page until the hyperlink W3 Search Engines is visible.

3. Click once on **W3 Search Engines**.

4. Move down the W3 Search Engines page until the hyperlink people is visible.

5. Click once on the **hyperlink people**

When we click on the People hyperlink, we arrive at an area of the University of Geneva page that shows us several search possibilities as shown in Figure 7-25.

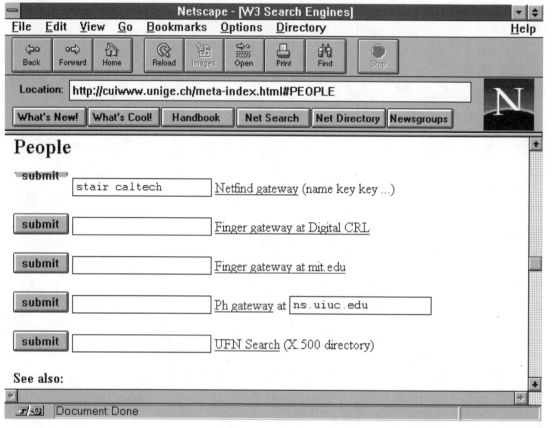

Figure 7-25
The Netfind Gateway

To see how this works, we will use the first tool in the list: Netfind Gateway. The Netfind Gateway runs at the Internet Network Information Center (the InterNIC.) It is actually a Gopher server, but Netscape hides much of this from you. We will use the Netfind Gateway to see what we can learn about Henry Stair, co-author of this book. We will assume for purposes of this activity that we do not know his E-mail address. We will use the Netfind Gateway to help us to find it.

We will use his last name, *Stair*, and the fact that we heard about his having gone to Caltech. The form for Netfind is quite simple. You are asked to provide a name and one or more "keys" or other bits of information. We will enter the keywords `stair` and `caltech` as shown in Figure 7-25.

Entering these two search terms and pressing **Enter** sends off the search to the Data Services section at the InterNIC. Now we wait for the result and in a moment it is returned as a Gopher Menu. We are getting closer, but we still do not have what we want: an actual E-mail address.

The list shows as its second item what appears to be something about CalTech alumni. This is shown in Figure 7-26.

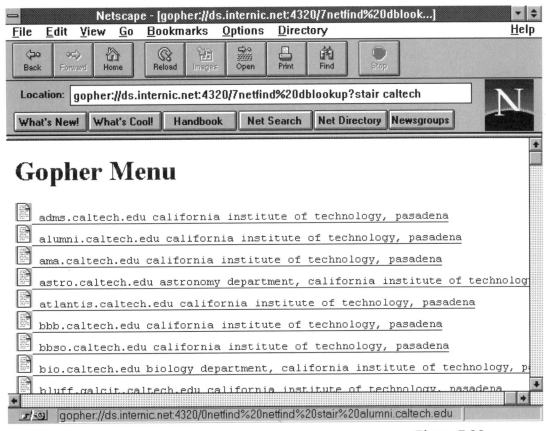

Figure 7-26
Gopher Results

If we now click on the second line of the Gopher Menu, the InterNIC Gopher returns what we are actually looking for. After reading through the response, we find that Henry Stair can most likely be reached at `stair@world.std.com`

The results screen is shown in Figure 7-27.

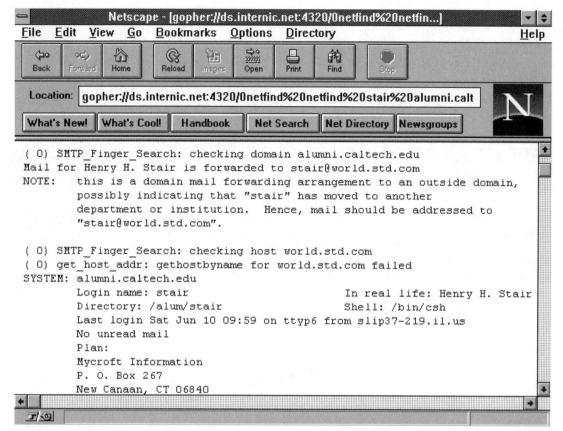

Figure 7-27
E-mail Search Results

In addition to learning an E-mail address, we also learn that Henry Stair is associated with Mycroft Information and we get a traditional postal address. This can be considered a pretty fast and successful search. However, it is important to note that we may not always be as successful or we may be too successful. That is, we could have found several thousand Smiths or Wongs or Suzukis.

Verifying the Address

Before sending E-mail to Henry Stair, we should check to see if the address we have been given is correct. To do this, we will use an old Internet tool called *Finger*. Although Netscape does not have Finger capability, there are many gateway machines around the Internet we can use.

We have chosen to use a Finger gateway at the following URL:

`http://www.america.net/cgi-bin/finger`

We use Netscape to open this URL and are presented with the screen shown in Figure 7-28.

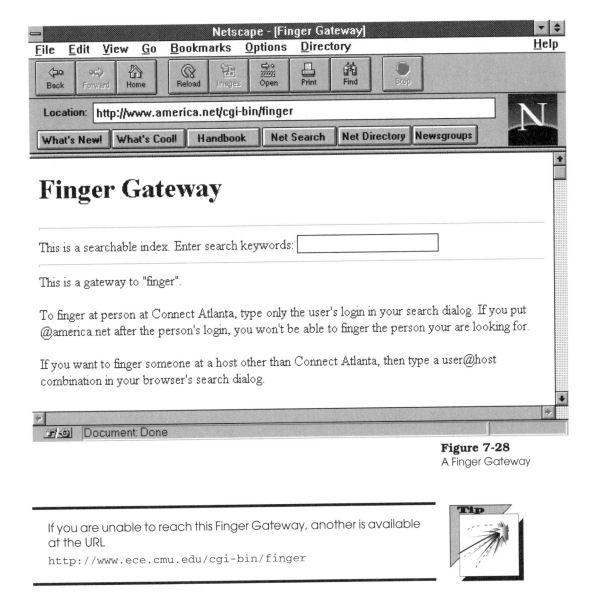

Figure 7-28
A Finger Gateway

If you are unable to reach this Finger Gateway, another is available at the URL

`http://www.ece.cmu.edu/cgi-bin/finger`

To use the Finger Gateway (or the finger command, if your system has that capability,) you need to use the full E-mail address. In our case that is `stair@world.std.com`

After moving the mouse to the keywords: area and clicking to position the typing cursor, we enter

`stair@world.std.com`

as shown in Figure 7-29.

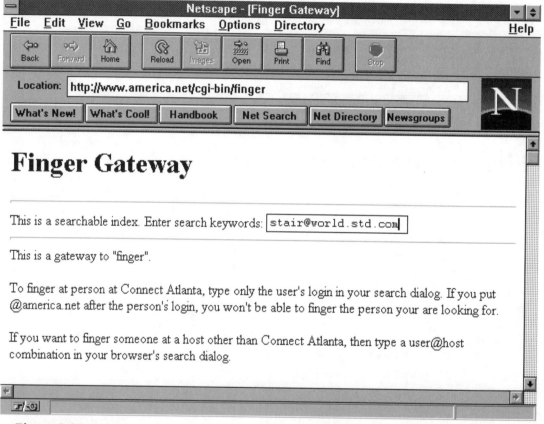

Figure 7-29
Entering the Search
Keywords

Notice that the Finger Gateway has some text to help us with our entry. Not all Finger Gateways provide such directions. When using Finger, you must enter the E-mail address as correctly as possible. Finger servers at the distant hosts will try their best to figure out what you mean, but it is best if you give them as much information as possible.

The result of our Finger Gateway search is shown in Figure 7-30.

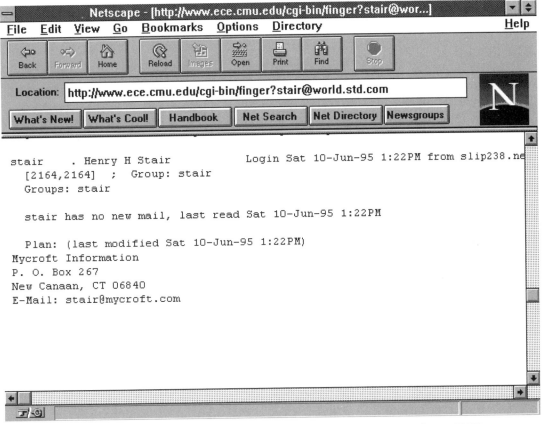

Figure 7-30
Finger Results

Now we can see that this is indeed the Henry Stair we are looking for and that E-mail to either of two addresses will work. He can be reached at `stair@world.std.com` or `stair@mycroft.com`

Other People Searches

We will describe two other methods that are used to find people and their E-mail addresses on the Internet. They are known as Knowbot and Four11.

The Knowbot

The *Knowbot* was developed at the Corporation for National Research Initiatives in Reston, Virginia and is a prototype of what are called

Intelligent Agents. That is, the Knowbot is a program that goes forth about the Internet on your behalf and looks for the information you have requested. This particular agent looks for names in lots of different places. The URL for the Knowbot is

```
http://info.cnri.reston.va.us/kis.html
```

Figure 7-31 shows the Knowbot's welcome page.

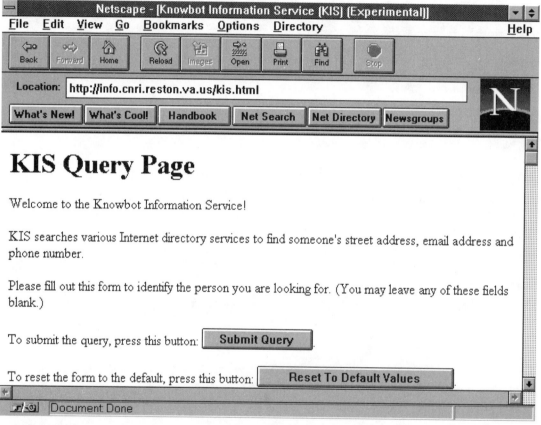

Figure 7-31
The Knowbot
Information Service

As we scroll down the page, we find a number of different blanks in which we might enter information. We do not need to use them all, but it makes the Knowbot's job easier. In our example we will enter the name `stair`, the organization `mycroft`, and the country `us`.

Our entries are shown in Figure 7-32.

Netscape - [Knowbot Information Service (KIS) [Experimental]]

File   Edit   View   Go   Bookmarks   Options   Directory   Help

| Back | Forward | Home | Reload | Images | Open | Print | Find | Stop |

Location: http://info.cnri.reston.va.us/kis.html

To submit the query, press this button: **Submit Query** .

To reset the form to the default, press this button: **Reset To Default Values** .

Enter a name: `stair`

Who does this person work for?: `mycroft`

What country? (Abbreviated): `us`

Which services should I try?

1. ☒ The Internic "White Pages" (North America)
2. ☒ MCImail Database
3. ☒ RIPE "White Pages" (Europe)

Figure 7-32
Knowbot Entries

Below the blanks are the places that the Knowbot will search on your behalf. The defaults are

1. The InterNIC "White Pages"

2. MCImail Database

3. RIPE "White Pages" (Europe)

4. Latin American InterNIC (not visible in Figure 7-32)

RIPE is an organization called Resaux IP Europeans (European IP Networks in French). There are other locations available to you to select, although they are not visible in Figure 7-32. You can select the other locations if you wish. They include the UNIX Finger service that we just used and a powerful tool called UNIX Whois. We'll leave Whois as a later exercise for you.

When we click on the **Submit Query button**, the Knowbot launches queries into the Internet to the locations indicated. The results come in and look like those displayed in Figure 7-33. Again, we seem to have found the information that we are seeking.

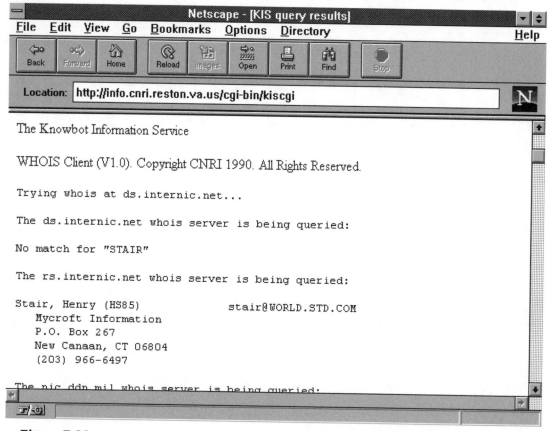

Figure 7-33
Knowbot Results

The Four11 Directory Services

A newer entry in the people finding business is the *Four11* (or 411) *Directory Services*. This is (as of today) a free service which offers listings in their pages. It is necessary to get a password, but you also get a free listing when you do so. As we have already obtained the password, we will skip the introductory screen that you will see at the URL

```
http://www.four11.com
```

After you have registered (which takes only a moment), you will arrive at a screen that looks like Figure 7-34.

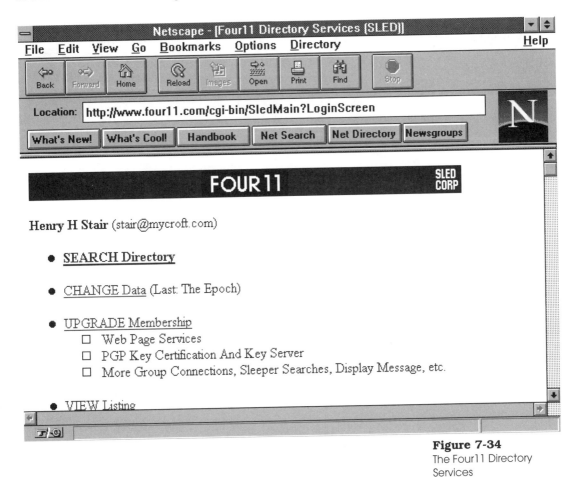

Figure 7-34
The Four11 Directory Services

Notice the many options for later exploration. We will just use the search function here, but you may wish to explore the others on your own.

When we click on **SEARCH Directory**, we are shown a screen with blanks (forms) for our entries. This screen looks like Figure 7-35.

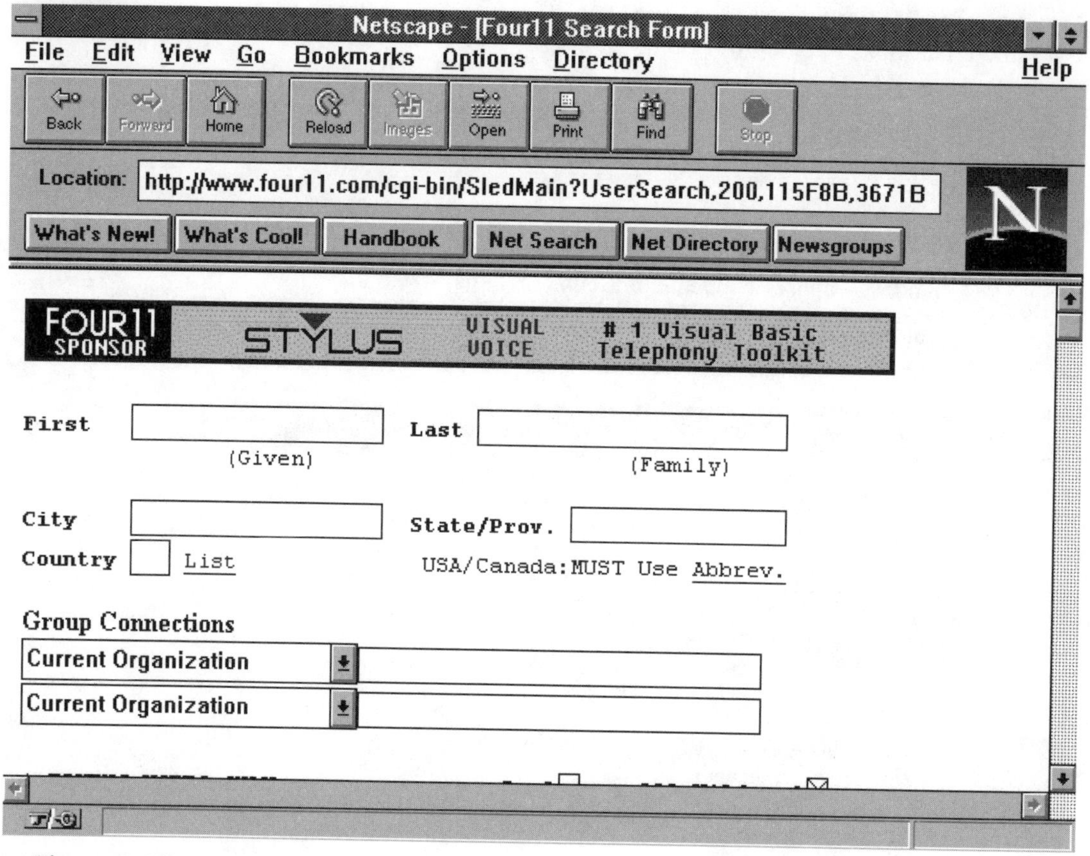

Netscape - [Four11 Search Form]

File   Edit   View   Go   Bookmarks   Options   Directory   Help

Back   Forward   Home   Reload   Images   Open   Print   Find   Stop

Location: http://www.four11.com/cgi-bin/SledMain?UserSearch,200,115F8B,3671B

What's New!   What's Cool!   Handbook   Net Search   Net Directory   Newsgroups

FOUR11
SPONSOR   STYLUS   VISUAL   # 1 Visual Basic
                   VOICE   Telephony Toolkit

First [   ]   Last [   ]
              (Given)   (Family)

City [   ]   State/Prov. [   ]
Country [   ] List   USA/Canada: MUST Use Abbrev.

Group Connections

| Current Organization ▼ | [   ] |
| Current Organization ▼ | [   ] |

Figure 7-35
The Four11 Entry
Screen

We will again look for Henry Stair in the United States so we will fill in
just these three blanks. Once we have done this, as shown in Figure
7-36, we scroll down and click on **Search button**.

Figure 7-36
Our Search Entries

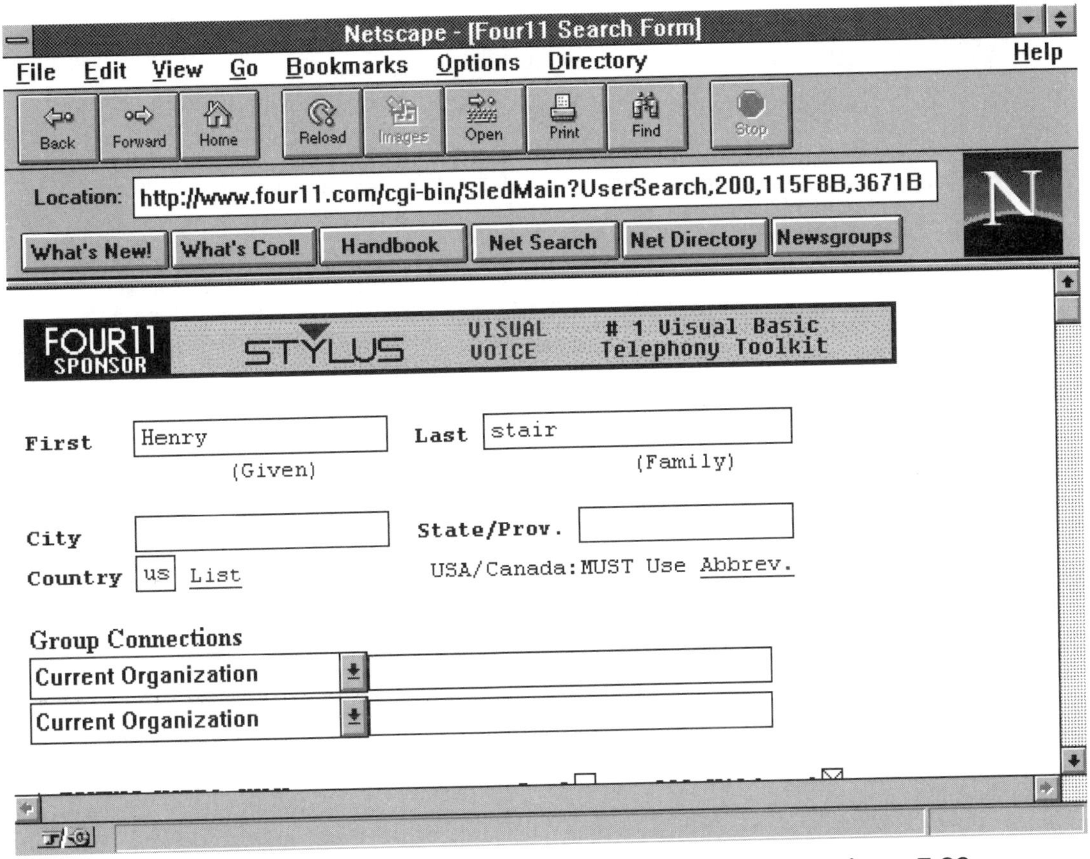

The Four11 Directory Services return two entries as shown in Figure
7-37. But, unlike our previous searches, it returns them as hyperlinks.

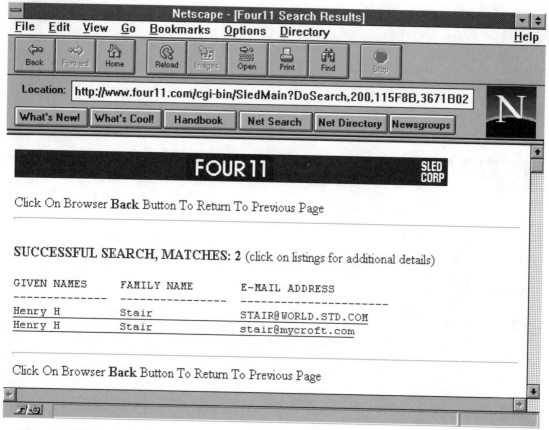

Figure 7-37
Search Results

If we now click on the lower hyperlink, we get a page of Henry Stair's listing on the Four11 Directory. This is a little like signing up for a telephone and getting a listing in the telephone directory. Of course, you also get a listing in the dial 411 service. The page listing Henry Stair looks like the one that is shown in Figure 7-38.

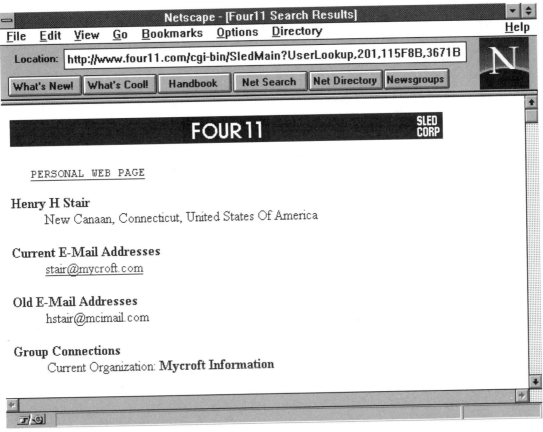

Figure 7-38
The Four11 Listing

Notice also that there is a place for a personal home page in hyperlink format. (If you click on **PERSONAL WEB PAGE**, you should arrive at Henry Stair's Home Page.) In addition, clicking on the hyperlink for his E-mail address will begin an E-mail message to him. For occasional E-mail this is a very fast and effective way to look someone up and send them E-mail.

Activity
Seven

Searching Tips and Tricks

To conclude our tour of Web searching, we will point out some tips and hints for searching. This should help you speed your searches throughout the World Wide Web. You will pick up additional ideas for quick and efficient Web searching as you continue to explore.

Search Engines versus Directory Searches

Search engines work best for you when you have relatively unique keywords. For instance if you were looking for World Wide Web browsers for UNIX, you could easily use search engines. The query might have a structure like Web *and* browser *and* unix

This would imply that you were pretty sure that you wanted to find information about this specific topic. That is, you knew what you wanted, but did not know where to locate it.

When you are less sure of what you are looking for, a directory search can be very helpful. For example, you might be looking for Web sites relating to outer space in general (for example, NASA) rather than doing a directed search with WebCrawler for a particular Shuttle mission. Once you have found the information in the general directory search, you could then browse through the results of your search.

Simple Search Terms

Watch out for simple search terms using common words or names. You may receive thousands of results. If you are searching for a common word (game) or name (smith), try adding some qualifiers such as (basketball) or (peter). That is, you should add some additional words that might help to reduce the size of the search.

Wildcard Searching

Most directories and search engines offer the ability to use "wildcard" characters in your searches. This means using a special character (often $ or *) to represent multiple possible search words. For example, using *Lobster** would enable you to get the following results:

Lobster, Lobsters, Lobsterman, Lobstering, Lobsterboat, and so on.

Complex Search Terms

Similarly, you don't want to start out with a set of search terms that are too complex. If the terms are too complex, you may receive no results at all. Usually a two- or three- word set will start you on your search better than will a one- or six-word set of terms.

Other Restrictions

If a search engine offers other ways to restrict search, such as time or geography, it's a good idea to use them. More often than not, you will receive far more results than you had anticipated and will need to narrow your search.

Synonyms

Also be careful of the fact that different people call things by different names. You may want to keep a thesaurus close by and try several different words for the same term.

Spelling Errors

Not yours! We know that you do not make spelling or typing errors. But perhaps the people who entered information into the source files may have goofed a little. Many search engines will allow "wildcards," that is, special characters such as * or & to indicate multiple beginnings or endings of terms.

Helps and Frequently Asked Questions (FAQs)

There's an old saying in the computer business called *RTFM*. It stands for *Read the F'ing Manual*. It's good advice to follow when using search engines. The help and Frequently Asked Question (FAQ) files of all the search engines and directories give many examples of what works best for that particular search engine or directory. Take a little time and learn that engine's tricks.

Falling in Love

It's easy to fall in love with a particular search engine or directory. But even if you're in love, you should try out the others. A similar set of terms provided to several different engines can often produce widely different results.

Session Summary

We have taken you through a number of different ways to browse and search the World Wide Web and the Internet. We began by investigating directory type browsing and searching using Yahoo. Then we showed how you could use topic search engines such as WebCrawler, Lycos, and InfoSeek. Finally, we searched for people with Finger Gateways, s and the Four11 search tool. Lastly, we provided some search tips and tricks that have worked for us. We hope that your own Internet and Web searches will be both enjoyable and productive!

Session

8

Activity 1:	Using Netscape for telnet Sessions
Activity 2:	Using Netscape for ftp Sessions: Getting an ASCII File
Activity 3:	Using Netscape and ftp to Get a Copy of pkz204g.exe
Activity 4:	Getting pkz204g.exe Ready to Use
Activity 5:	Using Netscape and ftp to Get Virus Protection Software
Activity 6:	Using PKUNZIP to Get scn-221e.zip Ready to Use
Activity 7:	Using Netscape for gopher Sessions
Activity 8:	Using Netscape for E-mail
Activity 9:	Using Netscape for Usenet

Movie 1:	File Transfer Protocol
Movie 2:	Gopher

Using Netscape for telnet, ftp, gopher, E-mail, and Usenet

Session Overview

As you may be aware, Netscape permits you to do all the Internet activities that are commonly described, including telnet, ftp, gopher, E-mail and Usenet newsgroups. In this session, we will look at how Netscape might be used to facilitate the use of these Internet tools.

The power of Netscape is made possible by the use of Uniform Resource Locators as we mentioned earlier. The *Uniform Resource Locators* (or *URLs*) enable you to access all of the "traditional" Internet functions in the same way. For example, here are the URLs for three major functions:

    telnet   telnet://fedworld.gov

    ftp   ftp: //ftp.netscape.com

    gopher   gopher://gopher.netmanage.com

In each instance, the protocol is to the left, followed by a colon and two slashes, and then the host name. As you will see in the following exercises, you can use Netscape as somewhat of a universal front end to these three major Internet activities once you have mastered how they work with Netscape. Here goes!

Using Netscape for telnet Sessions

Brief Review of telnet

telnet is one of the oldest of the Internet's tools. It allows you to go to a computer anywhere on the Internet and log in to that computer. At least, it gets you there. Most often, you need to have a valid account at the distant computer. Many computers such as libraries, however, allow anyone to access them. Here we will show you how to use Netscape for telnet sessions.

telnet addresses can be entered as you would enter other URL information. The format for this is always going to be telnet://address/ You will note that Netscape permits you to enter the URL information and then immediately switches you over to your local telnet client for the actual application.

There is one very important step that must be completed before you can use Netscape to access telnet sites. You will have to tell Netscape where to find your telnet client program so Netscape can use it when it needs to do so. We will provide you with directions on how to do this in a moment. However, it is important to realize that if you do not do this, you will be confronted with a screen resembling Figure 8-1. You have not done anything wrong; Netscape just does not have the information it needs to carry out the command you have given it.

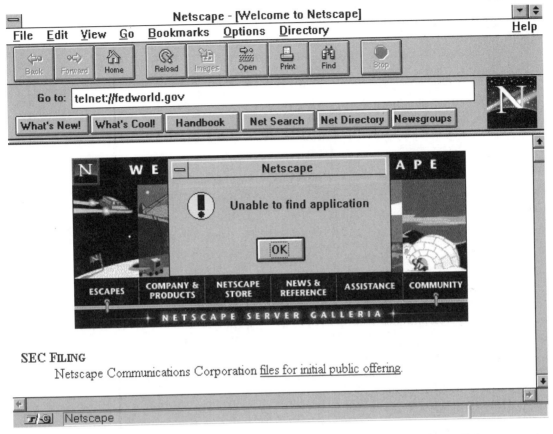

Figure 8-1
Netscape without
telnet Configuration

Here is how to prepare Netscape for accessing telnet sites:

1. Click on **Options** and then on **Preferences**

2. Click on the **down arrow** in the Set Preferences On: box. You should see a screen resembling Figure 8-2. (In later versions of Netscape, you will click on the file tab marked: **Applications and Directories**)

Preferences

Set Preferences On:

| Applications and Directories | ↓ |

Styles
Fonts and Colors
Mail and News
Cache and Network
Applications and Directories
Images and Security
Proxies
Helper Applications

Supporting Applica

Telnet Applicatio · · · · · Browse...

TN3270 Applicatio · · · · · Browse...

View Sourc · · · · · Browse...

Directories

Temporary Directory: C:\temp

Bookmark File: c:\netscape\bookmark.htm · · · · · Browse...

OK   Cancel

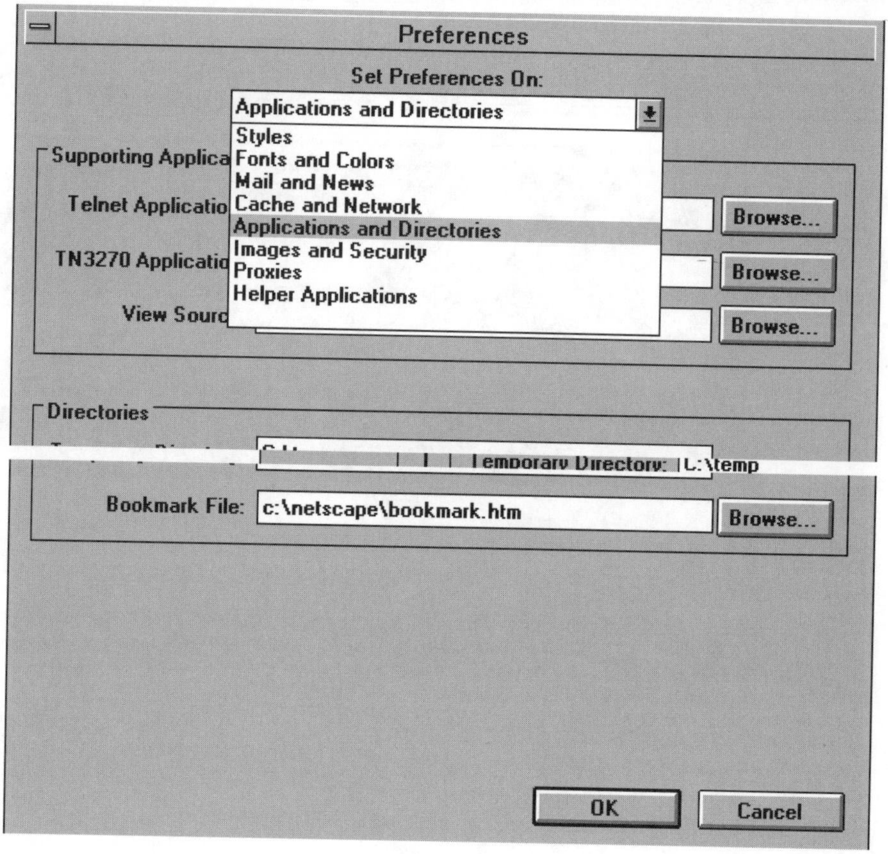

Figure 8-2
Set Preferences Box

3. Click once on **Applications and Directories** to make it active. You should see a screen resembling Figure 8-3.

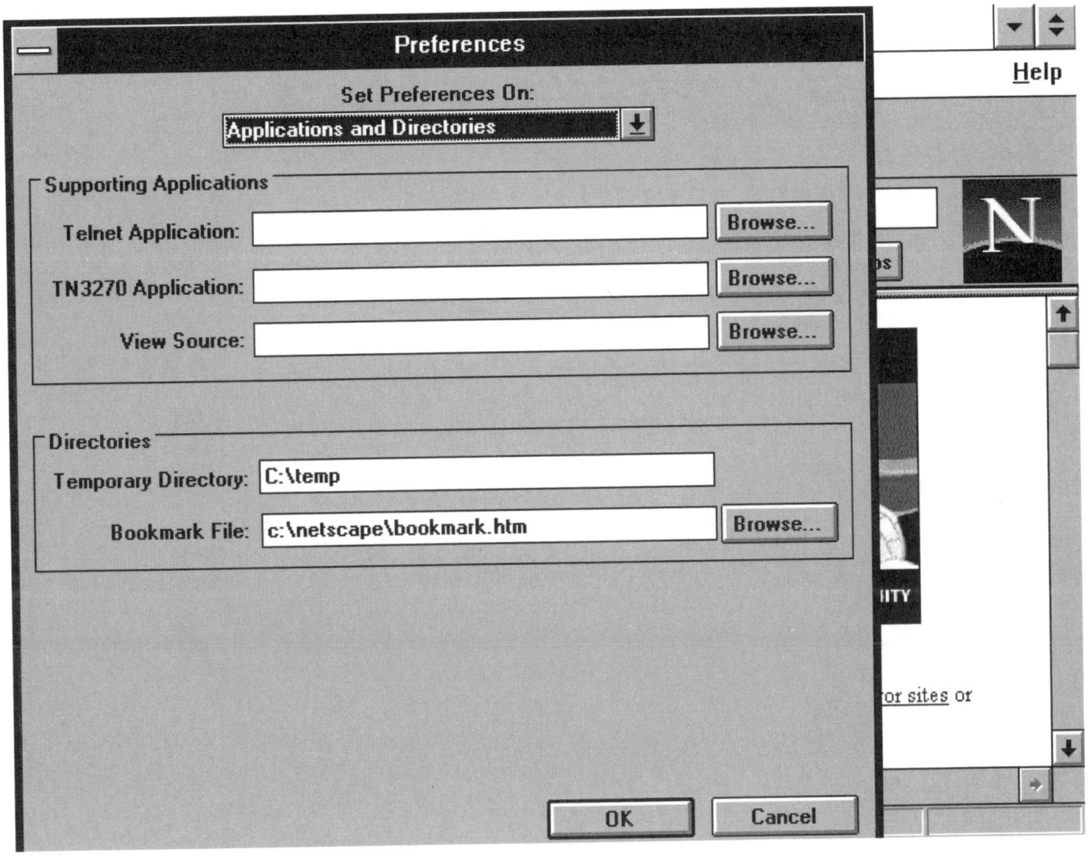

Help

Preferences

Set Preferences On:

Applications and Directories ▼

Supporting Applications

Telnet Application: [   ] Browse...

TN3270 Application: [   ] Browse...

View Source: [   ] Browse...

Directories

Temporary Directory: C:\temp

Bookmark File: c:\netscape\bookmark.htm Browse...

OK   Cancel

Figure 8-3
Applications and
Directories Selection
in the Set Preferences
On: Box

4. Click once in the **Telnet Application: box** and then on the **Browse... button** until your telnet.exe file is visible. In our case, telnet.exe is located in the netmanag directory; yours may differ. Your screen should resemble Figure 8-4.

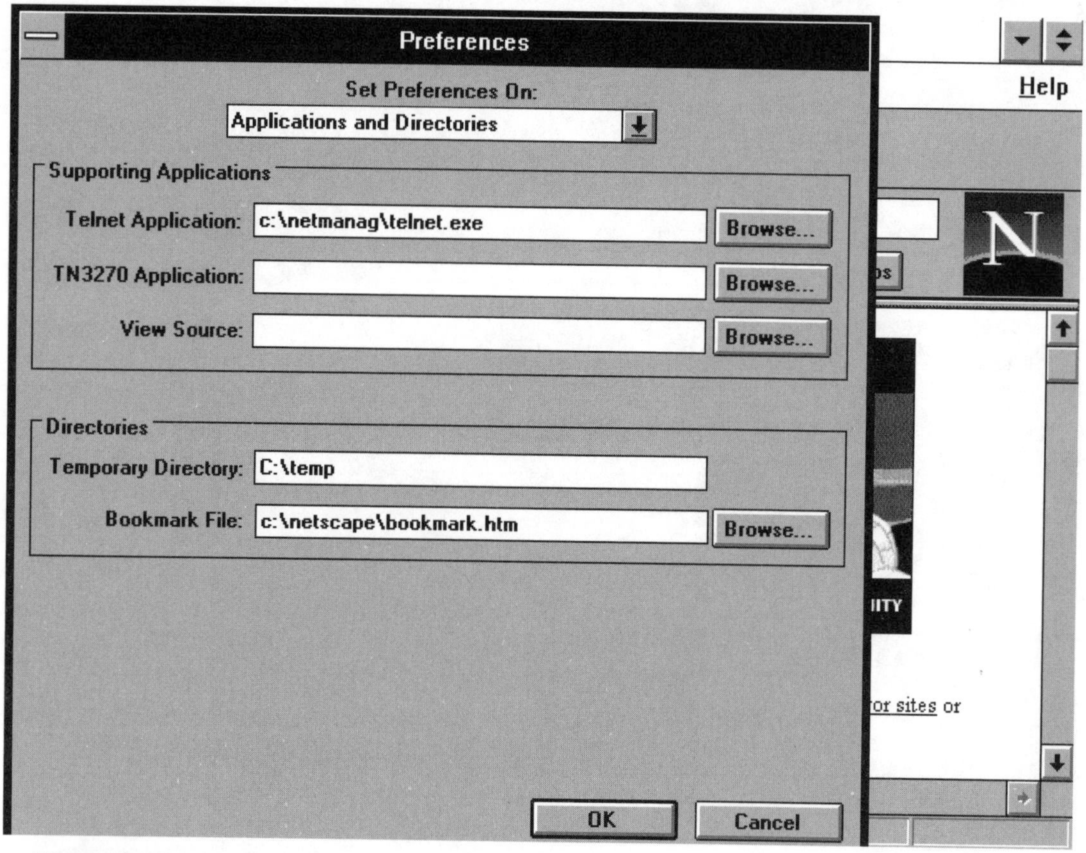

Preferences

Set Preferences On:

| Applications and Directories ⬇ |

Help

Supporting Applications

Telnet Application: `c:\netmanag\telnet.exe` — Browse...

TN3270 Application: Browse...

View Source: Browse...

Directories

Temporary Directory: `C:\temp`

Bookmark File: `c:\netscape\bookmark.htm` — Browse...

N

IITY

or sites or

OK   Cancel

Figure 8-4
Entering Telnet
Application
Information

5. Click on **OK**

Now you are ready to access telnet sites. Here is how to do so.

1. Connect to your Internet Service Provider and launch Netscape.

2. Click on **Open**

3. In the Open Location: box, type

   `telnet://fedworld.gov`

You should see a screen that resembles Figure 8-5.

You may want to maximize the telnet screen to make it easier to read.

```
┌────────────────────────────────────────────────────────────────┐
│ ▭              Telnet - fedworld.gov                    ▼ ▲ ▼   │
├────────────────────────────────────────────────────────────────┤
│ File   Edit   Disconnect   Settings   Script   Network   Help  │
│ * MajorTCP/IP by Vircom Inc. *                                 │
│                                                                │
│      ************************************************          │
│      *                                            *            │
│      *    Welcome to the FedWorld Information Network!  *      │
│      *                                            *            │
│      ************************************************          │
│                                                                │
│   The following destinations are available...                  │
│                                                                │
│                                                                │
│   [1]  FedWorld                                                │
│                                                                │
│   [2]  IRIS - IRS Tax forms, Publications and Information       │
│                                                                │
│                                                                │
│   [X]  Abort Connection                                        │
│                                                                │
│                                                                │
│ Please select an option from above and press <return>:         │
│                                                                │
│                                                                │
├────────────────────────────────────────────────────────────────┤
│ Ready                                    VT100          21, 57 │
└────────────────────────────────────────────────────────────────┘
```

Figure 8-5
Welcome to the
FedWorld Information
Network!

This is FedWorld, which is sponsored by the National Technical Information Service. Its mission is to disseminate scientific and technical information. NTIS FedWorld offers access to thousands of files from a wide array of subject areas.

4. Select [1] FedWorld and then press Enter

5. When prompted for a password, type in the word NEW   You will see a screen resembling Figure 8-6

Telnet - fedworld.gov

File   **Edit**   **Disconnect**   **Settings**   **Script**   **Network**   **Help**

```
                      What is NTIS FedWorld?
Each year, the U.S. Federal Government spends more than $70 billion on
scientific and technical research.  The National Technical Information Service
(NTIS) is tasked by Congress to help disseminate the vast amount of scientific
and technical information along with other, non-technical information.
As a central point of connectivity, NTIS FedWorld offers access to thousands
of files across a wide range of subject areas.  You can find information
from Environmental Protection to Small Business.  If you are interested in any
of the thousands of NTIS products, download the NTIS Products and Services
Catalog -- P&SCAT.TXT, in the NTIS Library of Files (opt. U on the TOP menu).

FedWorld Features include:
        Marketplace: Document ordering with popular DOWNLOADABLE products.
Subject Based Malls: Combined listings of services, files, and gateways.
   FedWorld Gateway: Gateway connections to other Govt systems/databases.
   Special Services: Whitehouse documents, Federal Job Announcements, etc.
      Subscriptions: ResearchBase, Davis-Bacon, Service Contract, etc.
   Library of Files: Collection of files/doc's on Govt info/other data.
    Internet Access: Telnet fedworld.gov, ftp.fedworld, http://www.fedworld.gov

These are some of the major features.  FedWorld provides such a broad range
of info we recommend you start with the above areas to locate your interests.
<Q> quit to prompt, <N> scroll, RETURN to continue
```

Ready   VT100   24,51

Figure 8-6
What is NTIS
FedWorld?

Notice several things.

a. You are actually using the telnet client software.

b. Documents are retrieved quite quickly, since there are no graphics.

Click on **File** and then **Exit** to return to the Netscape screen where you began.

Let's use Netscape for telnet once more. This time we will explore the Electronic Newsstand. Here is how to do so.

1.   Click on **Open**

2.   In the Open Location: box, type

    `telnet://internet.com`

3.   Click on **OK**

4.   At the login prompt, type enews and press **Enter**

You should see a screen resembling Figure 8-7.

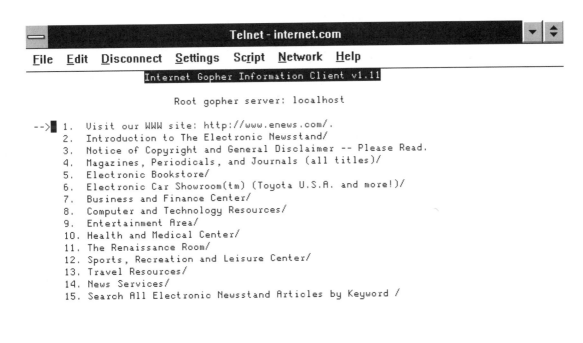

Figure 8-7
The Electronic
Newsstand

It happens that The Electronic Newsstand has chosen to use a gopher menu to provide their information, although we have used telnet to access it. Many Internet resources are rapidly becoming
commingled this way. Do not let it throw you; you are using telnet,
but you have arrived at a site that is providing its information using
gopher!

There is an enormous amount of information located at The Electronic
Newsstand. We will take a quick look now at their introductory screen
and then leave you to explore the resources that are of interest to you.
Use the up- and down-arrow keys to highlight the number of the
choice that interests you, or else type the number. Then press **Enter**.
You will be taken to your selection.

Here is a quick example:

1. Type the number 2 . (Introduction to The Electronic Newsstand)
    and press **Enter**

2. Once you are on the Introduction to The Electronic Newsstand
    screen, select **1.** (Introducing The Electronic Newsstand) and
    press **Enter**. You should see a screen resembling Figure 8-8.

```
  ___                    Telnet - internet.com                    ▼  ▲
File    Edit    Disconnect    Settings    Script    Network    Help
_____

            ----------------------------------------
                   This is The Electronic Newsstand
            ----------------------------------------

         The Electronic Newsstand was founded in July 1993 to provide
    the Internet community with easy access to a wide range of interesting
    information furnished by the world's leading publishers.

         Like traditional newsstands, The Electronic Newsstand is a
    place where you can browse -- for free -- through many publications
    and have your interest stimulated by a variety of subjects.  The
    Newsstand provides a window on the world of computers, technology,
    science, business, foreign affairs, the arts, travel, medicine,
    nutrition, sports, politics, literature and many, many other areas of
    interest.

         Every Newsstand publisher provides the table of contents
    and several articles from each current issue.  The Newsstand,
    which archives previously featured material, is also searchable by
    keyword.

 -- Hit SPACEBAR for more, q to quit --█




 Ready                                        VT100              23, 40
```

Figure 8-8
This is The Electronic
Newsstand

As indicated, tapping the space bar will take you to additional screens. Selecting **q** (for quit) and pressing **RETURN** will take you back to the menu from which you began. When you have finished exploring The Electronic Newsstand, enter **q** and **ENTER** several times which should take you back to the main telnet screen. Once there, just click on **File** and then **Exit** to return to Netscape.

Using Netscape for ftp Sessions: Getting an ASCII File

The ftp activities are extremely important. In order to install much of the software you will encounter on the World Wide Web, you will have to have compression software. If you are going to download binary files, you should have good virus protection software. By the end of this activity, you will be completely ready to download and install many of the compressed files you will encounter later in this book.

Brief Review of File Transfer Protocol (ftp)

As you may be aware, one of the most exciting aspects of using the Internet is the process of retrieving files from around the world to your own computer using the *file transfer protocol (ftp)*. File transfer protocol enables us to transfer ASCII and binary files from remote host computers to your own host computer. ASCII files are usually just text or human readable files. Binary files are usually programs, images, sounds, or movies.

Anonymous ftp is called anonymous because of an old convention on the Internet. When a server site wishes to share files with the Internet community, they allow a user ID of *anonymous* on their computers.

We will use Netscape in this and the following activities as we explore file transfer protocol (ftp). Using Netscape for file transfer protocol is a pleasurable and powerful way to experience anonymous ftp. It is a one-step process to move files from the remote host to your own computer using a very friendly point-and-click Windows interface.

Binary versus ASCII Files

As you are probably aware, *ASCII files* are the plain raw text that can be generated by many word processors (or spreadsheets). The files are stripped of all the code that might be particular to a given word processor, such as WordPerfect or Microsoft Word, and are, instead, just the text that forms those files. In addition, since you are retrieving "just text," you do not usually need to be concerned about introducing viruses to your computer or network.

Binary files, or graphics files or image files as they are also known, are all of the other files that are out there. Typically, binary files are software programs, pictures, sounds, images, or video clips.

Downloading binary files enables you to have a new software program or a new set of graphics files. Potentially problematic, however, is the fact that you also run the risk of bringing an unintended virus to your own computer or computer network. We will return to this point later in this session.

ftp addresses can be entered as you would enter other URL information. The format for this is always going to be ftp://address/

You will note that Netscape permits you to enter the URL information but does not require you to add the other information that ftp traditionally requires, such as a user name of anonymous and your actual Internet address as a password.

An excellent illustration of the power of using Netscape as the front end for ftp activities is provided in the following exercise. Initially, we will use our Netscape front end to enable us to connect to an ftp server provided by Netscape Communications Corporation. Here is how to do this.

1. Click on **Open**

2. In the Open Location: box type

    ```
    ftp://ftp.netscape.com
    ```

3. Then click on **Open**

If this works successfully, you should be connected to the ftp server provided by Netscape Communications Corporation and should see a screen resembling the one in Figure 8-9.

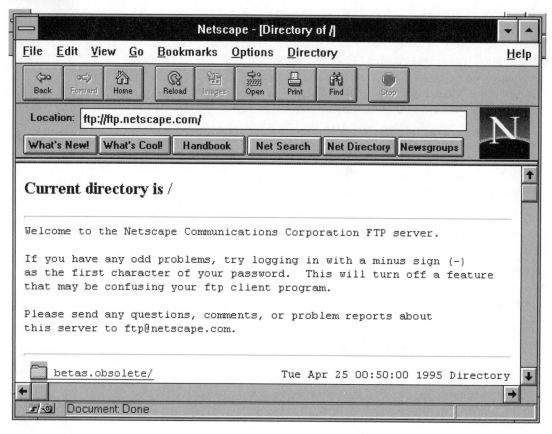

Figure 8-9
Netscape
Communications
Corporation ftp Server

Click on the **down arrow** on the scroll bar until you see a screen which should resemble Figure 8-10.

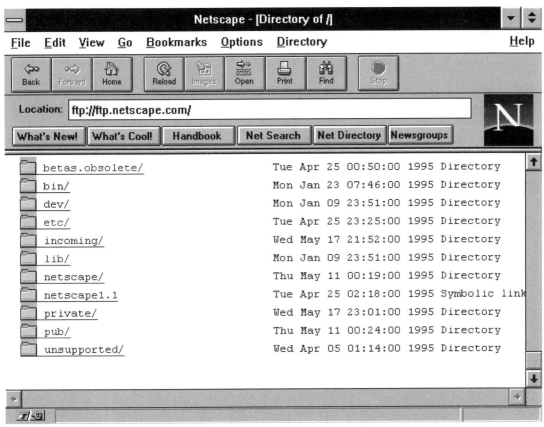

Figure 8-10
Netscape ftp Server
Menu Structure

Notice several important facts.

a. The ftp server contents are arrayed for you as a series of hyperlinks.

b. You are provided with clear information about where you are in the directory structure of this ftp server.

c. In each instance, should you make a selection, the ftp server will swing into action. You will move to the selected subdirectory, or you will be able to retrieve the particular file you have chosen.

Follow along as we explore these resources in greater detail.

1. Click on the hyperlink **netscape 1.1** (or the current version) and then on **Windows**. You should see a screen that resembles Figure 8-11.

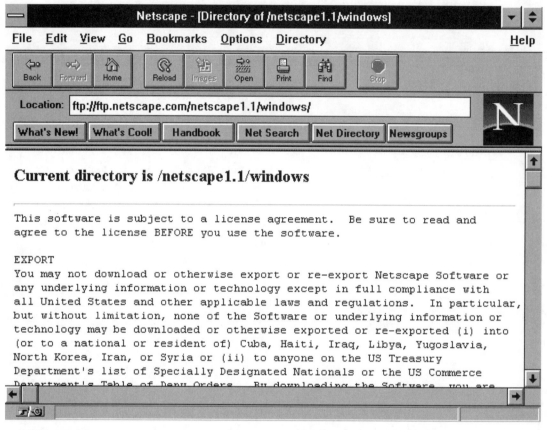

Figure 8-11
Netscape License
Information

2. Click on the **down arrow** on the scroll bar until you see a screen that resembles Figure 8-12. As we are told in the title bar, this is the directory of netscape 1.1 for Windows.

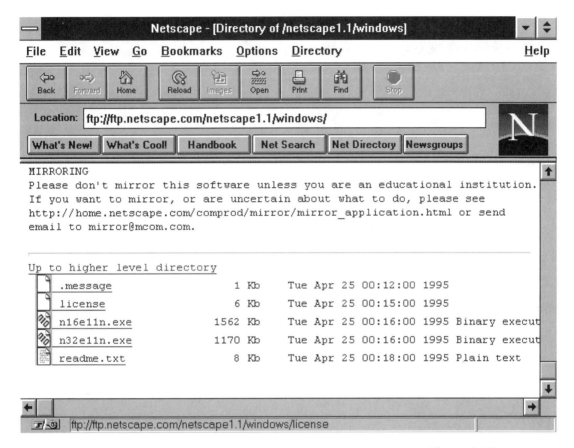

Figure 8-12
Netscape 1.1
Directory

Notice how much information is provided when we use Netscape as the front end to an ftp file server. In addition to the usual information about the date when a file was created, you also learn about the type of file that is available (either plain text or binary executable) and about the size of the file. All this is particularly helpful before you download a file. We will download a file now, to give you some practice.

3. Slide your cursor to the hyperlink license. Now, click once on the *right* **mouse button**. You should see a new window that affords you a variety of possibilities. The window should resemble the one that is shown in Figure 8-13.

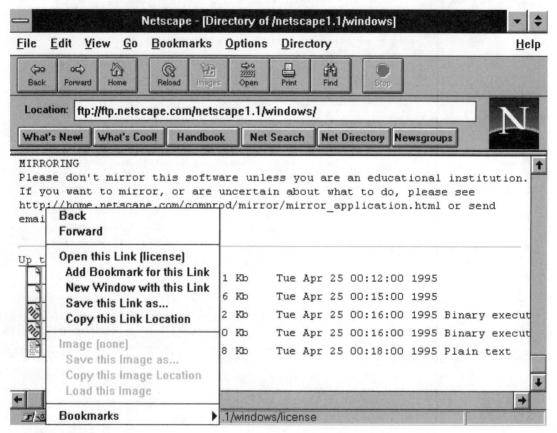

Figure 8-13
Right Mouse Options

4. Now, click on **Save this Link as...** with your *left* **mouse button**. As shown in Figure 8-14, a Save As... box will appear.

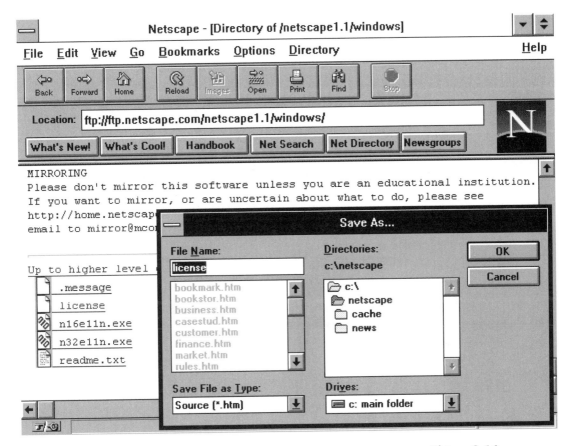

Figure 8-14
Save As... Box

5. Fill in the appropriate directory information (we have chosen to enter `c:\incoming\license`) and then click on **OK**

The file will be downloaded immediately to your computer!

NOTE: To read this file, just use your favorite word processor. It is a text file and should be accessible immediately. You may have to change the margins to one-half inch on each side in order to read it clearly.

Initial Observations about Using Netscape for ftp

There are several wonderful aspects to the ftp capabilities provided by Netscape.

a. Using Netscape to download a file using ftp is a simple, hyperlink activity.

b. As you may have noticed, you could have chosen to add a bookmark for a particular ftp site to your bookmark list. Had you done so, the ftp site would have become one more hyperlink in your bookmark list.

c. The actual download activity is a very traditional Windows/Save As set of procedures.

d. Finally, and perhaps most importantly, Netscape knows how to differentiate between text and binary files. There is no further action required on your part, except to point at the desired file and to click on **Save this Link as....**

Compressed Files

Binary files tend to be large. For example, it is not uncommon to find binary files that are 600,000 bytes or larger. It does take some time to transfer files of this size from one host computer to another. And, as you might imagine, there are costs affiliated with files of this size.

All the resources being used in this process cost time and money. There is a cost affiliated with your use of the remote host computer, as well as the cost affiliated with using your local host computer. Finally, there is a cost affiliated with using your own time.

Consequently, people have developed methods that are intended to minimize these costs. This work has focused on compressing files, so they will be much smaller than they were originally.

The advantages are many. First of all, the file can be stored in a much smaller space on its resident host computer. Second, the file can be transferred from one host computer to another in much less time. Finally, the file can be saved in much less space than would otherwise be required. When added together, all these represent sizable savings of time and money for all concerned.

Where Does Compression Take Place?

One location where compression may take place is on a remote computer. The person who has developed the program may wish to reduce its size before uploading it to a host computer, or before putting it on disks for distribution, and uses a file compression program to do so. Once you have retrieved such a file, you will need to have in your possession the compression program that can be used to uncompress the file. For example, if the program was *zipped* after it was created, it will need to be *unzipped* once it has been retrieved.

It is also possible that you may wish to compress files on your own computer in an attempt to conserve storage space. Once you begin to download large graphics and audio files using Netscape, you will quickly discover the value of being able to do this!

If the topic of compression is new to you, it is possible to become somewhat overwhelmed by it all. So, before learning about many of the possible methods of compression that can be used, let's just focus on a few of them. There are two parts to the compression discussion:

a. The first part has to do with the file extensions that are commonly used by those who have compressed files.

b. The second part has to do with the programs that are used to compress and uncompress software programs.

Typical File Extensions

In the DOS environment, you have probably seen file extensions such as the ones in Table 8-1.

Table 8-1

File Extension	ASCII or Binary	File Type
com	binary	executable file
doc	ASCII	text file
exe	binary	executable file
ps	ASCII	to be printed on a PostScript printer
txt	ASCII	text file
wp	binary	WordPerfect file

In this context, we are going to focus on files with some new file extensions. Some (of the many) are presented in Table 8-2.

Table 8-2

File Extension	ASCII or Binary	Program Required
gif	binary	graphics file
tif	binary	graphics file
zip	binary	PKZIP/PKUNZIP

Notice, first of all, that these new files are all binary files. In addition, you should notice that files ending in zip require compression programs to be used before you will be able to have a fully functional program on your personal computer.

Heads Up!

There is quite a bit of software available on the Internet. Some of it is known as *freeware*. This means that the people who developed it are purposely providing you with the software for free.

There is other software that is more properly thought of as *shareware*. In this latter instance, people develop software that they distribute in the hope that you will try their software, like it, and then decide to upgrade your program to the full version, for which there will be a fee paid to them. Several of the programs that we are about to acquire fall into this latter category.

In each case, we will make you aware of where it is possible to purchase the full version of the software with the complete documentation and files that may be missing from the shareware version. We would urge you to purchase the full version should the software have value to you. The cost of shareware licenses and full versions is typically small.

A much used file compression technique is known as PKZIP, and the files that are compressed this way typically have an extension of .ZIP. This program was developed by a company called PKWARE, Inc. To purchase the latest complete version of the software with all of the documentation, you can contact

PKWARE, INC.
The Data Compression Experts
9025 N. Deerwood Drive
Brown Deer, WI 53223

For us to use the shareware version of PKZIP, we will have to first have
a copy of pkz204g.exe. This file can be found most easily at Oakland or
at the University of Illinois.

Using Netscape and ftp to Get a Copy of pkz204g.exe

Hands-On
Activity
Three

Heads Up!

In this activity, we are going to show you an excellent software repository known as oak.oakland.edu in Rochester, Michigan. The
good news is that it has lots of software; the bad news is that sometimes it is very busy. If you encounter difficulty contacting this location, use Archie to help you to find others with the same file. A
recent Archie search for a file called PKZ204G.EXE (or pkz204g.exe)
provided us with the following alternate locations for the file:

Host	Path
ftp.bath.ac.uk	/pub/incoming
sunsite.doc.ic.ac.uk	/computing/comms/tcpip/nsco.netcom.com/eda
celtic.stanford.edu	/pub/tunes/abcwin
ftp.std.com	/customers/vendors/ellipsis
ugle.unit.no	/pub/msdos/arctool
isdec.vc.cvut.cz	/pub/mcafee/misc
ftp.vse.cz	/pub/msdos/mcafee/misc
gigaserv.uni-paderborn.de	/ftp/disk1/msdos/magazin/elrad/020
ftp.forthnet.gr	/pub1/simtel-dos/disk2/disc2/zip

Many files on the Internet have been compressed using PKZIP, and
you would be unable to use them if you were not able to unzip them
once you have retrieved them. We will learn how to unzip files shortly.

In this activity we will download a copy of pkunzip.exe. Here is how to do that.

1. If your computer is not already connected to the Internet, connect now.

2. Launch Netscape

3. Click on **Open**

4. In the Open Location box, type

    `ftp://oak.oakland.edu`

5. Click on **Open** to connect to oak.oakland.edu   Your screen should resemble Figure 8-15.

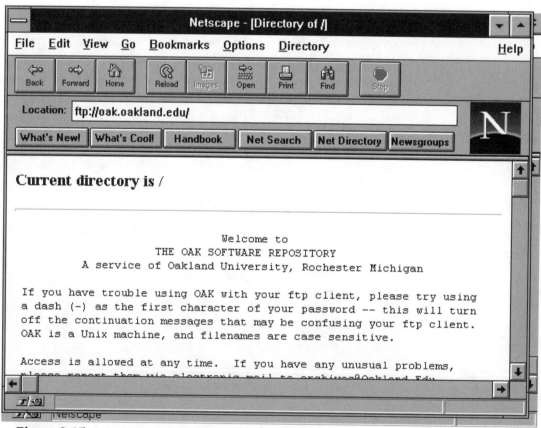

Figure 8-15
Directory of
oak.oakland.edu

6. Click on the **down-arrow** in the scroll bar until you come to the collection of files called SimTel

7. Click on **SimTel** so you can see the subdirectories it contains. Since we are looking for a file that can be used in an MSDOS environment, it seems logical to change to that subdirectory. Click on **msdos**

8. Click on the **down-arrow** in the scroll bar until you are able to see the sub-subdirectory called zip

---

It's a *long* way down!

---

9. Click on **zip** so you can change to that sub-subdirectory. Your screen should resemble the one that appears in Figure 8-16.

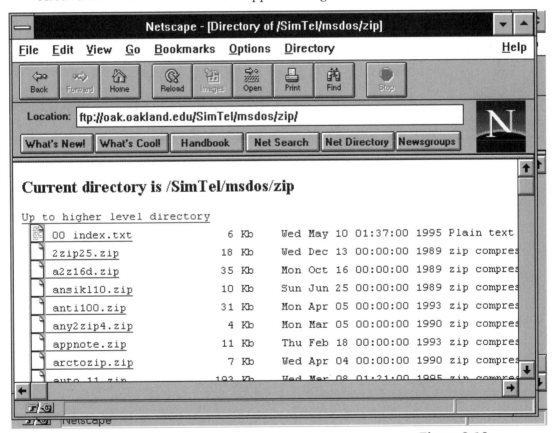

Figure 8-16
Directory of
/SimTel/msdos/zip

Once you have done so, click on the **down-arrow** in the scroll bar until the file called pkunz204g.exe is visible. Your screen should look like the one shown in Figure 8-17.

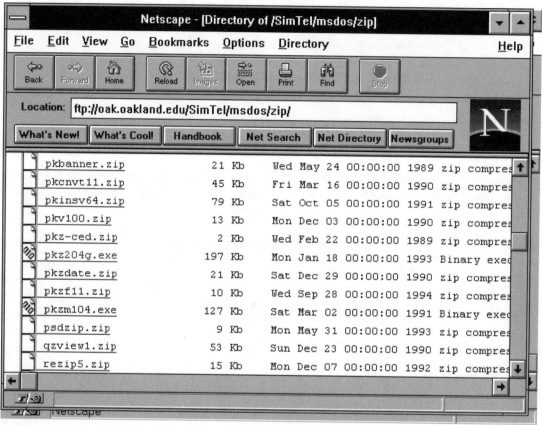

Figure 8-17
Locating pkz204g.exe

10. Click once on the *right* mouse button

11. Click once on **Save this Link as...**

12. In the Save As box, type

    ```
    c:\incoming\pkz204g.exe
    ```

    and then click on **OK**

Once the file has been successfully transferred to your computer, be sure to disconnect from oak.oakland.edu, as well as from your Internet service provider.

Getting pkz204g.exe Ready to Use

First, you should be aware that pkz204g.exe is what is known as an *executable* file. That is, it may be executed (run) by just typing the name of the file. For example, if you wish to run pkz204g.exe, you just have to type pkz204g. **WARNING: DO NOT DO THAT NOW!**

It is probably useful to have the pkunzip.exe file and the files that accompany it in their own subdirectory on your hard disk. We would suggest that you copy the pkz204g.exe file to a new subdirectory called c:\pkware To do this:

a. Use File Manager to create a subdirectory on your hard drive called pkware

b. Use File Manager to copy pkz204g.exe from the incoming subdirectory to the pkware subdirectory

c. Now, let's explode the files that are contained within pkz204g.exe. Use File Manager to make the pkware directory active.

d. Next, double-click on **pkz204g.exe**

If all goes according to plan, you should wind up with 17 files in this subdirectory; you should have your original copy of pkz204g.exe as well as 16 files that have been exploded.

The important file for our purposes is the one called pkunzip.exe. We will not do any more with this file at this time. However, we will return to it momentarily.

Using Netscape and ftp to Get Virus Protection Software

If you have been using anonymous ftp for the transfer of ASCII files, then you should not have had to worry too much about the transfer of viruses to your personal computer or to your network. However, as soon as you begin to transfer new binary programs to your computer, you should begin to think carefully about protecting your computer and its software from viruses that might harm some or all of your programs. You would be well advised to have a virus protection program installed on your computer and to use it regularly.

There are quite a few commercial programs available. In addition, there is a well-known shareware program called *SCAN*, developed by McAfee Associates, that is available to us on the Internet. If you wish to order the latest commercial version of the software, you can order it from

McAfee Associates
2710 Walsh Avenue
Santa Clara, CA 95051
(408) 988-3832

Here is how to get the shareware version of SCAN and how to use it. You will use Netscape and ftp to get the software.

1.   Connect your computer to the Internet if you are not already connected

2.   Launch Netscape

3.   Click once on **Open**

4.   Click on **Connect** and select oak.oakland.edu as the host

5.   Click on the **down-arrow button** in the scroll bar box, until you find the subdirectory SimTel

6.   Next, click on **SimTel** so that you can see which directories it contains.

7.   Click on the sub-subdirectory **msdos** to make it active.

8.   Click on the **down-arrow button** in the scroll bar until you find the sub-sub-subdirectory named virus. If you have done this correctly, your screen should resemble Figure 8-18.

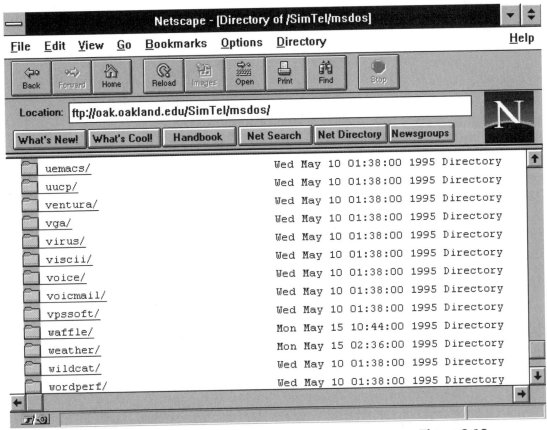

Figure 8-18
Directory of
/SimTel/msdos

9. Click on **virus** to make it active.

10. Click on the **down-arrow button** in the scroll bar to see the files that are contained in the virus sub-sub-subdirectory.

11. You will notice that one of the files is named scn- xxx.zip (When we did this, it was called scn-221e.zip.) This is the SCAN file you would like to retrieve.

Note: This file is a binary file that has (most likely) been compressed using the PKZIP/PKUNZIP compression program we referred to and retrieved earlier. First, we will retrieve scn-212e.zip; then we will use PKUNZIP to convert it into a usable program.

---

12. You will need to copy this program from the remote host (oak.oakland.edu) to your computer. We will copy this file into the subdirectory on drive c: called incoming.

    a. Move your cursor so that it is on top of *scn-221e.zip* to make the hyperlink active. Once you have done so, just click on the *right* **mouse button**. The special file transfer box resembling Figure 8-19 should appear.

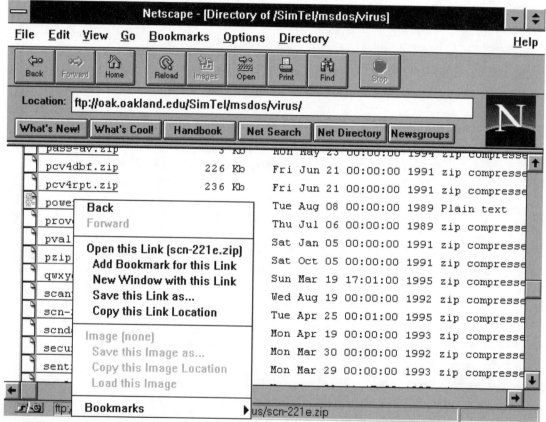

Figure 8-19
Save this Link as... Box

    b. Click once on **Save this Link as...**

    c. In the File Name: box, enter

        `c:\incoming\scn-221e.zip`

        and click on **OK**

Once the file has been successfully transferred to your personal computer, you may disconnect from the Internet. Now we just need to get the SCAN program ready for use!

Using PKUNZIP to Get scn-212e.zip Ready to Use

We will assume that you have followed all of the directions in Activity 4 and that your PKUNZIP.EXE file is on your hard drive in a subdirectory called pkware.

1.   First, you should put the SCAN program into its own directory. Use Windows File Manager to create a directory called scan

2.   Use Windows File Manager to copy scn-221e.zip from c:\incoming to c:\scan

3.   In addition to the scn-221e.zip file, we would like to also have a copy of PKUNZIP.EXE in that same directory. Use Windows File Manager to copy pkunzip.exe from c:\pkware to c:\scan

4.   Use Windows File Manager to make the SCAN directory active

5.   With Windows File Manager active, click once on **File** and then on **Run...**

6.   In the Command Line: box type

```
c:\scan\pkunzip scn-221e.zip
```

and press **ENTER**

All the files that have been compressed will be uncompressed, and you should wind up with approximately 19 files in your SCAN directory (the exact number will depend on the version of the program you are unzipping).

To use the SCAN program to check your computer for viruses is remarkably simple.

1.   At the c: prompt, change to the SCAN directory. Type `cd scan` and then type the word `scan` followed by the name of the drive you wish to check.

For example, type `scan c:` and the program will do the rest.

Summary of ftp Activities

Using ftp comfortably can add immeasurably to your computer enjoyment. The ftp activities in this session are intended to acquaint you with Netscape's marvelous ability to make downloading files from ftp servers an easy, pleasurable process. In addition, you have added two particular files (pkuzip and scan) to your set of software. We will use both of these files repeatedly when we begin to encounter multimedia files in Session Nine.

Using Netscape for gopher Sessions

Brief Review of gopher

gopher was developed by a team at the University of Minnesota and legend has it that they named it after the school's sports mascot. The gopher was among the first of the Internet's client-server tools and allows the gopher client (the one on your computer) to go-fer information to any of the Internet's gopher servers. The whole group was termed GopherSpace. Netscape has incorporated a gopher client in the Navigator and we will use it to demonstrate gopher.

gopher addresses can be entered as you would enter other URL information. The format for this is always going to be gopher://address/

You will note that Netscape permits you to enter the URL information and then accesses a traditional gopher menu. However, since you are now using Netscape as your front end to gopher, you will find that your experience with gopher is much more graphic than it has been before. We will try two quick exercises now to show you how easy it is to use gopher with Netscape as its front end. Try the following.

1. Launch Netscape and click once on **Open**

2. In the Open Location: box, type

    ```
    gopher://ds.internic.net
    ```

3. Click on **Open**

You are quickly taken to a gopher server for the InterNIC Directory and Database Services. Your screen should resemble the one shown in Figure 8-20.

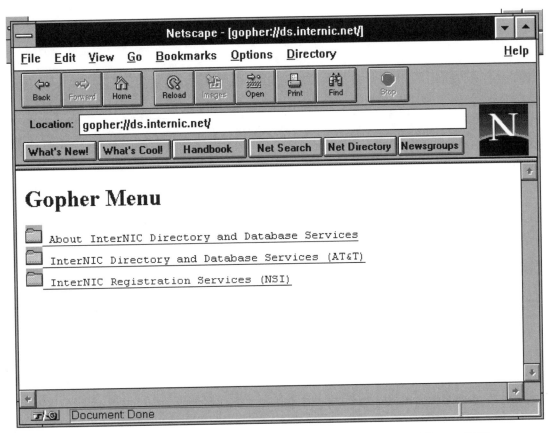

Figure 8-20
InterNIC Information
Services

Select whichever items are of interest to you. When you have finished, click on **Home** to return to the Netscape Home Page. Here's a second gopher exercise.

1. Click once on **Open**

2. In the Open Location: box, type

    ```
    gopher://gopher.netmanage.com
    ```

    and then click on **Open**

3. You should be taken to the gopher server provided by the Net-Manage Corporation. Your screen should resemble Figure 8-21.

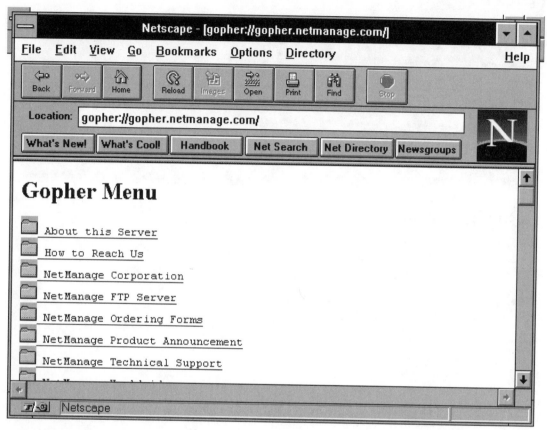

Figure 8-21
NetManage Gopher

There are many gopher resources accessible to you via Netscape. As you have seen in this activity, it is a quick and easy process to access them using Netscape.

Using Netscape for E-mail

While the Netscape Navigator may be used to send E-mail, it is not really an E-mail program or application. What we will demonstrate is how to send E-mail using Netscape. However, if you intend to use E-mail on a full-time basis, you should have (or should acquire) a tool to help you with E-mail. One reason you may want to set up Netscape for E-mail is so you might be able to send Web pages by E-mail. We will illustrate this after we show how to set up E-mail.

If you have Netscape Navigator Personal Edition, you have an excellent E-mail manager called Eudora Light. If you are using Netmanage's Chameleon product, you already have a Mail application included with the software. These are full (or nearly full) function E-mail programs. You should use these for your regular E-mail.

If you do choose to use Netscape to send E-mail, remember that you cannot use Netscape to receive E-mail.

Setting Preferences for E-mail

If you will be using Netscape to send E-mail, you must fill in all the necessary information in the Mail section of Mail and News preferences. Here's how to do that.

1. Click on **Options** and then on **Preferences**

2. Click on the **down arrow** in the Set Preferences On: box. (In later versions of Netscape, you will click on the file tab marked **Mail and News**)

3. Click once on **Mail and News** to make it active. You should see a screen resembling Figure 8-22.

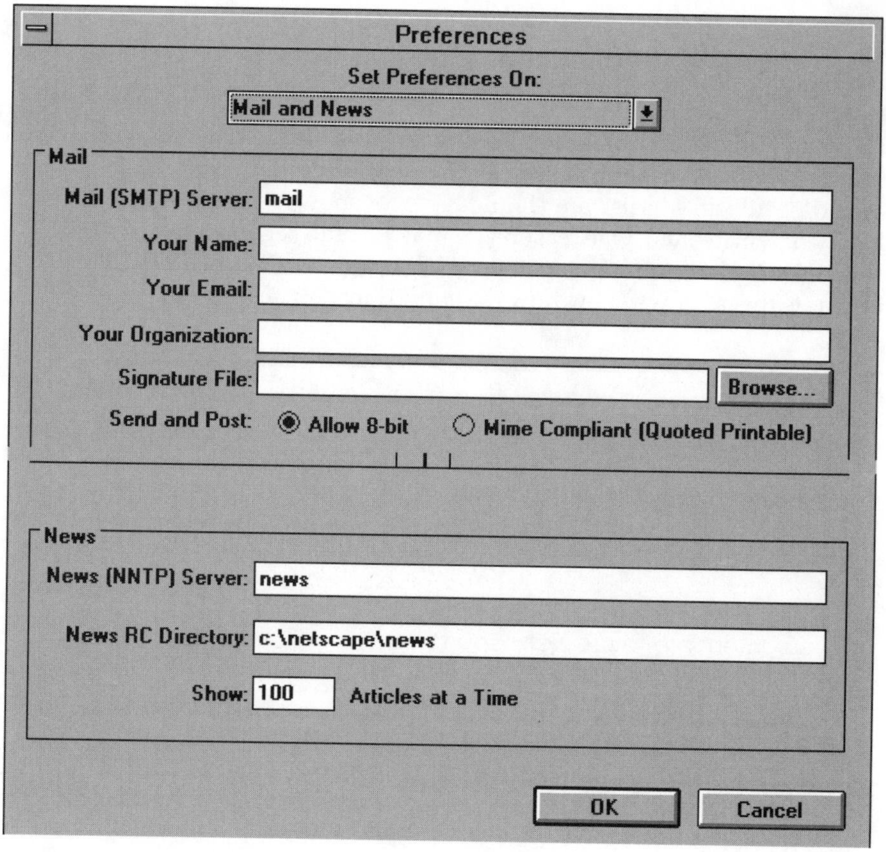

Preferences

Set Preferences On:

Mail and News ▼

Mail

Mail (SMTP) Server: mail

Your Name:

Your Email:

Your Organization:

Signature File: [Browse...]

Send and Post: ⦿ Allow 8-bit   ◯ Mime Compliant (Quoted Printable)

News

News (NNTP) Server: news

News RC Directory: c:\netscape\news

Show: 100   Articles at a Time

[OK]   [Cancel]

Figure 8-22
Set Preferences On:
Mail and News

4. Fill in the information requested. You will have to provide Netscape with the name of what is known as your Mail or Simple Mail Transfer Protocol (SMTP) server. If necessary, contact your Internet service provider or network administrator for this information. This will be a host address and may look something like

   pop03.ny.us.ibm.netnews.somehost.domain

5. Then fill in the rest of the information so your return address will appear when you send E-mail from Netscape.

6. If you have a file on your computer with your signature, that is, a small text file with your name, address, and so on, you can type in that complete file name on the Signature File: line.

7. Now click on **OK** and you will be able to send E-mail with the
Netscape Navigator.

We have shown an example of the mail screens you will see if you send
mail. Here is how you can send mail.

1. Click on **File and Open Location:** or just type the word `mailto:`
in the Open Location: box.

If you look closely at Figure 8-23, you will see that we entered
`mailto:` in the Go to: box followed by a real E-mail address.

Figure 8-23
Mailto:

2. After entering the word `mailto:` press **Enter**

You will be taken to a blank E-mail form. Here is where you can compose your E-mail note. The blank E-mail page is shown in Figure 8-24.

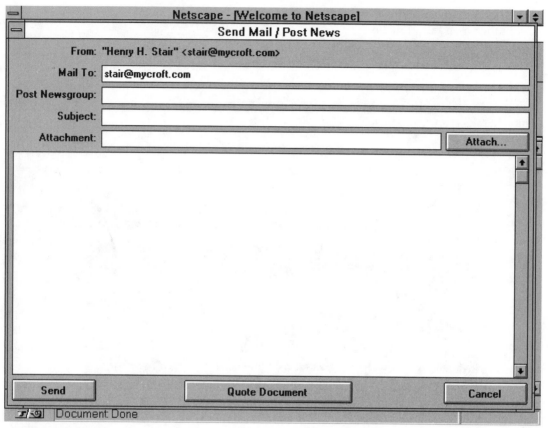

Figure 8-24
Send Mail/Post News
Page

Most of this form is self-explanatory. Once you have completed your E-mail note, just click on **Send** and your mail will be sent.

Quote Document

One nonobvious feature of Netscape's mail is the ability to put the text from a Web page in your E-mail. If, before you send your mail, you click on **Quote Document**, the current page's text will be placed in your note. This is illustrated in Figure 8-25.

```
┌─────────────────────────────────────────────────────────────────────────┐
│ ─                        Send Mail / Post News                            │
│         From:  "Henry H. Stair" <stair@mycroft.com>                       │
│       Mail To: ┌────────────────────────────────────────────────────────┐│
│                │ stair@mycroft.com                                       ││
│                └────────────────────────────────────────────────────────┘│
│ Post Newsgroup:┌────────────────────────────────────────────────────────┐│
│                └────────────────────────────────────────────────────────┘│
│      Subject:  ┌────────────────────────────────────────────────────────┐│
│                └────────────────────────────────────────────────────────┘│
│   Attachment:  ┌──────────────────────────────────────────┐ ┌──────────┐ │
│                └──────────────────────────────────────────┘ │ Attach.. │ │
│                                                              └──────────┘ │
│ >                          [Image]                                     ▲  │
│ >                                                                         │
│ > SEC FILING                                                              │
│ >      Netscape Communications Corporation files for initial public       │
│ >      offering.                                                          │
│ >                                                                         │
│ > WINDOWS 95 NAVIGATOR BETA                                               │
│ >      Download the latest beta release of Netscape Navigator,            │
│ >      specially tuned to take advantage of Win 95 interface              │
│ >      enhancements and features.                                         │
│ >                                                                         │
│ > SERVERMANIA THE WORLD OVER                                              │
│ >      Test drive a fully loaded Netscape Commerce or Communications      │
│ >      Server for 60 days and win the race for business server            │
│ >      solutions! This program is now available internationally, with     │
│ >      improved access for users behind a firewall.                       │
│ >                                                                         │
│ > ────────────────────────────────────────────────────────────────       │
│ >                         [NETSCAPE]                                    ▼  │
│ ┌───────────┐        ┌──────────────────────────┐      ┌──────────────┐   │
│ │   Send    │        │     Quote Document       │      │    Cancel    │   │
│ └───────────┘        └──────────────────────────┘      └──────────────┘   │
└─────────────────────────────────────────────────────────────────────────┘
```

Figure 8-25
Quote Document

This is a neat way to send text from a Web page by E-mail. It is possible that you might be at a Web page and decide that you want to send a note to someone without opening your E-mail program. This feature will permit you to do so. However, we would still recommend that you use your regular E-mail program for your usual E-mail activities.

Hands-On
Activity
Nine

Using Netscape for Usenet

Brief Review of Usenet News

Usenet News now has well over 10,000 newsgroups. The group names are largely self-explanatory in that they start with the main subject and then go on to more detailed subheadings. Some good examples are

k12.ed.math	mathematics education, grades K to 12
news.announce.answers	answers about Usenet itself
rec.skiing.nordic	recreation, skiing, cross-country
sci.space.shuttle	space shuttle discussions and news

Heads Up!

> Almost all of Usenet is free and uncensored. And there is something there to offend everyone. Use care and supervision particularly with children and young adults. There is, however, much of great value and usefulness on Usenet. You don't read all the magazines in the newsstand either.

As with E-mail, you will need to set up some information about news to get Netscape pointed correctly. Here is how to do this.

1. Click once on **Options**

2. Click once on **Preferences...**

3. Click on the **down arrow** on the Set Preferences On: box until Mail and News have been selected. You should see a screen that resembles Figure 8-22.

4. Look at the lower portion of the screen. You will need to know the address of a computer system that will act as your News or NNTP (Network News Transport Protocol) server. It will be something like the following: `news-s01.ny.us.ibm.net`

   You may have to contact your Internet service provider or systems administrator for this information.

After you have entered this information, you may click on the **News-groups button** on the directory bar (or click on **Directory, Go to News-groups** on the menu bar). You will receive a screen similar to the one shown in Figure 8-26.

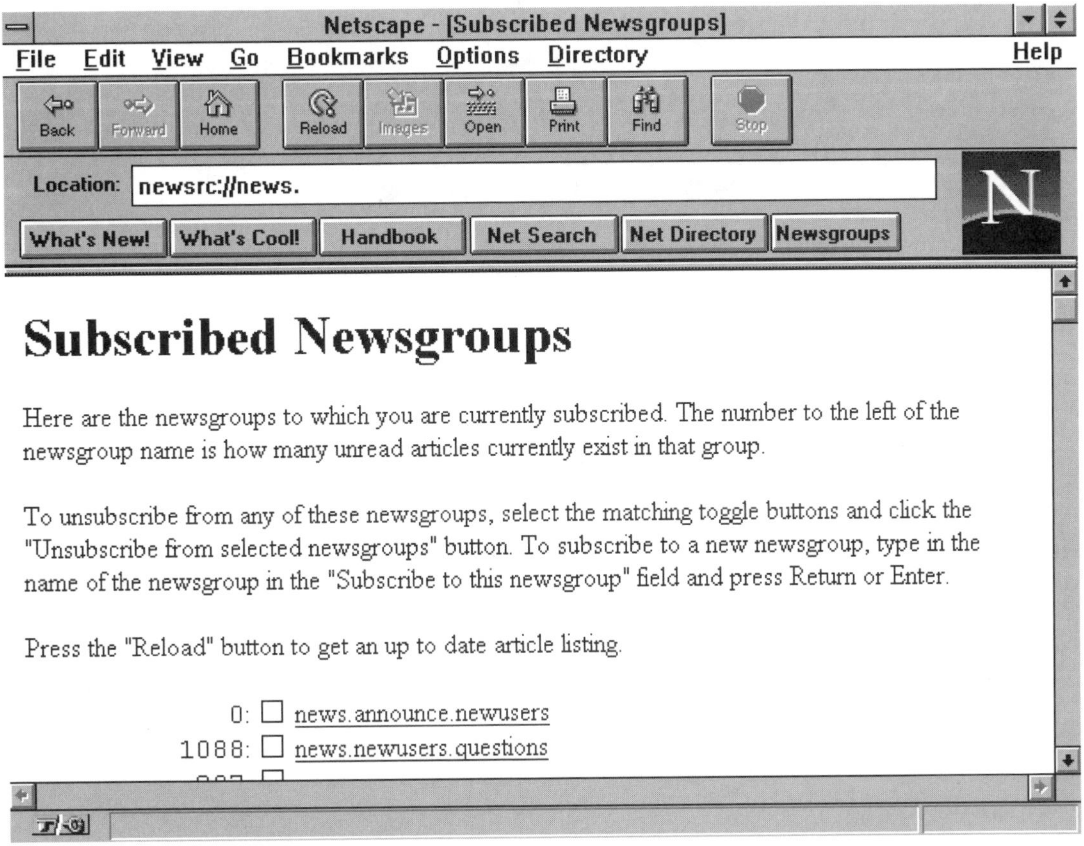

Netscape - [Subscribed Newsgroups]

File   Edit   View   Go   Bookmarks   Options   Directory   Help

Back   Forward   Home   Reload   Images   Open   Print   Find   Stop

Location: newsrc://news.

What's New!   What's Cool!   Handbook   Net Search   Net Directory   Newsgroups

Subscribed Newsgroups

Here are the newsgroups to which you are currently subscribed. The number to the left of the newsgroup name is how many unread articles currently exist in that group.

To unsubscribe from any of these newsgroups, select the matching toggle buttons and click the "Unsubscribe from selected newsgroups" button. To subscribe to a new newsgroup, type in the name of the newsgroup in the "Subscribe to this newsgroup" field and press Return or Enter.

Press the "Reload" button to get an up to date article listing.

    0: ☐ news.announce.newusers
1088: ☐ news.newusers.questions

Figure 8-26
Subscribed Groups

This screen shows you the newsgroups to which you are currently sub-scribed. In our example, you can see that we have subscribed to

news.announce.newusers   (with no new articles)
news.newusers.questions   (with 1,088 new articles)
and so on ...

If you scroll down this screen, you will see the Unsubscribe and Subscribe options, as shown in Figure 8-27.

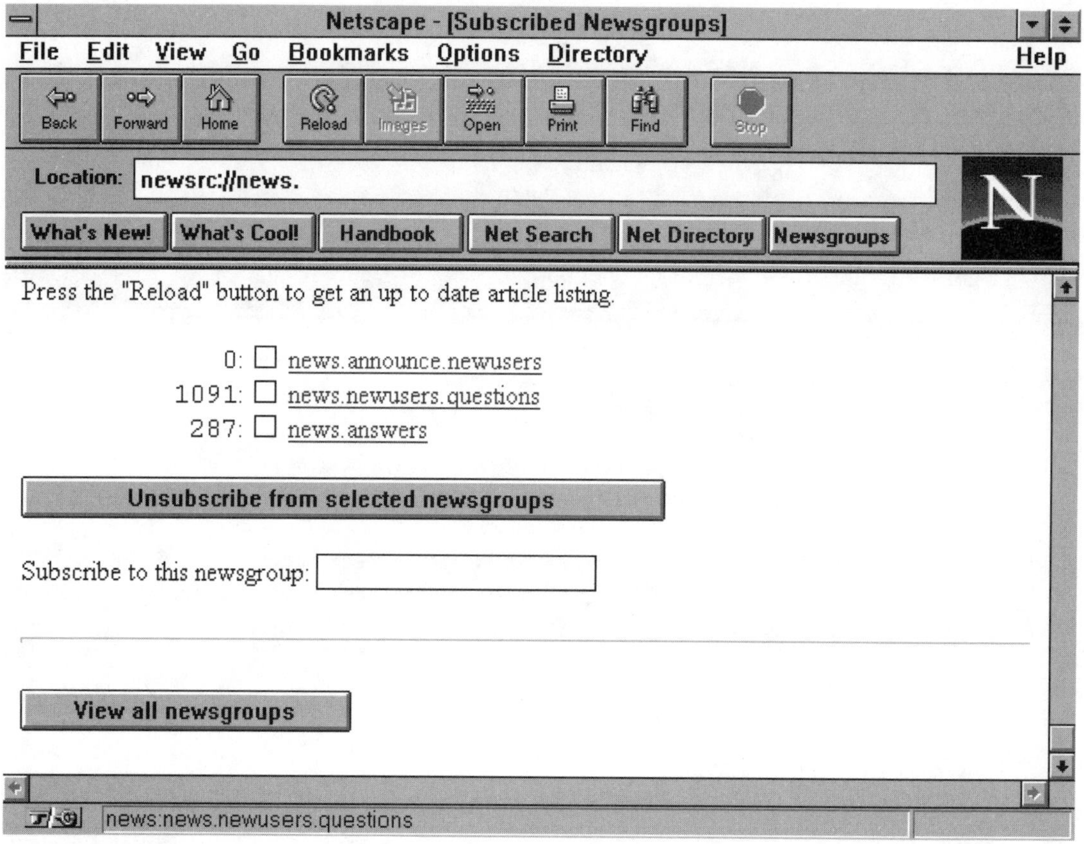

Netscape - [Subscribed Newsgroups]

File   Edit   View   Go   Bookmarks   Options   Directory   Help

| Back | Forward | Home | Reload | Images | Open | Print | Find | Stop |

Location: newsrc://news.

What's New!   What's Cool!   Handbook   Net Search   Net Directory   Newsgroups

Press the "Reload" button to get an up to date article listing.

    0: ☐ news.announce.newusers
1091: ☐ news.newusers.questions
 287: ☐ news.answers

Unsubscribe from selected newsgroups

Subscribe to this newsgroup: [_____]

View all newsgroups

news:news.newusers.questions

Figure 8-27
Subscribed
Newsgroups

If you wish to unsubscribe from a particular group, just click on the
box before a particular newsgroup name and then click on Unsubscribe from selected newsgroups.

To subscribe to a given newsgroup, just type a group name in the box
following the phrase Subscribe to this newsgroup: and then press
Enter to subscribe.

Obviously, you must know what the newsgroup names are. The good
news is that there are many books available with newsgroup names.
You can also ask your friends or associates.

Or, you may wish to get a list of all the newsgroups and then choose which ones to follow. You can do this by clicking on **View all newsgroups**. If you do that, you may receive the warning shown in Figure 8-28.

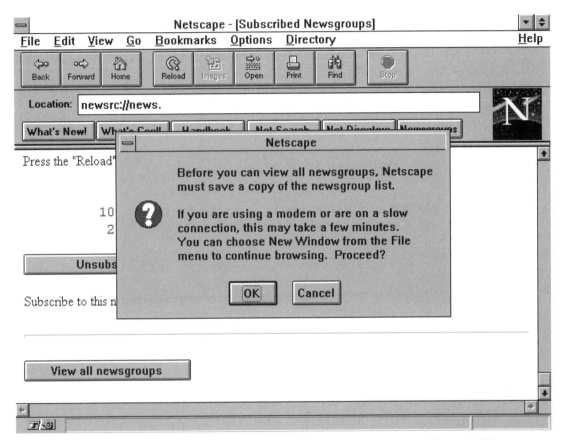

Figure 8-28
All Newsgroups
Warning

After you have subscribed to one or more groups, clicking on their hyperlinked name will bring in the article titles. We have clicked on **news.newusers.answers** to show what this looks like. Figure 8-29 shows the titles of the articles included in the newsgroup news.answers.

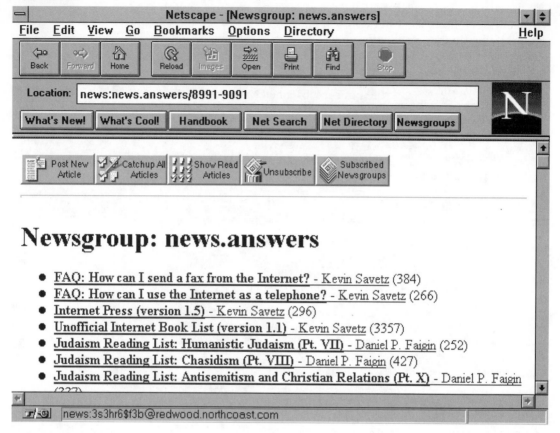

Figure 8-29
Newsgroup Titles

If you click on a title, the full text of that article will be brought to your screen.

Notice the new button bar at the top of the document area. Clicking on these buttons will allow you to do the following:

> *Post New Article* You can add to the discussion with a new article of your own.

You should follow groups that are of interest to you for a while before you contribute. You need to get a feeling for the group. You wouldn't break into a party conversation without listening first for a while, would you?

Catchup All Articles You can mark all the new news as read. (Just think about returning from a trip and finding 1,000 unread articles!)

Show Read Articles Go back to see some older titles. You can't go back forever, as very old articles are erased to save storage.

Unsubscribe You're no longer interested.

Subscribed Newsgroups Go back to the Subscribed Newsg roups page.

Session Summary

As you have seen in this session, you can do an amazing number of things with Netscape. You have complete access to all the Hypertext Transfer Protocol hosts out there on the World Wide Web. You can also use Netscape to access more traditional Internet tools such as ftp, telnet, gopher, E-mail and Usenet news. In our next session, you will learn how to use Netscape to access multimedia resources such as images, sounds, and movies.

Session

9

Activity 1:   Accessing the IBM Welcome Page

Activity 2:   Getting the PC Speaker Driver and WPLANY

Activity 3:   Viewing Images on the World Wide Web

Activity 4:   Viewing Documents Using Adobe Acrobat Reader

Activity 5:   Getting and Installing Movie Players

Movie 1:   Visiting the White House

Movie 2:   Adobe Acrobat Examples

Using Multimedia with Netscape

Session Overview

Netscape's ability to bring you text and images only begins to show you the breadth of the Internet and the World Wide Web. We will now introduce you to Netscape's ability to work collaboratively with other software programs to produce sound, brilliant images, and even video clips. These multimedia capabilities will allow you to access, view, and listen to information from all around the globe.

You can listen while corporate chief executives tell you about their companies. You can watch, in near-realtime, as space telescopes bring back planetary images. You can, with some patience, bring in film and animation clips to view at your leisure. You can look at some of the world's finest art treasures on your own PC.

As we write this, the range of sounds, images, and video clips is astounding. We can be sure that when you read this the range will have expanded tremendously! Let's look quickly at how Netscape can get and show you all this wonderful multimedia.

We have included four programs on the Hands-On Netscape CD-ROM that is included with Hands-On Netscape. They are listed in your CD Contents Menu under Netscape Helper Applications. All of them were current when Hands-On Netscape went to press. However, as is true with so much else on the Internet, they may have changed with time. If you would like to quickly install the software for the activities in this session, then feel free to use the software that is included on the CD-ROM. If your computer does not have a CD-ROM player, or if you wish to acquire the most current version of the software, then you should follow along as we go out onto the Internet to acquire each of the Netscape Helper Applications. More specific information about each of the software programs is provided in the appropriate activities in this session.

A Brief Multimedia Vocabulary Lesson

Before teaching you how to configure Netscape so you will be able to hear sounds and see pictures, we will take a moment to introduce you to the vocabulary you will encounter while doing so. It will also be helpful for you to understand the logic of what is taking place.

Most of the files you'll find while exploring the World Wide Web are what is known as MIME typed. The *MIME* (*Multimedia Internet Mail Extension*) *type* defines the type of file. For example, plain text, HTML files, image files, movie files, and audio files are specific file types that have a specific MIME type. Netscape uses MIME to determine what it needs to do to display the file correctly. Even though Netscape can reach computers around the world, it is capable of displaying only a few MIME types. These MIME types include text files, HTML files, gif files, and jpeg files.

When Netscape encounters a MIME type that it cannot directly display, it will send the file to a previously defined helper application (Netscape calls these *helper apps*) that has been associated with that MIME file type. Should such a relationship not exist, Netscape will ask you how to handle the given file.

MIME types are constructed of two parts: the main type and a subtype. For example, a MIME type could be labeled as video/mpeg. In this instance, the main type is video and the subtype is mpeg and we would expect to see movie files (more about movies later in this session).

There are various types of multimedia files that are available on the World Wide Web. In this session, we will focus on audio files, image files and movie files. Each one of these files may have one of several possible extensions. In addition, in order for you to be able to see or hear these multimedia files, you must have some additional software programs known as helper applications, viewers, players, or sound-playing programs. (We will refer to them as *helper applications* or *helper apps.*)

It is important to understand that several activities are required in order for these helper applications to work effectively with your copy of Netscape. You must:

1. Obtain the required helper application.
2. Install the helper application on your hard drive.
3. "Teach" Netscape where to find the helper application once it has been installed.

For each one of the files that we will download, we must make certain associations between Netscape and the files, so Netscape will know where to find the files when it needs to use them. In each of the following activities, we will walk you through all these steps.

Table 9-1 provides you with a listing of the files, their extensions, and the required helper applications or players.

Table 9-1
**Multimedia Files, Extensions, and
Required Helper Applications/Players**

File Type	Extension	Helper Application/Player
audio	.wav	speaker
audio	.au	wplany
image	gif	None needed (Netscape)
image	jpeg	None needed (Netscape)
Adobe	pdf	acroread

Table 9-1
Multimedia Files, Extensions, and
Required Helper Applications/Players

File Type	Extension	Helper Application/Player
video	mpg	Mpegplay
video	qt	QuickTime for Windows
video	mov	QuickTime for Windows

NOTE: If you already have a multimedia PC (or at least a sound-board such as SoundBlaster), you can play sounds right off of the Internet. Our first activity will do just that.

If you do not have a soundboard or multimedia PC, you can download a Microsoft Windows driver to send sounds to your PC speaker. If your computer presently has no sound capability, you may wish to skip ahead to Activity 2: Getting the PC Speaker Driver.

Accessing the IBM Welcome Page

In this first activity, we have chosen a well-known company that uses its Home Page to provide a multimedia welcome to all who visit. As you can see, Figure 9-1 shows a portion of the About International Business Machines Corporation page (Document URL: http://www.ibm.com/IBM). As you might imagine, clicking on the **Loudspeaker Icon** will send a sound clip to your PC. With your soundboard and speakers, you should then hear a clear, crisp audio clip from Lou Gerstner at IBM. We will show you how to do so in this activity.

We are venturing into tricky waters here as there are many variations in PCs equipped with soundboards. The following activity may
work flawlessly, or you may hear nothing. If your PC does *not* presently have sound capabilities, then skip ahead to Activity 2.

1. Connect to your Internet Service Provider and launch Netscape.

2. Click on **File** and then on **Open Location....** In the Open Location:
   box, enter the URL

   ```
   http://www.ibm.com/IBM
   ```

3. When the International Business Machines Corporation page
   appears, make sure that you can see a screen similar to the one
   shown in Figure 9-1. Be certain that you are showing the bor-
   dered Loudspeaker Icon.

4. Click on the **Loudspeaker Icon** labeled welcome. (If that icon is
   no longer there, find the nearest Loudspeaker Icon.)

5. On the status bar at the bottom of your Netscape screen, you
   should see a file coming in with the file extension .au The file is
   many tens of thousands of bytes, but when the transfer has been
   completed, you should hear the audio clip.

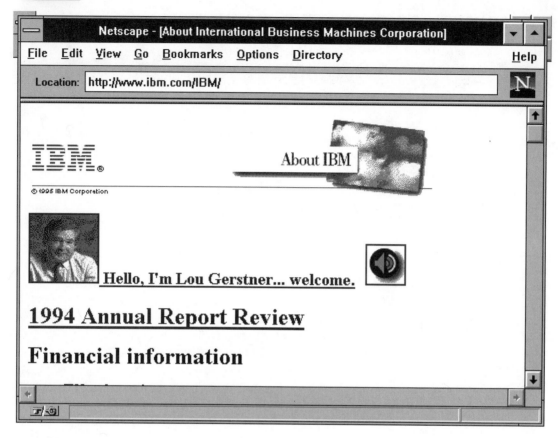

Figure 9-1
The International
Business Machines
Corporation Page

PC Speaker Driver

If you do not have sound capabilities on your PC, you may wish to try
the PC speaker as a sound driver. Although it will not produce very
good sound, you will be able to get some sense of the sound clip.

Getting the PC Speaker Driver and WPLANY

1. Connect to your Internet service provider and open Netscape. We
    wish to go to the document whose title is Mosaic and External
    Viewers and whose URL is

    `http://www.ncsa.uiuc.edu/SDG/Software/WinMosaic/viewers.htm`

2. Click once on **File** and then click on **Open Location**

3. In the Netscape Open Location: box, type the URL given in step 1. Your screen should resemble the one shown in Figure 9-2.

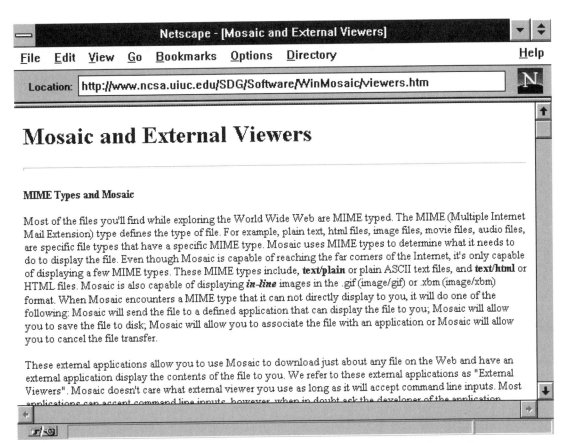

Figure 9-2
Mosaic and External Viewers

This page is provided by NCSA, the developers of Mosaic. Therefore, as you might expect, their focus is on Mosaic. Except for the fact that they call helper applications viewers, you should be aware that much of the information provided, as well as the many helper applications that are located here, apply equally well to Netscape. It is a good resource we would like you to know about. We will show you the Helper Apps page offered by Netscape later in this session.

4. Click on the **down arrow** on the scroll bar until you come to Tested Viewers. Your screen should be similar to Figure 9-3.

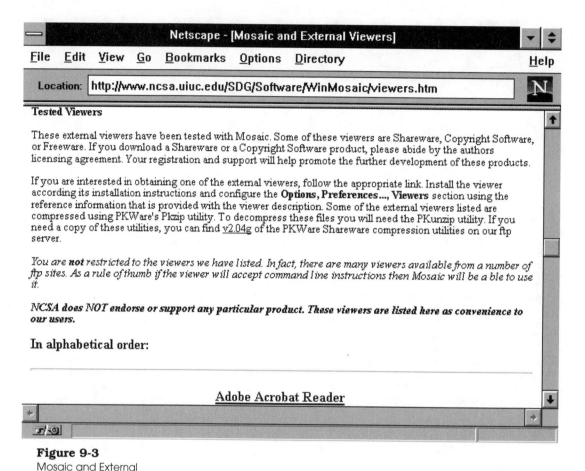

Figure 9-3
Mosaic and External
Viewers

You may wish to add this URL to your Bookmark List, since it contains a wealth of useful information and is one to which you may wish to return often.

5. Slide your cursor down the screen until you come to the hyperlink *PC Speaker Driver.* Click once on this hyperlink. Your screen should resemble Figure 9-4.

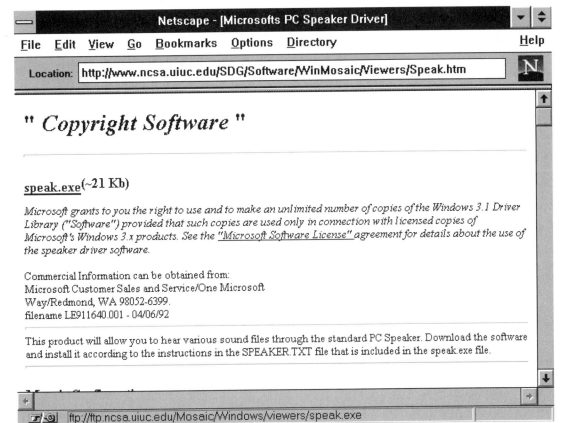

Figure 9-4
PC Speaker Driver

6. The file we wish to download is called speak.exe and the hyperlink indicates that it is about 21 Kb in size.

7. Slide your cursor to the hyperlink **speak.exe** Click once on the *right* **mouse button**, until the white box with the Save this Link as... option appears

8. Click once on **Save this Link as...**

9. In the Save As... box, indicate that the file name should be c:\incoming\speak.exe

10. Click once on **OK**. The file speak.exe will be downloaded to your hard drive.

11. Go back to the page that lists all of the external viewers (Mosaic and External Viewers)

12. Slide down to the hyperlink **WPlany**. Click on it once. Your screen should resemble Figure 9-5.

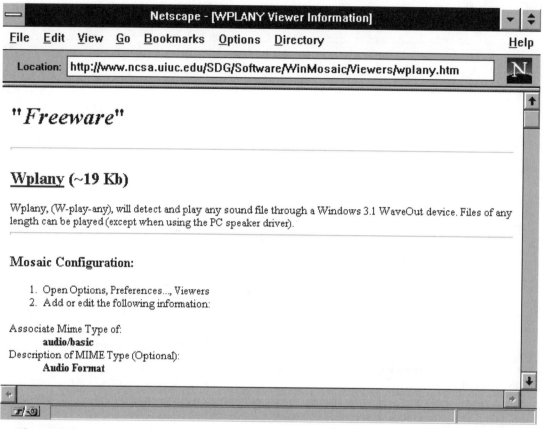

Figure 9-5
WPLANY Viewer
Information

We do wish to have the wplany file; however, the one that is presently at this location is an older file. Come with us now as we go elsewhere to acquire the latest version, which as of this writing is known as wplny11.zip. And, in the process, you will learn about a wonderful repository of files!

A copy of wplany.exe is on the CD-ROM that has been included with *Hands-On Netscape*. You can use this one or you may choose to follow the directions in this activity to acquire your copy of wplany.exe If you are using the copy of wplany.exe that is on the CD-ROM, then install the files as follows:

1. In File Manager, click **File** then **Copy**

2. Type

    From: `d:\wplany\wplany.exe`

    (If d is not your CD drive, then substitute the correct letter.)

    To: `c:\windows\wplany.exe`

3. Follow the directions included in this activity that show you how to tell Netscape that wplany.exe has been located in the c:\windows directory.

We will use the ftp capabilities of Netscape to download the wplny11.zip file. Here is how to do so:

1. Click once on **File** and then on **Open Location**

2. Enter the following URL:
    `ftp://ftp.sunet.se/pub/pc/windows/mirror-cica/sounds`

3. Click once on **Open**

4. You will be taken to the ftp repository in Sweden (the Swedish University Network) that contains the desired file. Your screen should resemble Figure 9-6.

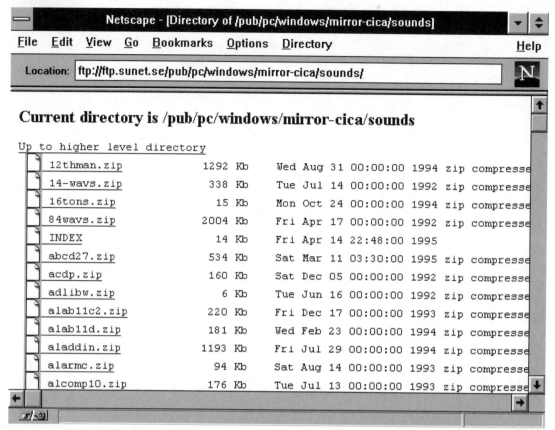

Netscape - [Directory of /pub/pc/windows/mirror-cica/sounds]

File   Edit   View   Go   Bookmarks   Options   Directory   Help

Location: ftp://ftp.sunet.se/pub/pc/windows/mirror-cica/sounds/

Current directory is /pub/pc/windows/mirror-cica/sounds

```
Up to higher level directory
    12thman.zip        1292 Kb     Wed Aug 31 00:00:00 1994 zip compresse
    14-wavs.zip         338 Kb     Tue Jul 14 00:00:00 1992 zip compresse
    16tons.zip           15 Kb     Mon Oct 24 00:00:00 1994 zip compresse
    84wavs.zip         2004 Kb     Fri Apr 17 00:00:00 1992 zip compresse
    INDEX                14 Kb     Fri Apr 14 22:48:00 1995
    abcd27.zip          534 Kb     Sat Mar 11 03:30:00 1995 zip compresse
    acdp.zip            160 Kb     Sat Dec 05 00:00:00 1992 zip compresse
    adlibw.zip            6 Kb     Tue Jun 16 00:00:00 1992 zip compresse
    alab11c2.zip        220 Kb     Fri Dec 17 00:00:00 1993 zip compresse
    alab11d.zip         181 Kb     Wed Feb 23 00:00:00 1994 zip compresse
    aladdin.zip        1193 Kb     Fri Jul 29 00:00:00 1994 zip compresse
    alarmc.zip           94 Kb     Sat Aug 14 00:00:00 1993 zip compresse
    alcomp10.zip        176 Kb     Tue Jul 13 00:00:00 1993 zip compresse
```

Figure 9-6
Directory of
ftp.sunet.se

5.   Use the right-hand scroll bar to move the screen until the file wplny11.zip is visible.

6.   Move your cursor until it is on top of the hyperlink **wplny11.zip**

7.   Click once on the *right* **mouse button**

8.   The white box with the Save this Link as... selection will appear.

9.   Click once on **Save this Link as...** until the Save As... box appears.

10. In the File Name box, enter the following

     c:\incoming\wplny11.zip

     and click on **OK**

You have just downloaded two files, speak.exe and wplny11.zip. Disconnect from your Internet service provider. We will now prepare these files for use.

Installing the PC Speaker Driver

1. Use File Manager to create a directory for your PC Speaker Driver. For example, we created one called speaker

2. Use File Manager to copy the file speak.exe to this directory.

3. Use File Manager to make the directory called speaker active and then double-click on **speak.exe**

speak.exe will self-extract all the PC Speaker Driver files into this directory.

4. Using your favorite word processor, you should print copies of two files: audio.txt and speaker.txt.

These files will provide you with the information you will need to correctly install the PC Speaker Driver.

Later in this session, we will show you how to use Netscape to install new helper applications; in this example, we will just follow the directions that have been provided by Microsoft.

5. We will follow the directions given by Microsoft to install the PC Speaker Driver.

a. In the Main Group, double-click the **Control Panel Icon**

b. In the Control Panel, double-click on **Drivers**

c. In the Drivers dialog box, click on **Add...**

d. In the List of Drivers box, click on **Unlisted** or **Updated Driver**. Then, choose **OK**

e. The Install Driver box will appear. If you have installed the files into a subdirectory called speaker, then type

```
c:\speaker
```

Then, click on **OK**

f. The Add Unlisted or Undated Driver box will appear. You will be told that the name for your file is Sound Driver for PC-Speaker

g. Since this is correct, click on **OK**

You should hear a sound emanating from your PC

IMPORTANT: When you install the SPEAKER.DRV, you will be shown a PC-Speaker Setup box. Change the Seconds to limit playback from its default to No Limit (right end of the bar). Then, click on **OK**.

---

     h.   Try hearing the sound by clicking on **Test**

6.   When you have finished installing your PC Speaker Driver, you should click on **OK** and then **Cancel** to return to the Control Panel.

Installing and Associating the Windows Play Any File (WPLANY)

1.   Use File Manager to create a directory on your hard drive entitled wplany

2.   Use File Manager to copy wplny11.zip from the incoming directory to the c:\wplany directory

3.   Use File Manager to copy the file pkunzip.exe from the pkware directory to the c:\wplany directory

4.   Use File Manager to make the wplany directory active

5.   In File Manager, click once on **File** and then on **Run**

     In the Command Line box, type

```
pkunzip wplny11.zip
```

6.   Two files will be created: WPLANY.DOC and WPLANY.EXE

7.   Using your favorite word processor, print out WPLANY.DOC

8.   Use File Manager to copy WPLANY.EXE to your Windows directory

9.   Launch Netscape. Click once on **Options** and then on **Preferences...**

10.   Click on the **down-arrow** in the Set Preferences On: box until the words Helper Applications are visible

11.   In the File Type box, highlight audio/basic

Netscape already comes with a sound player (NAPLAYER) but WPLANY seems to provide more capabilities.

---

12. Click once on **Launch Application**. Then click on the **Browse button** until you have highlighted the path:
c:\WINDOWS\WPLANY.EXE

13. Click once on **OK**

IMPORTANT: Repeat the above steps for audio/x-wav

Running the Windows Play Any File (WPLANY)

Sound files tend to be long files. If you are going to listen to sounds from the World Wide Web, you might find it best to download them first and then to listen to them. This way, if you like the sound, you will save yourself the time and trouble of having to download it again.

You can run WPLANY in either of two ways:

1. You can capture sound files (files that typically end in .au or wav) from the World Wide Web as you encounter them. We strongly recommend doing this! Then, using Netscape's File and Open File..., you will be able to play the sounds. We will show you how to do that shortly.

2. Or, you can associate particular extensions such as au or wav with the particular helper application wplany as we have just done. Once these helper apps have been associated correctly, you should be able to listen to sound clips from the World Wide Web when you next launch Netscape.

HINT: Remember that files must be fully received before they can be played. For long sound bites, this may take many seconds. You should also be aware that new software is being developed that will make this need to wait a thing of the past. However, we still recommend that you download files first and then listen to them after they have been downloaded.

Playing a Sound

An interesting example of how sound files are being put to use on the World Wide Web is provided in this next exercise. We will go to the

White House to hear a welcome message from President Clinton. To do this,

1. Click on **File** and then **Open Location:**

2. In the Netscape Open Location box, type

   `http://www.whitehouse.gov`

The Welcome to the White House Home Page will be downloaded to your computer. It should resemble Figure 9-7.

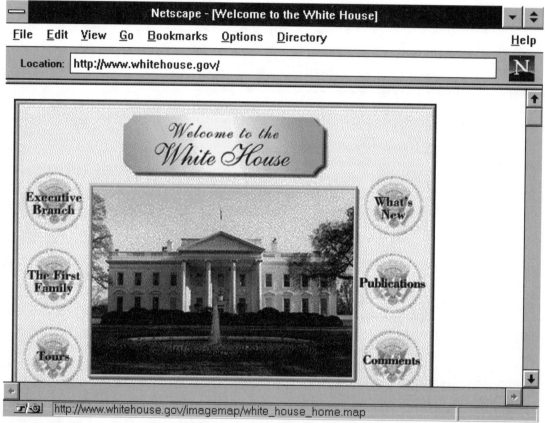

Figure 9-7
Welcome to the
White House Home
Page

3. Click on the hyperlink for **President's Welcome Message**

As noted in Figure 9-8, we can receive this message in three different formats.

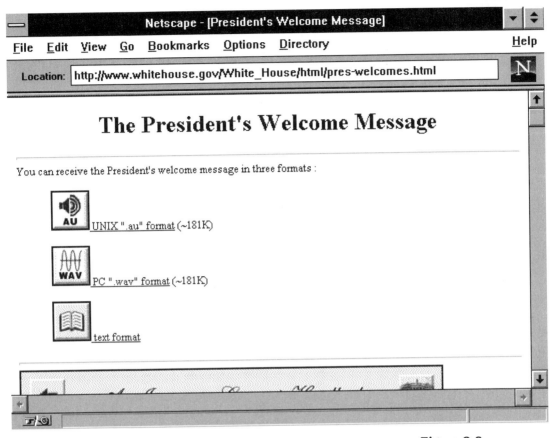

Figure 9-8
President's Welcome
Message

4. Slide your cursor to the hyperlink labeled **UNIX "au" format**

5. Click once on the *right* **mouse button**

6. Click on **Save this Link as...**

7. In the Save As... box, indicate where you would like the file to be saved.

8. Once the file has been saved, click on **File** and then on **Open File...**

The default extension in the File Open. box is *.htm—you will have to click on the **down arrow** in the List Files of Type: box to indicate that you wish to see all the files in a given directory, including the .htm files.

9. Highlight the name of the file that you have just downloaded (ours was called potus5.au) and then click on **OK**

Congratulations! If all has gone according to plan, you should now be listening to a welcome message from the President of the United States.

Let's take a break. When we return, we will learn about the many graphics images that Netscape permits us to see.

Viewing Images on the World Wide Web

On the World Wide Web, you can find a marvelous variety of images and video clips that are widely (and in many cases freely) available. For example, space photos from NASA, art from museums, photos of all descriptions, and near-realtime weather satellite views are all accessible if you know where to look.

Some of the "art" available on the Internet may be objectionable to some people and some of it may be objectionable to almost everyone. To prevent this material from being shown to children, always exercise care and supervision in the use of the Internet.

GIF and JPEG Images

Many formats and standards have evolved for the PC presentation and storage of images and documents. A few have become quite popular and are more commonly found than are others. These more common formats such as GIF and JPEG are supported by Netscape.

One of them called GIF is supported directly by Netscape. This format is very common throughout the Internet, and you will encounter many hundreds of GIF files in your travels. In fact, you have already seen Netscape receiving GIF images and then converting them for presentation on your PC's screen.

A second one, known as JPEG, is also directly supported by Netscape. The extensions .jpeg, .jpe, and .jpg tell Netscape to look for files that have been created in adherence to a standard called JPEG. *JPEG* stands for the *Joint Photographic Experts Group*. The key word *photographic* might give you a hint that some of these images will be like photos. In addition, you might expect to find paintings, and so on.

Let's take a few moments to look at some of the many marvelous images that can be found on the World Wide Web.

1. Open your WEBTOUR.HTM file from your CD-ROM or else access the one that is located at http://world.std.com/~stair and slide your cursor to **Art and Entertainment**.

2. Click once and select WebMuseum: The WebMuseum network The URL is http://sunsite.unc.edu/wm/ You should see a screen that resembles the one depicted in Figure 9-9.

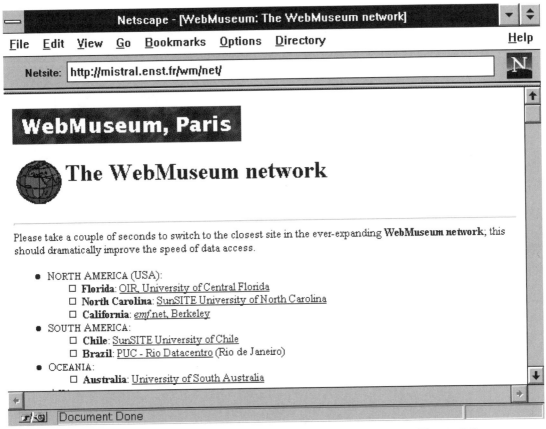

Figure 9-9
WebMuseum: The
WebMuseum network

3. Slide your cursor down the screen until you see the list of sites that is included in the WebMuseum network. Select the site that is closest to you. We selected to go to SunSITE, located at the University of North Carolina.

Many of the files that you might find here are large and will take some time to download. Be patient. The art work is wonderful and well worth the wait!

When we went to the WebMuseum, the featured exhibit was one on Gothic art. Undoubtedly, you will find another one when you visit. Moving through several introductory pages will usually take you to many of the paintings that are on display in the current exhibit. As you will see, many of them are JPEG files.

1. Click on file and then open file. Make sure that your CD-ROM (Drive D: or E:) is active. Click on the WEBTOUR.HTM file to make it active and select the WebMuseum site that is nearest to you.

2. Slide your cursor down until you find the hyperlink called **Visit Paris on a small tour**. Click on it once. Your screen should resemble Figure 9-10.

Figure 9-10
WebMuseum: Paris: Tours

As you will discover, each time you encounter a small thumbnail image, clicking on it will enable you to see the full JPEG image to which it is linked. Have a great tour!

Viewing Documents Using Adobe Acrobat Reader

This activity provides you with a wonderful way to view text that is becoming increasingly available on the World Wide Web. Documents that have been created using Adobe's portable document format (pdf) will appear on your screen as well as on your printer, exactly as they were created. Follow along as we download the necessary files and then learn how to use them.

A copy of Adobe Acrobat Reader is on the CD-ROM that has been included with *Hands-On Netscape*. You can use this copy, or you may choose to follow the directions in this activity to acquire your copy of Adobe Acrobat Reader. If you are using the copy of acroread.exe that is on the CD-ROM, then install the files as follows:

1. In Program Manager, click **File** then **Run**

2. Type d:\acroread.exe

    (If d is not your CD drive, then substitute the correct letter.)

    This program will install Acrobat Reader on your hard drive and will create an icon in Program Manager.

3. Follow the directions in this activity that show you how to tell Netscape that acroread.exe has been installed in the c:\acroread directory.

1. Return to the page entitled Mosaic and External Viewers

2. Slide down on the right-hand scroll bar until the **Adobe Acrobat Reader** hyperlink is visible. Click on it once to see the screen that is displayed in Figure 9-11.

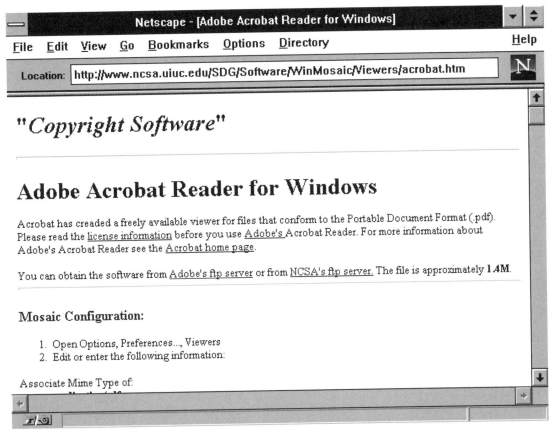

Figure 9-11
Adobe Acrobat
Reader for Windows

3. As noted, this reader is available from ftp servers located at both Adobe and at NCSA. Slide your cursor to the hyperlink that is to provide you with the file acroread.exe and click on the *right* **mouse button**

4. When the white box with Save this Link as... appears, click once on **Save this Link as...**

5. The file is named Windows on the Adobe ftp server and acro-read.exe on the NCSA ftp server; you should download it into your incoming directory. We have chosen to download the file called acroread.exe

6. In Windows, click once on **File** and then on **Run** and enter the following information:

    ```
    c:\incoming\acroread.exe
    ```

The file will be automatically installed in the directory acroread for you.

You must tell Netscape that the Adobe Acrobat Reader has been installed. Here is how to do so.

1. Launch Netscape and then click on **Options** and **Preferences...**

2. Click on the **down arrow** in the Set Preferences On: box

3. Highlight Helper Applications, as shown in Figure 9-12

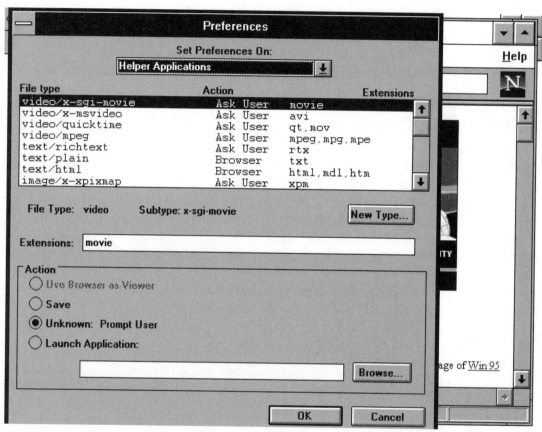

Figure 9-12
Preferences Box

4. Click once on **New Type**

You will be prompted to enter a Mime Type and a Mime Sub-Type.

5. In the Mime Type box, type `application`

6. In the Mime Sub/Type box, type `pdf`

7. Click on **OK**

8. In the Extensions: box, type `pdf`

9. Click on the radio button **Launch Application:**

10. Click on **Browse...** until the following information has been entered into the Launch Application: box

    `c:\acroread\acroread.exe`

11. Click on **OK** and Netscape will now be aware that all pdf files are to be handled by Adobe Acrobat Reader.

Now we must see if all of this is working. Here is an exercise that will let you see the power of the pdf format.

1. Click on file and then open file. Make sure that your CD-ROM (Drive D: or E:) is active. Click on the WEBTOUR.HTM file to make it active. Then click on **News** and then on **TimesFax**. The *New York Times* has chosen to put a special edition of its paper on the World Wide Web. It is known as TimesFax (URL: http://nytimesfax.com/). The TimesFax Home Page is shown in Figure 9-13.

Figure 9-13
TimesFax

Courtesy of TimesFax, The New York Times Company

2. Click once on **TimesFax** and you will be taken to the Internet edition of the *New York Times*. It is shown in Figure 9-14. You will note that TimesFax on the Web is presented in Adobe Acrobat (pdf) format.

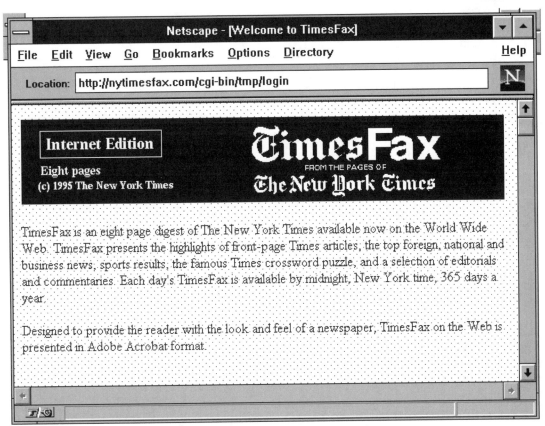

Courtesy of TimesFax, The New York Times Company

Figure 9-14
Welcome to TimesFax

Slide your cursor down the opening page until you see the registration form which appears. It is a simple form to complete, there is no charge, and you will only have to fill it in once. The response time is almost instantaneous. Once you have registered, you will be presented with today's edition of TimesFax.

1. Click once on the hyperlink for **TimesFax** and the TIMES.PDF file will be downloaded to your computer. The first part of the paper we saw is depicted in Figure 9-15.

Figure 9-15
TIMES.PDF

Courtesy of TimesFax, The New York Times Company

If your printer is capable of doing so, the entire issue of the TimesFax can be printed out for your reading enjoyment. However, you should be aware that it takes quite some time for all eight pages to be printed. Wait until you are not in a hurry to use your printer for other things!

Additional PDF Resources

It may be that you would like to see some pdf files other than the *New York Times*. Fortunately, Adobe has done a wonderful job of assembling them. Here is a way to find some of these marvelous resources.

1.   Click on **File** and **Open Location**. Type in the following URL:

```
http://www.adobe.com
```
Your screen should resemble Figure 9-16.

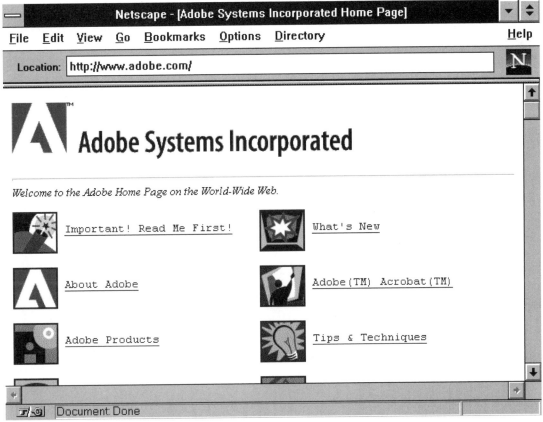

Figure 9-16
Adobe Systems Incorporated Home Page

2. Click once on the hyperlink **Elsewhere on the Web**
3. Once there, click on the hyperlink **WWW sites with PDF files**
   Your screen should show Web Sites with Cool PDF, as shown in
   Figure 9-17.

Figure 9-17
Web Sites with Cool
PDF

4. Click once on the hyperlink **here's how** in the first sentence. You
   will be taken to a page whose URL is

   ```
   http://www.adobe.com/Acrobat/AcrobatWWW.html
   ```

   There are many choices available to you. Have fun!

Getting and Installing Movie Players

You may be aware that in addition to the many graphical images you
have seen thus far Netscape can be used for downloading and displaying movies. In order to do so, there are additional helper applications
you will have to download and install with your copy of Netscape. We
are particularly interested in being able to play files that have the
extension mpeg, an abbreviation for *Motion Picture Experts Group*. Fol-

low along as we download the necessary files and install them. Then, we will go to the movies!

This next activity takes a little time to complete and is a bit complicated. You may wish to take a break before starting it. The good news is that the movies you will see once you have completed this activity are well worth the work to get them!

A copy of MPEGPLAY for Windows is on the CD-ROM that has been included with *Hands-On Netscape*. You can use this copy, or you may choose to follow the directions in this activity to acquire your copy of MPEGPLAY for Windows.

NOTE: MPEGPLAY for Windows will run successfully only if a copy of win32s has been installed on your computer. If you have not yet done so, then refer to the Appendix for directions on how to download and install win32s.

If you are using the copy of MPEGPLAY for Windows that is on the CD-ROM and if win32s has been installed on your computer, then install the files as follows:

1. In Program Manager, click **File** then **Run**

2. Type `d:\mpeg\setup.exe`

   (If d is not your CD drive, then substitute the correct letter.)

   The setup.exe program installs MPEG Player on your hard drive and creates an icon in Program Manager.

3. Follow the directions in this activity that show you how to tell Netscape that mpegplay.exe has been installed on drive c: in the win32app\mpegplay directory and subdirectory.

Let's return once again to the Mosaic and External Viewers page (URL: http://www.ncsa.uiuc.edu/SDG/Software/WinMosaic/viewers.htm). On that page, there is a section that includes a hyperlink for **Mpegplay**, a Shareware MPEG movie player. This is shown in Figure 9-18.

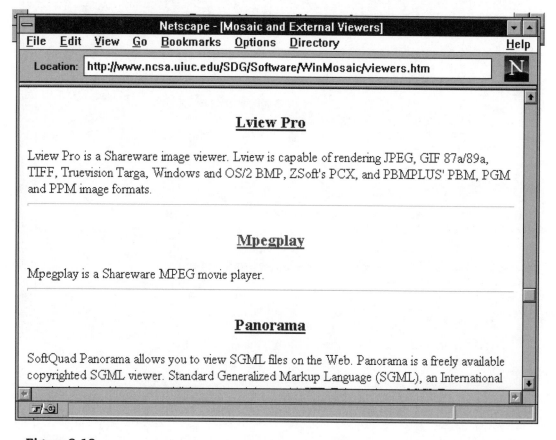

Figure 9-18
Mosaic and External Viewers

1.   Click once on **Mpegplay** and you will be taken to the location for MPEGPLAY v 1.61 (or whatever the latest version is) as shown in Figure 9-19.

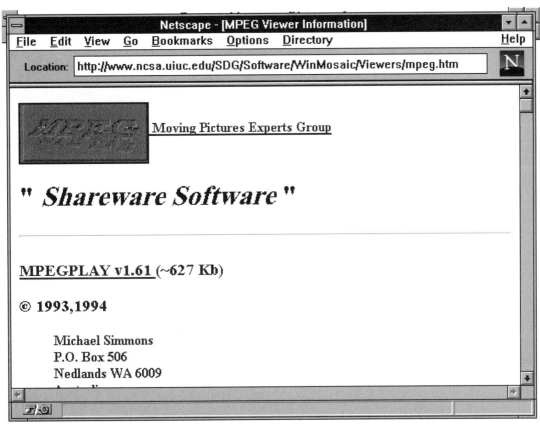

Figure 9-19
MPEG Viewer
Information

2. Slide your cursor to the hyperlink <u>MPEGPLAY v1.61</u> and click on the *right* **mouse button**. This will open the text box that includes the option to Save this Link as... so that you can store this file on your disk. This is shown in Figure 9-20.

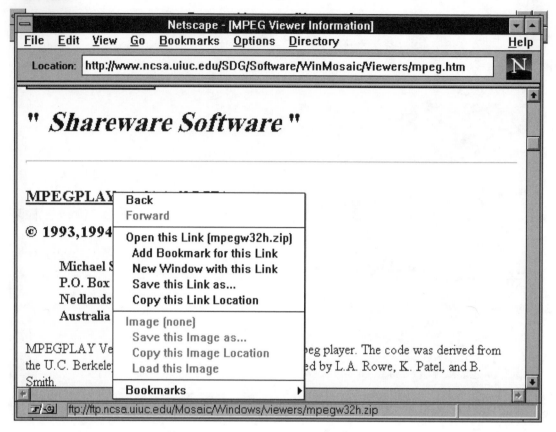

Figure 9-20
Save this Link as.

3. Click once on **Save this Link as...** and then verify that the file name in the Save As... box is mpegw32h.zip (or whatever the latest version is) and that the directory is incoming, as shown in Figure 9-21.

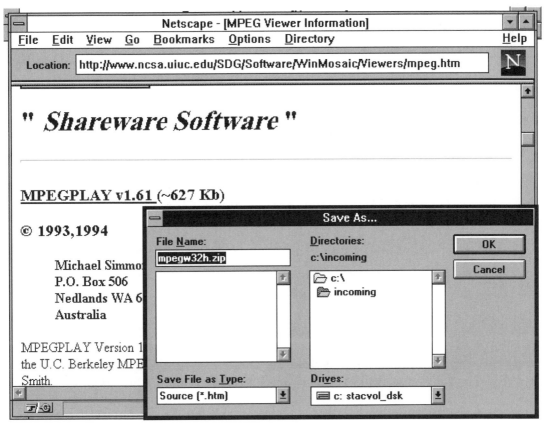

Figure 9-21
Downloading
MPEGW32H.ZIP

4. Click on **OK**

The file we are about to install requires you to have a copy of WIN32S already installed. If you need to install WIN32S, it is readily available from Microsoft as well as from NCSA. If this is more than you wish to deal with at this time, then just go on to the next activity, in which you will download and install a copy of QuickTime for Windows. It is easy to install QuickTime and it requires no additional software. Directions to download and INSTALL WIN32s are included in the Appendix

---

5. Once the file has been successfully downloaded, disconnect from your Internet Service Provider and we will install it.

6. Use File Manager to copy the file mpegw32h.zip to an empty temporary directory.

7. Use File Manager to copy the file pkunzip.exe to that same temporary directory.

There are some special directories that must be created as you are preparing mpegw32h.zip for use. You *must* include the -d after the command **pkunzip** or the files will not be unzipped correctly.

8. Use File Manager to make your temporary directory active. Select **File** and **Run** and in the Command Line: box, type

```
pkunzip -d mpegw32h.zip
```

9. Select **File** and **Run** and then in the Command Line: box, type

```
setup.exe
```

NOTE: All the files will be installed into the directory known as WIN32APP in the subdirectory called MPEGPLAY.

Now, we have to inform Netscape that these files have been installed and may be used, if necessary. Here is how to do so.

1. Launch Netscape

2. Select **Options** and then **Preferences**

3. Click on the **Set Preferences On: box** until the words Helper Applications are visible.

4. Highlight video/mpeg as shown in Figure 9-22.

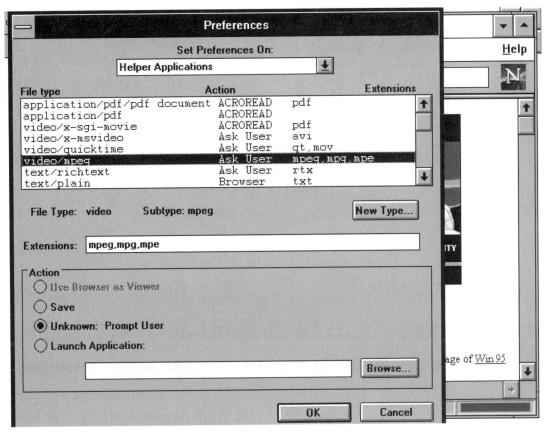

Figure 9-22
Selecting
Preferences/Helper
Applications

5. Click on **Launch Application:** and then on the **Browse... button**

6. When you have highlighted c:\win32app\mpegplay\mpeg-play.exe, as shown in Figure 9-23, click on **OK**

From here on in, Netscape will know what to do when it encounters mpeg files!

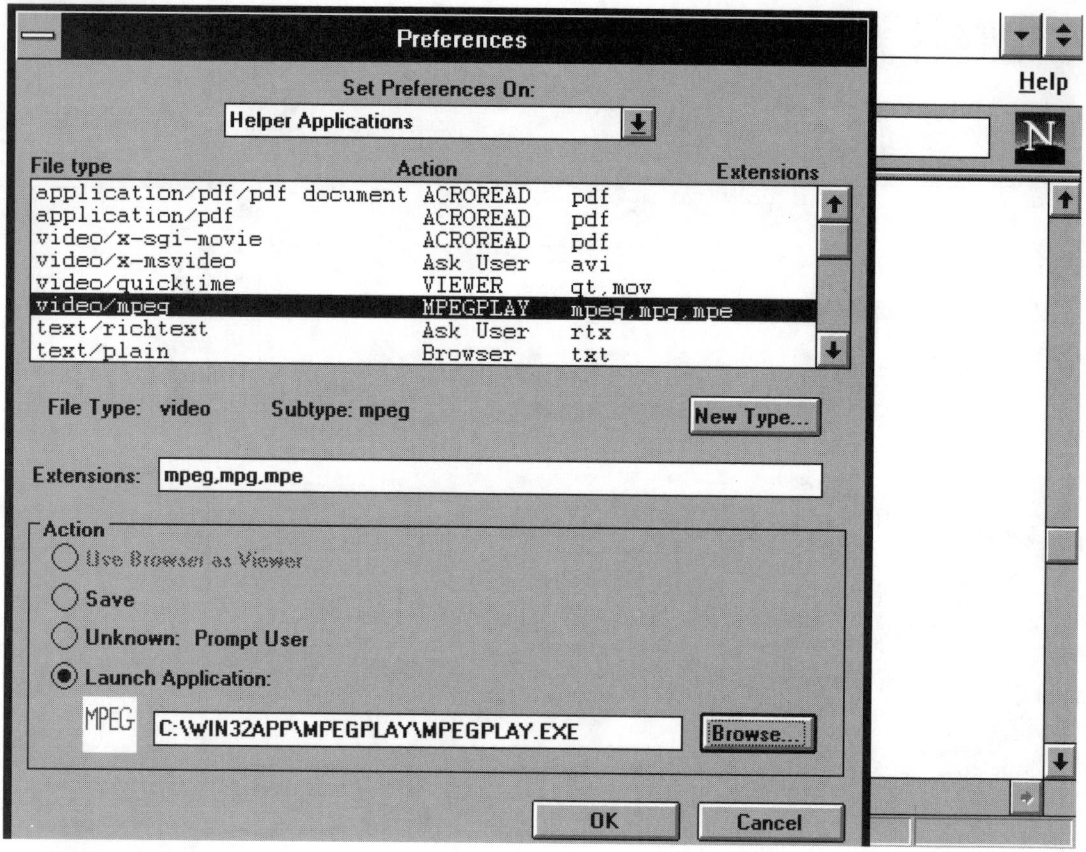

Help

Preferences

Set Preferences On:

Helper Applications

File type	Action	Extensions
application/pdf/pdf document	ACROREAD	pdf
application/pdf	ACROREAD	pdf
video/x-sgi-movie	ACROREAD	pdf
video/x-msvideo	Ask User	avi
video/quicktime	VIEWER	qt,mov
video/mpeg	MPEGPLAY	mpeg,mpg,mpe
text/richtext	Ask User	rtx
text/plain	Browser	txt

File Type: video   Subtype: mpeg

New Type...

Extensions: mpeg,mpg,mpe

Action

○ Use Browser as Viewer

○ Save

○ Unknown: Prompt User

◉ Launch Application:

MPEG C:\WIN32APP\MPEGPLAY\MPEGPLAY.EXE   Browse...

OK   Cancel

Figure 9-23
Preferences/Helper
Applications/video/
mpeg

Finding Movie Files

Like audio files, movie files are quite large. Although you have now prepared Netscape to play movie files as they are downloaded, we would suggest that you download movies first by clicking on the **right** mouse button and on **Save this File as...** and then opening the file locally once it has been downloaded.

Figures 9-24 through 9-27 are included to provide you with some ideas about where to go next for sounds and images. In each figure, the document name and document URL are shown by Netscape. To explore these, we will just show you the figures and not give you our usual step-by-step instructions. By now, we believe, you know how to do this on your own. Happy exploring!

Music, Images, and Multimedia

Document Title: Internet Resources List

Document URL: http://www.eit.com/web/netservices.html

Once the Internet Resources Home Page appears, just click on the
hyperlink **Music, Images, and Multimedia** to see the screen shown in
Figure 9-24.

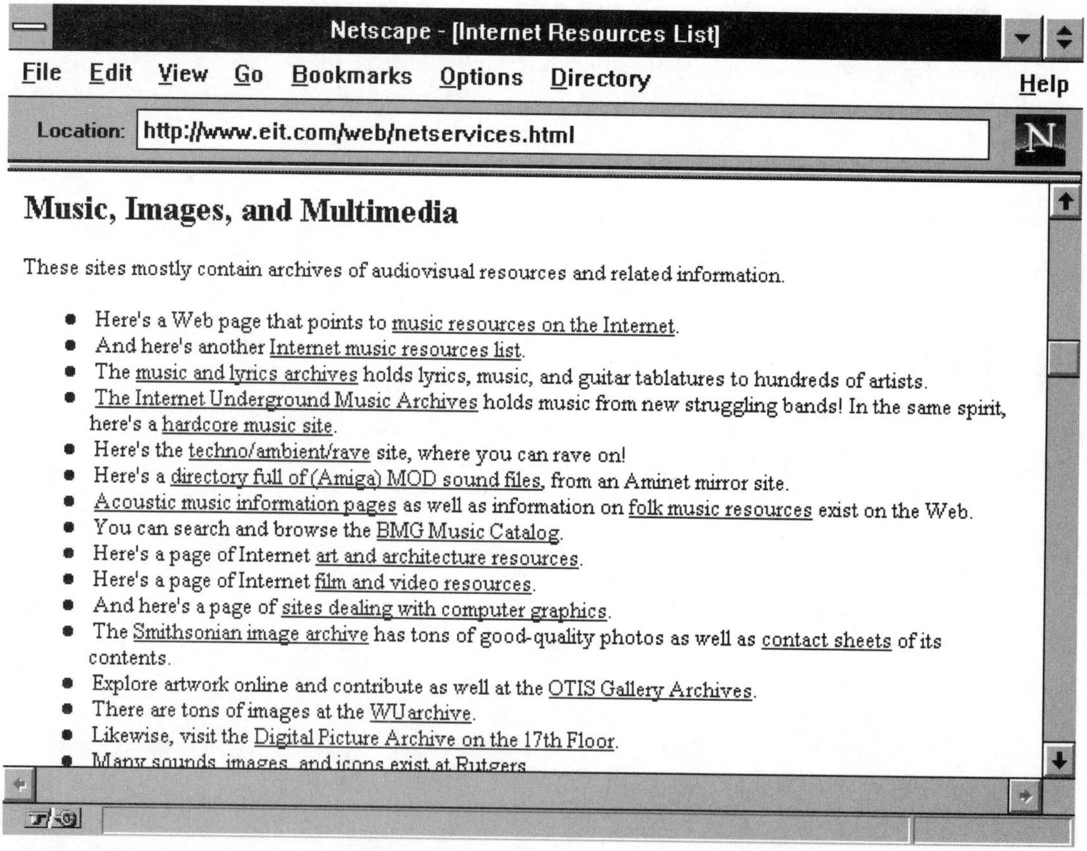

Netscape - [Internet Resources List]

File   Edit   View   Go   Bookmarks   Options   Directory   Help

Location: http://www.eit.com/web/netservices.html

Music, Images, and Multimedia

These sites mostly contain archives of audiovisual resources and related information.

- Here's a Web page that points to music resources on the Internet.
- And here's another Internet music resources list.
- The music and lyrics archives holds lyrics, music, and guitar tablatures to hundreds of artists.
- The Internet Underground Music Archives holds music from new struggling bands! In the same spirit, here's a hardcore music site.
- Here's the techno/ambient/rave site, where you can rave on!
- Here's a directory full of (Amiga) MOD sound files, from an Aminet mirror site.
- Acoustic music information pages as well as information on folk music resources exist on the Web.
- You can search and browse the BMG Music Catalog.
- Here's a page of Internet art and architecture resources.
- Here's a page of Internet film and video resources.
- And here's a page of sites dealing with computer graphics.
- The Smithsonian image archive has tons of good-quality photos as well as contact sheets of its contents.
- Explore artwork online and contribute as well at the OTIS Gallery Archives.
- There are tons of images at the WU archive.
- Likewise, visit the Digital Picture Archive on the 17th Floor.
- Many sounds, images, and icons exist at Rutgers.

Figure 9-24
Internet Resources List

Click on the hyperlink **film and video resources**, and you will be taken
to the next resource that is displayed in Figure 9-25.

Guide to Film and Video

Document Title: Film and Video Resources

Document URL:

http://http2.sils.umich.edu/Public/fvl/film.html

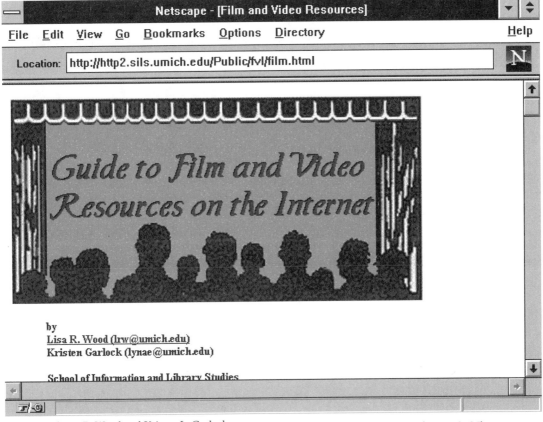

Courtesy of Lisa R. Wood and Kristen L. Garlock

Figure 9-25
Film and Video
Resources

Current Weather Maps/Movies

Document Title: Current Weather Maps/Movies

Document URL: http://wxweb.msu.edu/weather

The initial screen for this information is shown in Figure 9-26.

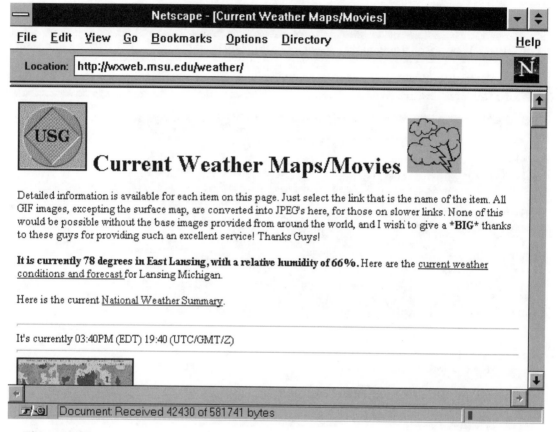

Figure 9-26
Current Weather
Maps/Movies

This resource contains an enormous number of GIF, JPEG, and MPEG files, just waiting for you to download them. Have fun!

Downloading and Installing QuickTime

Movies are also frequently to be found with either a qt or mov extension. Both of these can be accessed by using QuickTime from Apple. This file is included on your CD-ROM.

A copy of Quicktime 2.0 for Windows is on the CD-ROM that has been included with *Hands-On Netscape*. You can use this copy, or you may choose to follow the directions in this activity that show you how to locate and download your own copy of Quicktime 2.0 for Windows. If you are using the copy of Quicktime 2.0 for Windows that is on the CD-ROM, then install the files as follows:

1. In Program Manager, click on **File** then **Run**

2. Type `d:\qtw2\setup.exe`

   (If d: is not your CD drive, then substitute the correct letter.)

   The program installs Quicktime for Windows on your hard drive and creates an icon in Program Manager.

3. Follow the directions in this activity that show you how to tell Netscape that viewer.exe has been correctly installed on drive c: in the Windows directory.

If you choose to download QuickTime from the Internet, here is how to do so.

1. Launch Netscape

2. Enter the following URL:
   `ftp://ftp.ee.ualberta.ca/pub/dos/win3/local-winsock/viewer`

   You should be taken to a location that resembles Figure 9-27.

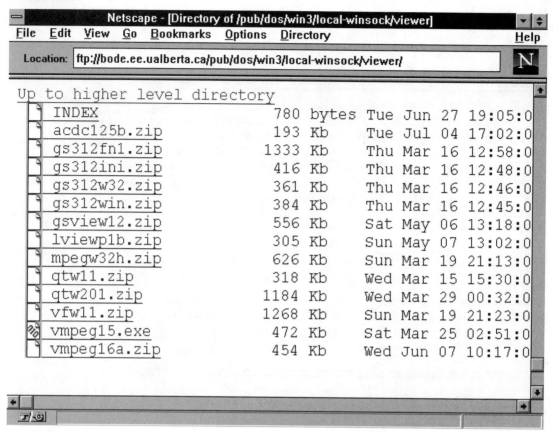

Figure 9-27

Directory of
bode/ee.ualberta.ca/
pub/dos/win3/local-
winsock/viewer

3. Highlight qtw201.zip (or the most current version)

4. Click once on the *right* **mouse button** and then highlight Save this Link as...

5. In the Save As box, make sure that the file will be saved into your incoming directory

6. Once the file has been downloaded (it is rather large,) disconnect from your Internet Service Provider

7. Use File Manager to create a directory into which to put qtw201 (we chose to call it qtw) and then copy the file into the new directory

8. As you have done before, copy the file pkunzip.exe into this directory

The file qtw201.zip must be uninstalled using the command **pkunzip -d** so that the files are correctly installed into several different directories. Failure to do this will mean that your program will not run.

9. Then type

```
pkunzip -d qtw201.zip
```

so that the files are correctly uncompressed.

10. Next, click on **File** and **Run** and then **Setup** so that the Quick-Time program will correctly install itself using the setup.exe file that has been included with the program.

11. Launch Netscape and then click on **Options** and then on **Preferences**

12. Once there, click on **Set Preferences On:** until Helper Applications is visible

13. Highlight video/quicktime and click on Launch Application: Then use the **Browse... button** to help you to find the exact directory and subdirectory where the file viewer.exe is located. It should be located in c:\windows\viewer.exe

14. Finally, click on **OK**

Having done this, you are probably eager to see how these new Quick-Time movies work. An excellent repository of sample movies for you to try is the National Museum of American Art. Here is how to get there.

1. With Netscape launched, click on file and then on Open File. Open the file **WEBTOUR.HTM** on your CD-ROM drive

2. Slide your cursor to the heading Art and Entertainment

3. Highlight the heading National Museum of American Art Home Page

4. Click on this bookmark and you will be taken to the National Museum of American Art, as shown in Figure 9-28.

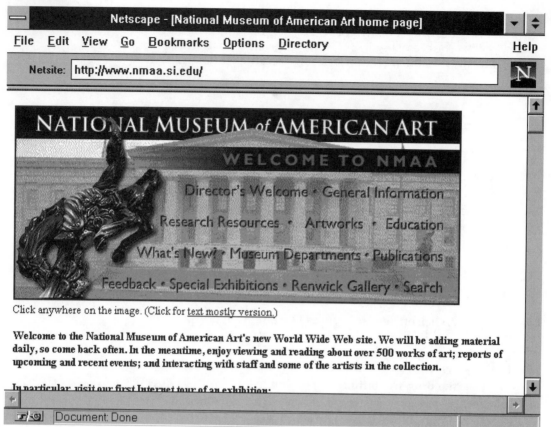

Figure 9-28
National Museum of
American Art

This site has a great many movies you might enjoy trying out. As you can tell, they are *very* large, and some of them will take you quite some time to download. As we suggested earlier, you should probably download the movies first, and then use Netscape, File, and Open File... to play them once they are safely on your computer. Enjoy!

Session Summary

In this session, you have begun to experience the multimedia aspects of Netscape and the World Wide Web. You installed software that permits you to hear many of the audio sounds that are available on the World Wide Web. The helper applications you installed make it possible for you to see an amazing number of images on your PC. As the last activity in this session illustrated, the array of sights and sounds on the World Wide Web is seemingly limitless. We hope you will enjoy many pleasurable hours exploring the multimedia universe that Netscape and these new software programs make available to you!

Session

10

Activity 1:   Setting Up an HTML Document

Activity 2:   Creating a List

Activity 3:   Adding Hyperlinks

Activity 4:   Checking Hyperlinks

Activity 5:   Additional HTML Resources

Movie 1:   HTML Document

Getting Started With Hypertext Markup Language (HTML)

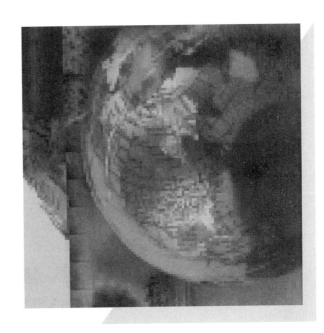

Session Overview

In this session you will learn about Hypertext Markup Language, the language that is used to create the documents that you have been looking at with Netscape. You will learn how Hypertext Markup Language is structured and about some of the conventions that are used. After creating a document using some of the fundamental HTML commands, you will learn about additional HTML resources. An important aspect of this session is that while you will be creating your HTML document, you will also be creating a good search tool for yourself.

Hypertext Markup Language Introduction

The *Hypertext Markup Language (HTML)* is a set of special codes that permits you to add formatting and linking information to the text that is to be made available to others who may be using browsers such as Netscape. It is important to realize that this information may be transmitted about the World Wide Web or to others within your own company or organization.

As you might imagine, Hypertext Markup Language is directly related to the Hypertext Transport Protocol (http) that we have been using with Netscape throughout this book. You will find that HTML is a relatively straightforward way to prepare information to be transmitted about the World Wide Web. Learning a little HTML is an interesting way to have a better understanding of how the World Wide Web does its magic. In addition, knowing HTML will permit you to develop some pages for local viewing by Netscape, as we will do later in this session. Now, let's get started!

Let's begin by looking at a typical home page, as we have done throughout this book. The document depicted in Figure 10-1 is the home page for Advantis, the U.S. provider of IBM's Global Network. The Advantis Home Page includes some graphics, some text, and some hyperlinks pointing you toward additional information. In all likelihood, you have not spent much time thinking about how all that information actually was developed, or what procedures or techniques were in place so that you could see the actual document that appeared on your screen.

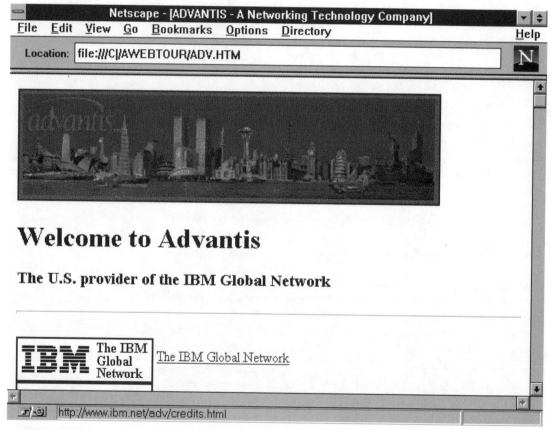

Figure 10-1
Advantis Home Page

Now, let's take a look at the Hypertext Markup Language that has been used to create this page. Once Netscape has been launched, you can easily look at this version of the document by clicking once on View and then on Source. Figure 10-2 shows the HTML that was used to create the Advantis Home Page that was shown in Figure 10-1.

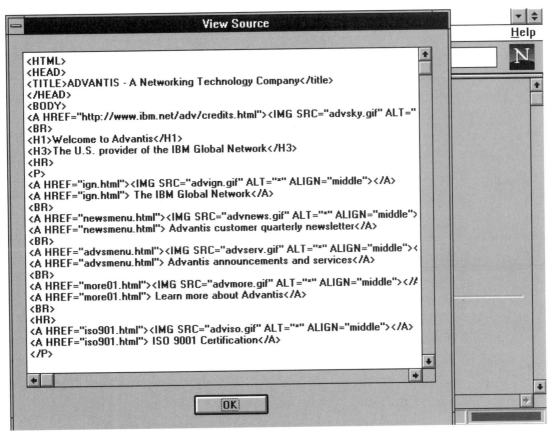

Figure 10-2
HTML Version of
Advantis Home Page

Notice several things about this page.

   a.   It begins with <HTML> and ends with <HTML>.

   b.   It has a heading, in which we find the title of the document.

   c.   It has a body, in which we find the main components of the document.

d. It includes quite a bit of text, surrounded by some items that are in brackets.

Let's see what this is all about.

First of all, it is important to realize that HTML documents are ASCII text files, stored on DOS computers with the extension htm and on UNIX computers with the extension html. Second, every HTML document is divided into two parts: a head and a body. The head contains some brief information about the document (in this case it is the title), and the body contains the text of the document.

We use what are known as *markup tags* (those items that were in brackets in Figure 10-2) to provide signals to the browser about how to present the text that is contained between the tags. Here is a very simplified version of the Advantis Home Page that was seen in Figure 10-1:

```
<HTML>

<HEAD>

<TITLE> ADVANTIS - A Networking Technology Company
</TITLE>

</HEAD>

<BODY>
```

Here is some information about Advantis.

```
</BODY>

</HTML>
```

Notice that many of the tags (HTML, HEAD, TITLE, BODY, H1, and H3) come in pairs (a starting tag and an ending tag). The starting tag will turn on a given feature, and the ending tag (which has a slash mark in front of it) will turn off that feature. For example, <TITLE> tells your browser where the title of the document begins; </TITLE> tells the browser where the title ends.

You should also be aware that some tags such as <BR> for BREAK and <P> for PARAGRAPH do not have ending tags. Look carefully at Figure 10-2 and you will see that the <BR> tag and the <P> tag appear by themselves.
 just adds a break between items; <P> indicates to your browser that it should start a new paragraph.

Notice also that the document begins and ends with <HTML> tags (you cannot see the closing HTML tag in Figure 10-2, but it is there!); the initial HTML tag <HTML> tells Netscape that it has encountered an HTML document and the ending tag </HTML> signals Netscape that the HTML document is finished.

The Hypertext Markup Language is used to send signals to Netscape. Each one of the tags provides Netscape with a particular set of information, and based on that given information, Netscape will display the information that is displayed on your screen.

It is also important to realize that HTML allows you to add formatting and linking information to an ASCII text document as well as to determine the relative size of the various headings that are presented, using a series of tags that range in size from <H1> (the largest) to <H6> (the smallest). The person viewing the document actually determines how large or small the fonts will be, but the heading tags are used to indicate the relative size of the headings as they are presented.

Be aware that there are many more tags than just the ones that we have shown. In addition, there are some tags, known as *anchors*, that will permit us to provide hypertext links in an HTML document. And, you should realize that as the World Wide Web becomes more popular and as people are trying to do a better and better job of sending information from one to another using HTML, they are working to add many more new and improved features to HTML than have been available to date. (More about that later.)

Rather than just looking at HTML documents that others have created, or just talking about HTML, let's begin to set up our own HTML document.

Setting Up an HTML Document

HTML documents are ASCII text files, which means that there are many different ways to create them. You could use a text editor, or you could use one of the many new software programs that have been created especially to make HTML creation easier and quicker. We will provide you with information about several of these software programs before the end of this session. However, for the exercises that follow, we are going to suggest that you work along with us as we use the Windows Notepad to create our HTML document.

If you use a word processor such as Microsoft Word or WordPerfect to create an HTML document, you must be sure to save the file as a plain ASCII text file.

The HTML document that we are about to create is a relatively simple one. However, it will provide you with a good introduction to the commonly used HTML vocabulary, as well as enable you to have a very powerful search tool at your disposal. We will create a set of Web-based Yellow Pages sites, each of which is a hyperlink that will take you directly to that site. The completed document, as shown when accessed by Netscape, resembles Figure 10-3.

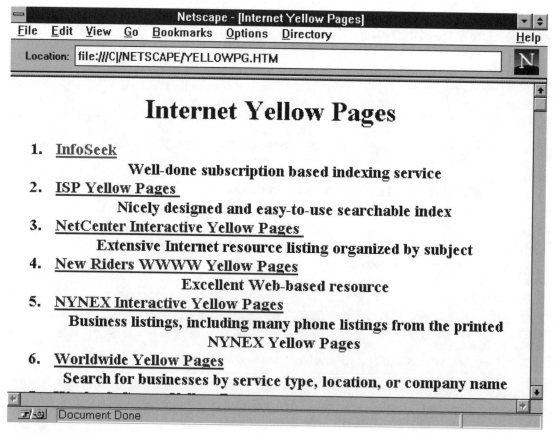

Figure 10-3
Internet Yellow Pages

Here is how to begin.

1. From the Windows Program Manager, click once on **Window**, then **Accessories**, and then on **Notepad**.

2. Type in the following information:

```
<HTML>
<HEAD>
<TITLE> Internet Yellow Pages </TITLE>
</HEAD>
<BODY>
Some sample text goes here for the moment!
</BODY>
</HTML>
```

We are about to save a series of text files in Notepad. You will want to access them frequently using Netscape, so it is very important that you know where you have saved your files. Also, since these will be HTML files (the DOS/Windows extension is htm) it is important that you give these files the extension htm when you save them.

3. Save your document as c:\NETSCAPE\YELLOW01.HTM The Notepad version of YELLOW01.HTM is shown in Figure 10-4. Yours should look very much the same.

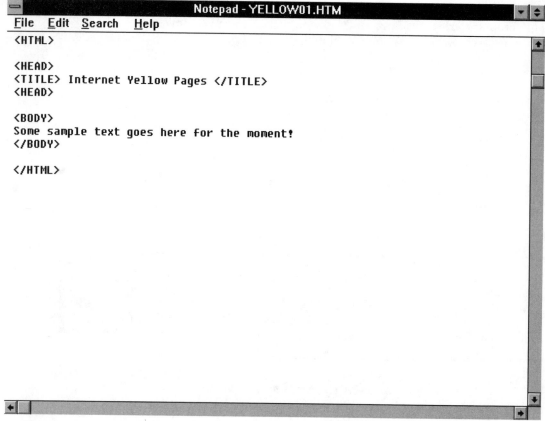

```
Notepad - YELLOW01.HTM

File   Edit   Search   Help

<HTML>

<HEAD>
<TITLE> Internet Yellow Pages </TITLE>
<HEAD>

<BODY>
Some sample text goes here for the moment!
</BODY>

</HTML>
```

Figure 10-4
Initial Yellow Pages
HTML Document in
Notepad

Now, let's see how Netscape will display the document.

1. Minimize Notepad

2. Launch Netscape

3. Click on **File** and then on **Open Local File**

4. Enter YELLOW01.HTM in the File Name box

5. Click on OK

You should see a screen resembling the one that is shown in Figure 10-5.

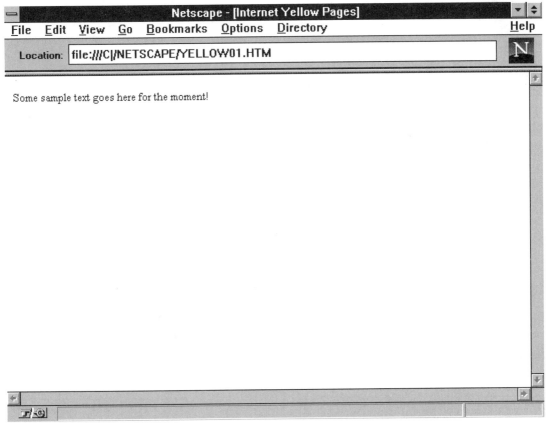

Figure 10-5
Initial Yellow Pages
HTML Document in
Netscape

Notice that the title of the document (Internet Yellow Pages) is displayed on the title bar, next to the word Netscape. Also, notice that your one line of sample text has been correctly displayed in the body of your document. (We will add more interesting information in a moment.)

The activities in this session are progressive. If for any reason, you do not have the same text as was shown in either the Notepad or Netscape version of YELLOW01.HTM, please stop now and enter that information into your document so that you can follow along.

Now, let's add some more information and, while doing so, learn more about HTML.

1. Go back to Notepad where we have our HTML text file.

You may switch between Notepad and Netscape by holding down the **ALT key** and pressing the **TAB key** until you see Netscape.

2. For the top line of the body of the document, let's add the following:

```
<CENTER> <H1> Internet Yellow Pages </H1>
</CENTER>
```

This will put the title of the page (Internet Yellow Pages) into the body of the document itself. Many people find it helpful to see the actual heading in the body of the document, in addition to the title that appears in the title line.

As you might imagine, the <CENTER> and </CENTER> tags, which at the moment are used only by Netscape, tell the browser to center and then to stop centering the enclosed text.

Headings

As mentioned earlier, headings, when viewed by Netscape and other browsers, can be one of six levels, with 1 being the largest and 6 being the smallest. Headings may be used throughout a document to provide added emphasis to given topics. We have chosen to make the words Internet Yellow Pages into a level 1 (the largest) heading, since they will be at the top of the document. The person who is using Netscape has total control over how large the <H1> heading (and all of the others) will actually be. The person creating the HTML document can use the <H1> tag to indicate that a particular heading should be the largest.

Creating a List

Now we will begin the actual list of items to be included in the document. Go to Notepad and type the following below the Internet Yellow Pages heading; then we will explain what you have typed.

```
<OL>
<LI> InfoSeek
<LI> ISP Yellow Pages
<LI> NetCenter Interactive Yellow Pages
<LI> New Riders WWW Yellow Pages
<LI> NYNEX Interactive Yellow Pages
<LI> Worldwide Yellow Pages
<LI> Works Software Yellow Pages
<LI> Yahoo
<LI> YellowPages.com
</OL>
```

Save your new Notepad document as YELLOW02.HTM. It should resemble the one that is shown in Figure 10-6.

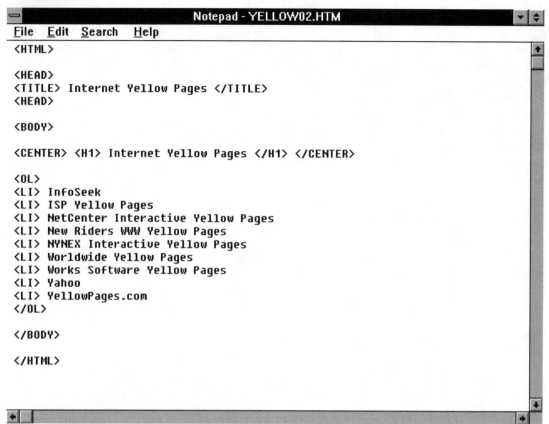

```
                    Notepad - YELLOW02.HTM
File   Edit   Search   Help
<HTML>

<HEAD>
<TITLE> Internet Yellow Pages </TITLE>
<HEAD>

<BODY>

<CENTER> <H1> Internet Yellow Pages </H1> </CENTER>

<OL>
<LI> InfoSeek
<LI> ISP Yellow Pages
<LI> NetCenter Interactive Yellow Pages
<LI> New Riders WWW Yellow Pages
<LI> NYNEX Interactive Yellow Pages
<LI> Worldwide Yellow Pages
<LI> Works Software Yellow Pages
<LI> Yahoo
<LI> YellowPages.com
</OL>

</BODY>

</HTML>
```

Figure 10-6
YELLOW02.HTM in
Notepad

Here's what you have just done.

a. You have set up a framework for an Ordered List of items by adding the tags <OL> and </OL> in the body of the document. HTML permits you to have either ordered (meaning numbered) or unordered (meaning bulleted) lists of items.

b. The tag <LI> tells Netscape and other browsers that the information following the tag is one of the list items that is to be included in the ordered or unordered list. If the list is to be an ordered one, then Netscape will automatically add the appropriate numbers for you, as you will see in a moment. Notice by the way, that the <LI> tag does not have an ending tag. Once you are inside an ordered or an unordered List, you just need to use <LI> to indicate the list items.

c. You have added information about nine different Yellow Pages providers, each of which has a particular location on the World Wide Web, and each of which may be accessed via a hyperlink. (More about that in a moment.)

Now, let's see what we have created. Go back to Netscape and then click once on **File** and then on **Open File**. Open the file whose name is YELLOW02.HTM If all has gone according to plan, you should see a document that resembles the one shown in Figure 10-7.

Figure 10-7
YELLOW02.HTM as
Seen by Netscape

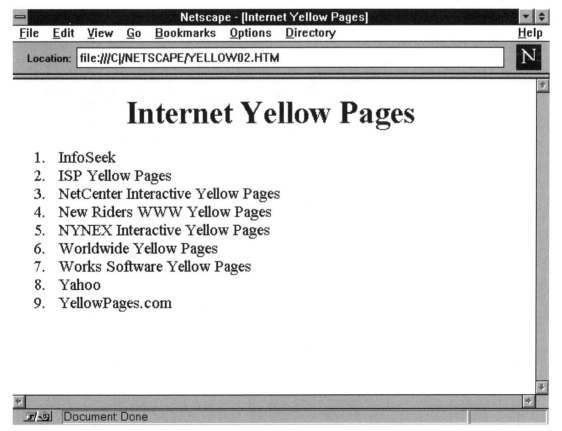

Several observations are in order.

a. Netscape has automatically numbered the items in your list. By using the tags <OL> and </OL>, you directed Netscape and other browsers to do this.

b. You have created an interesting list of Yellow Pages names, but there is no power to be had from this list at the moment. In the next activity, you will learn how to turn each of these list items into a hyperlink.

You should be aware that different browsers will present HTML information in different ways. If you are preparing information that is to be viewed only by those with Netscape, then what you see with your browser will, for the most part, resemble what others see with theirs. However, if your HTML document will be placed on a Web server for many to view, then it is important that you look at your document using a variety of browsers. Different browsers present HTML documents differently.

Adding Hyperlinks

As you have seen throughout your journey about the World Wide Web, it is hypertext and hyperlinks that provide the World Wide Web documents with their power. Hypertext links may take the viewer to another location within a document, or to another source anywhere on the World Wide Web. Although in this activity we will focus on links that are accessed using Hypertext Transport Protocol (http), you should be aware that all possible forms of URLs, such as ftp, gopher, or telnet, can be included as hypertext links.

The format to provide this power includes the concept of anchors and links. *Anchors* are text strings that delineate the beginning and the end of the hypertext links that are included between them. Here is an example of two anchors and an included hypertext link:

```
<A HREF="http://www.infoseek.com"> InfoSeek </A>
```

Notice the following:

a. There are anchor tags (<A> and </A>) at the beginning and the end of this text string.

b. Within the initial anchor tag is an attribute, HREF, that is an abbreviation for *Hypertext Reference*. *HREF* denotes that the attribute is the beginning of a hypertext link.

c. Following the HREF attribute, is an equal sign, followed by the actual hyperlink, which is always enclosed in quotation marks.

d. Following the hypertext link, the starting link is closed. Then we see the actual word or words (in this case the word InfoSeek) that will appear on the page when it is displayed by Netscape.

Now, let's enter the information into our text file that will convert the list of references that we have created into a set of hypertext links. In the following, we have indicated where to put the anchors, and how to enter the hypertext links. Here is the information to be entered in Notepad:

1. `<A HREF="http://www.infoseek.com"> InfoSeek </A>`

2. `<A HREF="http://www.index.org/"> ISP Yellow Pages </A>`

3. `<A HREF="http://netcenter.com/yellows.html"> NetCenter Interactive Yellow Pages </A>`

4. `<A HREF="http://www.mcp.com/nrp/wwwyp/"> New Riders WWW Yellow Pages </A>`

5. `<A HREF="http://www.vtcom.fr/nynex/"> NYNEX Interactive Yellow Pages </A>`

6. `<A HREF="http://www.yellow.com/cgi-bin/SearchWWYP"> Worldwide Yellow Pages </A>`

7. `<A HREF="http://planetcom.com/workmedia/wsyp.html"> Works Software Yellow Pages </A>`

8. `<A HREF="http://www.yahoo.com"> Yahoo </A>`

9. `<A HREF="http://theyellowpages.com/"> YellowPages.com </A>`

Once all your information has been entered into Notepad, be sure to save the new file as YELLOW03.HTM The completed document should resemble the one that is shown in Figure 10-8.

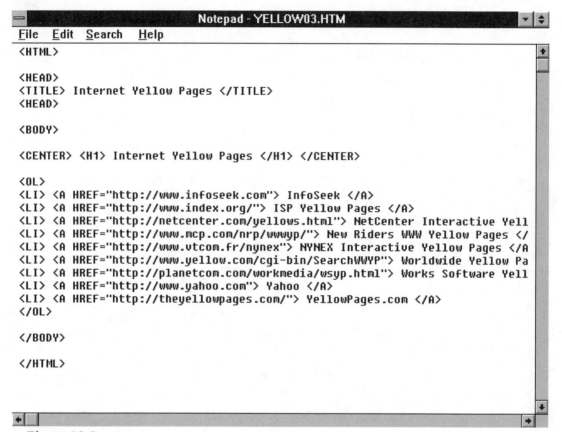

```
─                    Notepad - YELLOW03.HTM                      ▼│▲
 File  Edit  Search  Help
<HTML>

<HEAD>
<TITLE> Internet Yellow Pages </TITLE>
<HEAD>

<BODY>

<CENTER> <H1> Internet Yellow Pages </H1> </CENTER>

<OL>
<LI> <A HREF="http://www.infoseek.com"> InfoSeek </A>
<LI> <A HREF="http://www.index.org/"> ISP Yellow Pages </A>
<LI> <A HREF="http://netcenter.com/yellows.html"> NetCenter Interactive Yell
<LI> <A HREF="http://www.mcp.com/nrp/wwwyp/"> New Riders WWW Yellow Pages </
<LI> <A HREF="http://www.vtcom.fr/nynex"> NYNEX Interactive Yellow Pages </A
<LI> <A HREF="http://www.yellow.com/cgi-bin/SearchWWYP"> Worldwide Yellow Pa
<LI> <A HREF="http://planetcom.com/workmedia/wsyp.html"> Works Software Yell
<LI> <A HREF="http://www.yahoo.com"> Yahoo </A>
<LI> <A HREF="http://theyellowpages.com/"> YellowPages.com </A>
</OL>

</BODY>

</HTML>
```

Figure 10-8
YELLOW03.HTM with
Hyperlinks Added as
Seen in Notepad

When you look at the Notepad version of this document, there is not much that is visibly different from the earlier versions, except for the fact that you have added the new anchors and hyperlinks. However, the significant difference will be visible as soon as we open this new document using Netscape. Go back to Netscape and click once on **File** and then on **Open File**. If you open the file named YELLOW03.HTM, you should see a screen that looks like the one depicted in Figure 10-9.

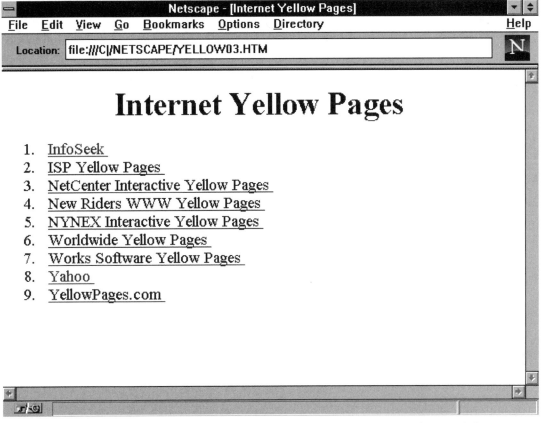

Figure 10-9
YELLOW03.HTM as
Seen Using Netscape

If all has gone according to plan, your document should consist of nine
hyperlinks, each of which is pointing toward its actual Yellow Pages
resource. Notice that each one of the hyperlinks is underlined and
appears in blue on your screen (unless you have changed either or
both of those options). We will test these links in just a moment after
we add just a little more information.

Often it is useful to add some brief comments about the hyperlinks
that are included in a document such as this one. They might be your
personal thoughts about the resource, or perhaps they are comments
that others have made. An easy way to do so, is to use the <CENTER>
tag; this will format your text nicely and the appearance on the screen
is pleasing. We will now add some comments about each of the hyperlinks you have just created.

1. Open the file YELLOW03.HTM in Notepad

2. Add the information about each resource on the line following the respective hyperlink as we have shown you in the following example.

3. When you have finished, save the document as YELLOWPG.HTM

Here is an example of how the information is to be added for *InfoSeek*. Add the information for all of the remaining hyperlinks the same way.

```
<A HREF="http://www.infoseek.com"> InfoSeek </A>
<CENTER> Well-done subscription-based indexing ser-
vice </CENTER>
```

Here is the information for the remaining eight hyperlinks:

ISP Yellow Pages

```
<CENTER>Nicely designed and easy-to-use search-
able index</CENTER>
```

NetCenter Interactive Yellow Pages

```
<CENTER>Extensive Internet resource listing
organized by subject</CENTER>
```

New Riders WWW Yellow Pages

```
<CENTER>Excellent Web-based resource</CENTER>
```

NYNEX Interactive Yellow Pages

```
<CENTER>Business listings, including many phone
listings from the printed NYNEX Yellow
Pages</CENTER>
```

Worldwide Yellow Pages

```
<CENTER>Search for businesses by service type,
location, or company name</CENTER>
```

Works Software Yellow Pages

```
<CENTER>A traditional name-and-address yellow
pages, with many computer-related and consultant
references</CENTER>
```

Yahoo

```
<CENTER>Quickly overwhelming listing of sites,
with a free-form search capability</CENTER>
```

YellowPages.com

```
<CENTER>The granddaddy of Internet Yellow Pages
contains thousands of links</CENTER>
```

Be sure to save the Notepad document as YELLOWPG.HTM when
you have finished. Figure 10-10 shows what it should look like.

Figure 10-10
YELLOWPG.HTM as
Seen Using Notepad

This final version of the Notepad document contains all the tags we entered during the last few activities. Figure 10-11 demonstrates the real payoff for all the work we have done to make this happen. You now are the proud owner of a set of Yellow Pages resources, each of which is carefully annotated so that you will know what each resource has to offer you and others who choose to view it.

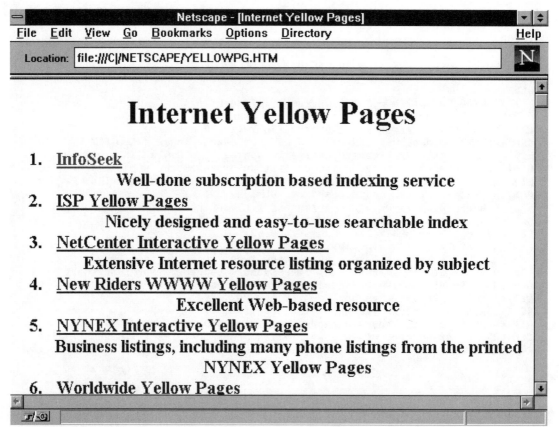

Figure 10-11
YELLOWPG.HTM as
Seen Using Netscape

Checking Hyperlinks

Setting up a document such as the one we created in this session is exciting; suddenly, the power of hyperlinks is at your disposal. However, it is important to complete the final step in this process. It is imperative that you check each one of the hyperlinks once to make sure that they are accurate. We have found in the process of designing many documents such as this one, that problems are often encountered in this final step. Given the complexity of hyperlinks, it is not uncommon to find that a typing mistake has been made while entering the information. Also, given the ever-changing nature of the World Wide Web and the Internet, hyperlinks that were correct one moment, may have changed the next.

> Should you find that a hyperlink you believed to be correct is not working when you try it out, we suggest the following. Enter the hyperlink address manually in Netscape. When doing so, enter just the host address of the desired resource first, without any of the more detailed directory and subdirectory information. We have found that the resources we were seeking were often still available, but that their actual directories or subdirectories may have been moved or changed since we had initially obtained the information.

Now, let's check out the resources included in the Internet Yellow Pages document.

1. Connect to your Internet Service Provider and launch Netscape

2. Click once on File and then on Open File

3. Enter YELLOWPG.HTM as the name of the file

4. Try each one of hyperlinks by clicking on it

If all has gone according to plan, you are now the proud owner of an HTML document that is filled with wonderful Yellow Pages resources. These resources should provide you with an efficient way to search the World Wide Web. In addition, you now have a better understanding of the Hypertext Markup Language.

Additional HTML Resources

In this session, we have just begun to show you some of the many aspects of Hypertext Markup Language. If you are interested in learning more about HTML, there is quite a bit of additional information to be found on the World Wide Web. Some of the many resources are listed below:

1. A Beginner's Guide to HTML

http://www.ncsa.uiuc.edu/General/Internet/WWW/HTMLPrimer.html

2. The HTML Quick Reference Guide

http://kuhttp.cc.ukans.edu/lynx_help/HTML_quick.html

3. How To Compose Good HTML

http://www.willamette.edu/html-composition/strict-html.html

4. HTML Editors

http://akebono.stanford.edu/yahoo/Computers/World_Wide_Web/HTML_Editors/

There are also several good HTML editors for Windows. Two of the best known are HotMetal and HTML Assistant.

There are numerous books on the subject too. Two well-known ones are *HTML Manual of Style* by Larry Aronson and *HTML for Fun and Profit* by Mary Morris.

Session Summary

As the interest in and the use of the World Wide Web have grown, interest in HTML has also grown. The good news is that HTML is relatively straightforward to implement. However, as you have probably noticed, it takes time to turn a document into the HTML format, and there is a fair amount of tedium affiliated with the actual process of adding all the required tags and the hyperlinks that are included. It is fair to say, however, that newer and better HTML editors appear to be removing some of that difficulty.

In addition, it is important to note that there remains an additional problem affiliated with HTML usage. Unlike the Adobe Portable Document Format that preserves the exact format of the document as it was created, HTML does not do that. The best that one can do with HTML is to provide browsers with a suggestion of what is to be done. Ultimately, the user has total control over the actual colors to be displayed and the size of the fonts to be used.

It is for all these reasons that significant work on HTML is underway. HTML 3.0 is the proposed new standard and it is intended to include new and more powerful tags. In addition, new software packages are appearing that should help to mechanize the actual creation of HTML documents. All these developments should improve the ability to create HTML documents quickly and efficiently.

We hope that this initial introduction to HTML whets your appetite for more!

Session

11

| **Activity 1:** | Customizing Netscape - Preferences |
| **Activity 2:** | Staying Up-to-Date |

| **Movie 1:** | Preferences |

Netscape, Your Way

Session Overview

Now you have seen what Netscape Navigator can do, have traveled the World Wide Web, and have added multimedia and HTML to your tool kit. There remain just two things to tell you about. These are:

1. Showing you how to customize Netscape to your tastes and preferences

2. Sharing our methods for keeping Netscape and your multimedia helper applications up-to-date.

We will focus on these two areas during this session. We begin with setting Netscape's Preferences.

Customizing Netscape - Preferences

Although we visited Options on the menu bar early in the book, we have not, as yet, walked together through the Preferences choice under Options. This is a really large area as almost everything about Netscape can be adjusted to *your* preferences.

We will go through each of the Preferences submenus and show you what you can and cannot do. We will also show you the *defaults*, that is, the *original factory settings*. This will permit you to return Netscape to its original look and feel if you have made too many changes and wish to begin again.

When you click on **Options** on the menu bar, and then click on **Preferences**, you will usually see one of the two following screens. The actual screen that you will see depends upon the version of Netscape you are using. The initial appearance differs, but the choices are nearly the same. Figures 11-1 and 11-2 show the two initial screens.

```
┌────────────────────────────────────────────────────────────────┐
│ ▬                        Preferences                            │
├────────────────────────────────────────────────────────────────┤
│                      Set Preferences On:                        │
│              ┌─────────────────────────────────┬──┐             │
│              │ Styles                          │ ▼│             │
│              ├─────────────────────────────────┴──┤             │
│  ┌─Window Styles──│ Styles                       │──────────────┐│
│                   │ Fonts and Colors             │              ││
│  Show Toolbar as: │ Mail and News                │  ures and Text││
│                   │ Cache and Network            │              ││
│                   │ Applications and Directories │              ││
│                   │ Images and Security          │              ││
│     Start With:   │ Proxies                      │ n:           ││
│                   │ Helper Applications          │              ││
│  └────────────────┴──────────────────────────────┴──────────────┘│
│                                                                  │
│  ┌─Link Styles──────────────────────────────────────────────────┐│
│                                                                  ││
│     Links are: ☒ Underlined                                     ││
│                                                                  ││
│  Followed Links: ○ Never Expire  ◉ Expire After: [30] Days [Expire Now]││
│  └──────────────────────────────────────────────────────────────┘│
│                                                                  │
│                                        ┌────────┐  ┌────────┐    │
│                                        │   OK   │  │ Cancel │    │
│                                        └────────┘  └────────┘    │
└────────────────────────────────────────────────────────────────┘
```

Figure 11-1
Preferences - Earlier
Versions

Figure 11-2
Preferences - Later
Versions

Notice that the choice of Styles, Fonts and Colors, Mail and News, and so forth are the same. In earlier versions, you select your preferences by clicking on the list in the center. In later versions, you click on the tabs at the top.

From here on, we will show the more recent versions in our figures, but the choices remain largely the same as they were for earlier versions. Your screen may look a little different from the ones we show, but you can do most of the same things. We begin with Styles.

Styles

The Styles area allows you to alter the appearance of the toolbar and to set the initial home page when you start Netscape. It also lets you change the way hyperlinks are shown. We explain these one at a time. Figure 11-2 shows the Styles page.

In the top box of Styles, you can make choices that will determine the appearance of your toolbar.

> If you use Options to turn off the toolbar, this won't make any difference. The choices here take effect whenever the toolbar is shown.

Toolbar Appearance

You can choose to show the toolbar icons in *one* of three ways:

1.   (Default) As both the small pictures and the words or text

2.   As pictures only

3.   As text only

Figures 11-3, 11-4 and 11-5 show these three options.

Figure 11-3
Toolbar - Pictures and Text

Figure 11-4
Toolbar - Pictures Only

Figure 11-5
Toolbar - Text Only

You make the choice about Netscape's actual appearance. We find that displaying the toolbar with pictures and text is a quick and easy way to use Netscape. However, we use pictures only or text only when we wish to have more screen area available so that we can see more of the actual document area of the information that has been downloaded. It's *your* choice.

Starting Page

Your next choice is to determine what page Netscape uses when you start browsing the World Wide Web using Netscape. There are three choices:

1. (Default) The Netscape Home Page

2. No page at all, that is, a blank screen waiting for your choice

3. Your choice of home page

If you choose to begin each Netscape session with your own home page, you must type in the URL of that place in the area where Netscape's Home Page is shown. Note that you can use any URL here. You might want a World Wide Web page or a gopher page or an ftp page. You might also want a page filled with all of your favorite references or areas of interest. It's *your* choice.

Hyperlink Appearance

The last choice in the Styles section concerns hyperlinks and their appearance. You can choose to show your hyperlinks underlined or not underlined. (Their color will be set on another Styles page.) You can also decide whether or not your hyperlinks will indicate a previous visit.

If Netscape displays previous visits to a given site, this is referred to as *followed links*. You may have noticed earlier that the normal blue hyperlink color changes to purple (or some other color) after you have visited a link.

You can now set *one* of three preferences:

1. (Default) Change back to blue (expire) after 30 days
2. Change back to blue (expire) after your setting in days.

If you type in 0 (zero) days, followed links will not change color.

---

3. Never expire, that is, hyperlinks will always be purple if you visit them just once

In the next section, you can select whatever colors you prefer for both hyperlinks and followed links.

You can also click on the Expire Now button, and clear (after an Are You Sure screen) all your followed links.

Fonts and Colors

The next Preferences page sets the appearance of text and color. In these two areas, you can vary the size and character shape (font) of displayed text and you can change almost all the special colors of Netscape.

Figure 11-6 shows the Fonts and Colors page.

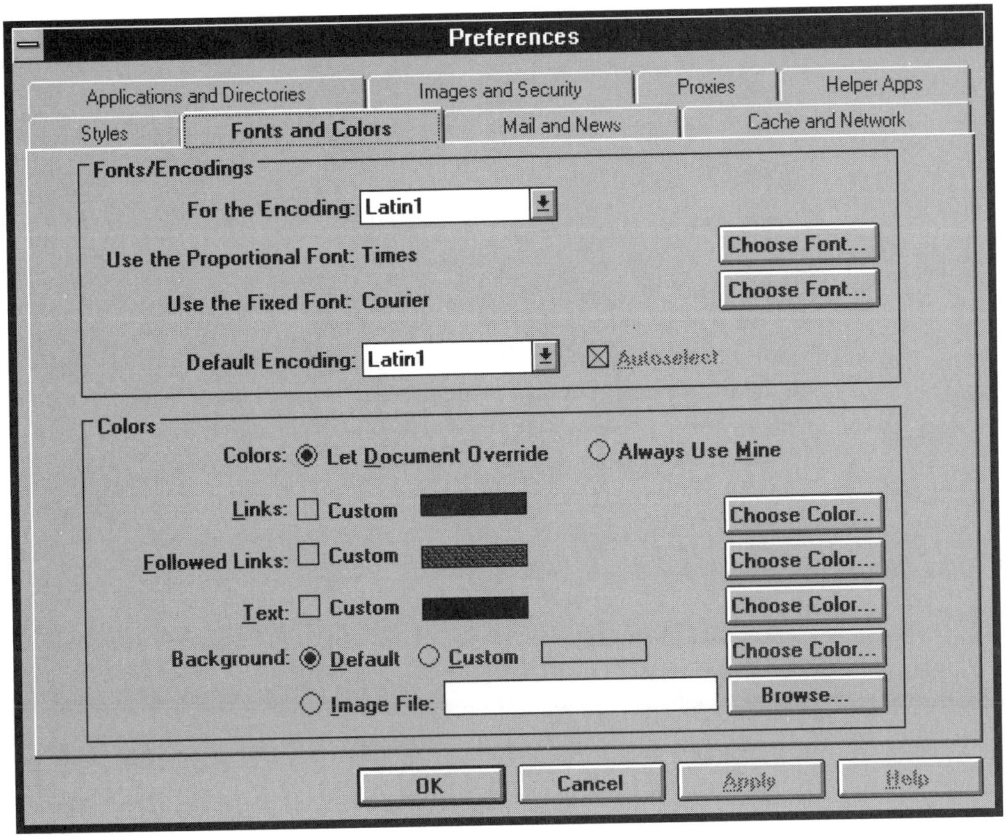

Figure 11-6
Fonts and Colors

Fonts and Encodings

Your first choice in the top box is encodings. In Netscape, this will currently select either the Latin alphabet or a Japanese character set.

As we write this, standards for Japanese character representation are still under discussion. We will focus only on the Latin encoding.

If you have experimented with different character styles and shapes before, you will have a better understanding of fonts. Basically, there are two choices in Netscape's fonts. You can select the size and appearance of the proportional fonts and of the fixed fonts.

Proportional fonts have characters of different widths, that is, a "W" is much wider than an "i" and the overall appearance is more pleasing.

Proportional fonts look like this.

Fixed fonts are like old typewriters. Each character is the same width. While less pleasing, tables of figures and columns of data are easier to read in fixed fonts.

Fixed fonts look like this.

Netscape's font option allows you to select the size and shape of each. You may want to experiment with these to see what font and size are best for you in both proportional and fixed fonts. You do this by clicking on the **Choose Font... buttons** in the upper box.

> You will have the choice of fonts that are already installed in Windows on your computer. Be careful not to select "wingdings" or "symbol" or you will get some very strange results.

The default fonts are

     Proportional – Times New Roman, 12 Point

     Fixed – Courier New, 10 Point

Colors

Here you have the choice of what colors you will use for Netscape. There are a number of different items you can choose to change in Netscape's appearance.

First, you can set your own colors or let the original HTML document control your colors.

     Default: Let Document Override

Next you can choose standard or custom colors for hyperlinks.

     Default: Blue for links and purple for followed links

You can choose to have text in black or your own custom color.

     Default: Black

Finally, you can set the background color to default (grey) or a custom color.

     Default: Grey

If you select to have your own colors, you will be presented with a color options menu. In addition, you can work from a complete color palette and create your own colors.

Unless you have a requirement to select custom colors due to perhaps red-green colorblindness, you will probably wish to leave the colors at their default values.

One other reason to change the colors is if you are capturing screens as we have done while writing this book. In that case, you may want to change the background to white as it looks better in black and white printed pages.

Mail and News

Figure 11-7 shows the Mail and News page.

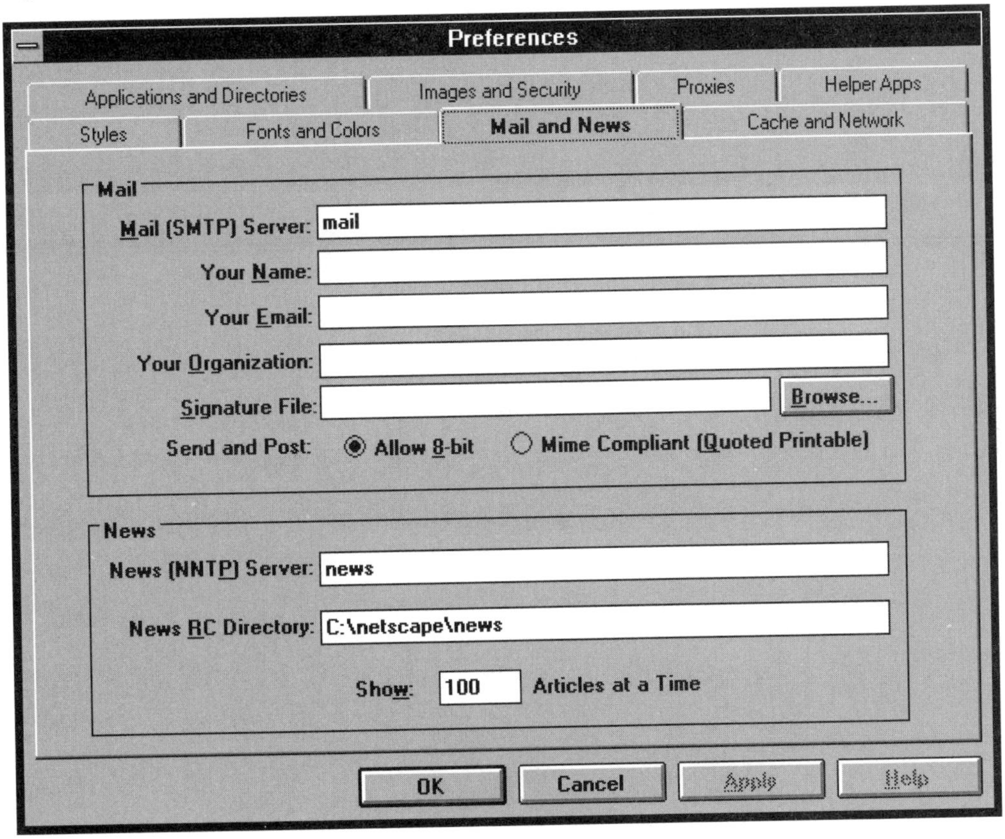

Figure 11-7
Mail and News

You should set your own E-mail address on the Mail and News Preferences page. Many Web sites request feedback or forms using E-mail. At a minimum, you will want to put your name and E-mail address on this page. If your provider offers an E-mail server, you can put this information on this form and use Netscape for E-mail.

It happens that this is one of the things Netscape doesn't do very well. You would be better off selecting an E-mail program such as Qualcomm's Eudora. (Netscape Navigator Personal Edition comes with Eudora Light.)

To subscribe to and to follow Usenet Newsgroups, you will need to enter the name of your provider's news server. You should contact your provider to see if they offer this service. If they do, then you will need to ask them for the name of their server. Put that in the News (NNTP) Server: form and you will then be able to use Netscape for Usenet newsgroups. (For more detail on Usenet News, see Session Eight.)

Cache and Network

Figure 11-8 shows the Cache and Network page.

Preferences

| Applications and Directories | Images and Security | Proxies | Helper Apps |

| Styles | Fonts and Colors | Mail and News | **Cache and Network** |

Cache

Memory Cache: `600` Kilobytes   [Clear Memory Cache Now]

Disk Cache: `5000` Kilobytes   [Clear Disk Cache Now]

Disk Cache Directory: `c:\netscape\cache`

Verify Documents: ⦿ Once per Session   ○ Every Time   ○ Never

---

Network Connections

Network Buffer Size: `6` Kilobytes

Connections: `4`   (Maximum number of simultaneous network connections)

[OK]   [Cancel]   [Apply]   [Help]

Figure 11-8
Cache and Network

This Preferences page allows you to tune the size of the memory (RAM) and also the amount of space on your hard disk that is used to "cache" information brought in from Web sites. You may have noticed that many images come in more quickly the second time you access a particular site. This is true because a copy of the images and the HTML have been placed on your computer in a directory called *cache*. On the Cache and Network page you can adjust the size of this storage.

Memory Cache: stores the pages you have just visited and allows you to navigate with the back and forward functions.

Disk Cache stores the HTML and images of places you have visited. As new space is needed, the older HTML and images are erased. You may keep more in the memory or disk cache by increasing the values.

Memory Cache Default: 600 Kilobytes

Disk Cache Default: 5000 Kilobytes (5 Megabytes)

You can also adjust the size of your network buffer to allow more data to be temporarily stored in your incoming buffer. You can also adjust how many simultaneous connections Netscape can use. With greater storage and a higher number of connections, you can increase Netscape's ability to bring in multiple images or to use multiple open Netscape Windows.

Network Buffer Size Default: 6 Kilobytes

Connections Default: 4 Maximum

Applications and Directories

Figure 11-9 shows the Applications and Directories page.

```
┌─────────────────────────────────────────────────────────────┐
│ ─                         Preferences                         │
├─────────────────────────────────────────────────────────────┤
│   Styles    │   Fonts and Colors  │   Mail and News  │  Cache and Network │
│ Applications and Directories │ Images and Security │ Proxies │ Helper Apps │
│                                                               │
│   ┌ Supporting Applications ───────────────────────────────┐ │
│   │                                                         │ │
│   │  Telnet Application: [                    ]  [Browse...] │ │
│   │                                                         │ │
│   │  TN3270 Application: [                    ]  [Browse...] │ │
│   │                                                         │ │
│   │  View Source:        [                    ]  [Browse...] │ │
│   │                                                         │ │
│   └─────────────────────────────────────────────────────────┘ │
│                                                               │
│   ┌ Directories ────────────────────────────────────────────┐ │
│   │  Temporary Directory: [C:\temp                     ]    │ │
│   │                                                         │ │
│   │  Bookmark File: [c:\netscape\bookmark.htm     ] [Browse...] │
│   └─────────────────────────────────────────────────────────┘ │
│                                                               │
│              [   OK   ]  [ Cancel ]  [ Apply ]  [ Help ]      │
└─────────────────────────────────────────────────────────────┘
```

Figure 11-9
Applications and
Directories

If you plan to use telnet to reach other sites on the Internet, you will need a telnet application program. To telnet to IBM systems with MVS or VM operating systems, you will need a TN3270 application program.

Those program directories and names should be entered here if you will use them from within Netscape.

The View Source allows you to specify your own choice of file viewer or editor. You can select a word processor program, but usually a simple editor is better.

      View Source Default: Netscape's viewer

Directories

You can pick your own directories and bookmark files here. The defaults are

      Temporary Directory Default: C:\TEMP
      Bookmark File Default: C:\NETSCAPE\BOOKMARK.HTM

Images and Security

Figure 11-10 shows the Images and Security page.

Preferences

| Styles | Fonts and Colors | Mail and News | Cache and Network |

| Applications and Directories | **Images and Security** | Proxies | Helper Apps |

Images

Colors: ⦿ <u>D</u>ither to Color Cube   ○ Use <u>C</u>losest Color in Color Cube

Display Images: ⦿ <u>W</u>hile Loading   ○ <u>A</u>fter Loading

---

Security Alerts

Show a Popup Alert Before:

☒ <u>E</u>ntering a Secure Document Space (Server)

☒ <u>L</u>eaving a Secure Document Space (Server)

☒ <u>V</u>iewing a Document With a Secure/Insecure <u>M</u>ix

☒ Submitting a <u>F</u>orm Insecurely

| OK | Cancel | Apply | Help |

Figure 11-10

Images and Security   The Images section of this Preferences: box allows you to set colors either closer to their intended color (*Dither*) or closest (*Closest*) to colors available on your computer.

         Colors Defaults: Dither to Color Cube

You can also choose the order of loading of images. You would do this if you were operating with a slow modem or low-speed connection and wanted to see the text first.

If you click on **After Loading**, the text will come in first and you will be able to click on the **Images button** on the toolbar to bring in an image of interest.

This is not the same as turning off Autoload Images in the Options menu. This choice only delays the loading of images until after the text has been downloaded. The Autoload choice either brings in images or waits for you to click on the Images button on the tool-bar.

Display Images Defaults: While Loading

Security

Netscape offers encryption security with certain Web servers. When the Netscape Navigator recognizes one of these servers, it will pop up warning alerts. You may chose to turn off these pop-ups. The default is

Security Default: Show All Alerts

Proxies

Figure 11-11 shows the Proxies page.

Preferences

| Styles | Fonts and Colors | Mail and News | Cache and Network |

| Applications and Directories | Images and Security | Proxies | Helper Apps |

Proxies

| ETP Proxy: | | Port: | 0 |

| Gopher Proxy: | | Port: | 0 |

| HTTP Proxy: | | Port: | 0 |

| Security Proxy: | | Port: | 0 |

| WAIS Proxy: | | Port: | 0 |

| No Proxy for: | | A list of: host:port, ... |

| SOCKS Host: | | Port: | 1080 |

| OK | Cancel | Apply | Help |

Figure 11-11
Proxies

The Proxies Preferences box allows you to use Netscape from *behind* a network "firewall" or "gateway." If you are connected to a local area network at a company, agency, or campus with a security system or firewall between your computer and the Internet, you will need to complete this screen to use the World Wide Web (and other services) on the Internet.

Contact your network or firewall administrator or technical support people and ask them for the types, names, and port numbers of the proxy servers and/or SOCKS gateway. Then complete this screen. You may need to seek technical assistance from within your enterprise.

If you are using a dial-up line, you will not need to do this.

If you are connected to an enterprise LAN *and* you are using a dial-up line with a modem to reach the Internet, contact your network administration people to be sure you are not creating a security problem.

Helper Applications

Figure 11-12 shows the Helper Applications page.

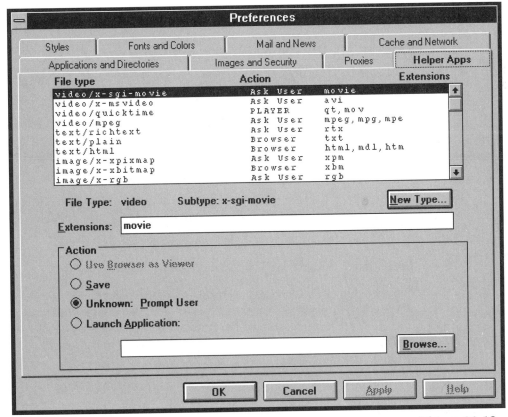

Figure 11-12
Helper Apps

The helper applications area was covered in some detail in Session Nine. Please refer to that session for details on setting up helper applications.

Staying Up-to-Date

The World Wide Web and Web browsers are evolving amazingly quickly. You will soon discover that there are newer (and perhaps better) versions of Netscape and its helper applications being offered.

There are three things to do here.

1. Become aware of newer versions.

2. Decide when to get the newer versions.

3. Obtain and install the newer versions.

We can offer you some guidance about each of these.

Becoming Aware of Newer Versions

To become aware of newer versions, you can do one of several things. The easiest is to visit Netscape's Home Page from time to time and to watch for announcements. You may also follow Usenet Newsgroups such as

comp.infosystems.announce

comp.infosystems.www.browsers.ms-windows

Finally, you can follow computer industry magazines and newsletters that cover the Internet and the Web. Two of our favorites are *Internet World* and *WebWeek.*

Deciding When to Get the Newer Versions

Some people like adventure and thrills more than others. Those who really enjoy thrills usually install new software the moment the first Alpha release becomes available. It's fun to be the first on your (electronic) block. It also takes considerable time as you are helping the developers find the bugs.

For those with less desire to be first, a Beta version will perhaps be more suitable. There will be fewer bugs and usually a more stable product.

Finally, there are people who just want to have the software work as well as possible and don't want to help test for bugs. These folks usually should wait for the shrinkwrap versions.

You will need to discover which type of person you are.

Obtaining and Installing the Newer Versions

Alpha and Beta software for newer versions of Netscape and its helper applications can usually be downloaded from the Internet. In Sessions Two, Eight, and Nine, we showed you how to find, get, and install both Netscape and the helper applications. You can follow these same techniques to get the newer versions.

You should always back-up your current versions and all their support files before installing a newer version. You may discover that the newer version is buggy or not quite ready for you. If you have backed up the previous version, you will have something to fall back on.

Session Summary

In this final session, we reviewed the ways you can set up Netscape Navigator to reflect *your own preferences*. We included the original default settings in case you want to return to the factory settings.

We concluded with suggestions on keeping up-to-date with the fast changing world of the Web and its premier browser - Netscape.

Happy Surfing!!

In this fourth part of Hands-On Netscape, we provide you with:

1. *A listing of Internet service providers.*

2. *A brief introduction to TCP/IP.*

3. *Instructions for downloading and installing win32s software.*

○ Internet Service Providers

○ TCP/IP Background

○ Downloading and Installing
   win32s Software

Appendix

A

Internet Service Providers

Every month, more providers are providing Internet connectivity. Since these providers exist all over the world, it could be tough finding them.

The following list from the Internet Society includes many many ISPs. There may be others closer to you, but this will give you a starting point.

NOTE: Not all providers offer SLIP or PPP services. You will have to contact them if you plan to use dial-up SLIP or PPP.

Internet Service Providers (Courtesy of the Internet Society)

AARNet (The Australian Academic and Research Network)

> GPO Box 1142
>
> Canberra ACT 2601
>
> AUSTRALIA
>
> Tel: +61 6 249 3385
>
> E-mail: aarnet@aarnet.edu.au

Area Served: Austrialia (Research and Education)

Services: FULL ACCESS

URLs: http://www.aarnet.edu.au, ftp://ftp.aarnet.edu.au/

Last Update: 7/23/94

a2i communications

1211 Park Avenue #202

San Jose, CA 95126-2924

E-mail: info@rahul.net

Area Served: San Jose, CA, area (408 area code)

Services: Terminal

ACM Network Services

PO BOX 21599, Waco, TX 76702

Tel: (817) 776-6876

FAX: (817) 751-7785

E-mail:: Account-Info@ACM.org

Area Served: world

Services: Terminal, UUCP

Last Update: 3/17/94

ACONET

Austrian Scientific Data Network

ACONET-Verein

Gusshausstrasse 25

A-1040 Wien

AUSTRIA

Attn: Florian Schnabel

Tel: +43 1 436111 or +43 222 58801 3605

E-mail: helpdesk@aco.net

schnabel@edvz.tu-graz.ada.at

schnabel@fstgss01.tu-graz.ac.at

C=at; ADMD=ada; PRMD=aconet; O=wep; S=helpdesk

C=at; ADMD=ada; PRMD=tu-graz; O=edvz;

S=schnabel

Area Served: Austria

Actrix Information Exchange

P.O. Box 11-410

Wellington NEW ZEALAND

Tel: +64 4 499-1708

FAX: +64 4 389-6356

E-mail: john@actrix.gen.nz

Area Served: New Zealand

Services: Terminal

Last Update: 2/23/94

Aimnet Corporation

20410 Town Center Lane, Suite 290

Cupertino, CA 95014

USA

Tel: 408-257-0900

Fax: 408-257-5452

E-mail: info@aimnet.com

Area Served: San Francisco Bay Area and Silicon Valley (408,
        415, 510 area codes)

Services: Terminal, Personal IP, FULL ACCESS

URL: http://www.aimnet.com

Last Update: 20 Feb 1995

Allied Access, Inc.

1002 Walnut St.

Murphysboro, IL 62966

Tel: (800)INET-DOM or (618)684-2255

E-mail: info@intrnet.net

Area Served: Southern Illinois and entire US

Services: Personal IP, nation-wide 800 access, Full Access

URLs: http://www.intrnet.net/, ftp://ftp.intrnet.net/

Last Update: 16 Apr 1995

Allura Inc.

> Postal Address:85 Merrimac Street; Boston, MA 02114
>
> Tel:617-723-8535
>
> FAX:617-723-2264
>
> E-mail: gourdj@allura.net
>
> Area Served: Washington DC & Boston, MA
>
> Services: Network Connections, IP, Business, Personal
>
> URL: http://www.allura.net
>
> Last Update: 2-Jun-1995

Alternex

> IBASE
>
> Rua Vicente de Souza 29
>
> 22251 Rio de Janiero
>
> BRAZIL
>
> Tel: +55 (21) 286 0348
>
> FAX: +55 (21) 286 0541
>
> E-mail: suporte@ax.apc.org
>
> Area Served: Brazil
>
> Services: Terminal, UUCP

America Online, Inc.

> 8619 Westwood Center Drive
>
> Vienna, VA 22182-2285
>
> USA
>
> Tel: 1-800 827 6364   or   +1 703 827 6364
>
> E-mail: joinaol@aol.com
>
> Area Served: US and Canada
>
> Services: Personal Information Service, Client/Server
>
> URL: FTP ftp://ftp.aol.com/

AMT Solutions Group Inc. - Island Net

    P.O. Box 6201 Depot 1

    Victoria B.C.

    V8P 5L5

    CANADA

    Tele: (604) 727-6030

    FAX: (604) 478-7343

    E-mail: mark@amtsgi.bc.ca

    Area Served: Victoria and area, British Columbia

    Services: Terminal

    Last Update: 1/28/94

Anomaly

    Anomaly - Rhode Island's Gateway To The Internet

    Tel: +1 401 273 4669

    E-mail   info@anomaly.sbs.risc.net

    Area Served: Providence RI (area codes 401, 508)

    Services: Terminal

ANS   CO+RE (Advanced Network and Services, Inc.

    1875 Campus Commons Drive, Suite 220

    Reston, VA 22091-1552

    USA

    Tel: 800 456 8267 or +1 703 758-7700

    Fax: 703-758-7717

    E-mail: info@ans.net

    Area Served: U.S. and International

    URLs: http://www.ans.net

        gopher://gopher.ans.net

    Services: Internet and WAN Services, Network Security

    Last Update: 16 Feb 95

ANTENNA

>Box 1513
>
>NL-6501 BM Nijmegen
>
>Netherlands
>
>Tel: +31(80)235372
>
>Fax: +31(80)236798
>
>Email: support@antenna.nl
>
>Area Served: Netherlands
>
>Services: Terminal, UUCP

Anterior Technology

>P.O. Box 1206
>
>Menlo Park, CA 94026-1206
>
>USA
>
>Tel: +1 415 328 5615
>
>FAX: +1 415 322 1753
>
>E-mail: info@radiomail.net
>
>Area Served: San Francisco Bay area
>
>Services: Terminal; UUCP; Wireless: E-mail.

APK, Public Access UNI*

>19709 Mohican Ave
>
>Cleveland, OH 44119
>
>Tel: data - 216-481-9436
>
>   216-481-1960
>
>   voice 216-481-9428
>
>FAX: 216-481-9428x33
>
>E-mail: zbig@wariat.org
>
>Area Served: Cleveland Ohio (216 area code)
>
>Services: Terminal, UUCP
>
>URLs: gopher://gopher.wariat.org/, http://wariat.org/
>
>Last Update: 6/17/94

ARIADNE

    NRC DEMOKRITOS

    153 10 Attiki-Athens

    Greece

    Tel: +30 1 6513392 or +30 1 6536351

    FAX: +30 1 6532910 o +30 1 6532175

    E-mail: postmaster@isosun.ariadne-t.gr

        postmast@grathdem (Bitnet)

        S=postmaster; OU=isosun; O=ariadne-t;

        P=ariadne-t;C=gr;

    Area Served: Greece

ARNES

    ARNES Network

    Jamova 39, Ljubljana

    SLOVENIA

    Attn: Marko Bonac

    Tel: +38 61 159199

    FAX: +38 61 161 029

    E-mail: helpdesk@ijs.si

        C=si; ADMD=mail; PRMD=ac; O=ijs; S=helpdesk

    Area Served: Slovenia

ARnet (Alberta Research Network)

    Director of Information Systems

    Alberta Research Council

    Box 8330, Station F

    Edmonton, Alberta

    CANADA, T6H 5X2

    Attn: RALPH PENNO

    Tel: +1 403 450 5188

    FAX: +1 403 461 2651

    E-mail: arnet@arc.ab.ca

        penno@arc.ab.ca

Area Served: Alberta, Canada

Services: Network Connectsions

Last Updated: 5 Jan 1994

ARNET

Ministerio de Relaciones Exteriores

Comercio Internacional y Culto

Reconquista 1088 - 1er Piso

(1003) Buenos Aires

Argentina

Tel: +54 1 315 4804

FAX: +54 1 315 4824

E-mail: noc-arnet@atina.ar, nic-arnet@atina.ar, postmaster@atina.ar

Area Served: Argentina (Government, Public Access and Academic inside Argentina)

Services: UUCP, Network Connections, Personal IP (experimental),

URLs: http://www.ar, gopher://gopher.ar, ftp://ftp.ar

Last Update: 7-May-1995

AT&T Mail

AT&T Mail Customer Assistance Center (ATTMAIL-DOM)

5000 Hadley Road

South Plainsfield, NJ 07080

Tel: 1 (800) MAIL-672   or   1-800-367-7225

in Canada   (613) -778-5815

in UK or the Republic of Ireland

0800-289-403 or ++44-

527-67585

in Europe +322-676-3737

in Japan 81-3-5561-3411

in the Pacific Rim   +852-846-2800

in Africa or the Americas +908-658-6175

E-mail: POSTMASTER@ATTMAIL.COM

Area Served: International

Services: Terminal; Messaging Access; Busniess Services

auroraNET Inc

5065 Anola Drive

Burnaby BC

Canada V5B 4V7

Tel: 604-294-4357 ext 115

FAX: 604-294-0107

E-mail: jcryer@aurora.net

Area Served: (Country or Region Served) Greater Vancouver,

Greater Toronto

Services: Full Access, Personal IP, Terminal, Website

hosting and development On-Line Information Services,

UUCP

URLs: WWW: http://www.aurora.net, FTP:
ftp://ftp.aurora.net

BALTBONE

Ants Work

Deputy Director

Institute of Cybernetics

Estonian Academy of Sciences

Akadeemie tee 21

EE 0108 TALLINN

ESTONIA

Tel: +007 0142 525622

FAX: +007 0142 527901

E-mail: ants@ioc.ee

Area Served: Baltic countries: Estonia,

Lithuania, Latvia.

BARRNet (Bay Area Regional Research Network)

    Pine Hall Rm. 115

    Stanford, CA 94305-4122

    USA

    Tel: +1 415 723 3104

    E-mail: info@barrnet.net

    Area Served: San Francisco Bay Area, Northern
        California

    Services: FULL ACCESS; Terminal, Personal IP.

    URLs: ftp://ftp.barrnet.net/

       http://www.barrnet.net/

    Last Update: 7/23/94

BCnet

    BCnet Headquarters

    515 West Hastings Street

    Vancouver, British Columbia

    Canada V6B 5K3

    Attn: Mike Patterson

    Tel: +1 604 291 5209

    FAX: +1 604 291 5022

    E-mail: Mike@bc.net

    Area Served: British Columbia, Canada

    Type of Service: FULL ACCESS

    URLs: ftp://ftp.bc.net/

       http://www.bc.net/

    Last Update: 7/23/94

BELNET (Belgian Research Network)

    DPWB-SPPS

    Wetenschapsstraat 8

    B-1040 Brussels

    Belgiun

    Tel: +32 2 238 3470

    FAX:

    E-mail: helpdesk@belnet.be

    Area Served: Belgium

BGnet

    Daniel Kalchev

    c/o Digital Systems

    Neofit Bozveli 6

    Varna - 9000

    BULGARIA

    Voice & FAX: +359 52 234540

    E-mail: postmaster@Bulgaria.EU.net

    Area Served: Bulgaria

The Black Box (blkbox.com)

    PO Box 591822

    Houston, TX 77259-1822

    Tel: 713-480-2684 voice, 713-480-2686 modem

    FAX: None

    E-mail: info@blkbox.com

    Area Served: Houston, Texas

    Services: Terminal, UUCP, Personal IP, Network

          Connections

    Last Update: 4/5/94

CA*net

> CA*net Information Centre
>
> Computing Services
>
> University of Toronto
>
> 4 Bancroft Ave., Rm 116
>
> Toronto, Ontario
>
> CANADA, M5S 1A1
>
> Attn: Eugene Siciunas
>
> Tel: +1416 978 5058
>
> FAX: +1 416 978 6620
>
> E-mail: info@CAnet.ca
>
>> eugene@vm.utcs.utoronto.ca
>
> Area Served: Canada

Capital Area Internet Service

> 6861 Elm Street, Suite 3E
>
> McLean, VA 22101
>
> USA
>
> Tel: +1 (703) 448-4470
>
> FAX: +1 (703) 790-8805
>
> E-Mail: info@cais.com
>
> Area Served: Washington-Baltimore Metropolitan
>
> Services: Terminal, Personal IP, FULL ACCESS, WWW
>
> Last Updated: 1 March 1995

CARNet (Croatian Academic and Research Network)

> J. Marohnica bb
>
> 41000 Zagreb
>
> Croatia
>
> Tel: +385 41 510 033
>
> FAX: +385 41 518 451
>
> E-mail: helpdesk@carnet.hr
>
> Area Served: Croatia (Non-Profit)
>
> Services: Network Connections, Terminal.

URLs: file://carnet.hr/

gopher://carnet.hr

Last Update: 7/23/94

CCAN (Computer Communication Access for NGOs)

121/72 Soi Chalermla, Phya Thai Rd.

Rajthevee, Bangkok 10400

Thailand

Tel: (66-2) 255-5552, 251-0704

FAX: (66-2) 255-5552

Email: ccan@peg.apc.org

Area Served: Thailand

CCI Networks, a division of Corporate Computers Inc.

4130 - 95 Street, Edmonton, AB, Canada, T6E 6H5

Tel: +1403 450 6787

FAX: +1 403 450 9143

E-mail: info@ccinet.ab.ca

Area Served: Edmonton, Alberta, Canada (1 Feb 1994)

Rest of Alberta during Q294

Services: Terminal, Personal IP, UUCP

Last Update: 3/24/94

CERFnet (California Education and Research Federation Network)

P.O. Box 85608

San Diego, CA 92186-9784

Tel: +1-800 876 2373   or   +1 619 455 3900

FAX: +1 619 455 3990

E-mail: help@cerf.net

Area Served: California and International

Services: FULL ACCESS; Terminal, Personal IP.

URLs: http://www.cerf.net, ftp://nic.cerf.net

Last Update: 2/16/95

Channel One Internet Services

 280-55 Metcalfe Street

 Ottawa, Ontario, K1P 6L5

 Canada

 Tel: +1 (613) 236-8601

 Fax: +1 (613) 236-8764

 Area Served: Canada & the U.S.

 Services: Full Access, Personal IP, On-Line Information

  Services, Messaging Access, UUCP, Wireless, ISDN,

  UUCP, Web Publishing

 URLs: WWW: http://www.sonetis.com

  Gopher: gopher://gopher.sonetis.com

  FTP: ftp://ftp.sonetis.com

 Last Update: 19-June-1995

Chasque

 Casilla Correo 1539

 Montevideo 11000

 Uruguay

 Tel: +598 (2) 496-192

 Fax: +598 (2) 419-222

 E-mail: apoyo@chasque.apc.org

 Area Served: Uruguay & Paraguay

 Services: Terminal, UUCP

CICNet (Committee on Institutional Cooperation Network)

 ITI Building

 2901 Hubbard Drive

 Pod G

 Ann Arbor, MI 48105

 Tel: +1 313 998 6102

 E-mail: info@cic.net

 Area Served: Minnesota, Wisconsin, Iowa,

  Illinois, Indiana, Michigan, and Ohio

Services: FULL ACCESS

Last Update: 7/23/94

Clark Internet Services

10600 Rt. 108

Ellicott City, MD 21045

VOICE: First dial Maryland Relay Service for hearing

impaired at 1-800-735-2258 then ask operator for

extension 410-730-9764

FAX: 410-730-9765

E-mail: info@clark.net (person)

all-info@clark.net (auto-reply info)

Area Served: Metro MD, DC, Northern VA

Services: Terminal, Full Access

Last Update: 3/17/94

Clinet Ltd

PL 503 / Tekniikantie 17

02150 Espoo

FINLAND

Tel: +358-0-4375209

FAX: +358-0-455 5276

E-mail: clinet@clinet.fi

Area Served: Finland

Services: Terminal

Last Update: 4/5/94

CNS (Community News Service)

1155 Kelly Johnson Blvd., Ste 400

Colorado Springs, CO 80920

USA

Tel: +1 719 592 1240   or   +1 800 748 1200

FAX: +1 719 592 1201

E-mail: service@cscns.com

Area Served: Colorado and US

Services: Terminal, UUCP, Business Services

Last Update: 2/24/94

Communications Accessibles Montreal (CAM.ORG)

2665 Ste-Cunegonde #002

Montreal, QC

H3J 2X3

Tel: +1 514 931 0749

FAX: +1 514 596 2270

E-mail: info@CAM.ORG

Area Served: Canada, QC: Montreal, Laval, South-Shore,

West-Island

Services: Terminal, Personal IP, UUCP

URLs: ftp://ftp.cam.org/CAM.ORG-info,
http://www.cam.org

Last Update: 7/23/94

CompuNerd Inc's DataBahn

408 S. Tejon, Suite 201

Colorado Springs, CO 80909 U.S.A.

Tel: 719 578-5425   FAX: 719 578-0478

e-mail: info@databahn.net

Area Served: Area Code 719 in Colorado, USA

Services: Full Access, Personal IP, UUCP, Terminal

URL: http://www.databahn.net

Last Update: 6-Jun-1995

Cooperative Agency for Library Systems and Services (CLASS)

1415 Koll Circle

Suite 101

San Jose, CA 95112-4698

USA

Tel: +1-800 488 4559   or   +1 408 453 0444

FAX: +1 408 453 5379

E-mail: class@class.org

Area Served: US

Services: Terminal; Special: Access for libraries in
the US.

COLNODO

Carrera 23 No. 39-82

Santafe de Bogota

Colombia

Tel: 57-2697181, 2444692, 2697202

E-mail: julian@colnodo.igc.apc.org

Area Served: Colombia

Colorado SuperNet

CSM Computing Center

Colorado School Mines

1500 Illinois

Golden, Colorado 80401

Attn: Ken Harmon

Tel: +1 303 273 3471

FAX: +1 303 273 3475

E-mail: kharmon@csn.org

info@csn.org

Area Served: Colorado

Services: FULL ACCESS

ComLink

Emil-Meyer-Str. 20

D-30165 Hannover

GERMANY

Tel: +49 (511) 350-1573

FAX: +49 (511) 350-1574

E-mail: support@oln.comlink.apc.org

Area Served: Germany, Austria, Switzerland, Zagreb, Beograd

Services: Terminal, UUCP

Community News Service

>1715 Monterey Road
>
>Colorado Springs, CO 80910
>
>USA
>
>Tel: +1 719 579 9120
>
>E-mail: klaus@cscns.com
>
>Area Served: Colorado Springs (719 area code)
>
>Services: Dialup Host.

CompuServe Information System

>5000 Arlington Center Boulevard
>
>P.O. Box 20212
>
>Columbus, OH 43220
>
>Tel: +1 614 457 0802   or   +1-800 848 8990
>
>E-mail: postmaster@csi.compuserve.com
>
>Area Served: U.S. and International
>
>Services: Personal Infortmation Service; Network
>>Connections.

CONCERT (Communications for North Carolina Education,
>Research, and Technology Network)
>
>P.O. Box 12889
>
>3021 Cornwallis Road
>
>Research Triangle Park, NC 27709
>
>USA
>
>Attn: Joe Ragland
>
>Tel: +1 919 248 1404
>
>E-mail: jrr@concert.net
>
>Area Served: North Carolina
>
>Services: FULL ACCESS , Terminal.

CONNECT

      The IBM PC User Group

      Attn: Alan Jay or Matther Farwell

      PO Box 360

      Harrow HA1 4LQ

      ENGLAND

      Tel: +44 0 81 863 1191

      FAX: +44 0 81 863 6095

      E-mail: info@ibmpcug.co.uk

      Area served: London area.

Connect

      Connect.com.au pty ltd

      129 Hawthorn Road

      Caulfield Victoria 3161

      AUSTRALIA

      Tel: +61 3 528 2239

      FAX: +61 3 528 5887

      E-mail: connect@connect.com.au

      Area Served: Australia: Melbourne, Sydney, Brisbane,

            Adelaide, Canberra, Perth

      Services: FULL ACCESS , Dialup Host, Terminal UUCP

      URL: http://www.connect.com.au/

      Last Update: 24 Feb 1995

Corinthian Internet Services

      PO Box 71,

      Artarmon, NSW 2064

      AUSTRALIA

      Tel 61 2 906 4333

      Fax 61 2 906 1556

      E-Mail: sales@ci.com.au

      Area Served: Australia: Sydney, Melbourne, Brisbane, Adelaide,
Perth, Canberra, Newcastle, Gold Coast and Cairns.

      Services: FULL ACCESS

URLs:

Last Update: 1 March 1995

CRL (CR Laboratories Dialup Internet Access)

Tel: +1 415 381 2800

E-mail: info@crl.com

Area Served: CA: San Francisco Bay Area;
continental US/800

Services: Dialup Host.

CRNet

National Academy of Sciences

Academia Nacional de Ciencias

San Jose

COSTA RICA

Tel: (506) 53 45 02

FAX:

E-mail: gdeter@NS.CR

Area Served: Costa Rica (Acedemic, NGO, and R&D
communities)

Services: Terminal, FULL ACCESS

Last Update: 4/5/95

CTS Network Services

A Division of Datel Systems, Inc.

4444 Convoy Street, Suite 300

San Diego CA 92111-3708

Tel: 619.637.3637

FAX: 619.637.3630

Data: 619.637.3660

E-mail: support@ctsnet.cts.com -- human response
info@ctsnet.cts.com -- automated responce

Area Served: San Diego County (619)

Services: dialup-host, personal information services,
FULL ACCESS, Messaging Access services,

UUCP, business services, special services

(include DNS, IDR, custom domain aliasing)

Last Update: 2/23/94

CYBER (The Cyberspace Station)

E-mail: help@cyber.net

Area Served: CA: San Diego (area code 619)

Services: Dialup Host.

CyberGate, Inc.

662 So. Military Trail

Deerfield Beach, FL 33442

Tel: +1 305 428 4283

FAX: +1 305 428 7977

E-mail: sales@gate.net

Area Served: Southeast & Central Florida

Services: Terminal, FULL ACCESS, Business

Services, UUCP, Personal IP

URLs: ftp://ftp.gate.net/,gopher://gopher.gate.net/,

http://www.gate.net/

Last Update: 7/23/94

DANTE

Lockton House

Clarendon Road

Cambridge CB2 2BH

UK

Tel: +44 223 30 29 92

FAX: +44 223 30 30 05

E-mail dante@dante.org.uk

s=sante; o=dante; p=dante; a=mailnet; c=fi

Area Served: Europe

Services:

URL: http://www.dante.net, gopher://gopher.dante.net

Last Update: 9/26/94

DASNET

>DA Systems, Inc.
>
>1053 East Campbell Avenue
>
>Campbell, CA 95008
>
>USA
>
>Tel: +1 408 559 7434
>
>Area Served: California and International
>
>Services: Terminal; Special: E-mail connectivity
>>services

Data Basix

>PO Box 18324
>
>Tucson, AZ 85731
>
>Tel: +1 602 721 1988
>
>FAX: +1 602 721 7240
>
>E-mail: Sales@Data.Basix.COM
>>RHarwood@Data.Basix.COM
>
>Area Served: Tucson, Arizona
>
>Services: Terminal.
>
>Last Update: 2/3/94

DataNet

>Telecom Finland
>
>P.O. Box 228
>
>Rautatienkatu 10
>
>33101 TAMPERE
>
>FINLAND
>
>Attn: Seppo Noppari
>
>Tel: +358 31 243 2242
>
>FAX: +358 31 243 2211
>
>E-mail: seppo.noppari@tele.fi
>
>Area Served: Finland

DENet (The Danish Network for Research and Education UNI-C)

    The Danish Computing Centre for Research and Education

    Building 305, DTH

    DK-2800 Lyngby

    DENMARK

    Attn: Jan P. Sorensen

    Tel: +45 45 93 83 55

    FAX: +45 45 93 02 20

    E-mail: Jan.P.Sorensen@uni-c.dk

              C=dk; ADMD=dk400; PRMD=minerva

              O=UNI-C; S=Linden; G=Steen

    Area Served: Denmark

DELPHI

    General Videotex Corporation

    1030 Massachusetts Ave

    Cambridge, MA 02138

    Tel: +1 800 544 4005

    E-mail: walthowe@delphi.com

    Area Served: U.S.

    Services: Terminal.

DFN

    DFN-Verein e. V.

    Geschaeftsstelle

    Pariser Strasse 44

    D - 1000 Berlin 15

    GERMANY

    Tel: +49 30 88 42 99 22

    FAX: +49 30 88 42 99 70

    E-mail: dfn-verein@dfn.dbp.de

              wilhelm@dfn.dbp.de

              rauschenbach@dfn.dbp.de

    Area Served: Germany

Digital Express Group

6006 Greenbelt Road, Suite 228

Greenbelt, MD 20770

Tel: 301-220-2020

FAX: 301-470-5215

E-mail: info@digex.net

Area Served: All regions, all areas, all communities

Services: Terminal, FULL ACCESS, Personal IP,

Messaging Access, Special

URL: http://www.digex.net

Last Update: 16 Feb 1995

Direct Connection

PO Box 931

London SE18 3PW

England

Tel: +44 (0)81 317 0100

Fax: +44 (0)81 317 3886

Email: helpdesk@dircon.co.uk

Areas Served: The UK (England)

Services: Terminal, UUCP

Last Update: 3/4/94

DKnet

EUnet in Denmark. See EUnet for further information.

DMConnection

> Doyle Munroe Consultants, Inc.
>
> 267 Cox St.
>
> Hudson, Ma 01749
>
> Tel: (508) 568-1618
>
> FAX: (FAX) (508) 562-1133
>
> E-mail: postmaster@dmc.com
>
> Area Served: New England
>
> Type of Services: FULL ACCESS, Terminal, UUCP
>
> Last Updated: 1/28/94

DPB

> Research and Technology Centre
>
> Section T 34
>
> P. O. Box 10 00 03
>
> D-W-6100 DARMSTADT
>
> Germany
>
> Tel: +49 6151 83 5210
>
> FAX: +49 6151 83 4639
>
> Email: G=walter; S=tietz; O=telekom; A=dbp; C=de
>
> Area Served: Germany
>
> Type of Services: X.400

EARN (European Academic Research Network)

> BP 167
>
> F-91403 Orsay CEDEX
>
> FRANCE
>
> Tel: +33 1 69 82 39 73
>
> FAX: + 33 1 69 28 52 73
>
> E-mail: grange%frors12.bitnet@mitvma.mit.edu
>
> Area Served: Europe and International
>
> Service: FULL ACCESS

EARN-France

European Academic Research Network - FRANCE

950 rue de Saint Priest

34184 Montpellier Cedex 4

FRANCE

Attn: Dominique Dumas

Tel: +33 67 14 14 14

FAX: +33 67 52 57 63

E-mail   BRUCH%FRMOP11.BITNET@pucc.Princeton.EDU

BRUCH@FRMOP11.BITNET (Bitnet)

Area Served: France

EarthLink Network, Inc.

3171 Los Feliz Blvd., Suite 203

Los Angeles, CA 90039

USA

Tel: 213-644-9500

Fax: 213-644-9510

E-mail: sales@earthlink.net

Area Served: Greater Los Angeles and Southern California area

Services: Personal IP, FULL ACCESS, Web servers

URL: http://www.earthlink.net

Last Update: 16 Feb 95

Ebone

 c/o TERENA, Singel 466-68,

 NL-1017 AW Amsterdam, The Netherlands

 Tel: +31 20639 1131

 FAX: +31 20639 3289

 E-mail: ebone@terena.nl

 Area Served: Europe and neighbouring countries

 Services: Network Services, Special - Global Internet connection

  for service providers

 URLs: http://www.ebone.net

 Last Updated: 26 Feb 1995

ECONNECT

 Sdruzeni Pro Snadne Spojeni

 Naovcinach 2 170 00 Prague 7,

 Czech Republic

 Tel: +42(02) 66710366

 Email: sysop@ecn.gn.apc.org

 Area Served: Czech Republic

EcuaNex

 12 de Octubre, Of. 504

 Casilla 17-12-566

 Quito

 ECUADOR

 Tel: +593 (2) 528-716

 FAX: +593 (2) 505-073

 E-mail: intercom@ecuanex.apc.org

 Area Served: Ecuador

 Services: Terminal, UUCP

ELCI

Box 72461

Nairobi

Kenya

Tel: +254 2 562 015 or +254 2 562 022

FAX: +254 2 562 175

Email: sysop@elci.gn.apc.org

Area Served: Kenya

Services: Terminal, UUCP

ELECTROTEX, Inc.

2300 Richmond

Houston, TX 77098

USA

Tel: +1 713 526-3456, 1 800 460-1801

FAX: +1 713 639-6400

E-mail: info@electrotex.com

Area Served: Houston, Texas, USA

URL: http://www.electrotex.com/

Services: Personal IP, FULL ACCESS, UUCP

Last update: 17 Feb 1995

EMAIL CENTRE

108. V. Luna Road, Sikatuna Village

Quezon City

Philippines

Tel: +632 921 5165

Email: postmaster@phil.gn.apc.org

Area Served: Philippines

Services: Email; local conferences

Last Update: 4/20/94

ENDA

> BP 3370
>
> Dakar
>
> Senegal
>
> Tel: +221 21 6027 or +221 22 4229
>
> FAX: +221 21 2695
>
> Email: sysop@endadak.gn.apc.org
>
> Area Served: Senegal
>
> Services: Terminal, UUCP

ERNET (Education and Research Community Network)

> Gulmohar Cross Road, Number 9
>
> Juhu, Bombay 400 049
>
> INDIA
>
> Tel: +91 22 436 1329
>
> FAX: +91 22 620 0590
>
> E-mail: usis@doe.ernet.in
>
> Area Served: India (Acedemic and R&D Communities)
>
> Services: UUCP, Network Conenctsion
>
> Last Update: 4/5/94

Eskimo North

> P.O. Box 75284
>
> Seattle, Wa. 98125-0284
>
> USA
>
> Phone:
>
> FAX:
>
> E-mail: nanook@eskimo.com
>
> Area Served: Seattle Washington Metro Area
>
> Services: Terminal
>
> URLs: file://eskimo.com/
>
> Last Update: 7/23/94

EUNET

Kruislaan 409

1098 SJ Amsterdam

NETHERLANDS

Tel: +31 20 592 5109

FAX: +31 20 592 5155

Fax problems: +31 20 592 9444

E-mail: info@eu.net

Area Served: Europe and International (Algeria,
Austria, Belgium, Bulgaria, Czech
Republic, Denmark, Egypt, Finland,
France, Germany, Greece, Hungary,
Iceland, Ireland, Italy, Luxembourg,
Morocco, Netherlands, Norway, Portugal,
Romania, Slovakia, Slovenia, Russia and
other parts of former Soviet Union,
Spain, Switzerland, Tunisia, United
Kingdom)

Service: FULL ACCESS , Personal IP, UUCP.

URLs: ftp://ftp.eu.net/
gopher://gopher.eu.net/
http://www.eu.net/

Last Update: 7/23/94

EuropaNET

DANTE (Delivery of Advanced Network
Technology to Europe Limited)

Lockton House

Clarendon Road

Cambridge, CB2 2BH

UK

Tel: +44 223 302 992

FAX: +44 223 303 005

E-mail: dante@dante.org.uk

Area Served: Europe (US, Canada, Rep. of Korea via
provision of intercontinental lines)

Services: FULL ACCESS, X.400, Special
(connection to a continental backbone)

EVERGREEN COMMUNICATIONS Libre Service

5333 N. 7th Street, Suite B-220

Phoenix, Az. 85014

USA

Tel: +1(602) 230-9330

FAX: +1 (602) 230-9773

E-mail: jennyu@libre.com

Area Served: Arizona (Phoenix,Tucson,Prescott,Casa
Grande,Sierra Vista,Flagstaff) Nevada
(Incline Village, NorthLake Tahoe, Reno,
Carson City, Las Vegas) New Mexico
(Albuquerque, Santa Fe) Mexico (Hispanic
Events) Four Corners (NM,AZ,UT,NV)
(Native American Events)

Services: FULL ACCESS , Terminal, UUCP,
Personal Information Services, Wireless

Last Update: 3/4/94

EZ-E-Mail

Shecora Associates, Inc.

P.O. Box 7604

Nashua, NH 03060

USA

Tel: +1 603 672 0736

E-mail: info@lemuria.sai.com

Area Served: USA and Canada

Services: Terminal.

FORTHnet

>Foundation for Research and Technology-Hellas (FORTH)

>FORTHnet - Institute of Computer Science

>Vassilika Vouton, P.O.Box 1385

>GR 711 10 Heraklion, Crete, Greece

>Tel: +30 81 391200

>FAX: +30 81 391201, 391601

>E-mail: pr@forthnet.gr, noc@forthnet.gr

>Area Served: Greece

>Services: FULL ACCESS , Personal IP (SLIP, PPP), UUCP, X.400.

>URLs: http://www.forthnet.gr/, gopher://gopher.forth-net.gr/,

>>ftp://ftp.forthnet.gr/

>Last Updated: 22 Feb 1995

Fnet Sylvain Langlois

>FNET Association

>11 rue Carnot

>94270 Le Kemlin-Bicetre

>FRANCE

>Tel: +33 1 45 21 02 04

>FAX: +33 1 46 58 94 20

>E-mail: contact@fnet.fr

>Area Served: France

Freelance Systems Programming

    807 Saint Nicholas Avenue

    Dayton, Ohio 45410

    USA

    Tel: +1 513-254-7246

    Data: +1 513-258-7745

    E-mail: Tkellar@Dayton.fsp.com

    Area Served: Dayton Ohio

    Services: Terminal

    Last Update: 2/23/94

FullFeed Communications

    359 Raven Lane

    Madison, WI 53705

    USA

    Tel: (608) 246-4239

    E-mail: info@fullfeed.com

    Area Served: Wisconsin

    Services: Terminal, Persional Information Services, Network
        Connections, Personal IP, UUCP, Business Services

    URLs:

      WWW: http://www.fullfeed.com

      FTP: ftp://ftp.fullfeed.com

      GOPHER: gopher://gopher.fullfeed.com

      LISTSERV: mailto:listserv@fullfeed.com

    Last Updated: 2/16/1995

FUNET (Finnish University and Research Network)

    P.O. Box 405

    SF-02101 ESPOO

    FINLAND

    Tel: +358 0 457 2711

    FAX: +358 0 457 2302

    E-mail: Markus.Sadeniemi@funet.fi

C=FI; O=FUNET; ADMD=fumail; S=Sadeniemi; G=Markus;

Area Served: Finland

URL: http://www.funet.fi

Last Update: 4/21/94

GARR (Gruppo Armonizzazione delle Reti per la Ricerca)

c/o CNR -Istituto Cnuce

Via S.Maria, 36

56126 Pisa

ITALY

Tel: +39 50 593360

FAX: +39 50 589354

E-mail: INFO@NIS.GARR.IT

C=IT; ADMD=GARR; PRMD=NIS; S=INFO

Area Served: Italy (Research and Education)

Services: Network Conenctions

URLs: ftp://ftp.nis.garr.it/garr/

Last Update: 7/23/94

GBnet

EUnet in Great Britain. See EUnet for further information.

GEONET

GeoNet Mailbox Systems

Tel: +49 6673 18881

E-mail: GmbH@geod.geonet.de

postmaster@geo5.geomail.org

Area Served: Germany

GLAIDS Internet BBS

    POB 20771 Seattle WA 98102

    Tel:206-323-7483

    FAX:

    E-mail:tomh@glaids.wa.com

    Area Served:Internet/Seattle

    Services:Terminal, UUCP.

    Last Update: 3/24/94

GlasNet

    Ulitsa Sadovaya-Chernograizskaya

    dom 4, Komnata 16, Third Floor

    107078 Moscow

    RUSSIA

    Tel: +7 (095) 207-0704

    FAX: +7 (095) 207-0889

    E-mail: support@glas.apc.org

    Area Served: Russia and other Commonwealth of

        Independent State's countries.

    Services: Terminal, UUCP

Global Enterprise Service, Inc.

    (was JvNCnet)

    John von Neumann Center Network

    6 von Neuman Hall

    Princeton University

    Princeton, NJ 08544

    Tel: +1 609 258 2400   or   +1-800 358 4437

    E-mail: market@jvnc.net

    Area Served: U.S. and International

    Services: FULL ACCESS , Terminal

GLUK - GlasNet-Ukraine, Ltd

    14b Metrologicheskaya str.

    Kiev, 252143 Ukraine

    Tel: +7 (044) 266 9481

    Fax: +7 (044) 266 9475

    E-mail: support@gluk.apc.org

    Area Served: Ukraine

    Services: Terminal, UUCP

GreenNet

    23 Bevenden Street

    London N1 6BH

    UNITED KINGDOM

    Tel: +44 (71) 608 3040

    FAX: +44 (71) 253 0801

    E-mail: support@gn.apc.org

    Area Served: International, Africa

    Services: Special: FTS (FidoNet) Polling Servies

Halcyon

    Dataway

    P.O. Box 555

    Grapeview, WA 98546-0555

    Tel: +1 206 426 9298

    E-mail: info@remote.halcyon.com

    Area Served: Seattle, WA

    Services: Terminal.

HEANET

    Higher Education Authority

    Fitzwilliam Square, Dublin

    IRELAND

    Attn: Mike Norris   or   John Hayde

    Tel: +353 1 612748 (Norris) +353 1 761545 (Hayden)

    FAX: +353 1 610492

E-mail: Mnorris@hea.ie   jhayden@vax1.tcd.ie

C-ie; ADMD=Eirmail400; PRMD=NRN; O=hes;

S=mnorris

Area Served: Ireland

HISTRIA (ABM-BBS)

Ziherlova 43 61

Ljubljana, Slovenia

Tel: + 38 61 211-553

Fax: + 38 61 152-107

Email: support@histria.apc.org

Area Served: Slovenia

HoloNet

Information Access Technologies, Inc.

46 Shattuck Square

Suite 11

Tel: +1 510 704 0160

FAX: +1 510 704 8019

E-mail: info@holonet.net

Area Served: Berkeley, CA (area code 510)

Services: Terminal, UUCP, FULL ACCESS .

Hong Kong Supernet

HKUST Campus

Clear Water Bay, Kowloon

HONG KONG

Tel: (+852)358-7924

FAX: (+852)358-7925

E-mail   info@hk.super.net

Area Served: Hong Kong and the ASEAN region

Services: Terminal, FULL ACCESS ,

Messaging Access, UUCP

Last Update: 2/23/94

HookUp Communications

>1075 North Service Road West
>Suite 207
>Oakville, Ontario, L6M 2G2
>Tel: (905) 847-8000
>FAX: (905) 847-8420
>E-mail: info@hookup.net
>Area Served: Ontario Canada, Canada-wide
>>(via 1-800 service)
>Services: Terminal
>Last Update: 4/5/94

HUNGARNET

>Computer and Automation Institute
>H-1132 Budapest
>18-22 Victory Hugo
>HUNGARY
>Attn: Istvan Tetenyi
>Tel: +36 11497352
>E-mail: postmaster@ella.hu
>Area Served: Hungary

IDS World Network Internet Access Service

>3 Franklin Road
>East Greenwich, RI 02818
>Tel: +1 (401) 884-7856
>FAX:
>E-mail: info@ids.net
>Area Served: Local Access in Rhode Island and
>>Miami, FL
>Services: Terminal, UUCP, Personal IP
>Last Update: 4/5/94

IEunet

> EUnet in Ireland. See EUnet for further information.

ILAN Israeli Academic Network Information Center

> Computer Center
>
> Tel Aviv University
>
> ISRAEL
>
> Attn: Ramat Aviv
>
> Tel: +972 3 6408309
>
> E-mail: hank@vm.tau.ac.il
>
> Area Served: Israel

INCA

> Internetworking Cape
>
> PO Box 6844
>
> Roggebaai 8012
>
> SOUTH AFRICA
>
> Tel: +27 21 4192690
>
> E-mail: info@inca.za
>
> Area Served: South Africa
>
> Services: FULL ACCESS , Terminal, UUCP

INDIALINK BOMBAY

> Praveen Rao, Indialink Coord. Bombay
>
> c/o Maniben Kara Institute
>
> Nagindas Chambers, 167 P.D'Mello Rd
>
> Bombay - 400 038
>
> Tel: 91-22-262-2388 or 261-2185
>
> Email: mki@inbb.gn.apc.org
>
> Area Served: India

INDIALINK DELHI

> Leo Fernandez, Coordinator Indialink
>
> c/o Indian Social Institute
>
> 10 Institutional area, Lodiroad,
>
> New Delhi

Tel: 91-11-463-5096 or 461-1745

Fax:91-11-462-5015

Email: leo@unv.ernet.in

Area Served: India

Individual Network e.V.

Tel: none

FAX Number: 02238/2593

E-mail: IN-Info@Individual.net

Area Served: Germany: Berlin, Flensburg, Kiel,
Hamburg, Bremen, Oldenburg,Muenster,
Osnabrueck, Hannover, Braunschweig,
Kassel, Dortmund, Magdeburg, Jena,
Chemnitz, Dresden, Rostock, Aachen,
Duisburg, Wuppertal, Koeln, Bonn, Kaarst,
Duesseldorf, Frankfurt, Saarbruecken,
Nuernberg, Ulm, Wuerzburg, Muenchen,
Konstanz

Services: FULL ACCESS , UUCP, Personal IP

Last Update: 3/23/94

INet

University Computing Services

Wrubel Computing Center

Indiana University

750 N. State Rd. 46

Bloomington, IN 47405

Attn: Dick Ellis

Tel: +1 812 855 4240

E-mail: ellis@ucs.indiana.edu

Area Served: Indiana

Services: FULL ACCESS .

Infiet, L.C.

> Internet Communications Services
>
> 211 East City Hall Avenue, Suite 236
>
> Norfolk, VA 23510
>
> USA
>
> Tel: +1 804 622-4289
>
> FAX: +1 804 622-7158
>
> E-mail: rcork@infi.net
>
> Area Served: Tidwater VA area,
>
>   USA via Compuserve Packet
>
> Network
>
> Services: Terminal, UUCP

InfoCom Networks

> P.O. Box 590343
>
> Houston
>
> TX 77259
>
> USA
>
> Tel: (713) 286-0399
>
> FAX:
>
> E-mail: sales@infocom.net
>
> Area Served: USA (713)
>
> Services: Full Access
>
> URLs: WWW: http://www.infocom.net
>
>   FTP: ftp://ftp.infocom.net
>
> Last Update: 19-Jun-1995

Infolan

> Infonet Service Corporation
>
> 2100 East Grand Avenue
>
> El Segundo, CA 90245
>
> Attn: George Abe
>
> Tel: +1 310 335 2600
>
> FAX: +1 310 335 2876

E-mail: abe@infonet.com

Area Served: International, including US, Europe,
    Canada, Hong Kong, Japan, Singapore, and
    Australia.

Institute for Global Communications (IGC)

(ECONET, PEACENET, CONFLICTNET, LABORNET)

18 De Boom Street

San Francisco, CA 94107

USA

Tel: +1 415 442 0220

FAX: +1 415 546 1794   TELEX: 154205417

E-mail: support@igc.apc.org

Area served: Worldwide

Services: Terminal; UUCP: Polling service.

InterAccess

9400 W. Foster Ave

Suite 111

Chicago, IL 60656

Tel: 800-967-1580

FAX: 708-671-0113

E-mail: info@interaccess.com

Area Served: Chicagoland

Services: Terminal, UUCP, Personal IP, Network
    Connections

Last Update: 4/5/94

Internet Africa

PO Box 44633

Claremont, 7735

SOUTH AFRICA

Tel: +27 21 6834370

FAX: +27 21 6834695

E-mail: info@iafrica.com

Area Served: Southern Africa

Services: FULL ACCESS , Terminal, Personal IP, UUCP

URLs: http://www.iaccess.za/

Last Updated: 2/16/1995

Internet(Bermuda) Limited

P.O. Box HM 2445

Hamilton   HM JX

BERMUDA

Tel: (809) 296-1800

Fax: (809) 295-7269

E-mail: info@ibl.bm

Area Served: Bermuda

Services: Personal IP, Network Services

URL: http://www.ibl.bm

Last Update: 26 Feb 1995

Internet Connect Services

202 West Goodwin

Victoria, Texas 77901

USA

Tel: +1 512 572 9987

Fax: +1 512 572 8193

E-Mail: staff@icsi.net

Area-Served: Victoria - Houston, Texas, USA

Services: Terminal, Personal IP, FULL ACCESS

URL: gopher://gopher.icsi.net, ftp://ftp.icsi.net,
    http://www.icsi.net/

Last Update: 21 Feb 1995

Internet Consult

abraxas dataselskab a/s

International House - Bella Center

2300 Koebenhavn S

DENMARK

Tel: +45 32 47 33 55

FAX: +45 32 47 30 16

E-mail: <info@ic.dk>

Area Served: Denmark

Services: UUCP, Personal IP

Last Update: 4/5/94

Internet Direct, Inc.

1366 East Thomas, Suite 210

Phoenix, Arizona 85014

USA

Tel: (602)274-0100

FAX: (602)274-8518

E-mail: info@indirect.com

Area Served: Arizonia

Service: Terminal

Last Updated: 1/28/94

Internet Initiative Japan, Inc. (IIJ)

Sanbancho Annex Bldg., 1-4 Sanban-cho,

Chiyoda-ku, Tokyo 102

JAPAN

Tel: +81 3-5276-6240

FAX: +81 3-5276-6239

E-mail: info@iij.ad.jp

Area Served: Japan

Services: FULL ACCESS , Personal IP, UUCP, etc.

URLs: http://www.iij.ad.jp

Last Update 21 Feb 1995

The Internet Solution

PO Box 3234

Parklands, 2121

SOUTH AFRICA

Tel: +27 11 447 5566

FAX: +27 11 447 5567

E-mail: info@is.co.za

Area Served: Southern Africa

Services: FULL ACCESS , Terminal.

URLs: http://www.is.co.za/

Last Updated: 6 Mar 1995

Internet Way

204 Blvd Bineau

92200 Neuilly sur Seine

FRANCE

TEL: +33(1)41 43 21 10

FAX: +33(1)41 43 21 11

E-mail info@iway.fr

Area Served: France

Services: Network Connections, Personal IP, Special

URL: http://www.iway.fr/

Last Update: 24 Feb 1995

InterNex Information Services, Inc.

1050 Chestnut St. Suite 202

Menlo Park, CA 94025

Tel: 415-473-3060

FAX: 415-473-3062

E-mail: info@internex.net

Area Served: San Francisco Bay Area

Services: Network Connection via ISDN, Messaging Access

Last Update: 4/5/94

Internex Online (Io)

1 Yonge Street Suite 1801

Toronto, Ontario Canada

M5E 1W7

Tel: 416 363-8676 voice

    416 363-4151 online registration/info

FAX: 416 369-0515

E-mail:: vid@io.org

Area Served: Toronto, Ontario, Canada

Services: Terminal

Last Update: 3/17/94

IntrepidNet

Intrepid Technologies, Inc.

PO Box 1322

Shepherdstown, WV 25443

Tel: 304 876-1199

Data:304 876-1175

E-mail: carl@intrepid.net

Area Served: Eastern West Virginia and the Tri-state area

Services: Personal IP, Dedicated access, Leased line access, WWW

URL: WWW http://www.intrepid.net

Last update: 7-Jun-1995

Ireland On-Line

West Wing, Udaras Complex

Furbo

Galway   Ireland

Attn: Barry Flanagan   <barryf@iol.ie>

Tel: +353 91 92727

FAX: +353 91 92726

E-mail: postmaster@iol.ie

Area Served: Ireland

Services: Terminal, Personal Information Services,

        Network Connections.

ISnet (The Icelandic Internet)

c/o SURIS

Taeknigardi

Dunhaga 5

107 Reykjavik

ICELAND

Attn: Marius Olafsson <marius@isnet.is>

TEL: +354 1 694747

FAX: +354 1 28801

E-mail: isnet-info@isnet.is

Services: FULL ACCESS

URL: http://www.isnet.is/

Area Served: Iceland

ITESM

Depto. de Telecomunicaciones y Redes

ITESM Campus Monterrey

E. Garza Sada #2501

Monterrey, N.L., C.P. 64849

MEXICO

Attn: Ing. Hugo E. Garcia Torres

Tel: +52 83 582 000 ext. 4130

FAX: +52 83 588 931

E-mail: hugo@mtecv1.mty.itesm.mx

Area Served: Mexico

IUnet

IUnet S.p.A.

V.le Monza, 253

I-20126 Milano

ITALY

Tel: +39 2 27002528

FAX: +39 2 27001322

E-mail: info@IUnet.it

Services: FULL ACCESS

URL: http://www.iunet.it, ftp://ftp.iunet.it

Area Served: Italy

Last Update: 2/16/95

Iway Internet Services

140 N. Phillips, Suite 404

Sioux Falls, SD 57102

USA

Tel: 1 800 386 IWAY / 605 331 4211

Fax: 605 335 3942

E-mail: info@iw.net

Area Served: USA - focused on South Dakota, Iowa, Nebraska, and Minnesota.

Services: FULL ACCESS , Terminal, Personal IP,

Messaging Access,Business Services

URLs: http://www.iw.net/

Last Updated: 15 Feb 95

JANET (Joint Academic Network)

JANET Liaison Desk

c/o Rutherford Appleton Laboratory

GB-Oxon OX11 OQX

UNITED KINGDOM

Attn: Chilton Didcot

Tel: +44 235 5517

E-mail: JANET-LIAISON-DESK@jnt.ac.uk

O=GB;ADMD=; PRMD=uk.ac; O=jnt;

G=JANET-LIAISON-DESK; (X.400)

Area Served: United Kingdom

JARING

MIMOS

7th Flr, Exchange Square

Off Jalan Semantan

50490 Kuala Lumpur, MALAYSIA

Tel: +60-3-254-9601 or +60-3-255-2700 ext 2101

FAX: +60-3-253-1898 or +60-3-255-2755

E-mail: noc@jaring.my

Area Served: Malaysia

Services: Terminal, UUCP, FULL ACCESS

URL: http://www.jaring.my

JIPS Joint Network Team

c/o Rutherford Appleeton Laboratory

Chilton Didcot

Oxon OX11 0QX

UNITED KINGDOM

Attn: Dr. Bob Day

Tel: +44 235 44 5163

E-mail: r.a.day@jnt.ac.uk

Area Served: United Kingdom

KAIWAN Corporation

12550 Brookhurst, Garden Grove, CA 92640

Tel: +1 714-638-2139

FAX: +1 714-638-0455

E-mail: info@kaiwan.com

Area Served: Southern California

Services: UUCP,Terminal, Personal Information
Services, FULL ACCESS ,
Messaging Access,Wireless,Business Services.

Last Update: 3/17/94

Karisi Communications, Inc.

61 Farrwood Avenue, Suite 11

North Andover, MA 01845, USA

Tel: +1 (617) 666-9559

Fax: +1 (617) 666-5299

E-mail: info@afrique.com

Area served: Africa

Services: UUCP, Special: FTS (FidoNet) polling.

Last Update: 16 Apr 1995

Karisi Communications Kenya Ltd.

    P.O. Box 49388

    Nairobi, Kenya

    Tel: +254 (2) 724349

    Fax: +254 (2) 724349

    E-mail: system@karisi.co.ke

    Area served: Kenya

    Services: UUCP, terminal.

    Last Update: 16 Apr 1995

Kuentos Communications, Inc.

    PO Box 26870

    GMF Guam 96921

    Tel: 671-637-5488

    FAX: 671-632-5641

    E-mail: pkelly@Kuentos.Guam.NET

    Area Service: Guam

    Services: Terminal, UUCP, Personal IP, Network

        Connections

    Last Update: 4/5/94

LANETA

    Tlalpan 1025, col. portales

    Mexico, df. Mexico

    Tel: (525) 2774791, (525) 5755395

    Fax: (525) 277-4791

    E-mail: soporte@laneta.igc.apc.org

    Area Served: Mexico

Latvian Internet Centre

    University of Latvia, Institute of Computer Science

    Rainis blvd. 29

    Riga LV-1459

    LATVIA

    Tel: +371 2 224730 or +371 2 212427

FAX: +371 8 820153

E-mail: postmaster@mii.lu.lv

Area Served: Latvia

Services: FULL ACCESS , Terminals, UUCP, USENet News

LavaNet, Inc.

733 Bishop St., Suite 1590

Honolulu, HI 96813

USA

Tel: 808-545-5282

FAX: 808-545-7020

E-mail: info@lava.net

Area Served: Island of Oahu (area code 808), Public Access

Services: Terminal, Personal IP

URLs: http://www.lava.net/

ftp://ftp.lava.net/pub/lavanet

Last Updated: 21 Feb 1995

Lega per L'Ambiente

via Salaria 280

I-00194 Roma

ITALY

Tel: +39/6-844-2277

E-mail: legambiente@gn.apc.org

Area Served: Italy

Los Nettos

  University of Southern California

  Information Sciences Institute

  4676 Admiralty Way

  Marina del Rey, CA 90292

  Attn: Ann Westine Cooper

  Tel: +1 310 822 1511

  E-mail: los-nettos-request@isi.edu

  Area Served: Los Angeles Area, Southern California

  Services: FULL ACCESS .

LvNet-Teleport

  204 Brivibas str

  Riga, LV-1039

  Latvia

  Tel: +371 2551133

  FAX: +371 2553261

  E-mail: vit@lynx.riga.lv

  Area Served: Latvia

  Services: FULL ACCESS , UUCP, Special (FTP-

      email gateway and Fax-email gateway)

Maestro Technologies, Inc.

  29 John Street Suite 1601

  New York, NY 10038

  USA

  Tel: +1 212 240 9600

  FAX:

  E-mail: info@maestro.com

  Area Served: New York

  Services: Terminal

  Last Update: 2/3/94

MANGO

    PO Box 7069

    Harare, Zimbabwe

    Tel: +263 4 303 211 EXT 1492

    Email: sysop@mango.apc.org

    Area Served: Zimbabwe

MBnet

    Director, Computing Services

    University of Manitoba

    603 Engineering Building

    Winnipeg, Manitoba

    CANADA, R3T 2N2

    Attn: Gerry Miller

    Tel: +1 204 474 8230

    FAX: +1 204 275 5420

    E-mail: miller@ccm.UManitoba.ca

    Area Served: Manitoba, Canada

MCI Mail

    1133 19th Street, NW

    7th Floor

    Washington, DC 20036

    Tel: +1-800 444 6245 or +1 202 833 8484

    E-mail: 2671163@mcimail.com

               3248333@mcimail.com

    Area Served: U.S. and International

    Services: Terminal; Messaging Access; Special: Business

        Services like FAX available

MichNet/Merit

    2200 Bonisteel Blvd.

    Ann Arbor, MI 48109-2112

    Tel: +1 313 764 9430

    E-mail: info@merit.edu or userhelp@merit.edu

Area Served: Michigan

Services: FULL ACCESS ; Terminal, Personal IP.

URLs: file://nic.merit.edu

Last Update: 7/23/94

MIDnet

Midwestern States Network

29 WSEC

University of Nebraska

Lincoln, NE 68588

Tel: +1 402 472 5032

E-mail: nic@westie.mid.net

Area Served: Midwestern States, including Iowa,
Kansas, Oklahoma, Arkansas, Missouri,
South Dakota, and Nebraska

Services: FULL ACCESS .

URLs: file://westie.mid.net/

Last Update: 7/23/94

MISNet   Mikrotec Internet Service

1001 Winchester Rd.

Lexington, KY, 40505, USA

Tel: +1 606-225-1488

Fax: +1 606-225-5852

E-mail: mailto:info@mis.net   mpolly@mis.net
mailto:wwweb@mis.net wwweb@mis.net

Area Served: Kentucky, U.S.A.

Services: FULL ACCESS, Personal IP, Dedicated (56k-T1)

URLs: http://www.mis.net/
gopher://gopher.mis.net

Last Update: 6/20/95

Milwaukee Internet X

    Mix Communications

    P.O Box 17166

    Milwaukee, WI 53217

    Tel: +1 414 962 8172

    E-mail: sysop@mixcom.com

    Area Served: Milwaukee, WI

    Services: Dialup Host.

MindVox

    Phantom Access Technologies, Inc.

    175 Fifth Avenue, Suite: 2614

    New York, NY 10011

    USA

    Tel: +1 800 - MindVox or +1 212 989 2418

    FAX: +1 212 989 8648

    E-mail: postmaster@phantom.com

    Area Served   New York

    Services: Terminal

    Last Update: 2/4/94

Mordor International BBS

    Tel: +1 201 432-0600 (data)

    FAX: +1 201 433-4222

    E-mail: ritz@mordor.com

    Area Served: New Jersey

    Services: Terminal

    Last Update: 3/17/94

MRNet

    Minnesota Regional Network

    511 11th Avenue South, Box 212

    Minneapolis, Minnesota 55415

    Tel: +1 612 342 2570

    E-mail: info@mr.net

Area Served: Minnesota

Services: FULL ACCESS , Personal IP.

URLs: ftp://ftp.mr.net/, gopher://gopher.mr.net/, http://WWW.MR.Net/

Last Update: 21 Feb 1995

MSEN, Inc.

628 Brooks Street

Ann Arbor, MI 48103

Attn: Owen Scott Medd

Tel: +1 313 998 4562

FAX: +1 313 998 4563

E-mail: info@msen.com

Area Served: U.S.

Services: FULL ACCESS , Terminal

URL: file://ftp.msen.com:/pub/vendor/msen"

Last Update: 7/23/94

MUKLA

Makerere University

Kampala, Uganda

Tel: +256-41-532-479

Email: sysop@mukla.gn.apc.org

Area Served: Uganda

Services: Terminal, UUCP

M V Communications, Inc.

P.O. Box 4963

Manchester, NH 03108-4963

USA

Tel: (603) 429-2223

FAX:

E-mail: mv-admin@mv.MV.COM

Area Served: New Hampshire

Services: Terminal

URL: file://ftp.mv.com:/pub/mv

Last Update: 7/23/94

NB*net

Director, Computing Services

University of New Brunswick

Fredericton, New Brunswick

CANADA, E3B 5A3

Attn: David Macneil

Tel: +1 506 453 4573

FAX: +1 506 453 3590

E-mail: DGM@unb.ca

Area Served: New Brunswick, Canada

NEARnet

New England Academic and Research Network

BBN Systems and Technologies

10 Moulton Street

Cambridge, MA 02138

Tel: +1 617 873 8730

E-mail: nearnet-staff@nic.near.net

Area Served: Maine, Vermont, New Hampshire,
        Connecticut, Massachusetts, Rhode Island

Services: FULL ACCESS , Terminal.

URLs: file://ftp.near.net

Last Update: 7/23/94

NeoSoft

3408 Mangum

Houston, TX 77092

USA

Tel: 1-800-GET-NEOSOFT or +1 (713) 968-5800

FAX: +1 (713) 968-5801

E-mail: info@NeoSoft.com

Area Served: Houston, Texas;New Orleans, LA; Northshore, LA

Services: Terminal, FULL ACCESS , UUCP, ISDN, Personal IP

URL: WWW: http://www.neosoft.com/

Last update: 2-June-1995

Netcom Online Communication Services

P.O. Box 20774

San Jose, CA 95160

Tel: +1 800 501 8649 or +1 408 554 8649

FAX: +1 408 241 9145

E-mail: info@netcom.com

Area Served: U.S.

Services: Terminal, Personal IP, FULL ACCESS , UUCP

URLs: ftp://ftp.netcom.com/

gopher://gopher.netcom.com/

http://www.netcom.com/

Last Update: 5/1/94

Net Direct

6251 N. Winthrop #5

Indianapolis, IN 46220

USA

Tel: +1 317-251-5252

FAX:

E-Mail: mrw@inetdirect.net

Services: Terminal, Personal IP, FULL ACCESS .

URLs: http://www.inetdirect.net/

Last Update: 1 Mar 1995

netILLINOIS

University of Illinois

Computing Services Office

1304 W. Springfield

Urbana, IL 61801

Attn: Joel L. Hartmann

Tel: +1 309 677 3100

E-mail: joel@bradley.bradley.edu

Area Served: Illinois

Services: FULL ACCESS , Personal IP.

netmbx

Feuerbachstr. 47/49, D-12163 Berlin

Tel: +49 30 855 53 50

FAX: +49 30 855 53 95

E-mail: netmbx@netmbx.de

Area Served: Berlin (Germany)

Services: Terminal, Personal Information Services,
FULL ACCESS , Messaging Access, UUCP

Last Update: 3/4/94

NETSYS COMMUNICATION SERVICES

992 SAN ANTONIO RD

PALO ALTO, CA. 94303

USA

Tel: +1 415 424 0384

FAX:

E-mail: info@netsys.com

Area Served: Palo Alto, California

Types of Service: Terminal

Last Update: 1/28/94

NevadaNet

University of Nevada System

Computing Services

4505 Maryland Parkway

Las Vegas, NV 89154

Attn: Don Zitter

Tel: +1 702 784 6133

E-mail: zitter@nevada.edu

Area Served: Nevada

Services: FULL ACCESS .

Nicarao

> CRIES
>
> Iglesia Carmen
>
> 1 cuadra al lago
>
> Apartado 3516
>
> Managua
>
> NICARAGUA
>
> Tel: +505 (2) 621-312
>
> FAX: +505 (2) 621-244
>
> E-mail: support@ni.apc.org
>
> Area Served: Central America, Panama.
>
> Services: Terminal, UUCP

NLnet

> Newfoundland and Labrador Network
>
> Department of Computing and Communications
>
> Memorial University of Newfoundland
>
> St. John's, Newfoundland
>
> CANADA, A1C 5S7
>
> Attn: Wilf Bussey   <wilf@morgan.ucs.mun.ca>
>
> Tel: +1 709 737 8329
>
> FAX: +1 709 737 3514
>
> E-mail: admin@nlnet.nf.ca
>
> Area Served: Newfoundland and Labrador, Canada
>
> Type of Services: Terminal, FULL ACCESS

NLnet

> EUnet in the Netherlands. See EUnet for further information.

NordNet

> Huvudskaersvaegen 13, nb
>
> S-121 54 Johanneshov
>
> SWEDEN
>
> Tel: +46-8-6000331
>
> FAX: +46-8-6000443

E-mail: support@pns.apc.org

Area Served: Sweden

NORDUNET

c/o SICS P.O. Box 1263

S-164 28 Kista

SWEDEN

Tel: +46 8 752 1563

FAX: +46 8 751 7230

E-mail: NORDUNET@sics.se

Area Served: Norway, Denmark, Finland, Iceland,
   Sweden.

North Shore Access

A service of Eco Software, Inc.

145 Munroe Street, Suite 405

Lynn, MA 01901

USA

Tel: +1 617 593 3110

FAX: +1 617 593 3110

E-mail: info@northshore.ecosoft.com

Area Served: Boston MA and Eastern Massachusetts

Services: Terminal, UUCP, USEnet News, Personal IP

URLs: gopher://gopher.ecosoft.com
   http://www.ecosoft.com

Last Update: 1/28/94

NorthWestNet

Northwestern States Network

NorthWestNet

2435 233rd Place NE

Redmond, WA 98053

Tel: +1 206 562 3000

E-mail: nic@nwnet.net

Area Served: Academic and research sites in Alaska,

Idaho, Montana, North Dakota, Oregon,
Wyoming, and Washington
Services: FULL ACCESS .
URLs: ftp://ftp.nwnet.net/, http://www.nwnet.net/
Last Update: 7/23/94

NovaNet, Inc. On-Line Communication Services
2007 N. 15 St. Suite B-5
Arlington, Va. 22201
USA
Tel: +1 703 524-4800
Fax: +1 703 524-5510
Email: sales@novanet.com
Area Served: U.S.
Services: Terminal, Personal IP, FULL ACCESS
URL: http://www.novanet.com/
Last Update: 21 Feb 1995

NSTN Nova Scotia Technology Network
General Manager, NSTN Inc.
900 Windmill Road, Suite 107
Dartmouth, Nova Scotia
CANADA, B3B 1P7
Attn: Mike Martineau
Tel: +1 902 468 6786
FAX: +1 902 468 3679
E-mail: martinea@hawk.nstn.ns.ca
Area Served: Nova Scotia, Canada

NTG / Xlink
Vincenz-Priessnitz-Str.3
D-76131 KARLSRUHE
GERMANY
Tel: +49 721 9652 0
FAX: +49 721 9652 210

E-mail   info@xlink.net

Area Served: Germany

Services: FULL ACCESS , UUCP, Terminal,

Special: PSI-Mail

Last Update: 3/17/94

NYSERnet

New York State State Education and Research Network

200 Elwood Davis Road

Liverpool, NY 13088-6147

USA

Tel: +1 315 453 2912

FAX: +1 315 453 3052

E-mail: info@nysernet.org

Area Served: New York State, U.S., and International

Services: FULL ACCESS , Terminal, Personal IP

URLs: http://nysernet.org

gopher://nysernet.org

Last Update: 16 Feb 1995

OARnet

Ohio Academic Research Network

Ohio Supercomputer Center

1224 Kinnear Road

Columbus, Ohio 43085

Attn: Alison Brown

Tel: +1 614 292 8100

E-mail: nic@oar.net

Area Served: Ohio

Services: FULL ACCESS , Terminal, Personal IP.

URLs: ftp://ftp.oar.net/

gopher://gopher.oar.net/

Last Update: 7/23/94

OLD COLORADO CITY COMMUNICATIONS

    2502 W. Colorado Ave. # 204

    Colorado Springs, CO, 80904

    USA

    Tel: +1 719-593-7575 or +1 719-632-4848

    FAX: +1 719-593-7521

    E-mail: thefox@oldcolo.com or dave@oldcolo.com

    Area Served: Colorado Springs

    Services: Terminal

    Last Update: 3/1/94

ONet ONet Computing Services

    University of Toronto

    4 Bancroft Avenue, Rm 116

    Toronto, Ontario,

    CANADA, M5S 1A1

    Attn: Eugene Siciunas

    Tel: +1 416 978 5058

    FAX: +1 416 978 6620

    E-mail: eugene@vm.utcs.utoronto.ca

    Area Served: Ontario,Canada

    Services: FULL ACCESS

    URLs: file://onet.on.ca/

    Last Update: 7/23/94

Opus One

    1404 East Lind Road

    Phoenex, AZ

    Tel: +1 602 324 0494

    FAX: +1 602 324 0495

    E-mail: info@opus1.com (machine)

                    jms@opus1.com (person)

    Area Served: Arizona

    Services: Terminal, FULL ACCESS

    Last Updated: 3/1/94

ORSTOM - Institut Francais de Recherche Scientifique pour le
          Developpement

     en Cooperation Service Informatique

    213, rue La Fayette

    75480-PARIS-Cedex

    FRANCE

    Tel: +33 48037609 or +33 67617510

    Fax:

    E-mail: renaud@PARIS.ORSTOM.FR

        michaux@ORSTOM.FR

    Area Served:

    Services: UUCP

    Last Update: 1/28/94

OLEANE

    35 Boulevard de la Liberation

    94300 VINCENNES

    FRANCE

    Tel: (33-1) 43.28.32.32

    FAX: (33-1) 43.28.46.21

    E-mail: info-internet@oleane.net

    Services: Network Services

    Area Served: FRANCE

    URL: http://www.oleane.net/

    Last Update: 07/23/94

OSLONETT Aksess

    Oslonett A/S Gaustadalleen 21

    N-0371 Oslo

    NORWAY

    Tel: +47 22 46 10 99

    FAX: +47 22 46 45 28

    E-mail: oslonett@oslonett.no

    Area Served: Norway

    Services: Terminal

    URLs: http://www.oslonett.no/index.html

    Last Update: 4/20/94

OTC Electronic Trading

    41 Mc Laren Street

    North Sydney,

    NSW 2060

    Australia

    Tel: +61 2 954 3055

    FAX: +61 2 957 1406

    E-mail: G=russell; S=fitzpatrick; O=et;

        P=easicom;A=otc; C=au

        S=helpdest; O=operations; P=enhanced;

A=otc; C=au

Area Served Australia

Type of Services: X.400

PACCOM

University of Hawaii

Department of ICS

2565 The Mall

Honolulu, HI 96822

U.S.A.

Attn: Torben Nielsen

Tel: +1 808 949 6395

E-mail: torben@foralie.ics.hawaii.edu

Area Served: Pacific Rim: Australia, Japan, Korea,
        New Zealand, Hong Kong, Hawaii.

Pacific Systems Group (RAINet)

9501 S.W. Westhaven

Portland, OR 97225

USA

Phone: (503) 297-8820

E-mail: rain-admin@psg.com

PACTOK

PO Box 284

Broadway 4006

Queensland, Australia

Tel: +61(7)257-1111

Fax: +61(7)257-1087

Email: pactok@peg.apc.org

Area Served: Pacific Islands

PADIS

Pan African Development Information System

Box 3001

Addis Ababa, Ethiopia

Tel: +251(1)511 167

Fax: +251(1)514 416

Email: sysop@padis.gn.apc.org

Area Served: Ethiopia

Services: Terminal, UUCP

PageSat, Inc.

8300 NE Underground Drive

Suite 430

Kansas City, Missouri

64161-9767

Tel: 800-989-7351 or 800-TYRELL-1

FAX: 816-741-5315

E-mail: root@tyrell.net

Area Served: U.S.

Services: FULL ACCESS , Terminal, UUCP,

Personal Information Services, Business

Services

Panix Public Access Unix

c/o Alexis Rosen

110 Riverside Drive

New York, NY 10024

Tel: +1 212 877 4854   or   +1 718 965 3768

E-mail: alexis@panix.com

jsb@panix.com

Area Served:New York City, NY

Services: Dialup Host, UUCP.

URLs: gopher://gopher.panix.com

Last Update: 7/23/94

PEACESAT   Pan Pacific Education and Communications Experiments

by Satellite

Social Science Research Institute

University of Hawaii at Manoa

Old Engineering Quad, Building 31

Honolulu, Hawaii 96822

Tel: +1 808 956-7794/8848

FAX: +1 808 956 2512

E-mail: peacesat@uhunix.uhcc.hawaii.edu

Area served: Pan Pacific region

Service: Special - Satellite stations with E-mail,
     network, and voice capability.

Pegasus Networks

PO Box 284

Broadway 4006

Queensland

AUSTRALIA

Tel: +61 (7) 257-1111

FAX: +61 (7) 257-1087

E-mail: support@peg.apc.org

Area Served: Australia, Pacific Islands, Southeast
     Asia

Services: Terminal, UUCP

Performance Systems International, Inc. (PSI)

510 Huntmar Park Drive

Herndon, VA 22070 USA

Tel: +1 800 827 7482 or +1.703.709.0300

FAX: +1.703.904.1207 or +1.800.fax.psi.1 (faxback info)

E-mail: info@psi.com

Area Served: U.S. and International

Services: FULL ACCESS , UUCP, Personal IP, Special

URLs: http://www.psi.net/
     gopher://gopher.psi.net/
     ftp://ftp.psi.net/

Last Update: 11 Mar 1995

Phantom Access Technologies, Inc. (MindVox)

    175 Fifth Avenue, Suite: 2614

    New York, NY 10011

    Tel: +1 800 - MindVox or +1 212 989-2418

    FAX: +1 212 989-8648

    E-mail: system@phantom.com or postmaster@phantom.com

    Area Served: New York

    Services: Terminal, Personal IP.

    Last Update: 7/23/94

Pingnet

    abraxas dataselskab a/s

    International House - Bella Center

    2300 Koebenhavn S

    DENMARK

    Tel: +45 32 47 33 93

    FAX: +45 32 47 30 16

    E-mail: adm@ping.dk

    Area Served: Denmark

    Services: UUCP

    Last Update: 4/5/94

Pioneer Neighborhood

    20 Moore St. #3

    Somerville, MA 02144-2124

    USA

    Tel: +1 617 646 4800

    FAX:

    E-mail: admin@pn.com

        autoreply@pioneer.ci.net

    Area Served: Boston MA

    Services: UUCP

    URLs: http://www.pn.com/

    Last Update: 7/26/94

The Pipeline

    150 Broadway, Suite 1710

    New York 10038

    USA

    Tel: (212) 267-3636

    FAX: (212) 267-4380

    E-mail: info@pipeline.com

    Area Served: New York and the World

    Services: Terminal, Messaging Access

    URLs: ftp://pipeline.com/

        gopher://pipeline.com/

        http://pipeline.com/infopage.html

    Last Update: 1/28/94

PIPEX

    Unipalm Ltd.

    Tel: +44 223 424616

    FAX: +44 223 426868

    E-mail: pipex@unipalm.co.uk

    Area served: United Kingdom

    Services: FULL ACCESS

    URLs: ftp://ftp.pipex.net/

        http://www.pipex.net/

    Last Update: 7/23/94

Piroska Giese KFKI-Research Institute for Particle and Nuclear
        Physics

    H-1121 Budapest

    Konkoly Thege ut 29-33

    HUNGARY

    Tel: (36-1) 169-9499

    FAX: (36-1) 169-6567

    E-mail: Piroska.Giese@rmki.kfki.hu

    Area Served: Hungary, High Energy Physics Community

    Services: Terminal, Personal Information Services

FULL ACCESS (dial-up and dedicated
network links to regional, national, and
international networks)

Prince Edward Island Network

University of Prince Edward Island

Computer Services

550 University Avenue

Charlottetown, P.E.I.

CANADA, C1A 4P3

Tel: +1 902 566 0450

FAX: +1 902 566 0958

E-mail: hancock@upei.ca

Area Served: Prince Edward Island, Canada

Services: Network Conenctions, Personal IP.

URL: ftp://atlas.upei.ca/

Last Update: 7/23/94

Portal Communications, Inc.

20863 Stevens Creek Blvd.

Suite 200

Cupertino, CA 95014

USA

Tel: +1 408 973 9111 or +1 800 433 6444

Fax: +1 408.725.1580

E-mail: info@portal.com or sales@portal.com

Area Served: U.S. and International

Services: Terminal, Personal IP, UUCP

URL: ftp://ftp.shell.portal.com, http://www.portal.com

Last update: 17 Feb 1995

PREPnet Pennsylvania Research and Economic Partnership
Network

305 South Craig Street, 2nd Floor

Pittsburgh, PA 15213-3706

Attn: Thomas W. Bajzek

Tel: +1 412 268 7870

E-mail: twb+@andrew.cmu.edu

Area Served: Pennsylvania

Services: FULL ACCESS .

URLs: file://nic.prep.net/

Last Update: 7/23/94

Prometheus Information Network Group, Inc.

Suite 284

4514 Chamblee Dunwoody Road

Dunwoody, GA 30338

USA

Tel: +1 404 818 6300

FAX: +1 404 458 8031

E-mail: questions@ping.com

Area Served: Georgia

Services: Network Connctions, Terminal, UUCP, Personal IP

Last Update: 2/3/94

PSCNET

Pittsburgh Supercomputing Center Network

Pittsburgh Supercomputing Center

4400 5th Avenue

Pittsburgh, PA 15213

Attn: Eugene Hastings

Tel: +1 412 268 4960

E-mail: pscnet-admin@psc.edu

Area Served: Eastern U.S. (Pennsylvania, Ohio, and

West Virginia)

Services: FULL ACCESS .

RARE

    RARE Secretariat

    Singel 466-468

    NL-1017 AW

    Amsterdam

    NETHERLANDS

    Tel: +31 20 639 1131

    FAX: +31 20 639 3289

    E-mail: raresec@rare.nl

    Area Served: Europe

    Services: Special: Network Information Center (NIC)

    URLs: WWW http://www.rare.net

        FTP ftp://ftp.rare.net

RCCN Vasco Freitas

    CCES

    Universidade do Minho

    Largo do Paco

    P-4719 Braga Codex

    PORTUGAL

    Attn: Dr. Vasco Freitas

    Tel: +351 53 612257 or +351 53 604475

    E-mail: ip-adm@rccn.net

        C=pt; ADMD= ; PRMD=fccn; O=ce; S=Freitas;

        G=Vasco;

    Area Served: Portugal (Research and Education)

    Services: FULL ACCESS

    URLs: file://ftp.rccn.net/

    Last Update: 7/23/94

RED400

>   Serge Aumont
>
>   CICB
>
>   Campus de Beaulieu
>
>   35042 Rennes
>
>   FRANCE
>
>   or
>
>   Paul-Andre Pays
>
>   INRIA
>
>   Domaine De Voluceau
>
>   Rocquencourt
>
>   BP 105
>
>   78150 Le Chesnay Cedex
>
>   FRANCE
>
>   Tel: +33 1 39 63 54 58
>
>   E-mail: contact-red@cicb.fr
>
>   > C=FR; ADMD=atlas; PRMD=cicb; S=contact-red;
>
>   Area Served: France

REDID

>   Asesor Cientifico Union Latina
>
>   APTD0 2972
>
>   Santo Domingo
>
>   REPUBLIC DOMINICANA
>
>   Attn: Daniel Pimienta
>
>   Tel: +1 809 689 4973   or   +1 809 535 6614
>
>   FAX: +1 809 535 6646   TELEX: 1 346 0741
>
>   E-mail: pimienta!daniel@redid.org.do
>
>   Area Served: Dominican Republic

Spanish Research & Academic Network

>   Centro de Comunicaciones CSIC RedIRIS
>
>   Serrano 142
>
>   Madrid E-28006

SPAIN

Tel: +34 1 5855150

FAX: +34 1 5855146

E-mail: infoiris@rediris.es

Area Served: Spain (Research & Academic)

Services: Full Access, On-Line Information Services,
   Messaging Access, X.400, X.500

URLs: WWW: http://www.rediris.es

   Gopher: gopher://gopher.rediris.es

   FTP: ftp://ftp.rediris.es

Last Update: 8-Jun-1995

Relcom (Russian ELectronic COMmunication)

6/1 Ovchinnikovskaya nab.

113035 Moscow

RUSSIA

Tel: +7 095 230 4022   or   +7 095 233 0670

FAX: +7 095 233 5016

E-mail: info@hq.demos.su

Area Served: Russia, CIS, and the Baltic States

URL: http://hpdemos.demos.su/

Last Update: 4/21/94

RESTENA

6 Rue Coudenhove Kalergi

L-1359

LUXEMBOURG

Attn: Antoine Barthel

Tel: +352 424409

E-mail: admin@restena.lu

   C=lu; ADMD=pt; PRMD=restena; O=restena;
   S=admin

RISCnet

      InteleCom Data Systems

      11 Franklin Road

      East Greenwich, RI 02818

      Attn: Andy Green

      Tel: +1 401 885 6855

      E-mail: info@nic.risc.net

      Area Served: Rhode Island, New England

      Services: FULL ACCESS , Terminal.

RISQ

      Reseau Interordinateurs Scientifique Quebecois

      Centre de Recherche Informatique de Montreal (CRIM)

      3744, Jean-Brillant, Suite 500

      Montreal, Quebec

      CANADA, H3T 1P1

      Attn: Bernard Turcotte

      Tel: +1 514 340 5700

      FAX: +1 514 340 5777

      E-mail: turcotte@crim.ca

      Area Served: Quebec, Canada

RustNet

      6905 Telegraph Road, Suite 315

      Bloomfield, MI 48301

      Tel: +1 810 650 6812

      E-mail: info@rust.net or help@rust.net

      Area Served: Southeastern Lower Michigan

      Services: Network Services, Personal IP

      URLs: ftp://ftp.rust.net, http://www.rust.net

      Last Update: 26 Feb 1995

SANET (Slovak Academic NETwork)

Vypoctove stredisko SAV

Dubravska cesta 9

842 35 Bratislava

Slovakia

Tel: +42 (7) 374422

FAX:

E-mail: bobovsky@savba.cs

Area Served: Slovakia

SANGONET

13th floor Longsbank Building

187 Bree Street

Johannesburg 2000

South Africa

Tel: +27 (11) 838-6944

Fax: +27 (11) 838-6310

E-mail: support@wn.apc.org

Area Served: South Africa

Services: Terminal, UUCP

SASK#net

Computing Services

56 Physics

University of Saskatchewan

Saskatoon, Saskatchewan

CANADA, S7N 0W0

Attn: Dean Jones

Tel: +1 306 966 4860

FAX: +1 306 966 4938

E-mail: dean.jones@usask.ca

Area Served: Saskatchewan, Canada

Services: Network Connections, Terminal, UUCP

Last Updated:

SatelLife

> Associate Director of Operations
>
> SatelLife-U.S.A.,
>
> 126 Rogers Street
>
> Cambridge, MA 02142 U.S.A.
>
> Attn: Jon Metzger
>
> Tel: (617) 868-8522
>
> FAX: (617) 868-6647
>
> E-mail: pnsatellife@igc.apc.org
>
> Area Served: International Medical Community

SatelNET

> 2269 S. University Drive, Box 159
>
> Davie FL 33324
>
> USA
>
> Tel: +1 (305) 434 7340
>
> FAX: +1 (305) 680-9848
>
> E-mail: root@satelnet.org
>
> Area Served: South-East Florida
>
> Services: Terminal
>
> Last Update: 3/4/94

SDSCnet

> San Diego Supercomputer Center Network
>
> San Diego Supercomputer Center
>
> P.O. Box 85608
>
> San Diego, CA 92186-9784
>
> Attn: Paul Love
>
> Tel: +1 619 534 5043
>
> E-mail: loveep@sds.sdsc.edu
>
> Area Served: San Diego Area, Southern California
>
> Services: FULL ACCESS .

Seicom Computer GmbH / NO Carrier e.V

    P.O BOX 7165

    72784 PFULLINGEN

    GERMANY

    Tel: +49 7121 9770-0

    FAX: +49 7121 9770-19

    E-mail: info@seicom.de / no-carrier@schwaben.de

    Area Served: Southern Germany { Tuebingen (07071)

            Reutlingen (07121), Stuttgart (0711) }

    Services: Terminal, Network Connection, UUCP, X.400

    Last Update: 3/17/94

SESQUINET

    Texas Sesquicentennial Network

    Office of Networking and Computing Systems

    Rice University

    Houston, TX 77251-1892

    Tel: +1 713 527 4988

    E-mail: info@sesqui.net

    Area Served: Texas

    Services: FULL ACCESS .

    URLs: ftp.sesqui.net/pub/sesquinet/"

    Last Update: 7/23/94

Sierra-Net

    PO Box 3709

    Incline Village, NV 89450

    USA

    Tel: 702-832-6911

    E-mail: giles@sierra.net

    Area Served: Northern Nevada

    Services: Personal IP

    URL: http://www.sierra.net

    Last Update: 2/16/95

SingNet

      Singapore Telecommmunications Limited

      31 Exeter Road, #02-00, Podium Block

      Comcentre, Singapore 0923

      Tel: +65 730-8079

      FAX: +65 732-1272

      E-mail: sales@singnet.com.sg

      Area Served: Singapore

      Services: Personal IP, Full Access, Terminal, UUCP, WWW

      URL: WWW http://www.singnet.com.sg

      Last Update: 7-Jun-1995

SoftAware

      4676 Admiralty Way

      Suite 410

      Marina del Rey, CA 90292

      Tel: +1 310 305 0275

      FAX:

      E-mail: info@softaware.com

      Area served: Los Angeles, U.S.

      Services: Full Access

      URLs: http://www.softaware.com/

      Last Update: 1-June-1995

South Coast Computing Services, Inc.

    P.O. Box 270355

    Houston TX 77277-0355

    USA

    Tel: +1 713-661-3301

    FAX: +1 713-661-0633

    E-mail: info@sccsi.com

    Area Served: Houston, TX

    Services: Terminal, FULL ACCESS , Personal IP,

        UUCP

    Last Update: 4/24/94

Speedway Free Access

    Tel: +1 503 520 2222

    FAX: N/A

    E-mail: info@speedway.net

    Area Served: Most of U.S. plus rest of world

    Services: Terminal, Personal Information Services,

        FULL ACCESS , UUCP

    Last Update: 3/17/94

Sprint/Centel-Florida

    1313 Blair Stone Rd.

    Tallahassee, Fl 32316

    USA

    Tel: +1 904-599-1373

    FAX: +1 904-656-6133

    E-mail: info@cntfl.com

    Area Served: North Florida

    Services: FULL ACCESS

    URLs: http://www.cntfl.com

    Last Update: 16 Feb 1995

Sprint NSFNET ICM

> Sprint NSFNET International Connections Manager
>
> Attn: Robert Collet
>
> Tel: +1 703 904 2230
>
> E-mail: rcollet@icm1.icp.net
>
> Area Served: International
>
> Services: International network Connections to NSFNET; operates under cooperative agreement with NSF and conforms to CCIRN guidelines.

SprintLink

> VARESA0115
>
> 12502 Sunrise Valley Dr.
>
> Reston, VA 22096-0002 USA
>
> Tel: +1 800 817 7755
>
> E-mail: info@sprintlink.net
>
> Area Served: U.S. and International
>
> Services: Dedicated Connections (56k-DS3)
>
> URLs: http://www.sprintlink.net,
>   ftp://ftp.sprintlink.net
>
> Last Updated: 24 Feb 95

Structured Network Services, Inc.

15635 SE 114th Ave

Ste. 201

Clackamas, OR 97015

USA

Tel: +1 503 656 3530 or 800 881 0962

FAX: +1 503 656 3235

E-mail: info@structured.net (auto reply) or sales@structured.net

Area Served: Oregon, Washington

Services: Dedicated Connections (56k-DS3)

URLs: http://www.structured.net

Last Updated: 16 Feb 95

SUNET

UMDAC

S-901 87 Umea

SWEDEN

Attn: Hans Wallberg or Bjorn Eriksen

Tel: +46 90 16 56 45

FAX: +46 90 16 67 62

E-mail: postmaster@sunic.sunet.se

Area Served: Sweden

SURAnet   Southeastern Universities Research Association Network

1353 Computer Science Center

University of Maryland

College Park, Maryland 20742-2411

Attn: Jack Hahn

Tel: +1 301 982 4600

E-mail: marketing@sura.net

Area Served: Southeastern U.S. (Alabama, Florida, Georgia, Kentucky, Louisiana, Mississippi, North Carolina, South Carolina, Tennessee, Virginia, and West Virginia)

Services: FULL ACCESS .

URLs: http://www.sura.net/, ftp://ftp.sura.net/

Last Update: 7/23/94

SURFnet

P.O. Box 19035

NL-3501 DA Utrecht

THE NETHERLANDS

Tel: +31 30310290

E-mail: info@surfnet.nl

   c=nl, ADMD=400net, PRMD=SURF, O=SURFnet,

   S=info

Area served: The Netherlands (Research and Education)

Services: FULL ACCESS

URLs: file://ftp.nic.surfnet.nl/surfnet/

Last Update: 7/23/94

SwipNet AB

P.O.Box 62

S-164 94 KISTA

Sweden

Tel: +46 8-6324058

Fax: +46 8-6324200

E-mail wallner@swip.net

Area Served: Sweden

Services: Terminal, UUCP

Last Update: 3/4/94

SWITCH

SWITCH Head Office

Limmatquai 138

CH-8001 Zurich

SWITZERLAND

Tel: +41 1 256 5454 or +41 1 268 15 15

FAX: +41 1 261 8133

E-mail: hostmaster@switch.ch

C=CH;ADMD=arCom;PRMD=SWITCH;O=SWITCH;

S=Hostmaster;

Area Served: Switzerland (Research and Education)

Services: FULL ACCESS

URLs: file://nic.switch.ch/network/

Last Update: 7/23/94

Systems Solutions (SSNet)

1254 Lorewood Grove Road

Tel: (302) 378-1386 (800) 331-1386

FAX: (302) 378-3871

E-mail:: sharris@ssnet.com, info@ssnet.com

Area Served: Delaware, (302)

Services: Terminal, UUCP

Last Update: 3/17/94

TANet

Computer Center, Ministry of Education

12th Fl, No. 106

Sec. 2, Hoping E. Road

Taipei, Taiwan

Attn: Chen Wen-Sung

Tel: +886 2 7377010

FAX: +886 2 7377043

E-mail: nisc@twnmoe10.edu.tw

Area Served: Taiwan (Research and Education)

Services: FULL ACCESS

URLs: http://www.edu.tw, ftp://ftp.edu.tw

Last Update: 7/23/94

TECHNET

    National University of Singapore

    10 Kent Ridge Crescent

    SINGAPORE 0511

    Tel: (65) 772-3119

    FAX:

    E-mail: help@solomon.technet.sg

    Area Served: Singapore (Research and Education)

    Services: Terminal, UUCP, Personal IP, FULL ACCESS

    URLs: ftp://ftp.technet.sg/, gopher://gopher.technet.sg,
        http://www.technet.sg/

    Last Update: 4/5/94

TELEMEMO (Telecom Australia)

    1/181 Victoria Parade

    Collingwood

    VICTORIA 3066

    Australia

    Tel: +61 3 4121539/4121535/4121078

    FAX: +61 3 4121548/4121545/6637941

    E-mail: G=peter; S=kelleher; O=telecom; A=telememo;
        C=au

    Area Served: Australia

    Services: X.400

Telerama Public Access Internet

    16 Southern Avenue

    Pittsburgh, PA 15211

    USA

    Tel: +1 412 481 3505

    FAX: +1 412 481 8568

    E-Mail: info@telerama.lm.com

    Area Served: Western Pennsylvania, USA

    Services: Terminal, Personal Information Services, Network

Connections, Personal IP, UUCP, Business services,

URLs: ftp://ftp.lm.com/info

http://www.lm.com/about.html

gopher://gopher.lm.com

Last Updated: 20 Feb 1995

Texas Metronet, Inc.

860 Kinwest Parkway (Suite 179)

Irving, Texas 75063-3440

Tel: +1 214 705 2900

FAX: +1 214 401 2802

E-mail :   info@metronet.com

Area Served: Terminal, UUCP, Personal IP

Last Update: 2/4/94

THEnet

Texas Higher Education Network

Computation Center

University of Texas

Austin, TX 78712

Tel: +1 512 471 2400

E-mail: info@nic.the.net

Area Served: Texas

Services: FULL ACCESS .

Last Update: 7/23/94

TIPnet

Technical Sales and Support

MegaCom AB

Kjell Simenstad

121 80 Johanneshov

Stockholm

SWEDEN

Tel: +46 8 780 5616

FAX: +46 8 686 0213

E-mail: info@tip.net or info-eng@tip.net for English

Area Served: Sweden

Services: Network Conenctions

Last Update: 7/23/94

TMX - The Message eXchange Pty Ltd

1st Fl, 2 King Street

Newtown NSW 2042

AUSTRALIA

Tel: +61 2 550-4448

FAX: +61 2 519-2551

E-mail info@tmx.com.au

Area Served: Australia: Sydney, Melbourne, Brisbane, Adelaide,
   Darwin

Services: FULL ACCESS , Personal IP, Terminal, Special

URL: http://www.tmx.com.au

Last Update: 24 Feb 1995

TUVAKA

Ege Universitesi

Bilgisayar Arastirma ve Uygulama Merkezi

Bornova, Izmir 35100

TURKEY

Attn: Esra Delen

Tel: +90 51 887228

E-mail: Esra@ege.edu.tr

              Esra@trearn.bitnet

Area Served: Turkey

UKnet

UKnet Support Group

Computing Laboratory

University of Kent

Canterbury

Kent CT2 7NF

UNITED KINGDOM

Tel: +44 227 475497, and +44 227 475415

FAX: +44 227 762811

E-mail   Postmaster@uknet.ac.uk

/S=postmaster/o=UKnet/PRMD=UK.AC

/ADMD=GOLD 400/C=GB/

Area Served: United Kingdom

UnBol/BolNet

Prof. Clifford Paravicini

Facultad de Ingenieria Electronica

Univ. Mayor de San Andres

La Paz

BOLIVA

E-mail: clifford@unbol.bo

Area Served: Bolivia

UNINETT

Postboks

6883 Elgeseter N-7002

Trondheim

NORWAY

Tel: +47 73 592980

FAX: +47 73 596450

E-mail: sekretariat@uninett.

Area Served: Norway

Service Network Connections

URLs:

ftp://ftp.aun.uninett.no

gopher://gopher.aun.uninett.no

http://aun.uninett.no

Last Update: 4/21/94

UNINET-ZA Project

    Foundation for Research Development

    P.O. Box 2600

    Pretoria 0001

    SOUTH AFRICA

    Attn: Mr. Vic Shaw

    Tel: +27 12 841 3542 or +27 12 841 2597

    FAX: +27 12 804 2679   TELEX: 321312 SA

    E-mail: uninet@frd.ac.za

    Area Served: South Africa

University of Alaska Tundra Services

    Tundra Services Coordinator

    UAS Computing Services

    11120 glacier Highway

    Juneau AK 99801

    Tel: +1 907 465-6452

    FAX: +1 907 465-6295

    E-mail: JNJMB@acad1.alaska.edu

              JXOPS@Tundra.alaska.edu

    Area Served: State of Alaska (Public, Government, Non-

          profits and the K-12 Education Community)

    Services: Terminal

    Last Update: 4/5/94

UUNET Canada Inc.

    1 Yonge Street

    Suite 1400

    Toronto, Ontario

    M5E 1J9

    CANADA

    Tel: +1 416 368 6621 or 1-800-INET-123

    FAX: +1 416 369 0515

    E-mail: info@uunet.ca

Area Served: Canada

Services: FULL ACCESS , Terminal, UUCP, Personal IP, Special

URLs: http://www.uunet.ca, ftp://ftp.uunet.ca/

Last Update: 21 Feb 1995

UUNET Technologies, Inc. (Alternet)

3060 Williams Drive

Fairfax, VA 22031

USA

Tel: +1 (800) 488-4864   or   +1 (703) 206-5600

FAX: +1 (703) 206-5601

E-mail: info@uunet.uu.net

Area Served: U.S., International

Services: FULL ACCESS , Terminal, UUCP;

URLs: WWW http://www.uu.net,

FTP ftp://ftp.uu.net/uunet-info/index

Last Update: 8-Jun-1995

UUNET India Limited

505B, Maitrivanam HUDA Complex

S.R. Nagar, Hyderabad

INDIA

Attn: I Chandrashekar Rao or Narayan D Raju

Tel: : +91 40 290933, 247787

FAX: +91 40 291933, 247747

E-mail: info@uunet.in

icr@uunet.in

ndr@uunet.in

Area Served: India and South Asia

Services: FULL ACCESS , Terminal, UUCP

URLs: ftp://ftp.uunet.in, http://www.uunet.in/

Last Update: 4/20/94

UUNORTH

    Tel: (416) 225-8649

    FAX: (416) 225-0525

    E-mail: uunorth@uunorth.north.net

    Area Served: Canada and the Northern USA

    Services: UUCP, Personal IP, Network Connection.

    Last Update: 4/5/94

ValleyNet Communications

    2300 Tulare, Suite 100

    Fresno, CA 93721-2226

    Tel: (209) 486-VNET (8638)

    Fax: (209) 495-4940

    E-Mail: info@valleynet.com

    Area Served: Central California (USA)

    Services:

    URL: http://www.valleynet.com, ftp://ftp.valleynet.com

       gopher://gopher.valleynet.com

    Last Update: 7-May-1995

VITA

    Volunteers In Technical Assistance

    1600 Wilson Boulevard 5th Floor

    Arlington, VA 22209

    USA

    Tel: +1 703 276 1800

    FAX: +1 703 243 1865 Telex: 440192 VITAUI

    E-mail: vita@gmuvax.gmu.edu

    Area Served: International

    Services: Special - FTS (FidoNet) Polling Service,

        Packet Radio, and Packet Satellite.

VERnet

> Virginia Education and Research Network
>
> Academic Computing Center
>
> Gilmer Hall
>
> University of Virginia
>
> Charlottesville, VA 22903
>
> Attn: James Jokl
>
> Tel: +1 804 924 0616
>
> E-mail: jaj@virginia.edu
>
> Area Served: Virginia
>
> Services: FULL ACCESS .

Vnet Internet Access

> PO Box 31474
>
> Charlotte, NC 28231
>
> USA
>
> Tel: +1 800 377 3282
>
> FAX: 704-334-6880
>
> E-mail: info@vnet.net
>
> Area Served: North Carolina (U.S. National access
>   also available via PDN.)
>
> Services: FULL ACCESS , Terminal, UUCP.
>
> Last Update: 2/16/94

WAMANI

> CCI
>
> Talcahuano 325-3F
>
> 1013 Buenos Aires
>
> Argentina
>
> Tel: +54 (1) 382-6842
>
> E-mail: apoyo@wamani.apc.org
>
> Area Served: Argentina
>
> Services: Terminal, UUCP

Web

    Nirv Centre

    401 Richmond Street West

    Suite 104

    Toronto, Ontario M5V 3A8

    CANADA

    Tel: +1 (416) 596 0212

    FAX: +1 (416) 974 9189

    E-mail: support@web.apc.org

    Area Served: International.

    Services: Terminal, UUCP

Westnet

    Southwestern States Network

    UCC

    601 S. Howes, 6th Floor South

    Colorado State University

    Fort Collins, CO 80523

    Attn: Pat Burns

    Tel: +1 303 491 7260

    E-mail: pburns@westnet.net

    Area Served: Western U.S. (Arizona, Colorado, New

         Mexico, Utah, Idaho, and Wyoming)

    Services: FULL ACCESS .

    URLs: file://westnet.net/

    Last Update: 7/23/94

Whole Earth 'Lectronic Link (WELL)

    27 Gate Five Road

    Sausalito, CA 94965

    Tel: +1 415 332 4335

    FAX: +1 415 332 4927

    E-mail: info@well.sf.ca.us or support@well.sf.ca.us

    Area Served: San Francisco Bay Area

Services: Terminal, UUCP

WIDE c/o Prof. Jun Murai

KEIO University

5322 Endo, Fujisawa, 252

JAPAN

Tel: +81 466 47 5111 ext. 3330

E-mail: jun@wide.ad.jp

Area Served: Japan

Services: Terminal, UUCP.

WiscNet

Madison Academic Computing Center

1210 W. Dayton Street

Madison, WI 53706

Tel: +1 608 262 8874

E-mail wn-info@nic.wiscnet.net

Area Served: Wisconsin

Services: FULL ACCESS .

URLs: file://nic.wiscnet.net

Last Update: 7/23/94

The World

Software Tool & Die

1330 Beacon Street

Brookline, MA 02146

Tel: +1 617 739 0202

E-mail: office@world.std.com

Area Served: Boston (area code 617)

Services: Dialup Host, UUCP.

WVNET West Virginia Network for Educational Telecomputing

837 Chestnut Ridge Road

Morgantown, WV 26505

Attn: Harper Grimm

Tel: +1 304 293 5192

E-mail: cc011041@wvnvms.wvnet.edu

Area Served: West Virginia

Services: FULL ACCESS .

wyoming.com

312 S. 4th

Lander, WY 82520

USA

Tel: +1 307 332-3030 or (800) WYO-I-NET

FAX: +1 307 332-5270

E-mail: info@wyoming.com

Area Served: Wyoming

Services: Personal IP, Network Service, Terminal

URLs: http://www.wyoming.com/

 ftp://ftp.wyoming.com/

 gopher://gopher.wyoming.com

Last Updated: 16 Feb 1994

Xlnet Information Systems

P.O. Box 1511

Lisle, IL 60532

USA

Tel: +1 708 983 6064

FAX: +1 708 983 6879

E-mail: : admin@xnet.com (auto-reply) info@xnet.com

Area Served: Chicago, IL

Services: FULL ACCESS , Terminal, UUCP, Personal IP

URLs: http://www.xnet.com, ftp://net.xnet.com/

Last Update: 7/23/94

XMission

PO Box 510063

Salt Lake City, UT 84151-0063

USA

Tel: +1 801 539 0852

FAX: +1 801 539 0900

E-mail: support@xmission.com

Area Served: Utah

Services: Terminal, Personal IP, UUCP, Business Services

Last Update: 7/24/94

XNet Information Systems

P.O. Box 1511

Lisle, IL 60532

USA

Tel: +1 708 983 6064

FAX: +1 708 983-6879

E-mail: admin@xnet.com

info@xnet.com

Area Served: Chicago, Illinois

Services: Terminal, UUCP

Last Update: 3/24/94

YUNAC

Borka Jerman-Blazic, Secretary General

Jamova 39

61000 Ljubljana

SLOVENIA

Tel: +38 61 159 199

FAX: +38 61 161 029

E-mail: jerman-blazic@ijs.ac.mail.yu

C=yu; ADMD=mail; PRMD=ac; O=ijs;

S=postmaster

Area Served: Slovenia, Croatia, Bosnia-Herzegovina

ZANGO

> Zambia Association for Research and Development
>
> Lusaka, Zambia
>
> Tel: +260 1 252 507
>
> Email: sysop@unza.gn.apc.org
>
> Area Served: Zambia
>
> Services: Terminal, UUCP

Appendix

B

TCP/IP Background

The TCP/IP Program

A communications program called TCP/IP runs on every computer on the Internet. Actually, the Internet is made up of all of the interconnected computers running some version of this program. It's really a whole set of programs that goes by the name TCP/IP. *TCP/IP* is an acronym that stands for *Transmission Control Protocol/Internet Protocol*.

Now, a *protocol* can be thought of as a way of reaching agreement. TCP/IP does just that. It lets all of the interconnected computers in the world talk to each other. We call that group of computers the Internet.

Think of it as similar to what is referred to as "business English." Most business people in the world speak just enough English to communicate with each other. They know a limited set of words that permits them to work together. The basic set of words allows people of many different languages to talk. That's what TCP/IP does for all different kinds of interconnected computers.

We don't know why TCP/IP came to be the common tongue, any more than we know why English became the common business language. Partisans for each claim many reasons, but for our purposes it is sufficient to know that they both function similarly. If you know business English, you can conduct business all over the world, and if your computer knows TCP/IP, it can communicate with all of the other computers on the Internet.

454

So, to make your PC talk to all the other Internet computers in the world, you have to teach it to talk TCP/IP. We have made doing that (relatively) easy for you. Session One show you how to find and get TCP/IP for your Windows PC.

There are lots of TCP/IP programs. Some can work on the big mainframe computers behind the glass walls. Some run on supercomputers and high-power workstations.

> TCP/IP is more than just a communications program; it also includes a number of applications (programs) and tools. These go by names like telnet, ftp, gopher and so on. Netscape allows you to do many of these things.

What TCP Does

TCP (Transmission Control Protocol) makes sure, to the best of its ability, that your information passes through the Internet complete and undamaged. TCP sets up sessions with other TCP programs across the Internet. This is very similar to a telephone call. Typically, you call another party, and when the connection is made, you talk. TCP does this with your data.

The TCP programs on the two different connected computers work to assure you of good communications. TCP tries to keep your information clean from telephone line errors and makes sure that all of the information is there.

What IP Does

IP (Internet Protocol) takes information from TCP and tries to get it across the Internet. Unlike TCP, IP just sends its datagrams into the network and hopes that they will arrive. This is like a postal system. You put a letter in the postal box and hope that it gets to its destination. If the datagram gets lost, IP doesn't worry; it has tried its best.

This may seem risky, but it works amazingly well. IP may lose an occasional datagram, but TCP assures you that the information will get through. TCP does this by getting a return receipt for all of its data. If IP loses some data, TCP will send it again. This means that if a line breaks, or a computer in the network fails, that data will still get through. It's a lovely combination.

Internet Addresses

Once you are running TCP/IP, there has to be a way to make your PC unique in the Internet world. As humans, we have learned how to find individuals by a complex system of names, addresses and telephone numbers. This works, most of the time, because there are a lot of people to ask.

However, with computers, it's more difficult because the computers don't really know how (or whom) to ask. The solution is for each computer on the Internet to have a consistent, worldwide computer address. The address is called the *Internet Protocol Address* or *IP Address*. Once a computer has been given an IP Address, it should be unique in the world. This means that no other computer should have that address.

Another convention we will use is to refer to the Internet computers as *hosts*. It's just a convention. The computer can be any size from the mainframes to your PC, but we will call them all hosts. This means that the *IP address* is also referred to as the *host address*.

The IP address is really just a binary number made up of ones and zeros. This system makes it easy for the host (computer) but tough on humans. To simplify the human problem, we have a way of talking about the addresses. We do this by converting the ones and zeros into four sets of numbers. Then, we can just say four numbers, and that's the IP address.

So when humans do talk about IP addresses, they say

>   One-ninety two **dot** sixteen **dot** forty-one **dot** twelve

after they have read

```
192.16.41.12
```

The numbers that are used for each of the sets of numbers which make up the IP addresses can range from zero (0) to two-fifty-five (255).

This means that the lowest number we will use is

```
0.0.0.0
```

and the largest number we use is

```
255.255.255.255
```

For at least the next few years, IP addresses will continue to look like this, and we will continue to say them this way.

Internet Names

While the hosts use IP addresses to find each other, this convention is often hard for humans. To make it easier, each host also has a name. Here's how the Internet uses names:

1. Your host (your own PC) can have any name which is acceptable to your Internet service provider.

2. That host name then becomes part of what is called a subdomain and a top domain (sort of like a family tree). There can be one or several parts to the whole name.

Let's look at some sample names to understand how it's done.

a. `panix.com`

b. `uiuc.edu`

c. `ncsa.uiuc.edu`

d. `microsoft.com`

e. `internic.net`

If we examine each of these, we can see that they are (almost) self-explanatory.

a. `panix.com` is the host address of an Internet service provider (Panix). The last part (.com) tells us that the address is a commercial enterprise.

b. `uiuc.edu` is not so easy, unless you have been to the University of Illinois at Urbana-Champaign (uiuc). You can also now guess that it's an educational institution (.edu).

c. `ncsa.uiuc.edu` is a host at UIUC which is used by the National Center for Supercomputer Applications (NCSA). NCSA is the developer of NCSA Mosaic, Netscape's predecessor.

d. `microsoft.com` should be pretty easy to decode. Microsoft is a commercial (.com) company, so that extension is pretty obvious.

e. `internic.net` refers to the interNIC, which is a shorthand name for the Internet Network Information Center (NIC). It has a number of functions, including giving out IP addresses and registering names, so it's part of a network (.net).

The last part of each name (.gov or .edu or .com) is called the highest level domain. When the entire host name is used, it is called the *fully qualified domain name (FQDN)*.

The final thing to notice about names is that we have printed them all in lowercase with no spaces. This is the usual convention in the Internet community, as many of the hosts treat upper- and lowercase letters differently. Although your PC treats upper- and lowercase letters the same, many hosts do not. So, you will find that many addresses use only lowercase.

This means that when you pick a name for your host (subject to the agreement of your Internet service provider), it will look something like this (notice the underline and dash to prevent spaces):

```
my_host.some-domain.provider.net
```

and is pronounced as we did the addresses, with a *dot* between each part. If you have been using America Online or Compuserve or Prodigy for E-mail, you will recognize the name forms

aol.com

compuserve.com

prodigy.com

Once you have an Internet service provider, you will give your PC a name. It can be your own name, or any kind of a (polite, we hope) name you wish. Since you may want to reserve your own name (Sally, Sam, or Smith) for your E-mail, the name you give your host could be different.

At this point, you may be asking how the Internet name and the Internet address relate to each other. That's a very good question. The answer is important and will be needed in the next session. Here's how it works.

Domain Nameservers

There are some special hosts all around the Internet called *nameservers*. Their function is to know the current IP address of each name.

This allows people to specify Internet names, which are easier for people to use and remember. And it allows hosts to use Internet addresses, which are faster for host computers to use.

That leads to the question: How does your host know the address of the nameserver? The answer is: You will learn the address of the nameserver from your Internet service provider.

Now, we are ready to talk about the third necessary element which is required for you (and your computer) to be on the Internet—a connection.

An Internet Gateway or Provider Connection

In earlier days on the Internet, universities and research labs banded together to connect to each other using TCP/IP. What they built has evolved into today's Internet. Now, more than half of the domains on the Internet are commercial. As such, a number of companies now offer Internet connectivity for a fee. Appendix A provides a reasonably complete list of Internet service providers.

When you select an Internet service provider, you will need to use two acronyms to tell the provider what kind of Internet connection you want. The acronyms are *SLIP* (which stands for *Serial Line Interface Protocol*) and *PPP* (which stands for *Point-to Point Protocol*). (There's that protocol word again.) You will need one or the other of these to become a full part of the Internet. We'll explain them next.

There are also Internet providers who use their own proprietary GUI interface programs for your PC. While these provide many of the Internet capabilities, most cannot use the common tools such as Netscape.

You will want to select a provider that offers either SLIP or PPP accounts.

SLIP and PPP

Earlier we discussed the fact that protocols are used to communicate between hosts on the Internet. Two of these are important to us here. These are *SLIP* (*Serial Line Interface Protocol*) and *PPP* (*Point-to-Point Protocol*). SLIP or PPP will be the protocol you will choose to connect to your Internet service provider. Some providers offer PPP and almost all providers offer SLIP.

SLIP is the older of the two and it is really not a standard protocol. It sort of happened and a lot of people started to use it. Later, the Internet community decided that a better and more complete standard should be used. They developed PPP and many providers, but not all, use it. What you really need to know is that there are two protocols, and you will have to choose one of them.

Actually, there are really three protocols. SLIP comes in a type called compressed and therefore is called *CSLIP* which stands for *compressed SLIP*. Unfortunately, some providers who use CSLIP call it SLIP.

That's really all you need to know about TCP, IP, SLIP, PPP, and CSLIP.

Appendix

C

Downloading and Installing win32s Software

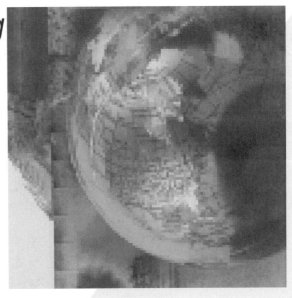

In order to run some of the newer software programs such as MPEG-PLAY, you will have to have a copy of a program called WIN32S. You will need to have the version known as win32s115a.zip (or a more recent version.)

It is possible to acquire win32s software from a variety of locations. Here are several hosts that recently had copies of the file known as win32s115a.zip. (You may wish to do an Archie search to see which hosts currently have this file.)

Host: ftp.univie.ac.at
Path: security/crypt/ftp.dsi.unimi.it/rpub.cl.msu.edu/pc/win

Host: ftp.funet.fi
Path: /pub/crypt/mirrors/ftp.dsi.unimi.it/rpub.cl.msu.edu/pc/win

Host: ftp.univ-lillel.fr
Path: /pub/pc/windows/infosys

Host: gwdu30.gwdg.de
Path: /www/msdos

The file that you are about to download, win32s115a.zip, is large (1,130,854 bytes). Be sure that the disk to which you intend to download it has ample room on it. Also, be prepared to wait a few minutes; even with a fast modem, this one takes some time!

Once you have located the file (or a more recent version) use Netscape's ftp capabilities to download the file. Here is how:

1. Click once on the **right mouse button**

2. Click on **Save this Link as...**

3. Store the file win32s11.zip (notice that the file name has been shortened a bit) in your incoming directory

4. Once you have downloaded the file, use File Manager to create a temporary directory on your hard disk. We have called ours temp32s

5. Use File manager to copy the file win32s11.zip to temp32s

6. Use File Manager to copy the file pkunzip.exe into the temp32s directory

7. Use File Manager to make the directory temp32s active

8. Now, unzip the file win32s11.zip

It is extremely important that you use the -d extension when you unzip these files so that the files are placed into the proper directories as they are unzipped.

    a. Click once on **File** and then **Run...**

    b. In the Command Line: box, type

```
pkunzip -d win32s11.zip
```

9. If all is working correctly, you should now have two disks in the temp32s directory in addition to pkunzip.exe and win32s11.zip. You should have

disk1

disk2

10. Make disk1 active

11. Double-click on **setup.exe** and Win32s will be installed.

At the end of the installation process, you will have the option of installing the Win32 game called Freecell. Freecell is a really neat game of solitaire; it is also a good way to test that your computer is working correctly. We would recommend that you choose to do this.

Congratulations! You now have successfully installed Win32s and will be able to install programs such as MPEGPLAY and others that require it.

Index

A

About the Internet, 78
About Netscape, 79
About Program Manager, 69
Access methods, Internet, 8-10
acroread.exe, 281
Add Bookmark, 106
Addresses, 89-90
Adobe Acrobat Reader:
    downloading, 281-82
    here's how URL, 288
    and Netscape Set Preferences box, 282-83
    and TimesFax, 283-86
    viewing documents using, 279-83
Adobe Portable Document Format (pdf), 279, 328
Adobe Systems Incorporated Home Page:
    hyperlinks, 287-88
    URL, 287
Advantis Home Page, 308
    HTML version of, 309
ALT key, shortcut using, 73

ALT key control, 68
America OnLine (AOL), 8, 11, 23, 31
Amtrak's Station on the World Wide Web, 145
Anchors, 320-22
    anchor tags, 321-22
        examples of, 321
        HREF attribute, 321
Anonymous ftp, 224
Applications and Directories page:
    bookmark file, selecting, 343
    customizing, 342-43
    directories, selecting, 343
    view source option, 343
Art: Children Page, 179
ASCII files, 224, 225
    and HTML, 311
.au, 261
    as top-level domain, 90
Audio files, 260-61
audio.txt, 271
Auto Load Images, Option menu, 112-14, 345

B

Back button, 47, 62
Back command, Go menu, 73
BankAmerica home page, 123
Beginner's Guide to HTML, The, URL, 328
Berners-Lee, Tim, 7, 38
Binary files, 225, 232-33
    compressed, 232-33
<BODY> and </BODY>, 310
Bookmark file, selecting, 343
bookmark.htm, 108, 145, 163
Bookmarks, 102, 105-8, 117-18
    Add Bookmark, 106, 146-50
    Add Bookmarks Under:, 160-61
    adding bookmarks:
        method #1, 146-48
        method #2, 148-50
    Bookmark List, 107, 117
        adding URLs to, 106-8
        building, 145-50
        editing, 162-63
        new headers, 153-58
        new separators, 158-59
        using, 108
    Bookmark List Edit box, 151-52
    Bookmark Menu:, 161-62
    Create Bookmark, 107
    organizing, 151-62
    View Bookmarks, 106, 107, 153
    window, 105
Bookmarks menu, 74-75

 tag, 310
Browsers, 7-8, 38-39, 91
    graphic, 39
Browsing the Internet, 8, 168-211
    casual browsing, 168
    directory searches, 175-80
    keyword searching, 168
    looking for information, 168
    Net Search button, 50, 65, 169
    people searching, 195-209
    search engines, 170-74

searching:
    with InfoSeek, 189-95
    with Lycos, 184-89
    for particular topics, 179-80
    tips and tricks, 210-11
    with WebCrawler, 181-83
    subject searching, 168
    topic browsing, 168
    See also People searching; Search
    engines

C

.ca, as top-level domain, 90
Cache and Network page:
    customizing, 340-42
    disk cache option, 341
    memory cache option, 341
    network butter size, 342
Casual browsing, 168
CERN World Wide Web Home Page, URL, 92
<CENTER> and </CENTER>, 316, 323
Choose Font... buttons, 338
CIA's World Fact Book, 133
City of Palo Alto, California site:
    URL, 99
    visiting (exercise), 99
Close, 70
Colors:
    changing, 336, 338-39
        for red-green colorblindness, 339
        for screen captures, 339
    defaults, 338
.com, 233
    as top-level domain, 90, 456
CommerceNet:
    home page, 125
    URL, 92
Communications, checking, 13
Comprehensive list of sites:
    URL, 101
    visiting (exercise), 101-2

Compressed files, 212, 232-33
    file extensions, 233-34
    pkz204g.exe, 235-39
Compressed SLIP, 459
CompuServe, 8, 10, 23, 31
    Internet connection, 15, 18
Control Menu Box, 61
Conventions, xxiii-xxiv
Copy, 71
Copy function, 70-71
CSLIP, defined, 17, 459
CTRL key control, 68
Current Weather Maps/Movies, URL, 300
Customizing Netscape, 331-47
    Applications and Directories page,
       342-43
    Cache and Network page, 340-42
    colors, 336, 338-39
    fonts, 336-38
    Helper Applications page, 347
    Images and Security page, 343-45
    Mail and News page, 339-40
    preferences, 331-33
    Proxies page, 345-47
    styles, 333-36
       hyperlink appearance, 335-36
       starting page, 335
       toolbar appearance, 334-35
Cut function, 70

D

.de, as top-level domain, 90
Default fonts, 338
Default preferences, 331-33
Dialing Settings box, Netscape Personal
    Edition, 34
Directories, selecting, 343
Directory buttons, 64-67
    Show Directory Buttons command, 76
Directory menu, 77-78
Directory searches, 175-80
    search engines vs., 210

.doc, 233
Document Info, 69
Domain nameservers (DNS), 47
    TCP/IP, 457
Domains, 89
    highest-level domain, 456
    subdomains, 89
    top-level domain, 89-90
Downloading:
binary files, 225
    Netscape Navigator using ftp, 22-24
       files needed for, 24
    WIN32S software, 461-63
Dumb terminal, 9

E

Edit menu, 70-71
.edu, as top-level domain, 90, 456
Electronic Newsstand, 221-23
E-mail, 10, 38
    finding/contacting ISPs through, 18-19
    and Mail and News page, 340
    Quote Document, 251
    setting preference for, 247-50
    using Netscape for, 247-50
Encodings, changing, 337-38
Eudora Light, 30
Europa Home Page, 135
.exe, 233
Experienced internet users, xxi

F

FedWorld, 219-20
File Drawer, 61
File extensions, 233-34
File menu, 68-70
File, Open Location choice, 64
Files:
    ASCII, 224, 225
    audio, 260-61
    binary, 225, 232-33

compressed, 232-33
gif, 260
graphics, 225
HTML, 260
image, 225, 260-61
jpeg, 260
movie, 261
text, 260
File transfer protocol, *See* ftp
Find, 71
Find button, 63
Find function, 70-71
Finger Gateway, 199-201
Fixed fonts, 338
Flat-rate charging structure, 18
Followed links, 335
Fonts:
changing, 336-38
default, 338
fixed, 338
proportional, 338
Fonts and Colors page, 336-37
Forward button, 62
Forward command, Go menu, 73
Four11 Directory Services, 204-9
entries, 207
listing, 209
results page, 208
Search button, 206
Search Form, 206
FQDN, *See* Fully qualified domain name
(FQDN)
.fr, as top-level domain, 90
Freeware, 234
Frequently Asked Questions (FAQs), 217
ftp (file transfer protocol), 10, 21, 23
anonymous, 224
downloading Netscape using, 23-24
obtaining a copy of pkz204g.exe with,
235-39
review of, 224-31

using Netscape for, 232-44
compressed files, 212
See also Netscape ftp server
Fully qualified domain name (FQDN), 456

G

Gateway access, 8-9
Gateways, 346
Finger Gateway, 199-201
Netfind Gateway, 196
SOCKS gateway, 346
Genie, 8
Getting started, 11-12
.gif, 261
GIF images, 260, 276-79
Go menu, 72-73
gopher, 10, 38, 244-46
Gopher Menu, 197
Go To:, Location Box, 64
.gov, as top-level domain, 90
Graphic browsers, 39
Graphics files, 225
Guide to Australia:
URL, 97
visiting (exercise), 97-98
Guide to Film and Video, URL, 299

H

<H1> and </H1>, 310, 317
Handbook button, 49, 65
Hands-On Netscape CD-ROM:
installation of, xvii-xviii
QuickTime 2.0, 301
WEBTOUR.HTM, 118
wplany, 269
Hard disk space requirements, 12-13
Hardware, checking, 12-13
<HEAD> and </HEAD>, 310
Helper applications (helper apps), 260
Helper Applications page, customizing,
347

Help menu, 78-80
History, 102, 103-5
   View History, 73, 104
Home button, 42, 43, 47, 62
Home command, Go menu, 73
Home pages, defined, 40-41, 43-47, 60
Host access, 10
Host names, 90
Hosts, 5, 10, 89
HotMetal, 328
How to Compose Good HTML, URL, 328
.htm, 313
html, *See* Hypertext Markup Language
   (HTML)
<HTML> and </HTML>, 310-11
HTML Assistant, 328
HTML Editors, URL, 328
HTML for Fun and Profit (Morris), 328
HTML Manual of Style (Aronson), 328
HTML Quick Reference Guide, The, URL,
   328
http (Hypertext Transport Protocol), 38-39,
   64, 91-92, 307, 320
Hyperlinks, 45-47
   adding to document, 320-26
   anchors, 320-21
   anchor tags, 321-22
      examples of, 321
      HREF attribute, 321
   changing appearance of, 335-36
   checking, 327
   clicking on, 82-84
   correcting, 327
Hypertext, 38-39
Hypertext Markup Language (HTML),
   92-93
   Advantis Home Page, 308
      HTML version of, 309-10
      simplified version of, 310
   <BODY> and </BODY>, 310

 tag, 310
   <CENTER> and </CENTER>, 316, 323

defined, 307
ending tags, 310
<H1> and </H1>, 310, 317
<H3> and </H3>, 310
<HEAD> and </HEAD>, 310
headings, 317
HTML 3.0, 329
<HTML> and </HTML>, 310-11
HTML document, setting up, 311-16
hyperlinks:
   adding, 320-26
   checking, 327
introduction to, 307-11
<LI>, 317-19
list, creating, 317-20
markup tags, 310
   purpose of, 311
<OL> and </OL>, 317-18, 320
<P> tag, 310
resources, 328
starting tags, 310
<TITLE> and </TITLE>, 310
YELLOW01.htm, 313
   adding title to document, 316
   displaying, 314-15
YELLOW02.HTM, 317-19
YELLOW03.HTM, 322-24
   adding hyperlinks to, 321
   as seen in Notepad, 322
   as seen using Netscape, 323
YELLOWPG.HTM, 324-26
   adding hyperlinks to, 324
   checking hyperlinks in, 327
   as seen using Netscape, 326
See also Hyperlinks

I

IBM Global Network, 15, 18
IBM Welcome Page, accessing, 262-64
Image files, 225, 260-61
Images button, 62, 113
Images and Security page:

customizing, 343-45
  order of loading images, 344-45
  setting colors, 344
Information service access, 8-9, 11
InfoSeek, 189-95
  commercial choices, 193-95
  InfoSeek hyperlink, 192
  search engine, 171, 190
  Search hyperlink, 193
  search results, 191
  Username and Password Required Box,
    193
Installation, 25-30
  Hands-On Netscape CD-ROM, xvii-xviii
  movie players, 288-96
  Netscape Icon group, 30
  Netscape Setup, 25-29
    conclusion of, 29
    Installation Location screen, 27
    Program Group Screen, 28
    progress screen, 29
    Welcome screen, 26
  newer versions of Netscape, 349
  PC speaker driver, 271-72
  Personal Edition, 31-35
  QuickTime, 301-4
  TCP/IP software, 14-15
  WIN32S software, 461-63
  wplany, 272-73
Installation Location screen, 27
Integrated Services Digital Network
  (ISDN) adapter, 13, 17
Intelligent Agents, 202
Internet:
  access methods, 8-10
  browsing/searching, 168-211
  connected networks, 4-5
  connections, 10-11
  defined, 4
  Internet Society, 4
  quick review of, 3-4

standards for, 4
  World Wide Web, 6
Internet access methods, 8-10
  gateway access, 8
  Internet Host, 10
  terminal emulator access, 9-10
Internet addresses (IP address), 89-90
  TCP/IP, 455
Internet Book Information Center:
  URL, 100
  visiting (exercise), 100-101
Internet connections, 10-11
  getting started, 11-12
  hardware/software, checking, 12-14
Internet Directory, 50-54, 175-79
  moving through series of hyperlinks,
    illustration of, 52-54
  Net Directory button, 50, 65
  value of, 52
  Yahoo Directory, 176-79
Internet Host, 10
Internet names, TCP/IP, 456-57
Internet Network Information Center
  (NIC), 456
Internet Protocol (IP) addresses, 89-90, 455
  TCP/IP, 455
Internet service providers (ISPs), 10,
  353-451
  access, 16
  cost of using, 17-18
  finding/contacting, 18-19
  flat-rate charging structure, 18
  local telephone access numbers, 18
  selecting, 15-19
    suggestions for, 17-18
  TCP/IP software from, 15
  variety of, 15
Internet users, classification of, xxi
Internet White Pages, 78
Internet Yellow Pages document, HTML
  for, 312-27

InterNIC Directory and Database Services Home Page, 137
ISDN adapter, 13, 17
ISPs, *See* Internet service providers (ISPs)

J

Joint Photographic Experts Group, *See* JPEG
.jp, as top-level domain, 90
jpeg (extension), 261
JPEG images, 260, 276-79

K

Keystrokes, 81-82
Keyword searching, 168
Knowbot, 201-4
  entries, 202-3
  Intelligent Agents, 202
  Knowbot Information Service (KIS) Query Page, 202
  results page, 204
  Submit Query button, 204

L

<LI>, 317-19
License, Netscape Navigator, 22
Load Images, 71
Local Area Network (LAN), 16
  adapter, 13
  connection, 11
Location Box, 63-64
Lycos, 184-89
  first Lycos result, 187
  Home Page, 184
  query, 186-87
  Search Form, 185
  second Lycos result, 188

M

McAfee Associates, 240
Mail Document, 69

Mail and News page, customizing, 339-40
Main type, MIME, 260
Markup tags, 310
Maximize button, title bar, 61
Menu bar, 61
Menus, 68-80
  Bookmarks menu, 74-75
  Directory menu, 77-78
  Edit menu, 70-71
  File menu, 68-70
  Go menu, 72-73
  Help menu, 78-80
  Options menu, 75-77, 109-13
  View menu, 71-72
Microsoft Windows PC users, xx
Microsoft Word, creating HTML documents in, 312
.mil, as top-level domain, 90
MIME (Multimedia Internet Mail Extension) types, 260
Minimize button, title bar, 61
Modem speed, 13
Mosaic, 6, 8, 38, 39
Mosaic and External Viewers, URL, 264, 290
Motion Picture Experts Group, *See* mpeg (extension)
Mouse:
  clicks, 81-82
  control, 67
  right mouse button, 82-84
.mov, 262
Movies:
  files, finding, 297-300
  players, getting/installing, 288-96
  QuickTime, downloading/installing, 301-4
Mozilla Team, 79-80
mpeg (extension), 288
MPEGPLAY for Windows, downloading, 289-93
mpegw32h.zip, 292-94

.mpg, 262
Multimedia:
 IBM Welcome Page, accessing, 262-63
 MIME types, 260
 PC speaker driver, 264-73
 using with Netscape, 259-305
Music, Images, and Multimedia:
 Internet Resources List, 298
 URL, 298

N

n16e11n.exe, 23, 25
n32e11n.exe, 23
Name lookup failure, 42-43
Name resolution, 41-43
Nameservers, 457
National Museau of American Art home
 page, 120-21, 304
National Organization of Women (NOW)
 Home Page, 143
NCSA Mosaic, 6, 8, 39
.net, as top-level domain, 90, 456
Net Directory button, 50, 65
Netfind Gateway, 196
Netscape 1.1 directory, 229
Netscape Communications Corporation, 64
 formation of, 39
Netscape communication servers, 64
Netscape ftp server, 226
 hyperlink license, 230
 menu structure, 227
 Netscape 1.1 directory, 229
 Netscape licence information, 228
 right mouse options, 230
 Save As... box, 237
Netscape Galleria, 78
Netscape Home Page, 40-41
 touring, 43-44
 What's New! page, 44-47
Netscape icon, 65
Netscape Navigator:
 ALT key control, 68

browsing/searching, 168-211
controlling, 67-68
CTRL key control, 68
customizing, 331-47
directory buttons, 64-67
downloading using ftp, 22-24
function of, xix-xx
Home Page, 40-41, 43-47, 60
installing, 25-30
Internet access methods, 8-10
Internet Directory page, 50-54
keystrokes, 81-82
license, 22
menu bar, 61
menus, 68-80
mouse clicks, 81-82
mouse control, 67
name resolution, 41-43
Net Directory button, 50, 65
Netscape icon, 65
Netscape Online Handbook, 49
Net Search button, 50, 65
newer versions:
 becoming aware of, 348
 obtaining/installing, 349
 when to get, 348
obtaining, 27-28
options, setting, 109-13
Personal Edition installation, 11, 31-35
security, 84-85
starting, 40-43
status bar, 66-67
staying up-to-date, 348-49
title bar, 61
toolbar, 62-64
touring, 59-85
using for E-mail, 247-51
using multimedia with, 259-305
using for Usenet, 252-57
web sites, visiting, 47
Welcome screen, 26, 60
What's Cool? page, 48, 93-96

Windows versions, 30-31
working area document, 65-66
and the World Wide Web, 8
See also Customizing Netscape; World
    Wide Web (WWW); Menus
Netscape Online Handbook, 49
Netscape Setup, 25-29
    conclusion of, 29
    Installation Location screen, 27
    Program Group Screen, 28
    progress screen, 29
    Welcome screen, 26
Net Search button, 50, 65, 169
Netsite:, Location Box, 64
Netsite server, 64
Network firewall, 346
Newsgroups button, Usenet, 253
News (NNTP) Server: form, 340
New Window command, 69
Novice internet users, xxi

O

<OL> and </OL>, 317-18, 320
Online Handbook, 49
Open button, 63, 64
Open File, 69
Open Location, 69
Operating system software:
    checking, 14
    TCP/IP, 14-15
Options menu, 75-77, 109-13
    Auto Load Images, 112-14
    Options window, 109
    Save Options, 114
    Show Directory Buttons command, 76,
        111-12
    Show FTP File Information, 114
    Show Location, 76, 110-11
    Show Toolbar, 110
    summary of, 114-15
.org, as top-level domain, 90

P

<P> tag, 310
Paste function, 70
PC speaker driver, 264-73
    installing, 271-72
    obtaining, 264-70
PCWEEK:
    URL, 96
    visiting (exercise), 96-97
.pdf, 261
pdf format, 279, 286-88
People searching, 195-209
    E-mail search results, 198
    Finger Gateway, 199-201
    Four11 Directory Services, 204-9
    Gopher Menu, 197
    Knowbot, 201-4
    Netfind Gateway, 196-97
    quick method for, 195
    verifying the address, 198-90
Personal Edition:
    Dialing Settings box, 34
    Icon group, 32
    installation of, 31-35
    obtaining, 12, 31
    Overview of Registration Wizard, 33
    Registration Wizard, 30, 32-34
    Welcome screen, 32
    What's Next? screen, 35
pkunzip.exe, 294, 303
pkz204g.exe:
    obtaining a copy of, 235-39
    running, 239
pkzip, 234-35
Pop-up warning alerts, turning on/off, 345
Portable Document Format (pdf), Adobe
    Acrobat Reader, 279,
    328
PPP (Point-to-Point Protocol), 23, 458-59
    account, 11

defined, 17, 458
  Internet Host access via, 10
Preference, Options menu, 76
Print, 70
Print button, 63
Print Preview, 70
Processor requirements, 12
ProComm, 9
Prodigy, 8, 10, 23, 31
Proportional fonts, 338
Proxies page, customizing, 345-47
.ps, 233

Q

.qt, 262
qtw201.zip, 302-3
Quote Document, 251

R

RAM memory requirements, 12
Refresh, 71
Registration Wizard, Netscape Personal
  Edition, 30, 32-34
Reload, 71
Reload button, 43, 62
Resources, World Wide Web, 87-89
Right mouse button, 82-84
  Graphic Menu, 83-84
  Text Menu, 82
RIPE (Resaux IP Europeans (European IP
  Networks), 203
RTFM, 217

S

Save As, 69
Save Options, 114
SCAN program, obtaining a copy of, 240-43
scn-221e.zip, 241-43
  unzipping with PKUNZIP.EXE, 243
Search engines, 170-74
  directory searches vs., 210

how they work, 170-72
  InfoSeek Search Engine, 171
  Looking for:, 174
  Search Engine Search, 172-74
  W3 Search Engines, 173
  See also Browsing the Internet
Searching:
  complex search terms, 210
  Frequently Asked Questions (FAQs), 217
  with InfoSeek, 189-95
  with Lycos, 184-89
  simple search terms, 210
  spelling errors, 217
  synonyms, 217
  tips and tricks, 210-11
  with WebCrawler, 181-83
  wildcard searching, 210
SEC EDGAR Database Home Page, 131
Secure status bar, 67
Secure Warning Window, 85
Security, 84-85, 345
  pop-up warning alerts, turning on/off,
    345
  Secure Warning Window, 85
  and status bar, 67
Serial Line Internet Protocol, *See* SLIP
  (Serial Line Internet Protocol)
Set Preferences Box, 216-18, 294-96
  Applications and Directories option, 217
  Telnet Application: box, 218
Shareware, TCP/IP, 14-15
Shell account access, 9-10
Shopping 2000 Home Page, 139
Show Directory Buttons command,
  Options menu, 76, 111-12
Show FTP File Information, 114
Show Location command, Options menu,
  76, 110-11
Show Toolbar command, Options menu,
  76, 110
Simple search terms, 210

SLIP (Serial Line Internet Protocol), 23, 458-59
 account, 11
 compressed SLIP, 459
 defined, 17, 458
 Internet Host access via, 10
SLIRP, 10
SmartComm, 9
Smithsonian Institution Home Page, 129
SOCKS gateway, 346
Software, checking, 14
SoundBlaster, 262
Sounds, playing, 273-75
speaker.drv, 272
speaker.txt, 271
speak.exe, 267, 271
Spelling errors in searches, 217
Starting page, changing appearance of, 335
Status bar, 46, 66-67
 and security, 67
 as thermometer, 66
Stolichnaya Vodka Home Page, 127
Stop button, 63
Subdomains, 89
Subject searching, 168
Subtype, MIME, 260
Synonyms, in searches, 217

T

Tattam, Peter, 14-15
TCP/IP:
 domain nameservers, 457
 Internet addresses (IP address), 455
 Internet gateway vs. provider connection, 458
 Internet names, 456-57
 IP (Internet protocol), function of, 454
 program, 453-54

software, 10-11
 finding/installing, 14-15
 from Internet service providers, 15
 shareware, 14-15
 TCP (Transmission Control Protocol), function of, 454
Telephone line connection, checking, 13
Telix, 9
telnet, 10, 34
 review of, 214-24
Terminal emulator access, 9-10
TIA, 10
TimesFax, 283-86
 Home Page, 284
 TIMES.PDF, downloading, 285-86
 URL, 283
<TITLE> and </TITLE>, 310
Title bar, 61
Toolbar, 62-64
 Back button, 62
 changing appearance of, 335
 Find button, 63
 Forward button, 62
 Home button, 62
 Images button, 62
 Location Box, 63-64
 Open button, 63-64
 Print button, 63
 Reload button, 62
 Show Toolbar command, 76
 Stop button, 63
Topic browsing, 168
Top-level domain, 89-90
Transaction security, *See* Security
Trumpet Winsock, 14
.txt, 233

U

Undo function, 70-71
UNIX Whois, 203

URLs (Uniform Resource Locators), 63, 69, 90-91, 213
  adding to Bookmark List, 106-8
  Adobe Systems Incorporated Home Page, 287
  Beginner's Guide to HTML, The, 328
  bookmarks, 102, 105-8
  CERN World Wide Web Home Page, 92
  City of Palo Alto, California site, 99
  CommerceNet, 92
  components of, 90-91
  comprehensive list of sites, 101
  Current Weather Maps/Movies, 300
  defined, 90
  examples of, 97
  Guide to Australia, 97
  Guide to Film and Video, 299
  history, 102, 103-5
  How to Compose Good HTML, 328
  HTML Editors, 328
  HTML Quick Reference Guide, The, 328
  Internet Book Information Center, 100
  Mosaic and External Viewers, 264, 290
  most common form of, 92
  Music, Images, and Multimedia, 298
  PCWEEK, 96
  probing the Web using, 93-102
  TimesFax, 283
  U.S. Bureau of the Census, 93
  WebCrawler, 181
  WebMuseum network, 277
  Welcome to the White House Home Page, 274
  What's Cool? page, 93
U.S. Bureau of the Census, URL, 93
Usenet:
  All Newsgroups Warning, 255
  Catchup All Articles button, 257
  Directory, Go to Newsgroups, menu bar, 253
  listing newsgroups, 255
  Newsgroups button, 253
  newsgroup titles, 256

  NNTP (Network News Transport Protocol) server, 252
  Post New Article button, 256
  Show Read Articles, 257
  Subscribed Newsgroups, 257
  Subscribed Newsgroups page, 253-54
  subscribing to a newsgroup, 254, 340
  unsubscribe, 257
  unsubscribing from a newsgroup, 254, 257
  using Netscape for, 252-57
  View all newsgroups, 255

V

View Bookmarks, 106
View History, 73, 104
Viewing images, 276-79
View menu, 71-72
View Source, 72
Virus protection software, obtaining, 239-43
VT-100, 9

W

W3 Search Engines, 173
.wav, 261
Web, *See* World Wide Web
WebCrawler, 181-83
  Search Results, 183
  URL, 181
WebMuseum network, URL, 277-79
WebSurfer, 38
WEBTOUR.HTM (exercise), 118-45
  art and entertainment, 120-21, 277
  banking, 122-23
  CD-ROM method, 118
  commerce, 124-25
  companies, 126-27
  education, 128-29
  finance, 130-31
  government, 132-33
  international, 134-35

Internet, 136-37
Internet method, 118
malls and marketing, 138-39
news, 140-41
organization, 142-43
travel, 144-46
Web Tour List, 119-20
Web Tour List, 119-20
Welcome screen, 26, 60
without telnet, 215
Welcome to the White House Home Page,
274-76
President's Welcome Message, 275
URL, 274
What's Cool? button, 48, 65
What's Cool? page, 48, 93-96
URL, 93, 94
visiting (exercise), 94-96
What's New! button, 44, 65
What's New! page, 44-47
Wildcard searching, 210
WIN32S software, 23
downloading/installing, 461-63
Windows 3.1, Netscape license file for, 23
Windows 95, 14, 24, 30
Netscape license file for, 23
Windows Notepad, 311
launching, 313
Windows NT, Netscape license file for, 14,
23
Windows for Workgroups 3.11, Netscape
license file for,
14, 23
winsock.zip, obtaining, 14-15
WordPerfect, creating HTML documents
in, 312
Working area document, 65-66
World Wide Web Consortium, 38
World Wide Web (WWW):
browsers, 7, 39, 91
concept, invention of, 7, 38
defined, 6, 37-39
global Internet, 37-38
graphic browsers, 39

growth of traffic on, 6
HTTP (Hypertext Transport Protocol),
38-39
hypertext, 38-39
and Netscape Navigator, 8
resources on, 87-89
sites, 7
touring, 117-45
traffic, 6
viewing images on, 276-79
.wp, 233
wplany:
on CD-ROM, 269
installing/associating, 272-73
obtaining a copy of, 268-73
running, 273
wplany.exe, 273
wplny11.zip, 268-70, 272
www, defined, 90

Y

Yahoo, 175
development of, 177
hierarchy, 178-79
home page, 176
Internet Directory, 50-54
Yahoo Directory, 176-79
YELLOW01.htm, 313
adding title to document, 316
displaying, 314-15
YELLOW02.HTM, 317-19
YELLOW03.HTM, 322-24
adding hyperlinks to, 321
as seen in Notepad, 322
as seen using Netscape, 323
YELLOWPG.HTM, 324-26

LICENSE AGREEMENT AND LIMITED WARRANTY

READ THE FOLLOWING TERMS AND CONDITIONS CAREFULLY BEFORE OPENING THIS CD PACKAGE, *HANDS-ON NETSCAPE CD—WINDOWS 3.1*. THIS LEGAL DOCUMENT IS AN AGREEMENT BETWEEN YOU AND PRENTICE-HALL, INC. (THE "COMPANY"). BY OPENING THIS SEALED CD PACKAGE, YOU ARE AGREEING TO BE BOUND BY THESE TERMS AND CONDITIONS. IF YOU DO NOT AGREE WITH THESE TERMS AND CONDITIONS, DO NOT OPEN THE CD PACKAGE. PROMPTLY RETURN THE UNOPENED CD PACKAGE AND ALL ACCOMPANYING ITEMS TO THE PLACE YOU OBTAINED THEM FOR A FULL REFUND OF ANY SUMS YOU HAVE PAID.

1.   **GRANT OF LICENSE:** In consideration of your purchase of this book, and your agreement to abide by the terms and conditions of this Agreement, the Company grants to you a nonexclusive right to use and display the copy of the enclosed software program (hereinafter the "SOFTWARE") on a single computer (i.e., with a single CPU) at a single location so long as you comply with the terms of this Agreement. The Company reserves all rights not expressly granted to you under this Agreement.

2.   **OWNERSHIP OF SOFTWARE:** You own only the magnetic or physical media (the enclosed CD) on which the SOFTWARE is recorded or fixed, but the Company and the software developers retain all the rights, title, and ownership to the SOFTWARE recorded on the original CD copy(ies) and all subsequent copies of the SOFTWARE, regardless of the form or media on which the original or other copies may exist. This license is not a sale of the original SOFTWARE or any copy to you.

3.   **COPY RESTRICTIONS:** This SOFTWARE and the accompanying printed materials and user manual (the "Documentation") are the subject of copyright. The individual programs on the CD are copyrighted by the authors of each program. Some of the programs on the CD include separate licensing agreements. If you intend to use one of these programs, you must read and follow its accompanying license agreement. You may not copy the Documentation or the SOFTWARE, except that you may make a single copy of the SOFTWARE for backup or archival purposes only. You may be held legally responsible for any copying or copyright infringement which is caused or encouraged by your failure to abide by the terms of this restriction.

4.   **USE RESTRICTIONS:** You may not network the SOFTWARE or otherwise use it on more than one computer or computer terminal at the same time. You may physically transfer the SOFTWARE from one computer to another provided that the SOFTWARE is used on only one computer at a time. You may not distribute copies of the SOFTWARE or Documentation to others. You may not reverse engineer, disassemble, decompile, modify, adapt, translate, or create derivative works based on the SOFTWARE or the Documentation without the prior written consent of the Company.

5.   **TRANSFER RESTRICTIONS:** The enclosed SOFTWARE is licensed only to you and may not be transferred to any one else without the prior written consent of the Company. Any unauthorized transfer of the SOFTWARE shall result in the immediate termination of this Agreement.

6.   **TERMINATION:** This license is effective until terminated. This license will terminate automatically without notice from the Company and become null and void if you fail to comply with any provisions or limitations of this license. Upon termination, you shall destroy the Documentation and all copies of the SOFTWARE. All provisions of this Agreement as to warranties, limitation of liability, remedies or damages, and our ownership rights shall survive termination.

7.   **MISCELLANEOUS:** This Agreement shall be construed in accordance with the laws of the United States of America and the State of New York and shall benefit the Company, its affiliates, and assignees.

8.   **LIMITED WARRANTY AND DISCLAIMER OF WARRANTY:** The Company warrants that the SOFTWARE, when properly used in accordance with the Documentation, will operate in substantial conformity with the description of the SOFTWARE set forth in the Documentation. The

Company does not warrant that the SOFTWARE will meet your requirements or that the operation of the SOFTWARE will be uninterrupted or error-free. The Company warrants that the media on which the SOFTWARE is delivered shall be free from defects in materials and workmanship under normal use for a period of thirty (30) days from the date of your purchase. Your only remedy and the Company's only obligation under these limited warranties is, at the Company's option, return of the warranted item for a refund of any amounts paid by you or replacement of the item. Any replacement of SOFTWARE or media under the warranties shall not extend the original warranty period. The limited warranty set forth above shall not apply to any SOFTWARE which the Company determines in good faith has been subject to misuse, neglect, improper installation, repair, alteration, or damage by you. EXCEPT FOR THE EXPRESSED WARRANTIES SET FORTH ABOVE, THE COMPANY DISCLAIMS ALL WARRANTIES, EXPRESS OR IMPLIED, INCLUDING WITHOUT LIMITATION, THE IMPLIED WARRANTIES OF MERCHANTABILITY AND FITNESS FOR A PARTICULAR PURPOSE. EXCEPT FOR THE EXPRESS WARRANTY SET FORTH ABOVE, THE COMPANY DOES NOT WARRANT, GUARANTEE, OR MAKE ANY REPRESENTATION REGARDING THE USE OR THE RESULTS OF THE USE OF THE SOFTWARE IN TERMS OF ITS CORRECTNESS, ACCURACY, RELIABILITY, CURRENTNESS, OR OTHERWISE.

IN NO EVENT, SHALL THE COMPANY OR ITS EMPLOYEES, AGENTS, SUPPLIERS, OR CONTRACTORS BE LIABLE FOR ANY INCIDENTAL, INDIRECT, SPECIAL, OR CONSEQUENTIAL DAMAGES ARISING OUT OF OR IN CONNECTION WITH THE LICENSE GRANTED UNDER THIS AGREEMENT, OR FOR LOSS OF USE, LOSS OF DATA, LOSS OF INCOME OR PROFIT, OR OTHER LOSSES, SUSTAINED AS A RESULT OF INJURY TO ANY PERSON, OR LOSS OF OR DAMAGE TO PROPERTY, OR CLAIMS OF THIRD PARTIES, EVEN IF THE COMPANY OR AN AUTHORIZED REPRESENTATIVE OF THE COMPANY HAS BEEN ADVISED OF THE POSSIBILITY OF SUCH DAMAGES. IN NO EVENT SHALL LIABILITY OF THE COMPANY FOR DAMAGES WITH RESPECT TO THE SOFTWARE EXCEED THE AMOUNTS ACTUALLY PAID BY YOU, IF ANY, FOR THE SOFTWARE.

SOME JURISDICTIONS DO NOT ALLOW THE LIMITATION OF IMPLIED WARRANTIES OR LIABILITY FOR INCIDENTAL, INDIRECT, SPECIAL, OR CONSEQUENTIAL DAMAGES, SO THE ABOVE LIMITATIONS MAY NOT ALWAYS APPLY. THE WARRANTIES IN THIS AGREEMENT GIVE YOU SPECIFIC LEGAL RIGHTS AND YOU MAY ALSO HAVE OTHER RIGHTS WHICH VARY IN ACCORDANCE WITH LOCAL LAW.

ACKNOWLEDGMENT

YOU ACKNOWLEDGE THAT YOU HAVE READ THIS AGREEMENT, UNDERSTAND IT, AND AGREE TO BE BOUND BY ITS TERMS AND CONDITIONS. YOU ALSO AGREE THAT THIS AGREEMENT IS THE COMPLETE AND EXCLUSIVE STATEMENT OF THE AGREEMENT BETWEEN YOU AND THE COMPANY AND SUPERSEDES ALL PROPOSALS OR PRIOR AGREEMENTS, ORAL, OR WRITTEN, AND ANY OTHER COMMUNICATIONS BETWEEN YOU AND THE COMPANY OR ANY REPRESENTATIVE OF THE COMPANY RELATING TO THE SUBJECT MATTER OF THIS AGREEMENT.

Should you have any questions concerning this Agreement or if you wish to contact the Company for any reason, please contact in writing at the address below.

Robin Short

Prentice Hall PTR

One Lake Street

Upper Saddle River, New Jersey 07458